THINKING
The Expanding Frontier

THINKING

The
Expanding
Frontier

Proceedings of the International, Interdisciplinary
Conference on Thinking held at the University of
The South Pacific, January, 1982

Edited by William Maxwell, *University of The South Pacific*
Preface by Jerome Bruner, *New School for Social Research*

Selected and Edited by
    John Bishop, *University of Auckland*
    Margaret Boden, *University of Sussex*
    William Connell, *University of Sydney and*
       Monash University
    Roderic Girle, *University of Queensland*
    Jack Lochhead, *University of Massachusetts*
    Jeanette Maas, *University of The South Pacific*
    D. M. Mackay, *University of Keele*
    S. Muralidhar, *University of The South Pacific*
    David Perkins, *Harvard University*
    R. A. C. Stewart, *University of The South Pacific*
    Ivan Williams, *University of The South Pacific*

THE FRANKLIN INSTITUTE PRESS℠

Published by THE FRANKLIN INSTITUTE PRESS[SM]
Philadelphia, Pennsylvania

Current printing (last digit):
5   4   3   2   1

Printed in the United States of America

Library of Congress Cataloging in Publication Data
Main entry under title:

Thinking, the expanding frontier.

   Proceedings of the Conference on Thinking, held in
1982 at the University of the South Pacific, Suva, Fiji
under the auspices of the School of Education.
   Includes bibliographies and index.
   1. Thought and thinking—Congresses.   2. Cognition
and culture—Congresses.   3. Bateson, Gregory—Congresses.
I. Maxwell, William, 1935–   . II. Conference on
Thinking (1982 : Suva, Fiji)   III. University of the
South Pacific. School of Education.
BF455.T535   1983   153   83-1586
ISBN 0-89168-047-0

FOREWORD

This book contains a selection of the papers delivered at the Conference on Thinking which was held at the University of the South Pacific, Suva, Fiji, in January, 1982. The Conference on Thinking was an international, interdisciplinary gathering of scholars from fourteen countries on all continents. The Conference was called by the School of Education of the University of the South Pacific to pursue further the question, "What is Thinking?" The primary goal of the Conference was to help accelerate the clearly evident educational trend toward giving more emphasis to teaching thinking skills.

The response to the call for papers was greater than expected; we received almost ninety papers from over forty universities.

The Conference itself was declared by many participants to be an exciting success. Perhaps the context contributed to these perceptions of success: a young, international university in a sunny peaceful Pacific setting; a collection of distinguished scholars of various nationalities, ages, races, academic backgrounds; and everyone excited about the prospects of thinking about thinking for three days.

One of the predecessors and models for the Conference on Thinking was the Woods Hole Conference described by Bruner (1960), "The Conference was... unique in composition.... Strange as it may seem this (1959) was the first time psychologists had been brought together with leading scientists to discuss problems involved in teaching their various disciplines" (p.ix). Another antecedent to the 1982 Conference on Thinking was the 1978 University of Massachusetts' Conference on Cognitive Process Instruction. That conference, organized by Jack Lochhead of the Department of Physics and Astronomy, University of Massachusetts, was important from several perspectives. For example, Dr. Lochhead's opening sentence in the introduction to the volume that contains most of the papers of that conference captured the conference's essence as well as the essentials of the curricular trends highlighted by the earlier Woods Hole Conference: "We should be teaching students how to think; instead we are primarily teaching them what to think" (Lochhead and Clement, p.1).

The Woods Hole Conference was a conference of some of the leading scientists and cognitive psychologists in the United States who were interested in examining and revising the structure of the curriculum in order to disseminate or teach more effectively current scientific *content* and *processes*. The University of Massachusetts Conference, in contrast, was much more sharply focused on the cognitive processes themselves, more than on the content or object of those processes.

Our Conference attempted to broaden the perspective from which we may examine the phenomena of cognitive processes, or thinking. We at the University of the South Pacific felt that while many inquiries benefit from the division of scientific labor into the traditional disciplines, when we seek to understand more deeply the processes of inquiry itself, a cooperative, interdisciplinary approach seems imperative. To think about our own thinking we need to pool resources and perspectives. The Conference on Thinking provided such an opportunity. A good deal of the proceedings of this 1982 Conference continued the pedagogical themes of its two predecessors. But the multidisciplinary net was cast wider in Suva to include philosophers, sociologists, administrators, anthropologists, linguists, mathematicians, political scientists, educators with various specialties, and others. The Conference generated much local and regional interest, and, as can be seen from the list of participants, the interest went beyond professional teachers, researchers and academics: in harmony with an ancient academic tradition, the dialogue among experts was open to the general public.

If the 1982 Conference sought a broader than usual range of participants, it may still be asked, perhaps, whether our representation was broad enough. Only one creative artist presented a paper; the music presented was for pure entertainment, *i.e.*, there was no paper on musical or architectural thinking and the like; and the Anglo-Saxon cultures were disproportionately represented. Further expansion of the range of disciplines and expertise may be attempted at similar future conferences. Indeed, the 1982 Conference ended with an informal agreement to meet again in the northern hemisphere during the summer of 1984 — and we of the South Pacific hope that the interest and momentum can be maintained to justify a return to Fiji in January, 1987, of another international interdisciplinary Conference on Thinking.

The organization of this book illustrates the multifaceted approach of the Conference: the chapters or sections group the papers somewhat logically and somewhat arbitrarily into six parts, "Some Philosophical Perspectives;" "Thinking and Culture;" "Teaching Thinking;" "Thinking About Teaching Thinking;" "Artificial Intelligence" and "The Symposium on Gregory Bateson's *Mind and Nature: A Necessary Unity.*"

The title of the book, "Thinking: The Expanding Frontier," is intended to describe a clearly manifest and universal phenomenon and is not intended to suggest that the authors represented here or that the Conference participants alone are expanding that frontier or horizon. The frontier is expanding through the efforts of many thinkers and teachers all around the planet. It was our pleasure to note that expansion and, to a modest degree, to encourage and further that expansion.

William Maxwell
The University of the South Pacific

REFERENCES

Bruner, Jerome. *The Process of Education.* Cambridge: Harvard University Press, 1960; and New York: Random House, 1960.

Lochhead, Jack and Clement, John. *Cognitive Process Instruction: Research on Teaching Thinking Skills.* Philadelphia: The Franklin Institute Press, 1979.

ACKNOWLEDGMENTS

This acknowledgement is basically divided into two parts: to those institutions and individuals whose contributions especially helped to make the Conference on Thinking a success and to those who made this book possible.

We would like to thank the School of Education, of the University of the South Pacific, where the Conference was conceived. We would also like to express our gratitude to the Committee for International Cooperation in Higher Education of the British Council, especially Mr. T.H.L. Matthews, which gave the Conference increased stature by supporting three eminent scholars, Dr. Richard Dawkins of Oxford, Professor Margaret Boden of Sussex, and Professor D.M. MacKay of Keele, who not only served as intellectual magnets to attract other scholars but graciously pitched in to help with the countless chores of a large and complex gathering.

The Governments of Fiji and Kiribati further enriched the Conference proceedings by sending articulate ministerial representatives who filled several active roles. The Government of the United States through its International Communications Agency funded the participation of Dr. Jack Lochhead of the University of Massachusetts whose 1978 Conference on Cognitive Process Instruction helped to inspire this Conference. The Government of Finland is similarly thanked for helping to make possible the visit of sportspsychologist Laura Jansson from that country's pioneering Sports Academy.

So as not to bore the reader, we will omit the names of the countless people at the University of the South Pacific who labored long hours to help welcome the Conference guests. However, we must thank the University's Estates Department, and Mrs. Anita Naidu and Mrs. Cyrilla Waqa who labored diligently the entire month before the Conference sorting out endless logistical and financial details.

The book takes on an added dimension by having been influenced by the unusually positive spirit of the participants at the Conference. We are grateful to the publisher for constant encouragement, long before the Conference actually met, and, more specifically, to the publisher's director, Ms. Julia Hough, who provided invaluable encouragement, guidance and, sometimes, solace.

The members of the Editorial Committee, especially Margaret Boden, Jack Lochhead, William Connell, D.M. MacKay, and David Perkins, sacrificed a glorious four-day weekend in the balmy South Pacific in order to participate in the selection of the articles that would fill this volume. Then they worked tirelessly to offer editorial suggestions to the authors before flying back to their normal academic work. The Committee is especially grateful also to John Bishop who translated these several suggestions into coherent letters or reviews (or sometimes almost short essays) to the several authors.

Finally, we wish to thank each author and each presenter at the Conference. The concept that an idea is the product of one or two minds may be a fundamental error. Some ideas are born out of the context, lending, in the words of Bateson, a necessary unity to mind and nature.

The Conference on Thinking Organizing Committee:

CONTENTS

Preface, *Jerome Bruner* xi
Introduction, *Jack Lochhead* xiii

PART I. SOME PHILOSOPHICAL PERSPECTIVES
Introduction   3
Seeing the Wood and the Trees, *D.M. MacKay*.   5
Can There be Thought Without Language?, *John C. Bishop*. . . . 13
Hegel on Pure Thought, *Leonard E. Ninnes* 25

PART II. THINKING AND CULTURE
Introduction 41
Thinking in Tongan Society, *I. Futa Helu* 43
Social Structure, Speech, and Silence: Fijian Reactions
    to the Problems of Social Change, *Christopher M. Griffin*. . . . 57
Beliefs About Human Nature Held by Young People in the
    South Pacific, *Robert A.C. Stewart* 69
Cognitive Mapping Features of Micronesian Navigation
    Systems, *Graham R. Davidson* 79

PART III. TEACHING THINKING
Introduction 91
Systematic Development of Thinking Skills Through a
    Language Arts Curriculum, *Doris C. Crowell* 93
Games Children Play: Powerful Tools That Teach Some
    Thinking Skills, *William Maxwell* 101
The Cognitive Research Trust (CoRT) Thinking Program,
    Edward de Bono 115
Teaching Thinking in Secondary Science, *John Edwards and
    Richard B. Baldauf, Jr.* 129
A Top-Down Approach to the Teaching of Reasoning Skills,
    Roderic A. Girle 139
Educating for Creativity: A Holistic Approach, *Delores Gallo* 149

PART IV. THINKING ABOUT TEACHING THINKING

Introduction 161
A Second Look at de Bono's Heuristics for Thinking,
     John E. McPeck 163
Difficulties in Everyday Reasoning, D.N. Perkins, Richard Allen,
     and James Hafner 177
Mental Training: Thinking Rehearsal and Its Use,
     Laura H. Jansson 191
The Analysis of Problem-Solving Strategies: Implications for
     Psychometric Testing, Kristina Macrae 199
Teaching Toward Intelligent Behavior, Arthur L. Costa 211

PART V. ARTIFICIAL INTELLIGENCE

Introduction 225
Educational Implications of Artificial Intelligence,
     Margaret A. Boden 227
Heuristic Theorem Proving, Francis Jeffry Pelletier and
     Dan C. Wilson 237

PART VI. THE SYMPOSIUM ON GREGORY BATESON'S
MIND AND NATURE: A NECESSARY UNITY

Introduction 253
Mind and Nature: Teaching and Thinking, Victor N. Kobayashi . 255
Gregory Bateson and Cybernetics, Patrick Pentony 261
The Pattern That Connects, Jeannette P. Maas 271
Some Criticisms of Mind and Nature, Robert A.M. Gregson 275
The Symposium on Mind and Nature: A Brief Summary,
     Victor N. Kobayashi 281

Appendix A. List of Participants 287
Index 295

PREFACE

Jerome Bruner

It is an interesting twist in cultural history that a gifted group of scholars should gather in the year 1982 in Suva, Fiji, to discuss the nature of human thought and the possibilities inherent in taking thought about thought. One would be tempted to guess that the motive for such a meeting was an educational one: thought and its perfection are, after all, what education is (or should be) all about. And it is altogether understandable that responsible scholars resident in or invited to the Third World for consultation should be thinking about educational implications. That may indeed have been the hidden agenda of the planners. But in fact, the actual scope of the meeting (as reflected in this book) was so much broader as to be worth a comment on its own. The Fiji Conference was indeed about the nature of mind. That, in any case, was its starting point, wherever else it went. And it traveled far. I was not there, alas, and now that I read these pages, I am full of regrets.

For while this volume is *not* in any conventional sense a treatise on education but a treatise on mind, it approaches mind in a proper spirit of instruction: it is concerned with its perfectibility, the shape it imposes on knowledge, the prosthetic devices (like language) to which it can be linked or *must* be linked in order to achieve effectiveness, the manner in which it expresses not only its own inherent form but the form of the culture that nurtures it. You will find in the pages of this book discussions that range from conjectures about Hegelian pure thought, through contention about the specialness of deductive reasoning, through inquiries into whether Puluwat navigation is a mapping of star tracks or of the myths of the culture as well, through the issues of "mental practice" of skilled action, to the question of whether the modeling of problem solving on a computer tells you anything about mind or even about problem solving.

Yes, in the unconventional sense, I suppose, this book is about education. And in fact, there is a certain amount of hot debate right in the middle of the proceedings on whether you can teach people (children and adults alike) how to think, without particular regard for what it is that they are to think *about*. Is thinking (as people in Artificial Intelligence often seem to insist) a set of component skills, and is there something about the orchestration of those skills across a wide range of mental activities that can in fact be taught? If there is a strategy of thinking that generalizes from chess to war to courtship to investment—in the spirit of von Neumann and Morgenstern's theory of games, say—is there not some means of inducting people into its mysteries?

J. Bruner is a member of the Graduate Faculty in the New School for Social Research, New York.

Perhaps it will depend—the answer to the last question—on whether or not thought which the problem solver employs is in fact dedicated to explicating concrete contexts, or whether it is of that abstract nature that creates general propositions, or at least a propositional attitude. This book has some interesting points to make on this matter and does so in terms of examples that grow out of the cultures of Oceania where the conference, indeed, took place.

There is treasure awaiting the reader of these pages, treasure rich and varied that comes from bringing together talented philosophers, psychologists, anthropologists, cognitive scientists, and educators. The themes that surface and resurface relate not only to the problems of thought provoking education, wherever it may be pursued, but to the problems of knowledge generally, knowledge of the natural world and of culture. And though the book bristles with brand-new ideas out of Artificial Intelligence and cognitive anthropology and contemporary analytic philosophy, I think both Locke and Leibniz would have found it familiar enough to have experienced a shock of recognition, had they been lucky enough to have encountered it in their times.

INTRODUCTION

Jack Lochhead

It is appropriate to begin this volume by asking: is thinking about thinking healthy? Could it be that if we came to understand thought, we would destroy our own ability to think and lose the pleasure we now find in it? Concern over this issue has troubled Mankind ever since we were first driven from the Garden of Eden. MacKay opens the first chapter with a discussion of whether we can keep the fruit of the tree of knowledge and eat it too. Fortunately for the other authors, he concludes that the enterprise is safe, or at least, that no amount of thinking about thinking can ever eliminate the need and responsibility we have to think for ourselves.

Thought seems essential to our nature as human beings, but are we the only such beings? Bishop considers the question of whether thinking is possible among the animals with no language. The root of Bishop's interest is philosophical but there are other important implications. Is human thought primarily driven by language or are there essential non-linguistic components as well, and, if so, how should we teach in order to develop them? Our ignorance of this issue is perhaps the most appallingly clear in our misuse of the word ''dumb'' which we habitually use as a synonym for ''stupid.'' Bishop's paper should help make all of us less susceptible to such misnomers, and in the process, make us more considerate of our fellow travelers on this planet. In the next chapter, Ninnes introduces one of the recurring themes of this book: the inadequacy of formal logic as an all-encompassing model of effective thought. Many readers will be uncomfortable with the overall direction of his argument, which is based on Hegel's notion of pure thought. But the underlying issues are important, regardless of your particular perspective.

The next papers deal in various ways with the interaction between thinking and the social-cultural tradition. It is easier for most of us to accept cultural diversity than the idea that there are different but equally valid logics for mental processing; this section helps to widen our view of what constitutes good thinking. One of the special strengths of the Fiji Conference was that its cultural diversity forced each participant to break some of the confines of his or her particular mental habit. We were more open than usual to considering a wider view of reasoning, logic and thought. Although the quality of that atmosphere cannot, unfortunately, be recreated in a book, this section works towards that goal.

Helu argues that although the content and form of thought is often bound by social forces, there are basic universals to human reason. He claims that societies often limit the domain of thinking by substituting belief for reason, and in some societies these constraints are so numerous that there is little room left in which to

J. Lochhead is Director of the Cognitive Development Project at the University of Massachusetts, Amherst.

think. Stewart and Davidson each consider one aspect of South Pacific thinking. Stewart looks at beliefs about the trustworthiness of other people, while Davidson views the famous south sea navigational systems as cognitive maps, based on a dynamic system of knowledge about the course stars follow through the night sky.

From the centuries-old traditions of Pacific sailing, we move to an even earlier culture: the games children play. Maxwell shows how this world-wide heritage contains within it the roots of most adult knowledge and skill. He offers a system for evaluating games in terms of their educational benefit and concludes with a review of some of the world's best known games.

Games are important, in part, because they add meaning and purpose to what might otherwise appear to children as senseless drills. Crowell considers reading instruction in that light. She describes a program in which children first learn reading and writing from the perspective of effective communication. Thus, they can better appreciate and remember the mechanical aspects, since these have been shown to have a purpose.

Of all the efforts to teach thinking explicitly, the CoRT program is probably the best known and most widely used. DeBono provides us with an outline of the objectives of his program and a summary of evidence for its effectiveness. He also shares with us some of the practical concerns that have guided him in his work. Edwards and Baldauf describe their experience with CoRT and, in particular, explore whether or not training in the general skills described by deBono can be transferred over to improve science performance. Girle, continuing a theme first described by Ninnes, describes why traditional courses in formal logic fail to capture the nature of human reasoning. He then suggests a different approach based on dialogue and a simple informal structure. In the subsequent chapter, Gallo builds on Girle's theme and lays out a full, graduate-level program for creative thinking.

It is no secret that educational innovation has not shared the prestige or success of science. Undoubtably one reason is that educators have been insufficiently critical of their own methods. Here, however, McPeck provides a lively and well-constructed critique of deBono's curriculum. Though, for my own part, I find he has too much faith in the effectiveness of the current curriculum and a tendency to take deBono's words too literally, McPeck's comments should prove useful to anyone using CoRT. Perkins, *et. al.,* once again consider the limitations of formal reasoning. They show that in everyday situations, the appropriate premises are usually unclear. They suggest that a major portion of people's thought needs to be devoted to generating and testing such premises. In conclusion, they argue that education should devote more time and effort to that facet of thinking.

From everyday logic we jump to Olympic sports competition. Jansson describes the dramatic effect that armchair thinking can have on peak athletic performance. She challenges the traditional mind/body separation inherent in so much of education and provides exciting evidence of the potential power of training in thinking. Returning to school, Macrae considers fallacies in the fundamental assumptions of classical test theory. Her discussion has implications for learning theory, education and all of standardized testing. In this book, there is little said about the I.Q. controversy: is good thinking learnable or is its source primarily genetic? Macrae's paper casts doubts on the current technology of I.Q. measurement, thus giving strong support to those who feel the debate is far from settled. Finally, Costa closes our review of educational practice by considering training for thinking in the context of the entire school situation. He shows how much of education works at cross purposes to the goal of developing good thinking skills and he suggests that we are not likely to make progress until we can come to terms with these pressures.

Costa and Helu have each described some of the educational and social pressures which work against the development of our full potential to think. Fortunately, some intervention to counter these pressures may indeed be available in the form of the computer and artificial intelligence (A.I.). Boden reviews some of the effects that the computer revolution may have on education. She stresses ways in which the study of artificial intelligence helps us to better understand our own intelligence and how that understanding can be used to improve education. I believe these developments will bring about the most exciting and significant educational changes of this century. However, I differ with Boden's acceptance of A.I.'s current phase of seeing intelligence as largely a collection of special-purpose skills. These skills are undoubtedly important but there are also some powerful ideas, such as those developed by CoRT, which can be used in almost every form of human endeavor. This is why we believe in wisdom and why an expert is rarely expert in only one area. Pelletier considers one such general-purpose skill, the ability to use heuristic reasoning. He compares it to algorithmic processing and shows that for both humans and machines, heuristic thinking has definite advantages, in spite of its relative lack of rigor.

Pellitier's paper is the most technical in this volume, yet it adds one more note to the theme that formal reasoning cannot capture all that is important in thinking. That idea was central to Gregory Bateson's view and is the principle subject of the final contributions. While most of us can accept the premise in its general form, it is much more difficult to see how it can be applied rigorously, without simply lapsing into sloppy thinking. Some of those issues were argued by Pentony, Gregson and Maas in the Bateson symposium and they are expanded further in Kobayashi's final paper. Here, in trying to find man's proper place in our environment, and in thinking about how our modern modes of thought may be responsible for many of our problems, we come full circle, back to MacKay's woods and trees.

PART I.

SOME PHILOSOPHICAL PERSPECTIVES

Diogenes

INTRODUCTION

This book commences its study of thinking by reexamining the age-old questions of mind and matter, the physical and the metaphysical, and intentionality or will. This first part pursues the arguments advanced by some of the major protagonists on these fundamental issues. To what extent is mind independent of matter—that is, free? Is mind conditioned entirely by neural capacities, by genetic blueprints (cybernetic programs)? For a long time in human history these questions only rarely arose, and then by infrequently read philosophers and a few theologians. But of late, these questions have resurfaced on man's consciousness because, in part, we have become aware that thinking is not a simple manifestation of human consciousness. Thinking is more complicated than some of its physical analogues, breathing, for example.

Some readers may find this opening section a bit difficult. However, a little persistence, the editors feel, will reward the effort. If the reader finds this opening section a bit too difficult, we suggest beginning with Part II, and then returning to Part I.

In Part I, Don MacKay asks if human thought can be reduced to a recording or a consciousness of "nothing but" neural activity, or the like. Drawing upon more than two decades of brain science research, Professor MacKay invites you to join him in solving a most interesting and somewhat complex (but not excessively difficult) logical puzzle to better understand the interplay of mind and matter, the interactions of the physical and the metaphysical, the cognitive and the metacognitive.

John Bishop's paper, "Can There Be Thought Without Language?" further elucidates, from an entirely different perspective, somewhat the same basic issues as discussed by Don MacKay: intentionality or, more classically, the will. John Bishop's question is illuminated by the age-old question, "Do dumb creatures engage in behavior that can be called 'thinking'?" His answer is a fascinating reaffirmation of the central role that language plays in the higher processes we all agree to call thinking. John Bishop does not entirely solve the problems, but his reasoning is a brilliant survey of one aspect of the problem, "What is thinking?"

Leonard Ninnes' essay, "Hegel on Pure Thought" summarizes the Hegelian criticisms of formal logic to anticipate why cognitive psychologists had to coin the term "metacognition" to denote, among other things, a process, an interplay between the reality, perceiving, and knowing. Ninnes' logic again establishes a necessary unity between *Geist* or "spirit" and Nature as it really is.

In summary, one of the fascinating aspects of the mind is its ability to observe itself. One artistic expression of this aspect of mind is the infinity mirror: one light source between two mirrors, with one of the mirrors allowing light to escape, partially. As one looks at that mirror, one sees that light extending infinitely into the distance. Once thought escapes from inside the organism, if the metaphor holds, the limits of that extension cannot be found. The mind, then, might start from nothing and go on looking at itself from an ever-increasing level of detachment.

All three papers in this section will provide teachers of thinking skills with some ideas for recreational exercises to help their abler students develop an abiding interest in the subject of pure thought, or thinking that will have gone through the evolution from nothingness to concreteness to abstractness to a unity with the universe.

Such reflections are no longer restricted to philosophical or theological debates for the simple reason that thinking is now a popular topic, popular with an increasing proportion of experts and laypersons.

SEEING THE WOOD AND THE TREES[1]

D. M. MacKay

ABSTRACT

It is sometimes suggested that thinking has no determinative efficacy, and that neurophysiological explanations can, in principle, supplant those in terms of cognitive agency. Such reductionism ignores a vital distinction between determination of *force* and determination of *form*. Even if the brain were physically determinate, the outcome of a choice need not be inevitable for the chooser.

Brain science is unique in having two different kinds of fact to which to do justice: on the one hand, those of conscious experience, expressed typically in the first person (I see . . ., I think . . ., I have to decide whether to . . .); on the other hand, the facts of neurophysiology and other scientific "observer-stories" about the brain. The object of brain science, ideally, is to discover a correlate in the "brain-story" for each entry in the "I-story." Another object is to discover coherent, systemic connections between the different entries in the brain-story so that the physical, bodily system can be understood in purely mechanistic terms. In pursuing this aim, the brain scientist is willing (and indeed obligated) to pick up clues, both from conscious experience and from neurophysiology. The study of optical illusions, for example, has much to tell us about ways in which cerebral information-processing mechanisms can go wrong, and thus can give us clues about the principles on which they normally function (MacKay, 1970).

Early neurophysiological studies of single-cell activity predisposed theorists towards speculative models in which "pontifical neurones" were supposed to be responsible for the "decision-making" involved in pattern-recognition and similar discrete changes of brain state. Today, however, evidence is accumulating to suggest that in most neural networks, the cells engage in "cooperative" activity so that information-processing functions may be distributed over a large population of cells, and decision-making may be represented by transitions from one cooperative mode to another, rather than by changes in a single neurone (MacKay, 1978a).

This said, it would be a mistake to see brain function as so holistic that one could not hope to find localizable correlates for different conscious experiences or to im-

---

D.M. MacKay is in the Department of Communication and Neuroscience at the University of Keele in Staffordshire, England.

1. Two sections of this paper follow fairly closely the arguments published by this author, MacKay (1978b).

agine that all parts of the brain are equally necessary for consciousness. There is much clinical evidence that even the cerebral cortex can sometimes be adequately stimulated physiologically without giving rise to any correlated conscious experience; and that, conversely, quite complex sensorimotor acts can be carried out by the brain and body of a patient who is clinically unconscious (Penfield, 1952).

Over the past 30 years, I have been concerned with the development of information-engineering models of intelligent acts or behaviors in order to provide a conceptual bridge, or working link, between the data of physiology and of experimental psychology (see, *e.g.*, MacKay, 1956, 1966, 1981). These models have indicated a need for a multi-level type of organization, dominated by a supervisory system, with two main functions. The first function is the maintenance and updating of an internal state of conditional readiness at the lower organizing level, in matching response to sensory demands, and on the basis of internal experiments of an anticipatory or planning kind. The second function is the ongoing adjustment or re-ordering of goal-priorities and criteria of evaluation. Without going into detail here, such evaluative supervisory activity seems to offer a natural correlate for such conscious experiences as perceiving, thinking and deciding (MacKay, 1969, 1970, 1978a).

HAS THINKING ANY DETERMINATIVE EFFICACY?

I have given the foregoing brief sketch not so much in order to commend its details (though they do have relevance to the mechanics of thinking) as to provide a concrete image that can serve to illustrate a commonly-posed problem. Thinking is supposed (sometimes at least) to determine what we do. Brain science, however, as indicated above, does its best to trace the causes of all bodily movement in ultimately neurophysiological terms. What room, it may be asked, would be left for the determinative efficacy of thinking, if brain science were (one day) to succeed completely?

In answer to this question, some physiologists have suggested that an appeal to psychological concepts like thinking and deciding represents merely a temporary phase of the science of man, which ultimately will be displaced by physiological understanding of what goes on inside our heads. More extreme ontological reductionists also suggest that this will render obsolete and prescientific all our traditional moral and spiritual assessments of human nature.

Against such reductionist views, writers like Sir Karl Popper and Sir John Eccles (1977) argue for a "dualist interactionist" position that locates such mental activities as thinking and deciding in another "world," from which they are presumed to interact with the brain through some specific cortical area, the "liaison brain."

What is the educator who is concerned with improving the efficiency of human thinking—or indeed, the man in the street—to make of all this? Do we have to choose between a speculative interactionism that might seem to limit the possibility of the scientific explanation of human behavior on the one hand, and, on the other, a dogmatic, materialistic view that (even where it admits the need for so-called "emergent" properties) would reduce the mind-body problem to a brain-rest-of-the body problem (Bunge, 1977)?

I think not. I believe there is a third option which allows us to affirm what the thinkers at each extreme rightly wish to safeguard, without having to sacrifice what either think it necessary to deny.

KEEPING OUR FEET ON THE GROUND

Where should we start, if we want to keep our feet on solid ground? The materialist would have us take the concept of matter as primary; but this is a heavily theory-laden abstraction from the facts of our experience. Should we then start with mind? I do not think so, for the same reason. Instead, I suggest that our most solid starting point is in our immediate experience of what it is like to be a cognitive agent—the facts to which the "I-story" bears witness. In calling this starting point solid, I do not wish to enter into the hoary debate over the notion of "privileged access."[2] What I am pointing to might be better labeled *obligated access;* for what I want to emphasize is that the facts of experience to which the I-story bears witness are facts we would be *lying* to deny. They may sometimes be difficult to put into words; but they demand our best efforts to reckon with them accurately. They are facts to which all our thinking is obliged to do justice.

In the I-story and the brain-story, we do have a kind of irreducible dualism, both of data and of categories. But does this require us to postulate a dualism of interacting, quasi-substantial entities? That I must sometimes engage in deliberate thinking and deciding in order to determine what I do is a fact that I would be lying to deny. But is interaction between entities the only conceptual model available to us? Surely not. Consider, for example, a computer solving an equation. The operator can easily demonstrate that its behavior is determined by the equation; and it is important (for his reputation) that this be true. Yet there is no suggestion here that the components of the computer are being interfered with, or influenced quasi-physically, by the equation it is solving. Again, we are familiar nowadays with the principles on which automata can be designed to do jobs we would deem intelligent if done by human beings (MacKay, 1951, 1962, 1965, 1980). Of such systems we can say that their behavior is determined by the goals they are pursuing in their changing world, without denying that strict physical causality determines what each component is doing.

All appearance of conflict here is avoided if we recognize the distinction between two conceptual levels of determination:

1. *Physical* analysis is concerned, broadly speaking, to account for the determination of one *force* by another *force*.
2. *Informational* analysis, especially as applied to machines and living organisms, is concerned to account for the determination of one *form* by another *form*.

There is clearly no self-contradiction in saying that a given process was determined as to its energetics by a certain pattern of energy flow, and as to its form by a certain pattern of information flow.

The suggestion I have put forward elsewhere (*e.g.* 1951, 1954, 1966, 1978a and 1980) is that our bodily activities as cognitive agents depend on our conscious thinking and deciding for the determination of their form, in something of the sense in which the bodily activity of a goal-pursuing automaton depends on the calculations and other information-processing procedures in its computing networks. I am not, of course, suggesting that our brains are no more than computers, still less that we ourselves are insensate automata. The boot here is on the other foot; for it is as conscious agents that we are considering the whole question! My point is only that there

---

2. A discussion of "privileged access" as a perennial problem in the philosophical literature on thinking is carried forward by John Bishop in the following paper.

is no more need to consider physical and informational explanations (or determinations) as mutually exclusive rivals in the one case than in the other. By distinguishing (as a communication engineer does) between two levels of determination—the *energetic* and the *informational*—we can see how, even if the chainmesh of physical causality were unbroken at the energetic level, the *form* of our bodily actions can still be determined by our thinking and deciding, leaving us as much responsible for them as we ever were. The essential condition, I suggest, is that our conscious form-determining activity is *embodied in*, rather than running alongside, the cooperative activity of the supervisory system of the brain.

ARE WE NOTHING BUT PHYSIOLOGICAL MECHANISMS?

To the question whether we are really nothing but physiological mechanisms, then, our answer must be, "yes and no." Viewed from the outside, there seems no reason to doubt that the components of our brains work according to physico-chemical principles, as do other parts of our bodies. We know pitifully little of the details, but it looks as if at that level, and in that sense, our brains are indeed physiological mechanisms. What this does *not* imply, however, is that we are not also and equally really conscious, thinking, self-determining agents. In the case of the human being, as in that of the computer, to insist on giving the first description priority as "more parsimonious"—by appeal to Occam's Razor or whatever—would be simply to miss the point validly made by the second. Occam was concerned that our descriptions be no more elaborate than our data demanded—but in the case of ourselves as cognitive agents the facts of our conscious experience are data even more solidly demanding than those about our nervous system.

Of course, as with the computer, one level of description and explanation may be more relevant to a given purpose than another; but there is no question of conflict. In all such cases we must simply settle down to learn, quite easily and peacefully, to see both the wood and the trees. Reality can have many levels, all of which must be reckoned with in appropriate circumstances if we are to be truly realistic.

This point seems to be missed in much popular scientific writing about human beings. Instead there is a subtle (or sometimes blatant) indoctrination of the readers with the fallacy of ontological reductionism or "nothing-buttery." Typically, this is introduced by terms like "really" or "merely," with the implication that because the "reduced" account is a scientific one, the dismissal of metaphysical aspects of human nature has the prestige of science behind it. The truth is otherwise. The good name of science is needlessly damaged by discreditable propaganda of this sort. To disparage other accounts of human nature in the name of science, on the grounds that humans are really just a network of biological computing systems, or really just naked apes, or really "throwaway survival machines for our immortal genes" (blurb on the cover of Richard Dawkins' *The Selfish Gene*) is, wittingly or otherwise, to attempt to deceive the public. It is simply false to suggest on any of these grounds that we are warranted to deny or neglect more traditional assessments of human beings as conscious moral and spiritual agents. Naturally, we all want to be realistic in our view of ourselves. To the extent that any of these scientific pictures is backed by good evidence, we must surely accept that we *really are* what each describes. What I would urge is that our realism be *comprehensive*, recognizing that we really are not just one of these but *all of them and more*. To be human is to be a mysterious reality, with many aspects, both inside (witness the facts of the I-story) and outside (witness the facts of the brain-story and other observer-stories). I see no objection to describing these as complementary aspects of a unity; and in that specific sense—which, incidentally, I believe to be consonant with the view of man presented in the Christian Bible—I have some sympathy with monists, as well as with dualists (MacKay, 1980). The comprehensive realism I am advocating, however, is poles apart from the ontological reductionism that would deny reality to all but one level or aspect, whether material or spiritual, of the complex unity that is our human nature. Only by learning to recognize and do justice to all of these aspects can we hope to achieve the full potential of what it is to be human. Perhaps there is scope for some useful educational research here, as to the best ways of teaching *methodological* reductionism (as a valid and, in principle, innocuous scientific habit of mind) without illicitly inculcating the unfounded *ontological* reductionism of "nothing-buttery."

BRAIN AND WILL

So far, my argument has been independent of the precision with which we may suppose that the physical state of brain-plus-environment determines its future. Strict determinism is out of fashion in physics, and it is not part of my purpose to reinstate it. Let me end, however, by summarizing an argument presented elsewhere (*e.g.* MacKay, 1956, 1957, 1958b, 1960, 1964, 1973), which shows among other things that the I-story is no mere translation of the brain-story, and that there is no need to *deny* physical determinism (in the scientific sense) in order to prove that our immediate future as cognitive agents is *not inevitable for us,* even if it were predictable for detached non-participants. The basic point I want to establish is that talk about the immediate future of cognitive agents is inescapably *relativistic,* so that what is valid from the standpoint of a non-participant may be systematically invalid from the standpoint of the agent himself. Furthermore, where what is in question is the outcome of a cognitive process, a principle of indeterminacy applies, according to which *there does not exist,* even unknown to the agent, a completely determinate specification of his immediate future, with an *unconditional* claim to his assent. To put it otherwise, even in a physically determinate world (in the scientific sense), the mechanistic future brain-story that we might imagine being told by an omniscient Laplacean observer is systematically invalid for the agent whose brain it is, and so has no claim to be a translation of, let alone to supplant, the voluntaristic story that the agent himself can tell about his thinking and deciding. Without going into details, the proof of the above "non-existence theorem" is simple: assuming that conscious, cognitive processes and brain processes are correlated (not necessarily one-to-one, but so that *no significant change in cognitive state can take place without a correspondingly significant change in brain state*), then no complete specification of an immediately-future brain state could be equally accurate, whether or not the agent himself believed it. If accurate only on the assumption that the agent would *not* know or believe it, it clearly has no claim to his assent, since it would be inaccurate if the agent were to believe it. If, however, we imagine a specification adjusted so as to become accurate if (and only if) the agent believed it, then, although the agent would (*ex hypothesi*) be correct to believe this one, he would not be mistaken to disbelieve it (since it is inaccurate unless believed by the agent).

Even this specification, then, would have no *unconditional* claim to represent what the agent would be correct to believe, and mistaken to disbelieve, about the immediate future, if only he knew it. Note that this says much more than that the agent cannot predict his own future, or cannot learn or believe a prediction of it. We are saying that no prediction exists that can establish (even behind his back) an unconditional beliefworthiness-by-him. If calling the agent's future inevitable implies that it has one and only one specification, with an unconditional claim to the assent of all, including the agent if only he knew it, then the foregoing proves that his immediate future *is not completely inevitable* for a cognitive agent, even were his brain as mechanically determinate as a piece of clockwork (which, incidentally, it is not).

RESPONSIBILITY

Of course, the mere fact that a future event is indeterminate for an agent would not of itself imply that that agent had any responsibility for determining it. But the future events we are talking about are precisely those events whose form depends (in the sense explicated earlier) on the outcome of the cognitive information-processing activity we call making a decision. It is because the agent consciously decided to do what he did that he has *prima facie* responsibility for having done it. What we have been asking is whether this responsibility could be deemed reduced or abolished if the brain were a physically-determinate mechanism, on the grounds that the outcome would then be inevitable for the agent. What our non-existence proof does is to rule out this potential objection, leaving unchallenged the positive grounds for recognizing the agent's responsibility (namely, that it was he who consciously and deliberately made up his mind to do what he did).

Conversely, it is no part of our argument that responsibility for a future action would necessarily be diminished if the agent *could* predict it. Indeed, when the agent finally says, "O.K.—I'll do X," we could regard this as *both* determining *and* predicting that he will do X. By making up his mind that he will (or will not) do X, the agent makes it the case (other things being equal) that he does (or does not) do X. Here, the agent's thinking and believing is part of what *determines* the outcome. He can be correct in believing that he will do X; but he would not have been incorrect had he believed that he would not do X—for his coming to that conclusion would have ensured (*ex hypothesi*) that X would not be done. This is precisely what distinguishes foreknowledge of a free action from foreknowledge of an inevitable future event, such as the setting of the sun.

Note, however, the relativistic element here. Nothing in the foregoing argument proves that the outcome of an agent's thinking and deciding must be indeterminate for detached non-participants. The point is that even an outcome predictable-for-detached-non-participants need not be inevitable-for-the-agent. For cognitive agents in dialogue, of course, the above indeterminacy generalises, so that no complete specification of the future course of the dialogue exists, with an unconditional claim to the assent of *any* of the participants. In this sense, participants in dialogue know one another as free beings (MacKay, 1967).

IMPLICATIONS FOR TEACHING

How then, in teaching the analytical (methodologically reductionist) sciences of man, can we help students to see both the wood and the trees? Not, I think, by attempting abstract arguments such as the above, at least in the first place; but by taking pains to present data from different levels as positively complementary (in the sense that they are shown to be by the above argument), rather than as exclusive alternatives jostling for acceptance (MacKay, 1958a). The example of the two complementary levels of explanation of a computing process can help to expose the unjustified thought processes in "nothing-buttery," though it must not be taken to imply that brains operate like computing machines, or that minds are like equations! Most important of all, perhaps, is the need constantly to remind ourselves and our students that we are conscious agents first and foremost: that it is only as such that we learn anything about the physical world, including our brains: so that if there were any real conflict between the different levels of description, it is to our first-hand knowledge of what it is like to be conscious agents that all our thinking must do justice. This recognized, the immense and ever-growing value of knowledge gained by scientifically reductionist methods can be thankfully accepted, without any need to set limits *a priori* to its completeness-in-principle in order to admit the determinative efficacy of our thinking, and our responsibility for its consequences.

There is, after all, nothing so very exceptional about learning to see both the wood and the trees.

REFERENCES

Bunge, M. "Emergence and the Mind," *Neuroscience,* 1977, *2,* 501–510.

MacKay, D.M. "Mindlike Behavior in Artefacts," *British Journal for the Philosophy of Science,* 1951, *II,* 105–121.

MacKay, D.M. "On Comparing the Brain with Machines," *The Advancement of Science,* 1954, *40,* 402–406. Reprinted in *American Scientist,* 1954, *42,* 261–268, *Annual Report of Smithsonian Institute,* 1954, 231–240.

MacKay, D.M. "Towards an Information-flow Model of Human Behavior," *British Journal of Psychology,* 1956, *47,* 30–43. Reprinted in *Modern Systems Research for the Behavioral Scientist,* Buckley, W. (ed.), Chicago: Aldine Publishing Company, 1968.

MacKay, D.M. "Brain and Will," *The Listener,* 1957, May 9th and 16th. Reprinted (revised) in *Body and Mind,* Vesey, G. N. A. (ed.), London: Allen & Unwin, 1964.

MacKay, D.M. "Complementarity II," *Aristotelian Society Supplement,* 1958a, *32,* 105–122.

MacKay, D.M. "On the Logical Indeterminacy of a Free Choice," *Proceedings of the XIIth International Congress of Philosophy, Venice,* 1958b, G. C. Sansoni, 249–256. Also (expanded) in *Mind,* 1960, *69,* 31–40.

MacKay, D.M. "The Use of Behavioural Language to Refer to Mechanical Processes," *British Journal for the Philosophy of Science,* 1962, *XIII,* 89–103.

MacKay, D.M. "From Mechanism to Mind," In Smythies, J. R. (Ed.), *Brain and Mind.* London: Routledge and Kegan Paul, 1965.

MacKay, D.M. "Cerebral Organization and the Conscious Control of Action," In Eccles, J.C. (Ed.), *Brain and Conscious Experience.* New York: Springer, 1966.

MacKay, D.M. "The Mechanization of Normative Behavior." In Thayer, L. (Ed.), *Communication: Theory and Research.* Springfield, IL: Charles C. Thomas, 1967.

MacKay, D.M. *Information, Mechanism and Meaning.* Cambridge, MA: M.I.T. Press, 1969.

MacKay, D.M. "Ways of Looking at Perception." In Dodwell, P. C. (Ed.), *Perceptual Processing.* New York: Appleton-Century-Crofts, 1970.

MacKay, D.M. "The Logical Indeterminateness of Human Choices," *British Journal for the Philosophy of Science,* 1973, *24,* 405–408.

MacKay, D.M. "The Dynamics of Perception." In Buser, P. A. and Rougeul-

Buser, A. (Eds.), *Cerebral Correlates of Conscious Experience.* Amsterdam: Elsevier, 1978a.

MacKay, D.M. "Selves and Brains," *Neuroscience,* 1978b, *3,* 599–606.

MacKay, D.M. *Brains, Machines and Persons.* London: Collins, 1980.

MacKay, D.M. "Neural Basis of Cognitive Experience." In Székely, G., Lábos, E. and Damjanovich, S. (Eds.), *Neural Communication and Control.* Oxford: Pergamon and Budapest: Akadémiai Kiado, 1981.

Penfield, W. "Epileptic Automatism and the Centrencephalic Integrating System." Association for Research in Nervous and Mental Disorders, Proceedings, (1950), 1952, *30,* 513–528.

Popper, K.R. and Eccles, J.C. *The Self and its Brain—An Argument for Interactionism.* Berlin: Springer International, 1977.

CAN THERE BE THOUGHT WITHOUT LANGUAGE?

John C. Bishop

ABSTRACT

This paper surveys the range of "thought and language" issues, gives brief consideration to the notion of a language of thought, and focuses on the applicability of the purposive explanations of human folk psychology beyond the community of language-using beings. Two types of argument for restricting thought to language-users are examined and found wanting. But it is argued that those who believe that dumb creatures can engage in practical reasoning and intentional action have no more than a *prima facie* case in their favor. There is room to doubt whether a developed explanatory science of dumb animal behavior need employ purposive explanations at all.

THE RANGE OF ISSUES

Is thought possible without language? This is not one question, but many. First, there are empirical questions about connections between levels of thought and grades of linguistic skill. Second, there is the question whether thought must always take place in language, even if its "speech" is silent. And, third, there is the question whether our folk psychology is applicable only within the community of language users. My focus will be on the second and, especially, on the third of these issues.

The first set of questions is, of course, very important. Perhaps it is only language-users who possess certain levels of consciousness and reasoning ability. If so, does language learning trigger new levels of thought, or are these rather its preconditions? Knowledge of the precise function of various linguistic skills in the *repertoire* of intelligence would show us their relative importance in a total educational strategy. We might discover, for instance, what contribution multilingualism makes to intelligence—are there, indeed, some thoughts which just cannot be had except "in" a certain language? To what extent is abstract thinking possible only through extending the resources of existing languages? Are there some sorts of thinking which *cannot* be promoted by improving a person's linguistic skills? And

J.C. Bishop is in the Department of Philosophy at the University of Auckland in New Zealand.

13

so on. For answers to these questions, we look to the research of educationalists, psychologists and—let me stress—neurophysiologists, who seek to uncover the actual mechanisms of intelligence and language use. The philosopher may assist such empirical research with conceptual clarification and methodological critiques, but his true interest in the "thought and language" issue rests on those questions which concern the total vision we have of our world and our place in it. The second and third of our questions are of this character.

IS THINKING ESSENTIALLY LINGUISTIC?

Must thinking always express itself in language? We typically represent our own or somebody else's thoughts as a sequence of linguistic expressions. This tempts us to suppose that all thinking is linguistic. Yet it is fallacious to infer that since we must employ linguistic expressions to describe what a person is thinking, he must also use these same expressions in his thinking. For one thing, he may not share our language. But it does not even follow that he should use *any* language in his thinking. Human beings often behave intentionally without conscious, let alone verbal, deliberation. Recall, for example, the last time you took judicious evasive action in traffic. In retrospect you may verbally reconstruct the chain of reasoning which led to your action, but you are still sure that your actual reasoning involved no verbal imagery or silent speech.

Despite this, belief in a "language of thought" attracts some philosophers. (See, for example, Fodor [1975] and Dennett's discussion of the notion of an internal code in which all thinking occurs [Dennett, 1979, Chapters 3, 6, 7 and 9]). Within the class of representations generally, common sense does, however, recognize a sub-class whose meanings can be interpreted only through a knowledge of the conventional rules for their use. These are the linguistic representations. Now, it is uncontentious to say that thinking requires representation: a system capable of intentional action must somehow represent its goals to itself and have a means of mapping its environment. But these representations need not be embodied in the symbols of some language. Indeed, a representing system need not *itself* understand any symbolic code at all. Consider, for example, those fiendish heat-seeking missiles deployed to human shame in some theaters of war. An engineer who knew the missile's design would be able to pick out states of its guiding system which register information about the target's position, and this knowledge of the missile's mechanisms would show how these states modify its trajectory. But it would be absurd to suppose that the missile itself uses a rudimentary symbolic language in representing its environment. Of course, we do not suppose that such a missile can think: it can represent only a narrow range of states of its environment, and cannot learn new ways of modifying its behavior to serve its goals. Still, this example does establish that the argument, "thought must be linguistic because it must be representational and representations must occur in a language," can be dismissed on the grounds of the falsity of its second premise. It *may* be true that representations may be *represented* only in a language, but that is another matter.

Not all representations which modify behavior count as genuine thinking. This assertion leaves room for the suggestion that those which do have some intrinsic connection with the use of language. But this is implausible. Our experience of non-deliberative, intentional action shows, *prima facie,* that we do not do all our thinking in language. This presumption could be rebutted if there were an intrinsic connection between any kind of process of representation, however unconscious, and the use of some sort of language. But we have just argued that there is no such connection. And we have already noted the fallacy in seeking to derive such a con-

nection from the plausible claim that, in representing a thought, we have to express
its content verbally. The truth of the matter seems to be that, however important
the use of language is for some types of reasoning, genuine thinking can occur
without the thinker's using any language at all.

INTENTIONAL STATE EXPLANATIONS
AND THE INTENTIONAL-LINGUISTIC THESIS

Even if thinking does not have to take place in language, there may still be a different sort of connection between thought and linguistic ability. We have been
distinguishing genuine thinking (such as I perform when I judge a safe path across
the street) from a mere sequence of behavior-modifying representations (such as the
missile goes through when it alters course). What is the basis of this distinction? It is
grounded in our *folk psychology*—that inter-connected set of beliefs about
ourselves and how we differ from other creatures which provides the background to
our everyday explanations of human behavior. As Wilfrid Sellars in particular has
argued cogently (Sellars, 1963 and 1968), this set of beliefs is similar in structure to
a scientific theory. We think of ourselves as *intentional agents,* beings with some
direct control over events, principally certain types of movements of our own
bodies. We are capable of *acting for reasons:* acting intentionally as a consequence
of practical reasoning from beliefs and intentions. We can also reason theoretically
in working out the implications of what we already (think we) know. Our folk
psychology requires the use of a distinctive schema of explanation which we may call
Intentional State explanation (IS-explanation, for short). To give an IS-explanation
for the occurrence of behavior b is to show the reason for which the agent performed
b. And this requires establishing that the agent had beliefs and intentions which
made performing b-type behavior reasonable, and which contributed causally to his
doing b. (For example: why did Jones cross the street? Because he saw Smith approaching, wanted to avoid him, and believed that if he crossed the street Smith
wouldn't notice him.)

In this framework, the difference between genuine thinking and mere representation may be understood as follows: if b is rightly IS-explained, then b counts as an
intentional action and the sequence of representational (or, as philosophers'
technical usage has it, *intentional*) states, which are crucial in the causal production
of b, has the status of the agent's thoughts—whether or not they were conscious
and deliberate. But if b is not properly IS-explained, because, for example, it can be
fully understood as a conditioned response to a stimulus, no representational state
which may have contributed causally to b's occurrence counts as a thought. There is
thus a set of concepts which form the package deal of folk psychology: being a
thinker, being able to reason from intentions and beliefs, acting for reasons rather
than just responding to stimuli, having at least a minimal responsibility for one's
behavior, and so on. We apply any member of this set only if we are prepared to apply all.

The question remains how we may justify regarding some systems—principally
other humans—as intentional agents, while other systems whose behavior
resembles human action are denied this status. Much popular fascination is sparked
by the idea that we may eventually be obliged to regard some artificial systems as intentional agents. (I vividly recall how I first experienced this fascination while
watching Kubrik's "2001" with its portrayal of the computer, Hal.) There is a
serious philosophical problem at the root of this fascination. Under what conditions
would it be correct to extend our use of IS-explanations, with all that it carries with

it, to highly sophisticated computers, newly discovered alien beings, or even known terrestrial species whose intellectual virtuosity comes to be better appreciated? This question suggests a more radical one: is our folk psychology well-founded anyway? Certainly Intentional State (IS) explanations are important for everyday social and moral interaction, but do they provide a rigorous, scientific way of understanding human behavior? The suspicion that they do not has several sources. Many are convinced that teleological notions have no place in a scientific understanding of reality: physics and chemistry have no need of the notion of action guided by a purpose, and it is arguable that teleological terminology may, in principle, be eliminated from biology. But even if one repudiates prejudice against the teleological, it is hard to deny that significant advances in understanding human behavior—in psychology and, even more strikingly, in the neurosciences—have resulted from methodologies which avoid IS-explanation altogether. Perhaps, then, our folk psychology, like so many past scientific theories, will be displaced by a better theory of human action, and we shall one day look back with the same puzzlement on ancient talk of beliefs and intentions as the modern medical student feels for 17th century talk of humours.

Thus, we want to know: (a) whether IS-explanations are ever genuinely explanatory or not; (b) if they are, what are the criteria for their proper use and the associated demarcation between intentional action and mere well-adapted responses to stimuli; and finally, (c) if IS-explanations are really explanatory, whether it is conceivable that their use should be displaced by a more satisfactory theory of intentional action.

I cannot try to answer these questions here, but it is essential to bring them to light in order to show the significance of our third, and philosophically most significant, "thought and language" issue. Let us agree without further debate that IS-explanations can be genuinely explanatory: the answer to (a) is yes. In that case, (b) demands attention, and we must be prepared to discover, in the light of a clear view of the relevant criteria, that some creatures or machines which we do not commonly regard as persons have at least the capacity for intentional action. It is in the search for these criteria that our third "thought and language" issue emerges, for some philosophers have held that IS-explanations can apply only for behavior exhibited by language-users. Among classical philosophers, both Descartes and Kant accepted versions of this claim, which I shall call the "Intentional-Linguistic," or "I-L," thesis. For recent critical defenses of the I-L thesis, see Davidson (1975), Bennett (1964) and Stich (1979). It is important to note that I-L theorists may consistently agree with my earlier view that genuine thinking need not involve the use of language. Their claim is, rather, that only a language-user can have the status of an intentional agent and so be a genuine thinker. In what follows, I shall discuss briefly and selectively aspects of the recent debate on the I-L thesis. My own view, which I shall support but cannot fully defend here, is that although Intentional-Linguistic (I-L) theorists have failed to meet the onus of proof which is theirs, their opponents—whom I shall call brute intentionalists—have only a *prima facie* case in their favor. They have not decisively established that intentional agents do not need language.

Hume's Argument from Analogy: The Personification Challenge And an Instrumentalist Solution

A straightforward argument from David Hume's *A Treatise of Human Nature* apparently establishes the falsity of the I-L thesis. Some dumb animal behavior is so similar to human intentional action that, to be consistent, it must be explained in the same way—as the outcome of practical reasoning from beliefs and intentions. (See Hume, 1978, pp. 176-179.) Sometimes, of course, we may doubt whether a dumb creature acted for a reason or not, but all such cases will simply involve uncertainty about how strong an analogy the behavior bears to intelligent human action. It seems, as Hume said, "incontestable," that lack of a language does not preclude intentional action.

This argument from analogy, however, has its force blunted by the following "personification" challenge. As Davidson has warned, our tendency to IS-explain some dumb animal behavior may be pure anthropomorphism (see Davidson, 1975, p. 7). There is a difference between behaving *as if* for a reason and *actually* acting for a reason. Accordingly, the sort of behavior Hume appeals to may merely simulate intentional action and have causes quite distinct from those which count as practical reasoning. The personification challenge rests on the assumption that we should accept an IS-explanation of behavior only if there is no satisfactory alternative causal explanation, free of reference to beliefs or intentions. But this assumption is a corollary to a widely-accepted scientific principle of economy: if you *can* explain in terms purely of innate, genetic predisposition, the distraction display of a plover, for example, as it feigns injury or simulates the escape of a small mammal to entice a predator from its ground nest, then surely this account is to be preferred to the purposive, IS-explanation, which its behavior first suggests?

The puzzle is this: do the analogies between dumb animal behavior and human intentional action form independent evidence which confirms that these animals think, or is our perception of these analogies rather the result of anthropomorphic habit? One apparent solution is to argue, as Hume would (see Bishop, 1980a, p. 5), that the distinction between genuinely explanatory attribution of reasons and their merely personificatory use is a false one. For Daniel Dennett, for example, what matters is whether a system's behavior is best predicted from the "intentional stance"—that is, by treating it as reasoning out its responses. (One would, for instance, naturally and advisedly adopt such a stance in playing chess with a computer.) Given that a system is, in this sense, intentional, Dennett finds it unnecessary to wonder whether it really reasons from intentions and beliefs (see Dennett, 1979, Chapters 1 and 14). Yet he apparently ignores an important difference between prediction and explanation: the way the observer has to think of a system in order to predict its behavior *need not* correspond to the truth about how the system works. For example, in Chapter 14 (Dennett, 1979, p. 272), Dennett relates an anecdote about the habitual use of the intentional stance by loggers: "They will say of a young spruce, 'He wants to spread his limbs, but don't let him; then he'll have to stretch up to get his light.'" Dennett remarks, "This way of talking is not just picturesque . . . it is simply an efficient way of making sense of, controlling, predicting *and explaining* the behavior of these plants in a way that nicely circumvents one's ignorance of the controlling mechanisms" (my emphasis). But this way of talking is explanatory only in the barest instrumentalist sense: ignorance of controlling mechanisms provides no excuse for maintaining that the spruce's straight growth is intentional action! If we seek only a satisfactory instrument for making predictions, then causal mechanisms need not be known, and any concern whether or not they count as the system's own reasoning is out of place. But if we seek to know why a system behaves as it does—a question which may remain unanswered long after we have mastered the art of predicting its behavior—the difference between an IS-explanation and genetic or behavioristic explanations will matter a lot. Dennett shows how we can dissolve our puzzle by ceasing to care about finding true explanations for behavior. If we do still care, however, the puzzle remains.

TWO ARGUMENTS FOR THE INTENTIONAL-LINGUISTIC THESIS

It is interesting to speculate on the modern philosophical motivation for maintaining some form of Intentional-Linguistic (I-L) thesis. Perhaps it is hoped that its defense will provide new support for the perennial prejudice in favor of human uniqueness. Now that belief in immortal souls as the guarantee of our special status is unfashionable, the I-L thesis offers a suitably ontologically defused basis for it: we are different because we are the only beings who act for reasons, and this because we alone can use language. It may be, of course, that other true language-using species will be—or have been—found. Then, to avoid the accusation of "speciesism," believers in human uniqueness will need a different defense—or else will be obliged to face the consequences of conceding the existence of intentional agency in other species. (I assume it obvious that linguistic ability is sufficient for intentional agency. But see my discussion in Bishop, 1980b, section IV.) One acutely embarrassing possibility would be to discover that a species we use for food is capable of language. For, as Alice found in *Through the Looking Glass,* it is very difficult to carve a pudding to which—to whom?—one has just been introduced. A being with a language must be granted a point of view which, in principle, another language-user can come to understand, and this has important moral consequences. What the I-L thesis affirms is that *only* language-using beings need be afforded the treatment proper to intentional agents. We shall now consider two sorts of arguments for this claim. Their merits must be assessed quite independently of any facts or assumptions about the motivations of their proponents.

The gist of the first sort of argument is that it makes sense to attribute thoughts only if there is, at least in principle, a means of verifying their existence, but the only way to do this is through their linguistic expression, and so only language-users can sensibly be said to think. Even if the verificationist premise of this argument remains unchallenged, the question is still begged against a brute intentionalist who relies on Hume's argument, according to which much non-linguistic behavior provides adequate evidence for thought. Can any further reason be given for holding that the only satisfactory proof of thinking is the thinker's own linguistic reports, or, better still, his thoughts aloud?

Those who believe so, base their case on an appeal to what we may call *the indeterminacy problem* (see Stich, 1979). To give an IS-explanation for M's behavior, beliefs and intentions which make that type of behavior reasonable must be correctly attributed to M. This can be done only if the *content* of these states is specified: it may be true that M behaved thus because he believed *something* and intended *such-and-such,* but to say just this is hardly explanatory. When we seek to IS-explain a dumb creature's behavior, the determination of the content of its thoughts presents a certain difficulty. The dog sniffs at the ground, settles on a particular spot, digs and finally unearths a bone. What was it thinking as it did so? How can we justify a simple IS-explanation of its behavior in terms of wanting something to chew and believing a bone to be buried at that spot? Can we be sure that the dog thinks of the object it unearths as a bone, rather than just as something chewable, or—more likely, since dogs have greater olfactory sophistication than we do—as a bone at a particular state of maturity fit for chewing? We must surely dismiss any presumption that the dog deals with the world through just the same conceptual framework as we do. Just because of this, however, some philosophers will conclude that IS-explanations of the dog's behavior are inappropriate. When observers disagree about the right IS-explanation of a human action, the matter can, in principle, be settled by the agent's sincere reports of his practical thinking. Does it follow, however, that where this possibility of determining the content of thought is absent, IS-explanation is senseless, or, at least, of no scientific worth?

The brute intentionalist will say not, and for three reasons. First, even if we do not know the precise contents of a dumb creature's thoughts, we may still be certain of crucial references they make. The dog is certainly thinking about *what we call* the bone, digging, and its desire to chew, even if we don't know *how it thinks* of these things. There are grades of determinacy in the attribution of thought—and those we achieve with the higher mammals at least suffice to support IS-explanation. Second, it is a commonplace that the meaning of an expression in our language can never be fully determinately translated in another. (See Quine, 1960, Chapter II.) Accordingly, if it is suggested that *any* degree of indeterminacy renders IS-explanation illegitimate, the absurd consequence will be that the behavior of humans who do not understand my language cannot correctly be IS-explained by me. Finally, even with those who can speak my language, since they do much of their intelligent reasoning without using any language at all, my task in determining what they think cannot always consist in specifying the linguistic expressions they use. Thus, the use of IS-explanation to understand behavior produced through non-linguistic reasoning, if acceptable at all, cannot have its legitimacy affected by the presence or lack of linguistic ability.

The I-L theorist's only comeback is, first, to reject the imputation that he regards *any* degree of indeterminacy as precluding IS-explanation, and, second, to explain further why that level of indeterminacy which arises once linguistic evidence is unavailable does rob IS-explanation of its legitimacy. Human agents whose practical reasoning is non-linguistic may still give, in retrospect, a linguistic reconstruction of their thoughts which helps the observer decide between competing IS-explanations of their actions. If this type of independent confirmation must be possible and can be supplied only by linguistic behavior, then a version of the I-L thesis would follow. But independent evidence about a dumb creature's thought may perhaps be obtained by observing the general context of behavior in which its apparent intentional action occurs—or, better still, by discovering that its neural mechanisms resemble those which realize intentional thinking in humans. So this argument from the difficulty of establishing just what dumb animals think does not decisively support the I-L thesis.

A second type of argument proposes that the capacity for practical reasoning from beliefs and intentions has complex corequisites, some of which could only be satisfied by a language-user. Davidson (1975) offers an influential argument of this kind: in order to have beliefs, as an intentional agent must, it is necessary also to have the concept of belief; but only a language-user can have this concept, so no dumb creatures can be intentional agents.

To have the concept of belief is to be able to have beliefs about beliefs, whether one's own or another's. Davidson argues that, to have beliefs at all, one must grasp the possibility of mistaken belief. But this involves recognizing the contrast between true and false belief, and so is possible only for a system which has the notion of belief itself. This argument has force. As we have seen, a system is not regarded as believing, intending or thinking, just because it exhibits what an observer can best think of as behavior-modifying representations. (Recall the heat-seeking missile.) To grant that a system has beliefs, we need to know that it appropriates the contents of its intentional states in reasoning of its own. Arguably, this condition is satisfied only if the system can usually recognize when its representations do not represent things as they truly are, and modify its behavior accordingly. Insects, for example, do not think because when their representational systems lead them astray, they persist in the mistake to a point of exhaustion or even destruction. (See, for example, Wooldridge's description of the wasp *Sphex,* quoted by Dennett, 1979, p. 65.) As I have argued elsewhere (Bishop, 1980a, Section IV), we may doubt the validity of inferring that since to be mistaken is to have a false belief, any system which can recognize its own mistake must have the concept of belief. I shall, however, ignore this doubt for present purposes, and consider Davidson's other premise: why is the capacity for higher-order intentional states restricted to language-users?

Davidson argues that the concept of the contrast between true and false belief "can emerge only in the context of interpretation (*sc.*: of linguistic utterances), which alone forces us to the idea of an objective, public truth" (Davidson, 1975, p. 22). His case depends on a subtle analysis of linguistic interpretation. He shows that an interpreter must understand the difference between a speaker's holding an utterance to be true and its actually being true, and so must have the concept of belief. His argument for the converse thesis—that only an interpreter can ever develop the concept of belief—is harder to follow. (See my discussion, Bishop, 1980a, Section III.) Consider the following version, which may have some affinity with Davidson's own.

Beliefs as such are not observable. They have strikingly similar status to the postulated entities of a scientific theory. (See Sellars, 1963 and 1968, and Bishop, 1980b, for further discussion and references.) An agent's beliefs and intentions do not confront the observer: rather, the observer's folk psychological theory for interpreting the agent's behavior requires reference to them. As Davidson shows, behavior cannot be radically interpreted as linguistic without reference to beliefs and intentions. So an interpreter of language is obliged to operate with these theoretical concepts of belief and intention. No concept belongs to a system unless it has a sufficient reason for its use. There is a sufficient reason for its use only if the system could not function as it does without that concept. We have seen that there is sufficient reason for a language-user to have the concept of belief. Beyond the context of linguistic interpretation, however, there is no sufficient reason for its possession. So, only language-users can have this concept, and—if its possession is indeed essential for intentional agency—only language-users, therefore, can act for reasons.

It is plausible that if there is no aspect of its behavior for which a system needs to use a given concept, then there is no point in attributing it. The brute intentionalist need not disagree: his best reply is to argue that there are behavioral contexts in which a dumb animal must employ the concept of belief to function as it does. The most promising of such contexts are those where a dumb creature appears to practice intelligent deceit. For, to try to deceive is to try to produce a false belief. So only one who has the concepts of belief and truth can intend to deceive. Thus, a single authentic case of intentional deception by a dumb animal would overthrow the argument, and provide as well proof positive that IS-explanations sometimes rightly apply to dumb behavior. Because the promise of vindicating brute intentionalism is now involved, we should turn to a wider discussion of strategies for argument on this side of the debate. Let us remind ourselves, however, that neither of the types of argument considered in this Section prove the I-L thesis, though the second *may* succeed, if there is no clear evidence for higher-order beliefs amongst creatures with no language.

ARGUMENTS FOR BRUTE INTENTIONALISM

The appeal to alleged deception typifies a general strategy for emphasizing the force of Hume's argument from analogy. With much animal behavior, the suspicion that IS-explanation is inappropriate persists because we envisage simpler possible explanations in terms, for example, of stimulus-response conditioning or genetic predispositions. But when animal behavior shows inventiveness, IS-explanations are harder to resist. Consider this case which Dennett had from his friend Peter Ashley:

> One evening I was sitting in a chair at my home, the *only* chair my dog is allowed to sleep in. The dog was lying in front of me, whimpering. She was getting nowhere in her trying to convince me to give up the chair to her. (Then) she stood up, and went to the front door where I could still easily see her. She scratched the door, giving me the impression that she had given up trying to get the chair and had decided to go out. However, as soon as I reached the door to let her out, she ran back across the room and climbed into her chair, the chair she had forced me to leave (Dennett, 1979, pp. 274-275).

Such behavior must surely have an IS-explanation attributing a *third*-order intentional state to the dog, namely the intention to make Ashley believe that she wanted to go out. If so, we have a counter-example to Davidson's premise that only language-users can have the concept of belief. It turns out, however, that this IS-explanation can be resisted in favor of a behaviorist account, as Dennett points out in his discussion. (This does not finally bother Dennett, of course, given his instrumentalism noted earlier.) For, the dog can learn the connection between her scratching the door and Ashley's opening it, without recognizing that this connection is causally mediated by a belief of her master's.

Is there, then, any form of non-linguistic behavior which must be IS-explained? Robert Kirk (1967) and Donald Weiss (1975) have argued that there could be. If we describe the behavior of a research scientist, but exclude from it any reference to the use of written or spoken language, we may still (by dint of certain compensatory devices) retain a description of behavior which can be interpreted only as intelligent inquiry. Since such behavior is logically possible, Kirk and Weiss argue, there can be no conceptually necessary connection between intentional action (of which scientific inquiry is a very sophisticated variety) and linguistic ability. Kirk and Weiss each describe imaginary non-language-using creatures whose behavior strongly suggests that they are undertaking some scientific inquiry and so maintain that, even if we have our doubts about applying Hume's analogy to *actual* dumb animal behavior, we can still be sure that there is *possible* dumb behavior to which it would certainly apply.

Kirk and Weiss do demonstrate that the onus of proof lies with the I-L theorist if he wishes to hold the conceptual incoherence of practical reasoning without language. But they establish no more. It is a bothersome feature of dialectical appeals to the imagination that they invite the challenge of alternative descriptions of what is allegedly imagined. A convinced I-L theorist can thus insist that the imaginary creatures Kirk and Weiss describe would, just because they are clearly intentional agents, have to have a *secret* language. Accordingly, Kirk and Weiss do not prove that *there cannot be* a satisfactory proof of the I-L thesis. In the absence of any such proof, however, they do underline the *prima facie* evidence in their favor.

A further weakness in this strategy emerges once we note that the I-L theorist need not hold so strong a version of the thesis. Some I-L theorists, no doubt, do see conceptual confusion or category error in attributing thought to dumb creatures. But others, while agreeing that it is coherent to IS-explain dumb animal behavior, will insist, nevertheless, that an adequately rigorous scientific theory of animal behavior cannot be based on extending human folk psychology. Against this weaker form of I-L thesis, a stronger brute intentionalism maintains that IS-explanation does play an important part in an organized theory of animal behavior. Because Kirk and Weiss have to appeal to imaginary dumb animal behavior, their argument offers no support for this strong brute intentionalism.

A different brute intentionalist strategy is to appeal to the possibility of psychophysical correlations. (See, for example, Armstrong, 1973, pp. 33–34.) If we discovered that when language-users believe that p, they are uniformly in neural state s, and then found an analogue of s in the neural organization of a dumb animal, when its behavior suggests that it believes that p, such a connection would surely establish that the animal did believe that p, and show that language is not necessary for belief. A strong I-L theorist could reply, however, that it is a corollary of his thesis that there can be no psychophysical theory which would yield such correlations. Thus, for this theorist, the discovery of s's analogue would *falsify* the hypothesis that whenever a creature exhibits an s-type state, it uses the belief that p in its practical reasoning. Here the I-L theorist may call to aid recent advocates of functionalism in the philosophy of mind, who provide reasons for doubting the very possibility of psychophysics. (See, for example, Putnam, 1975.) But this reply is justifiable only given a proof of the I-L thesis: without this, even the bare logical possibility of psychophysical evidence for dumb animal thoughts is a further element in the *prima facie* case for brute intentionalism.

Once again, this strategy appeals only to a possibility: we do not yet have a psychophysical theory of the sort envisaged. So it can hardly support the stronger brute intentionalism—but, even if we did have such a theory, and found the correlates of specific beliefs and intentions in dumb creatures' brains, it would still not *follow,* as the stronger version of brute intentionalism maintains, that the right way to explain their behavior must involve Intentional-State-explanations.

Once we have the sort of neurophysiological knowledge which such a psychophysical theory would require, it may well be that the real work of explaining behavior can be carried on entirely on the neurophysiological level. This will, as admitted earlier, be a possibility for human as well as dumb animal behavior. MacKay's contribution in this volume offers an argument for the necessity of retaining IS-explanation for human purposive behavior, no matter what developments may be achieved in the neurosciences. But, even if these arguments succeed, it is a further question whether they could be applied to justify IS-explaining the behavior of any dumb creature.

We have seen, then, how the apparently innocuous question whether there can be thought without language raises fundamental issues about the extent of application of a form of explanation, basic to our present understanding of ourselves and our distinctness. Much more needs to be said. But in the meantime we may conclude as follows: no justification has been found for the strong claim that Intentional-State explanations make no proper sense when applied to the behavior of dumb creatures. Neither has it been shown that there can be no such justification.

Nevertheless, there is room for modest scepticism about the use of IS-explanations beyond the community of language-users. While linguistic behavior does force the use of some IS-explanations, it remains doubtful whether any actual forms of dumb animal behavior fail to be adequately explained in causal terms which make no essential reference to beliefs or purposes, reasons or intentions.

REFERENCES

Armstrong, D.M. *Belief, Truth and Knowledge.* Cambridge: University Press, 1973.

Bennett, Jonathan. *Rationality: an Essay Towards Analysis.* London: Routledge and Kegan Paul, 1964.

Bishop, John. (1980a) "More Thought on Thought and Talk," *Mind,* 1980, *89,* 1–16.

Bishop, John. (1980b) "The Analogy Theory of Thinking," *Australasian Journal of*

Philosophy, 1980, *58,* 222–238.

Davidson, Donald. "Thought and Talk." In *Mind and Language,* Guttenplan, S. (Ed.). Oxford: Clarendon Press, 1975.

Dennett, Daniel C. *Brainstorms: Philosophical Essays on Mind and Psychology.* Hassocks, Sussex: Harvester Press, 1979.

Fodor, J. *The Language of Thought.* New York: Crowell, 1975.

Guttenplan, S. (Ed.) *Mind and Language.* Oxford: Clarendon Press, 1975.

Hume, David. *A Treatise of Human Nature,* L. A. Selby-Bigge (Ed.), 2nd edition, revised by P. H. Nidditch. Oxford: Clarendon Press, 1978.

Kirk, Robert. "Rationality without Language," *Mind,* 1967, *76,* 369–386.

Putnam, Hilary. "Mind and Machines" and "Philosophy and our Mental Life," *Mind Language and Reality, Philosophical Papers, Vol. 2.* Cambridge: University Press, 1975.

Quine, W.V.O. *Word and Object.* Cambridge, MA: M.I.T. Press, 1960.

Sellars, Wilfrid. *Science, Perception and Reality.* London: Routledge and Kegan Paul, 1963.

Sellars, Wilfrid. *Science and Metaphysics: Variations on Kantian Themes.* London: Routledge and Kegan Paul, 1968.

Stitch, Stephen P. "Do Animals have Beliefs?" *Australasian Journal of Philosophy,* 1979, *57,* 15–28.

Weiss, Donald. "Professor Malcolm on Animal Intelligence," *Philosophical Review,* 1975, *84,* 88–95.

HEGEL ON PURE THOUGHT

Leonard E. Ninnes

ABSTRACT

Hegel claims to have shown how each individual thinker can attain the standpoint of Absolute Knowledge or Pure Objective Thought. This paper considers three aspects of that claim: first, how one reaches the level of Pure Thought; second, the failure of formal logic; and thirdly, the way Hegel begins his logic.

Hegel is concerned to demonstrate how we attain to the unity of thought and being, a level of comprehension Hegel calls Absolute Knowledge. This concern with unity is not, however, limited to Hegel. We find this concern with unity, with the attempt to integrate or interrelate seemingly disparate phenomena a current concern as well. For example, in his recent book Bateson (1980) similarly argues for the necessary unity of mind and nature.

Hegel, however, more than any other thinker, has attempted to demonstrate that this unity is achieved through the *failure* of all other ways of thinking about the world. Thus, it is instructive to consider Hegel's arguments concerning the faults of inferior or inadequate modes of thought. If he is correct, we may need to change our way of thinking.

Hegel claims to have shown how each individual thinker can attain the standpoint of Absolute Knowledge. This standpoint is positively free from error or one-sidedness, and it grasps reality as it really is. For this standpoint there is nothing beyond its conceptual comprehension—no reality transcendent to its knowledge. This standpoint is the conclusion to Hegel's *Phenomenology of Spirit*, and the level at which his *Science of Logic* is to be developed.

This is indeed an amazing claim. It is also the desire of all who seek knowledge—to know reality as it truly is, without prejudice arising from a one-sided or limited point of view, without bias due to method or presupposition. But it is generally recognised by scientists that such a desire is a will-o'-the-wisp. That the reality under investigation is a reality from the point of view of the scientist *only*. Change the point of view or experimental situation and you change the reality as well.[1]

L.E. Ninnes is in the Department of Politics and Sociology at the Paisley College of Technology in Scotland.

1. As an example we cite Davies (1980): "Neils Bohr, the originator of the quantum atom argued that it is meaningless to regard an atom, or any other denizen of the microcosmos as

This view that Absolute Knowledge, or knowledge of things as they really are, is impossible, has its counterpart in various philosophical viewpoints. The general view can be expressed as follows: there is a bifurcation of reality into an objective material realm and a subjective mental realm. Knowledge then becomes a subjective affair where we, in the subjective realm, are either caused to hold certain ideas but are unable to know the causal agency (for to know it would be to simply have more ideas in the mind—we are unable to vacate our subjectivity and view the world from without) or, we impose upon the world certain constraints—that is we experience it. We are here likewise unable to relinquish our experience, such that we can grasp reality in an unconditioned manner. We also note this view in Bateson (1980, pp. 38–39).

And following this bifurcation is the problem of adequately dealing with human existence itself. For it would appear at first glance that human beings appear to occupy the interface between the two realms. We are both bodily beings, amongst other things, *and* we are aware of our world or bodily existence.

The attempt to deny this bifurcation of reality and assert a monist view (*i.e.*, that there is but one reality) involves the problem of showing how one reality can contain properties that appear to be irreconcilable, *i.e.*, how one reality can be both extended and unextended.

It is Hegel's claim that he has done just this, that he has reconciled being and thought in his conception of the Absolute, or Spirit. This paper will consider three aspects of this claim. First, how one enters the Hegelian Science. Second, how Hegel evaluates formal logic. And thirdly, how Hegel's Logic—"the science of Pure Thought"—begins.

THE ENTRANCE TO THE HEGELIAN SCIENCE

Entrance to the Hegelian Science is via the *Phenomenology of Spirit*. (We have translated Hegel's *"Geist"* as "Spirit" throughout this paper.) This work considers Spirit (the only Reality) in its immediate existence as consciousness. The first appearance of consciousness (at the most primitive or fundamental level) is what Hegel calls the level of "sense-certainty." Here the object, of which the senses are certain, appears to consciousness as immediate, as unmediated by thought.

It is Hegel's intention to simply describe each level of knowledge as it arises, in terms of its own criteria. Each form of knowledge contains both the object we seek to know and a concept of knowledge which seeks to know the object. In the case of sense-certainty, the concept of knowledge is that the object can be known truly in its immediate apprehension by the senses. Hegel then examines whether the object which sense-certainty seeks to know can, in fact, be known with the concept of knowledge we have adopted. This examination is internal to the form of knowledge under investigation; no presuppositions or assumptions are made by Hegel himself. (There is much controversy over this point in philosophy. See, for example, DeNys [1978] and Dove [1971].)

This examination separates Hegel's phenomenological procedure from epistemology, the latter of which Hegel sees as always requiring assumptions or presuppositions concerning the fundamental nature of knowledge itself. Hegel gave

really existing in a particular condition before we observe it. Only within the context of an actual experiment does a concrete reality appear. Change the experiment and you change the reality. That may seem hard to swallow but it is the least bizarre of the various interpretations of quantum theory that have since been proposed" (p. 11).

as a first title to his Phenomenology, the "Science of the Experience of Consciousness;" thus the work documents each experience consciousness is involved in, as it seeks to upgrade knowledge of its object and (in so doing) of specifying its own concrete relations to the object. Experience is for Hegel a dialectical process, each experience containing within it, in an immanent form, the impulse to adequacy—or the necessity of knowledge working from lower to higher forms. Each form of knowledge is a necessary development from the preceding one (*i.e.*, perception arising out of the failure of sense-certainty) and contains within it the seeds of a more adequate form (the form of Understanding). It is typified by Hegel as a "highway of despair," consciousness seeing its knowledge continually being sublated (*i.e.*, annulled and reformulated at a higher level). This development, however, retains the lessons ("truth") of the previous forms of knowledge. For example, the examination of sense-certainty establishes for all future forms the impossibility of immediate knowledge; all knowledge must henceforth be recognised as mediated through universals. The examination of the next form, perception, establishes for all future forms the necessity of including a knowing subject actively employed in the determination of its object (and so on).

Thus, each form is positive; it makes a contribution to the advancement toward the Absolute standpoint. Each form is also necessary in that it provides the ground for the next form. This has its analogy in the way memory functions. Here a present experience becomes superseded by another experience, the first is retained as negated (*i.e.*, it is a memory, a present experience that is retained in the present as "overcome"). It is this abiding memory structure that provides the ground for the succession of present experiences.

One further point to be made here is that the *Phenomenology of Spirit* presents each form of experience from two points of view—the first from the consciousness involved in that particular form, and the second from the position of Absolute Knowledge. It is only from this latter standpoint that the necessity of the development can be grasped (that we can see the progression as a "scientifically constituted sequence").

The terminus is reached when knowledge is no longer compelled to go beyond itself to a more advanced form. This is the level of Hegelian science. At this level the object or substance has become entirely mediated by thought, and thought has become a "substantial content" (that is, a concept). Here, says Hegel, "substance shows that it is in reality subject" (Hegel, 1966, p. 97). That is, the dualities and oppositions evidenced in experience are now seen as undivided aspects of Spirit. This is the level of Hegelian praxis; that is, of the self-developing, self-comprehending activity of Spirit. At this level the oppositions found in lower inadequate forms of knowledge, between thought and being, finite and infinite, subject and object, freedom and necessity, *etc.*, have been sublated. We have then transcended experience and arrived at the level of "ideal" reality. Here we, as Spirit, are in a position to consider concepts as pure determinations. "With this, the Phenomenology of Spirit is concluded. What Spirit prepares for itself in it, is the element of [true] knowing" (Hegel, 1966, p. 97).

This level of true conceptual knowing is the level of science. It is the level of Hegelian Logic. For Hegel, a concept is not a subjective ideal item; it is a unity of substance and subject, or a real-rational and as such it is "self-developing." Philosophy, for Hegel, does not operate with any bare sensuous content (an abstraction) nor with some other universal form (also an abstraction) but with their concrete synthesis.

In this view any one concept is a representative of the complete conceptualization (the Absolute).

Further, any one concept is determinate. Therefore a concept is a determinate presentation of the Absolute and herein lies its problem. For, by *being* a determination, it must be existing in a way that is not true to the Totality of which it is a presentation. Thus, says Hegel, it appears in a manner at odds with its essence. It appears as only a moment of Totality.

Now it is the contradiction in the way Totality (as Pure Thought) presents itself that is documented in Hegel's Logic. The contradiction lies in each concept leading continually to further self-determinations of Totality (of itself). This process terminates in the Absolute Idea, Absolute self-comprehension.

A concept is then determinate, it is a determination of pure thought, *and* it is an "object in its own self." As issuing from the Absolute, concepts express in a determinate and, therefore, finite manner a seemingly necessary property of reality. But because they are determinate, they exhibit a particular, finite reality, not the Absolute itself. Thus as characterizing reality as determinate, they characterize it as it is not. This entails that reality is in contradiction, as depicted by any particular finite concept or set of concepts. Thus, simply by being posited, each concept will reveal its inadequacy in depicting reality. This inadequacy or contradiction in the concept as objective leads to the transformation of both its real and its rational moments.

We shall examine later the way Hegel begins his logic. First it is useful to see how Hegel evaluates formal logic. For Hegel's criticism of the way logicians understand identity, difference and contradiction (the so-called "Universal laws of thought") highlights the difference between formal logic and Hegel's Speculative Logic.

HEGEL'S EVALUATION OF FORMAL LOGIC

In his discussion of logic, Hegel seeks to demonstrate that the way identity, difference and contradiction are understood by formal logic is quite inadequate. His aim is to show that identity, in its formal logical presentation, fails to deal with identity as such, and that this presentation contradicts itself. As he puts it: "The several propositions which are set up as absolute laws of thought are, therefore, more closely considered, opposed to one another, they contradict one another, and mutually sublate themselves" (Hegel, 1969, p. 411).

And, further, Hegel sees no reason why these laws should be limited to three. Why not include "everything is"; "everything has a quality"; "everything has a determinate being," for all the logical categories are true of everything?

So, how does Hegel show these contradictions? Let us take each law in turn and develop Hegel's argument as above.

Identity

The law of identity states that if A is anything at all, then A = A. As Hegel puts it, "everything is identical with itself." This relationship is held to be transitive and symmetrical.

Now Hegel's question is: how can we show that this law is a properly scientific production, rather than a mere presupposition? For it is generally admitted that no deductive proof of such a law can be given. There are some answers to this. Some claim that it is plain common sense that A = A; that it is intuitively obvious; that it is apodeictically or indubitably self-evident; or that it is the minimum presupposition of rational thought itself.

The problem with these answers is that they either presuppose identity in their arguments, or they ground identity in the non-discursive beyond; that is, they make the ground beyond the domain of rational investigation in principle. This means that science, insofar as it rests upon this law, rests upon a law that cannot be scientifically proven. For Hegel this is to be arbitrary and dogmatic.

In Hegel's view *all* existence is scientifically knowable. The world of our experience can be totally grasped by conceptual thought, as it contains both thought and being. Hegel is then an objective idealist in contrast to, say, Kant. Hegel would see Kant as a subjective idealist, allowing no scientific access to the objective real world itself. Hegel, then, insists on the reality of the object *and* of our concepts.

A further way the law of identity is justified is through the appeal to experience. Through our experience we see the truth of such judgements as "a tree is a tree," or "a raven is a raven." Hegel's reply to this is to say that such judgements as these, if taken abstractly, are incoherent. In abstraction from their context and from the reflective process, such judgements of identity fail to make sense. Because we import more into the simple identity judgement than we think, it appears to be true. That is, the subject of such a judgement, considered in itself, is indeterminate. It is the business of the predicate to state what the subject is. This is not done. So either we begin with a *determinate* subject (hence involving more than abstract identity) or we fail to determine the subject at all (this being a contradiction in the judgement itself).

Further, Hegel's argument here is that such concrete examples do not prove the absolute truth of the Law of Identity because such examples deal with the relation of a concrete or determinate object to a whole, which is different from it. As he says:

> Expressed as a proposition, the concrete would just be a synthetic proposition. It is true that abstraction might succeed in extracting by analysis the Law of Identity from the concrete itself or from its synthetic proposition; but then it would not have left experience as it is, but would have changed it (1929, p. 41).

And, finally, Hegel would see such concrete examples as failing to be *concepts* anyway because "the form of simple relation to self does not properly belong to such limited and finite content, it is a form applied and lent to it by subjective understanding" (1929, p. 100).

Hegel's counterclaim is in fact, that experience manifests just the opposite of this law,

> ...for the fact is that experience contains identity in unity with difference and is the immediate refutation of the assertion that abstract identity as such is "something true" (Hegel, 1969, p. 415).

Part of Hegel's claim here can be substantiated through a particular view on the nature of predication. Part of his claim also relies upon a particular view of experience. In the former view, the notion of an abstract particular appears nonsensical. To abstract here is to fail to grasp the mechanics of predication. In the latter view, Hegel would claim to have shown that to abstract is to falsify.

I shall return to Hegel's notion of predication shortly. With regard to his view of experience, Hegel argues in his *Phenomenology of Spirit* that experience begins in an act in which a subject (consciousness), "distinguishes from itself something to which at the same time it relates . . . there is something for consciousness" (1966, p. 139).

This is the subject-object complex of experience, in which at every level there is manifest this activity of *relating-to* and *distinguishing-from*. Without such activity, Hegel argues, there can be no ground or basis for making any distinctions at all.

In this view, we cannot simply analyze the something we are conscious of, without at the same time bringing the other aspect—our consciousness of it—into view. For Hegel, they are mutually mediating. The attempt to have one without the other, to have knowledge of the object in exclusion from knowledge of the consciousness of it, ends in contradiction. His argument will be to show that identity, as abstract, is a denial of itself. That properly understood, identity contains the movement of reflection, and that identity as determinate, is a product of, and embodies reflection.

Prima facie, there appears to be corroboration of this view in certain areas of modern science, for example, the case already noted concerning the reality of the atom. Here it was claimed that it was only in a particular experiment that a "reality" appears. Vary the experimental conditions and you vary the "reality." Thus the experiment and its "reality" are mutually mediating. There are no such things as atoms in abstraction from the experimental conditions.

A similar case would appear to be that of the relationship between space and matter in Einsteinian physics. As it has been put in one slogan, "space tells matter how to move; matter tells space how to curve." Thus an understanding of matter in motion requires an understanding of the context or negative in which matter is in existence. So, it could be argued, matter in motion cannot be understood in abstraction from its spatial context.

In discussing identity, Hegel's first comments are concerned with the abstract nature of identity, as formal logic sees it. This is the position Hegel calls external reflection. Abstract identity is identity in exclusion from difference. "A" can be seen to be self-identical without the notion of difference arising. A is A simpliciter.

This, for Hegel, is an error. Identity, properly understood, is "the determination of identity as against non-identity"; it is a reflection. As abstract, the individual A is indeterminate, there is a *lack* of individuality. The abstract identity A is then unthinkable. The proposition A is A does not inform us as to the nature of A; thus, for Hegel, it contradicts itself. Consider the following:

A
A is what?
A is A.

We begin with the undetermined, simple A. We then proceed to determine A as A. That is, we proceed to characterize A with a predicate in a proposition. But the determination of A as something is denied, for the predicate fails to determine the subject at all. Hence A as self-identical is still indeterminate. For Hegel it is the dissolution of itself. The propositional form, which makes a distinction between subject and predicate is contradicted by the law of identity.

One of the problems with this formal process is that it separates identity from difference, and then separates identity from the reflective process embodied in the assertion that A is A. Thus, we end up with an abstract, static indeterminateness. To say of A what it is, we would need to characterize A as something else in a proposition, *i.e.,* A is X. To understand what happens in asserting of A that it is A, we need to see that in making such an assertion we are placing A in a context of mediation, A is A as against −A. That is, to assert of A that it is A, is to determine A, to deny its abstractness by setting it in relation to what it is not. Identity then can only be grasped as identity in difference.

Hegel's conclusions to the investigation of identity are: that the *law* of identity, which claims to express abstract identity, is no law. And, secondly, that this so-called law contains more than is meant by it, *i.e.,* it requires identity through difference. It involves the process of reflection. Perhaps this could be made more clear by the following argument derived from M. Kosok (1972).

When we reflect on the initial indeterminate A, we transform A into the assertion of A. By so doing, we place A in a context that is not A, we affirm the A is present in the field of consciousness. But A, as the assertion of A is changed from its original state and implies that something other exists, the other of A. This has not yet been determined, it is just the other of A. It has no positive content. A, through the process of reflection, is asserted to be A and it is A as against not A, meaning that A is determined as what it is by exclusion from what it isn't. This is why Hegel can say of the proposition A = A that both it and its opposite, "present themselves with equal necessity and, as *immediate* assertions, are equally correct" (1969, p. 410).

It is Hegel's view that formal logic eliminates the reflective aspect. It eliminates the reflective *process* of determining A as self-identical. By so doing, it is forced to consider identity by itself, reducing identity to emptiness. It also denies the temporal nature of thought.

Kosok makes the point nicely as follows:

> If we did not have a temporal logic, a reflection on A would simply be A itself. But a temporal logic regards reflection as an activity in which the very questioning of an initial posit changes the nature of the posit present. Thus we have a conceptual counterpart to the indeterminacy principle in physics, which states that the very activity of a subject measuring an object modifies the object (and also subject) involved (1972, p. 256).

Hegel also claims that the form of the proposition is not adequate to express the truth. It is perhaps appropriate here to say a little concerning Hegel's notion of predication. (A fuller discussion of this notion is given by Aquila, 1973).

First, it needs to be pointed out that for Hegel there is only one reality—Spirit or the Absolute as becoming. Reality is what it is by virtue of the fact that it is merely becoming, *i.e.*, that it is *not* what it is.

Secondly, a judgement is true insofar as it expresses the ontological structure of the Absolute. Thus the "is" of predication is also an "is" of identity. But further, if the nature of the Absolute is to be becoming, then a judgement which deals with the relation of a finite subject to a finite predicate, will be inadequate to the task. The Absolute—the concrete universal and true individual—is the ongoing system of relations between finite individuals. To know what a thing is, we need to know the total set of relations it involves. But in any one specification or proposition, the subject appears in abstraction from this total set, in abstraction from the whole. Thus what the individual subject *is* will be excluded from the proposition. We then are unable to state what the subject is. For Hegel, this propositional form is sublated through the reflective process. The logical subject as fixed and inert is taken up with the predicate in a *thought unity*. Hegel puts this as follows:

> The nature of judgement or the proposition in general, which involves the distinction of subject and predicate, is subverted and destroyed by the speculative judgement; and the identical proposition, which the former becomes (by uniting subject and predicate), implies the rejection and repudiation of the above relation between subject and predicate. This conflict between the form of a proposition in general, and the unity of the notion (concept) which destroys that form, is similar to what we find between metre and accent in the case of rhythm. Rhythm is the result of what hovers between and unites both (1966, p. 120).

The unity achieved by the speculative view of the subject and predicate in a proposition is seen as a "harmony of the elements." The proposition thus viewed, expresses one thought, the logical subject has been transformed through unification with the predicate in reflective thought. Without this speculative development, Hegel argues that the subject becomes unreal and vanishing.

As an example, we could consider, perhaps, the way a person's character or personality is taken up. We do not produce a set of discrete propositions that in an additive manner express a person's character through time, such discreteness would be laughable.

It is by taking up such propositions in a developing unity that we know this person's nature. It is then by taking the subject of such propositions in more than a logical way, and by thinking of the determinations made with respect to this subject as more than finite predicates (universals) that one unified concept of that person emerges. A concept, incidentally, that is continually developing. So one says, "I get to know him better." This is the fluidity of concepts that Hegel demands of philosophical thought.

Thus the subject is not an identity simpliciter, because we are continually coming to know him; but neither is the subject an ineffable substance of which we can only catch discrete temporal glimpses. He is both an identity (that is, a given being) and a non-identity (the negation of this given being) in unity.

Hegel's conclusion to his investigation of the concept of identity, and the law of identity could be put as follows:

The statement $A = A$ is asserting self-identity by determining A as A. But this can only be achieved if the predicate does in fact determine A. This can be achieved by virtue of the fact that $A = A$ is a reflection which asserts-of-A, or determines-of-A, that it is A. The predicate then sets A in a context of assertion (and by implication, denial). This context mediates the initial A; A is taken up in a particular mode of thought. It thus becomes polarized. It is the assertion of A as against all else. It becomes ideal.

The law of identity then must also involve difference, the difference between A and the assertion of A. This leads to a discussion of the nature of difference as formal logic understands it.

Difference

The law of the excluded middle states that "something is either A or not A: there is no third." A and not A are separated; there is no middle ground, no manner in which they can be brought into relation.

In Hegel's view, two problems arise. Firstly, how do we get negation from abstract identity? The conclusion to the investigation of identity as formal logic sees it is that identity as abstract, is the denial or dissolution of itself. There is but indeterminateness. The law of the excluded middle is asserting that no two things are the same, but it is providing no basis or ground upon which such an opposition or difference could be reached. And abstract identity can provide none. As Hegel says, if everything is different, then A is not equal to A, nor is it opposed to A; there is just indifference. For difference cannot be derived from abstract identity, just as negation cannot be derived from affirmation alone, without destroying the distinction between the two terms. Difference is difference of something, negation is negation of something.

The logician, to be consistent, must then posit difference as another fundamental axiom to complement abstract identity but cannot show in a scientific manner the connection between the two. There is but a separation between the two, which, because the ground of such a separation is excluded, is not seen as an opposition. There is then, on the one hand, indeterminate abstract identity and on the other, indifferently or unrelated different terms.

The second problem with the law of the excluded middle is that, taken by itself, it is internally contradictory.

To specify difference, it is necessary to affirm the identity of the determination in which the two differ. Without this affirmation it is impossible to determine the difference. Hence, if we assert separately that $-A \neq A$, then no two things are the same, in which case there is no basis on which they can be compared or related. A universe of pure abstract identities provides no basis for distinction between them. Hegel puts this point as follows:

> The Maxim of Excluded Middle is the maxim of the definite understanding, which would fain avoid contradiction, but in so doing falls into it. A must be either $+ A$ or $-A$, it says. It virtually declares in these words a third A which is neither $+$ or $-$, and which at the same time is yet invested with $+$ and $-$ characters (1892, p. 220).

The something A, is then the third term which the law was supposed to be excluding. Difference then cannot be taken in isolation from identity, any more than identity can be taken in isolation from difference. One necessarily involves the other, they are opposed and therefore related moments. (Just as to distinguish-from is also to relate-to.)

For Hegel, because the separation of identity and difference is laid down, together with the exclusion of the reflective process at the beginning, we get a series of contradictions both in each law itself, and in their relations to each other. The resolution of this situation is seen in the notion of contradiction as resolving identity and difference.

It can be noted here that Hegel's logic would offend the law of the excluded middle, for his "mind-blowing idea" is the denial of the separation of identity and difference. It would seem in Hegel's view that the law of the excluded middle would only apply, if at all, to the Concept or complete comprehension itself. For Hegel, identity is the conception that itself demonstrates the impossibility of having $A = A$. Such identity would again only be true of the Concept, that is of a non-temporal structure. But in any temporal structure the attempt to define $A = A$ fails.

Contradiction

The law of contradiction states that nothing can be both A and -A. Contradiction is impossible in the sense of something existing that has both of two contradictory qualities, or is typified by two contradictory predicates.

This law expresses the result of the other two laws. The laws of identity and the excluded middle were shown to stand in contradictory relations, if traditionally conceived. How then can a law which unites these fare any better?

Secondly, in logical terms, contradiction must result in nullity (nothingness), in a return to ground as Hegel says, for the only recourse available upon arriving at a contradiction is to return to the pre-contradictory state of affairs, in the hope of being able to provide a better account that avoids this contradiction. For Hegel this is impossible. The attempt to avoid contradiction simply illustrates the problems involved in the form in which the logician is attempting to know something; what might be called the form of the Understanding, a term derived from Kant.

To put it simply, Kant had three forms of Reason: these being sensibility, understanding and reason. The first two are responsible for scientific knowledge—knowledge of things as they appear, or phenomenal knowledge. Reason, however, attempts to know things as they are in themselves. It seeks the principle of unity underlying the determinations of the understanding. Reason is unscientific in this attempt, for all that we can know are things as they appear and they appear to us through various intuitions, concepts and categories which are subjective. We cannot get behind as it were, the conditionedness of our experience to grasp truth. Reason, for Kant, "Cannot acquire knowledge of any true content or subject matter and in regard to absolute truth must be directed by faith" (Hegel, 1969, p. 61).

For Hegel, Kant was a subjective idealist, in that he was unable to resolve the opposition between subject and object. For Hegel, the conditions of any experience are not to be found in the human faculty of thought, but are to be found in the Absolute.

Hegel then took over Kant's three forms of Reason and welded them into one: the Absolute. For Hegel, as we stated earlier, nothing is transcendent to knowledge, all reality is scientifically knowable, all concepts are distinguishable but inseparable developments (moments) of the Absolute. Hegel's system is then monistic and dynamic.

For Kant, contradictions arise in our knowledge, not in reality. For Hegel, contradictions arise in reality which includes our conceptualizations. Even common experience verifies that there are contradictions in reality, "sensuous motion" being one example (Hegel, 1969, p. 440). For Hegel, contradictions can exist. They exist or are real solely as illusion and they become superseded. The contradictions arise much in the way the contradictions arose in the consideration of identity. In his logic Hegel showed that the real determination does not square with the ideal nature of that determination. Each determination of thought embodies its negation or opposite determination; these two determinations then resolve themselves at a higher, more concrete level. Every concept in the logic passes over into contradiction, leading to a return to ground wherein the opposition between the real objective existence of the concept and its ideal existence will be resolved, yet retained as resolved.

This is the life—the impulse—in the system. As Hegel says, "something is therefore alive only in so far as it contains contradiction within it, and moreover, is this power to hold and endure contradiction within it" (1969, p. 440).

It needs to be pointed out again that Hegel is operating in his logic at the level of the Concept. The only objects dealt with are concepts—"real-rationals." These arise out of Pure Thought.

Thus for any other level of analysis, other conditions will apply. If we are considering only the relation of one finite determination of consciousness to another, we are involved in the form of the understanding where formal logic holds sway. But this level does not deal with ontological determinations, it deals with determinations in their formal aspect i.e., one-sidedly. Hegel puts it thus: "Aristotle is thus the originator of the logic of the understanding; its forms only concern the relationship of finite to finite, and in them the truth cannot be grasped" (Sarlemijn, 1971, p. 94).

Formal logic provides the correctness of the argument, not the truth of thoughts as they correspond to reality. It leads to distinguishing the formal aspects of things, but it is unable to grasp the underlying unity of opposed determinations or aspects. It is, then, a static analysis. Things are reduced to a set of independent universal determinations, but these latter are then not shown to be unified with the reality they are supposed to present.

Hegel's speculative logic shows that supposedly independent determinations or concepts are dependent (i.e., independence is being-separated-from, which is then to relate to that which the independence is of, hence dependence). The consideration of any concept at this level will show the underlying negation inherent in it, which, when brought into opposition with it, will contradict itself. Let us take the first transition in Hegel's logic to illustrate this.

THE BEGINNING OF THE SCIENCE OF PURE THOUGHT

Hegel begins his logic with Pure Being. Why? He presupposes (as proved by the *Phenomenology of Spirit*) the level of pure conceptual knowledge. He claims that the beginning must be made with that which is first in the process of thought (of the all-encompassing activity of the absolute thought). Now, what is first for thought is thought itself without distinction, and as his absolute thinking is the only real object for Hegel, it must, prior to its self-becoming, be but Pure Being. But, on the other hand, there is nothing yet and there is to become something. The beginning is a nothing from which something is to proceed.

The beginning has to be made with something that is without determination, this being a contradiction. A pure being without determination is then no different from non-being. But, for Hegel, it is absolutely different in that it is Pure Thought. Pure Thought is then neither non-being nor being, but the constant ''vanishing'' of one into the other, *i.e.,* Becoming.

Obviously, if the beginning is made with nothing, no beginning will be made. Likewise if the beginning is made with being, then reflection will already have been at work; that is, we would be dealing with a result, not with the beginning. What I think Hegel is trying to demonstrate is that his system does not have a beginning in the normal understanding of that term. Understood from the Absolute viewpoint, the beginning is a false notion, due to the argument that the system is circular. We are always dealing with the Absolute through its becoming or process.

J. Piaget is interesting in this respect. He claims that ''objectivity begins as a process not a state; and it is achieved with difficulty through gradual approximations'' (1977, p. 82).

> The first results of psychogenetic analysis suggest that knowledge arises neither from a self-conscious subject, nor from objects already constituted (from the point of view of the subject) which would impress themselves on him; it arises from interactions that take place mid-way between the two and thus involve both at the same time, but by reason of their complete indifferentiation rather than of any interplay between different kinds of things (1977, p. 19).

It would appear that Piaget is trying to describe the nature of psychogenesis by pointing to a state of indifferentiation out of which is arising the knowledge experience. This, it would seem, is the psychogenetic counterpart to Hegel's notion of Becoming.

Hegel's first concept is in fact Becoming and is an example of what C. Taylor calls Hegel's ''most mind-blowing idea,'' (that is, ''the identity of identity and non-identity'' [1975, p. 49]). Becoming is a unity of Pure Being (Identity) and Pure Nothing (non-Identity). Hegel gives as the first, purest and most abstract definition of the beginning that it is ''the identity of identity and non-identity'' (1929, p. 86).

For Hegel, the moments of Being and Nothing pass over into each other because Pure Being is Being without determination, *i.e.,* it is no different from Nothing, yet it is not just Nothing but Pure Thought. Nothing more can be said of Pure Being and Nothing because no determinations can be made. So, prior to the concept of Becoming, we have the non-identity of Being and Nothing—a contradiction.

With the advent of Becoming, we are able to grasp the unity of the mutual mediation of Pure Being and Nothing. Becoming is the state of transition between Being and Nothing and contains within it, as negated, the moments of Pure Being and Nothing. They are negatively present (just as memory is a negative presence). Due to the two moments it contains, Becoming is an *unrest*.

Becoming is then considered in its turn and found to contain the two moments of arising and passing away, which latter are seen to be unified in the concept of

Determinate Being. As this process continues we are dealing with the same one reality, Pure Thought, as it presents itself through conceptual development. This is the process of the Absolute Thought thinking itself. It is a temporal ontological development of an ever-expanding structure of concepts. There is in this logic, no way of returning by a logical double negation to the original situation. This is because reflection has transformed the content of the object (here a concept) reflected upon.

A parallel example is the impossibility of reliving an experience as "new." The reliving is never the same as on the first occasion, due to the structure of memories which have been modified through the inclusion of the experience that is due to be relived. This structure of memories provides the meaning context (or ground) for the second occasion of the "same" experience.

CONCLUSION

Hegel's discussion of formal logic aims at demonstrating the incoherence in the development of its fundamental laws—identity, difference (excluded middle), and contradiction. It is Hegel's claim that identity must be understood in unity with difference. All concepts embody this unity and are for this reason self-developing. We attempted to demonstrate this in Hegel's first concept, Becoming.

This argument requires as its presupposition that logic is the conceptual unfolding of Pure or Absolute thought. Hegel would claim to have demonstrated the truth of this presupposition in his Phenomenology. This latter is the ladder by which the consciousness is able to become one with the Absolute as it works its way from naivete to Science, through the dialectical process of experience.

There is then, for Hegel, only one reality, which is Spirit. This latter contains, as negated, the process of experience. We then become one with Pure thought and are able to think concepts, *i.e.,* to see the conceptual process that constitutes Spirit as Pure thought. This idealism is not subjective, for the thought in question is not human thought but the thought of Reality. "This realm is truth as it is without veil and in its own absolute nature" (Hegel, 1969, p.50).

REFERENCES

Aquila, R.E. "Predication and Hegel's Metaphysics," *Kant - Studien*, 1973, *64*, 231–245.

Bateson, G. *Mind and Nature.* London: Fontana, 1980.

Davies, P. "The Subatomic Anarchy Show," *The Guardian*, May 1, 1980, p. 11.

DeNys, M.J. "Sense Certainty and Universality: Hegel's Entrance into the Phenomenology," *International Philosophical Quarterly*, 1978, *18*, 445–464.

Dove, K.R. "Hegel's Phenomenological Method." In *New Studies in Hegel's Philosophy*, W. Steinkraus (Ed.). New York, 1971.

Hegel, G.W.F. *The Phenomenology of Mind.* (J.B. Baillie, trans.) London: Allen and Unwin, 1966. (Originally published, 1807.)

Hegel, G.W.F. *The Science of Logic.* (W.H. Johnson and L.G. Struthers, trans.) London: Allen and Unwin, 1929. (Originally published, 1812–16.)

Hegel, G.W.F. *The Science of Logic.* (A.V. Miller, trans.) London: Allen and Unwin, 1969. (Originally published, 1812–16.)

Hegel, G.W.F. *The Logic of Hegel.* (W. Wallace, trans.) Oxford: Clarendon, 1892. (Originally published, 1817).

Kosok, M. "The Formalization of Hegel's Dialectical Logic." In *Hegel*, A. MacIntyre (Ed.). New York: Anchor, 1972.

Piaget, J. *Principles of Genetic Epistemology.* (W. Mays, trans.) London: Routledge and Kegan Paul, 1977. (Originally published 1970.)

Sarlemijn, A. *Hegel's Dialectic.* Dordrecht, Holland: Reidel, 1971.

Taylor, C. *Hegel.* London: Cambridge University Press, 1975.

PART II.

THINKING AND CULTURE

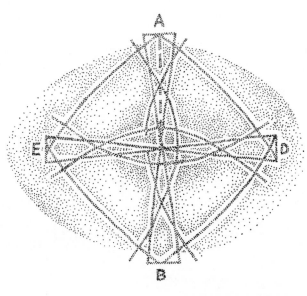

Polynesian navigational chart

INTRODUCTION

How much does culture influence the content, the processes of thinking? How much does culture account for the obvious differences in human abilities to solve problems which require thinking? McClelland (1961) analyzed several societies and found that several psychological variables (particularly the need for achievement) vary enormously over time. Hagan (1962) in studying Japan found that while certain elements of the culture were apparently very constant over time, other elements were easily amenable to control. Crocombe (1973) pointed out that in the mix of elements in South Pacific cultures, all elements seemed to change at different rates.

Thinking ability — and we normally measure that ability through intelligence tests or IQ tests — obviously will vary similarly across cultures and within cultures, and, of course, over time, both for individuals and for cultures or societies. Interestingly, none of the four papers in this section discusses directly the relationship between intelligence (one manifestation of thinking) and culture.

When the *Encyclopaedia Britannica* asserts that "a common finding in European and North American research is that seventy to eighty percent of human variation in intelligence is ascribable to genetic difference ... twenty to thirty percent to environmental factors" (15th Edition, Vol. 9, 1978, pp. 672–3), it is implicitly acknowledging a possible failing of "European and North American (Psychometric) research" to see other cultures' manifestations of intelligence. Perhaps that research on intelligence, and especially on differences within and between cultural groups, has been too narrowly focused.

The biographer of Sir Cyril Burt wrote, "If we have over the last half-century increased our understanding of the nature of intelligence, it has not been so much because of work in psychometrics (the field in which Burt was the acknowledged dean), which has told us very little, but because of work in developmental psychology, in the pathological field (brain injuries, psychoses, senescence), in comparative psychology, particularly with primates, in experimental studies of thinking, and finally in the field of artificial intelligence" (Hearnshaw, 1979, p. 71).

Hearnshaw earlier stated that "... the psychometric road which Burt persisted in following ran into relatively arid country" (p. 53). The "nature — nurture," the "genetic versus environment or culture" controversy will not be stilled for a very long time. But the four essays in this section, while not really cast as arguments in the "nature — nurture" debate, may provide several possible clues to paths out of the apparent *culs-du-sac* that psychometric studies of intelligence have led us to. Futa Helu's paper shows how myths or belief systems can both restrict and expand intelligence. His case in point is the Tongan Culture.

Chris Griffin uses the Fijian Culture to illustrate the dangers of a culture resisting the forces that would continually expand the linguistic powers of its members. If actions, including cognitive actions, are influenced by beliefs, educators should continually remind themselves that deeply held beliefs may play a greater role both in how we respond to opportunities to learn, and how we improve our own intelligence, or how learners and teachers respond to each other, than we have acknowledged thus far. Chris Griffin's paper is a case study that will have implications beyond the one culture on which he focused.

Robert Stewart's paper continues the focus on the importance of beliefs. He demonstrates the usefulness of one research mode in understanding beliefs about human nature held by different sexes and different ethnic groups in the South Pacific. The significance of the paper is that people tend to "see" confirmation of their deeply held beliefs. The phenomenon of "selective perception" (going back to Bruner and Goodwin, 1947) is well documented in psychology. Thus, behavior toward others is partly explained by the beliefs held about others.

Graham Davidson's paper on Micronesian Cognitive Mapping nicely closes this section by offering an example of how cultures other than European and North American have frequently demonstrated a capacity to invent and to learn skills. These extraordinary capabilities illustrate that we are a long way from knowing the limits of the human power to image and to think.

REFERENCES

Bruner, J.S. and Goodwin, L.C. "Value and Need as Organizing Factors in Perception," *Journal of Abnormal and Social Psychology,* 1947, *42,* 33–44.

Crocombe, R.G. *The New South Pacific.* Wellington, N.Z.: Reed Education, 1973. (Rev. Ed., 1978).

Hagan, E.C. *On the Theory of Social Change.* Homewood, IL: Dorsey Press, 1962.

Hearnshaw, L.C. *Cyril Burt — Psychologist.* London: Hodder and Stoughton, 1979.

McClelland, D.C. *The Achieving Society.* Princeton: Van Nostrand Reinhold. 1961.

THINKING IN TONGAN SOCIETY

I. Futa Helu

ABSTRACT

This paper examines certain aspects of thinking which are determined by social factors. It does this by distinguishing between *what we think* and *how we think* and comes to the conclusion that society determines the *focus* or content of thinking but not how we think. Some forms of cognition, *eg.,* believing, knowing, awareness, *etc.,* are considered to illustrate this point and to show that they are *formally* the same.

The second part of the paper discusses two ecological myths to show how religious changes in prehistoric Tonga gave rise to certain "systems of thought." This section also discusses a study of self-concept conducted by a social psychology class at the 'Atenisi Institute in Tonga in 1978.

The paper concludes with the somewhat unpleasant recognition that in the context of social action people are rarely directed by a desire for truth but are, most of the time, motivated by utility, fashion, and irrational aims.

This paper addresses the question of the sociology of knowledge as defined by Mannheim (1936) and others. A complete solution cannot be presented here, yet the argument has relevance and can form part of other attempts at a more thorough treatment. One thing is clear: a solution cannot even be attempted without some examination of the nature of thinking. It seems to me that the position of the sociologists has always been weakened by a refusal to consider seriously what the actual characteristics of thinking are. The question that interests them is not, "what are minds?" but, "what are the relations that mind enters into?" and this is akin to the psychologist's pet question, "what can minds do?" In the case of the behaviorists, because of their insistence on "observability" (or an erroneous account of it) thinking tends to be denied existence altogether and so no account of mind can be given.

There is another minor difficulty, and that is that sociologists do not, as a rule, define their terms with sufficient rigor to permit either comment or criticism. Mannheim, for example, uses "knowledge" and "thinking" interchangeably and does not differentiate sharply enough between the nature and the content of knowledge. The thesis of this paper, however, is that society determines the *focus* or scope of thinking but not its nature, *i.e.,* it determines *what we think* but not *how we think*. Mannheim, in fact, in discussing sociology of knowledge as theory, says,

---

I.F. Helu is affiliated with the 'Atenisi Institute in Nuku'alofa, Tonga.

"...It is a purely empirical investigation through description and structural analysis of the ways in which social relationships, in fact, influence thought" (Mannheim, 1936, pp. 266–267). And further on:

> The existential determination of thought will also have to be regarded as a fact (b) if the influence of these existential factors on the concrete content of knowledge is of more than mere peripheral importance, if they are relevant not only to the genesis of ideas, but penetrate into their forms and content and if, furthermore, they decisively determine the scope and the intensity of our experience and observation *i.e.*, that which we formerly referred to as the "perspective" of the subject (Mannheim, 1936, p. 267–268).

Here, if Mannheim means simply that society influences the scope and content (what he calls the "perspective") of our thoughts, then we cannot dispute him. However in the course of the discussion, he unmistakingly implies that thinking as a *process* is radically changed by social processes (Mannheim, 1936, p. 268). The Mannheim approach, in my view, is typical of sociological methodology in its imprecision, lack of definition, and reluctance to distinguish sharply between closely-related questions. Rex (1972) in criticizing psychometry and its use by Eysenck, goes on to argue that in evaluating intelligence power, one should take into account all environmental factors and all the complex history of not only the patient, but his race as well. The implication that all aspects of thinking are conditioned by society and history comes out very strongly.

For the above reasons, this essay is divided into two main sections: one on the nature of thinking, and the other on the influence of social forces on thinking (in this case, the influence of a specific society, Tongan society, on the thinking of its members). Tonga is a Polynesian island-kingdom in the South Pacific. The results of this discussion, however, are not culture-specific to Tongans but may apply to society in general.

The approach in this inquiry is *logical* rather than experimental. Logical questions will be uppermost, although some statistics from actual field studies in Tonga will be examined for the light they throw on the questions at issue.

THE NATURE OF THINKING

In this section, I discuss some attributes traditionally regarded as belonging to the cognitive domain of the mind *viz., believing, knowing, understanding, awareness, learning, remembering, experiencing, recognizing, etc.* As for the passions or emotions, I shall follow the tradition of philosophers in regarding them as falling outside the purview of epistemology and will not discuss them here. The aim here is to inquire whether there is a common denominator, if at all, to all these cognitive activities.

Believing

When we believe something, we believe it to be true. It is quite inconceivable to believe something and yet hold at the same time that what is believed is false. This would be a contradiction. Put thus, the following definition of belief must be accepted: *belief is taking something to be the case.* Therefore, when we say we believe something, we assert that something is the case.

The assertions we make stating our beliefs are always made in the form of categorical propositions *e.g.,* X is Y. But this is the general form of any assertion.

How then is the expression of a belief different from any other assertion? It differs in this: the truth claim is *explicit* in beliefs. We conclude, therefore, that the *logical form* of belief is "X is Y is true."

The question of whether our beliefs are true or false is, of course, a separate issue. When a belief, *e.g.*, that X is Y is true, is true, the statement "X is Y" is simply true. It does not affect the separate question of whether or not the believer is actually claiming that X is Y is true.

The pragmatic view of belief, *viz.*, we believe what eases our minds (Peirce 1878), is really an account of what we are *disposed* to believe, not what believing is. And although it is important to know what our dispositions are, it still cannot serve as an account of believing as a process. Pragmatism professes to tell us *what* kinds of things we believe, but not *how* we believe, and only the latter forms part of the answer to the question "what is thinking?" The pragmatic view, however, defines the *limits of* thinking, in so far as we cannot go beyond belief. As Peirce explains it, belief is the resolution of Doubt, and Inquiry (or thinking) can be regarded as the search for Belief. Hence pragmatism implies *mental inertia* and explains the *power* of belief. Put crudely: people, as a rule, do not want to think, and to believe is to economize mental energy. Thus belief can greatly promote ignorance and is therefore a tool for social control. Yet all this is not an account of what believing is, only of *what* we believe.

Knowing

We divide knowing into awareness and understanding. In both cases, however, some state of affairs is *recognized*.

> *Awareness.* When we are aware of some situation, we see it *in the context of its relations to other situations.* This is the process we sometimes refer to as *identification.* But any situation whatsoever is complex and thus, to be aware of something, is to recognize the interelationships between things. Therefore, the form of the mental process involved in awareness in *this* (*or that*) *is* X or, more generally *X is Y.*
>
> *Understanding.* In understanding we recognize the *passage* from one situation to another, or we recognize that one situation is implied by another. Formally, however, this is to recognize that X is Y (this can be analyzed, of course, into A is B, therefore, P is Q, *etc.*).

In this sense, awareness and understanding are not radically different but are, as processes, structurally the same. However, we commonly regard awareness as somehow more "primitive" than understanding, as being more spontaneous and sudden. But what must be borne in mind is that awareness is *always posited on the cognitive level,* which is also the level of analyzability, and on this level, we can only characterize it in the manner I have indicated. Thus, taking knowing as a whole, we see that it is, like believing, simply to take something to be the case.

Learning

It should also be pointed out that in our dealings with things we are engaged in the activity of learning, the end-point of which is knowledge. The classic experiments of Thorndike (1898) demonstrate that we learn by trial-and-error. In our theory, the Thorndike result can be explained in this manner: the mind grappling with things given in sensation, though not in fact, as distinct, succeeds in "seeing" that they are interrelated though only a finite number of relations are discoverable by the mind at any one time. *Insight,* as defined by Kohler (1925) and demonstrated by Birch (1945) and Harlow (1949), is based upon this discovery (awareness) of the relatedness of things. So, if insight (inference) based on trial-and-error leads to discovery, then we must not think of insight as a different species of knowing but as the mind's way of using its discoveries. Insight is an extension of, and continuous with, awareness. All in all, we must concede that both these phases of mental activity are fundamentally the same in their general ends: they both result in taking something to be the case. The scope of insight (inference) is unpredictable for any given case and may be large or small. The limit is set by our interests. We stop inquiring when we have found enough for our present purposes or have satisfied our curiosity. But we never find out everything about a particular situation or thing.

Remembering

The earliest discussion of a technical nature involving recollection and remembering is found in Plato's dialogues (Meno, Phaedo, *etc.*) where Socrates tries to prove that knowledge is a form of reminiscence. We are, he says, reminded of Simmias the man on seeing his portrait. This recognition, Socrates rightly points out, depends on prior acquaintance with (or knowledge of) Simmias. But the Socratic view does not explain how we come to know Simmias (or the Forms for that matter) in the first place. And here we come back to Thorndike's trial-and-error or Russell's "knowledge by acquaintance" (Russell, 1912), though this can only mean that we know Simmias through interacting with him in a variety of ways and this is not what we ordinarily mean by recollecting or remembering. At any rate, remembering appears to be formally the same as awareness in that they are both a "waking up" to some relationship. Their logical form must therefore be the same: *This is X,* or, more strictly, *X is Y.* In actual situations, when we are reminded of someone on seeing his portrait, we usually exclaim, "Oh, but that is so-and-so."

There are, it is true, instances of remembering something where there is no identifiable occasion or reason for remembering that particular thing. We simply cannot see any connection between the remembered thing and what we have been entertaining in our mind at the time of remembering it. The act was spontaneous and apparently unrelated to any prior thoughts.

Unless it was a case of "mental punning" (one which we cannot, for the moment, point to), there is one possible explanation: the process (or processes) leading to remembrance can, at times, be quite unconscious. This solution is not impossible because *external* stimulation to memory, so far as we know, is entirely absent. Nevertheless, this account of memory, whether correct or not, does not invalidate our general conclusion that to remember is to take something to be the case.

We now summarize the general results of the discussion as to the nature of thinking as follows:

1. Thinking in any form — believing, knowing, awareness, remembering, *etc.* —is *taking something to be the case.*

2. The logical form of thinking is *X is Y.*

3. Thinking, being a mental activity whereby the mind is related to things mental or non-mental, is therefore a *relation.*

THE INFLUENCE OF SOCIETY ON THE THINKING OF TONGANS

On the basis of the foregoing remarks, we can distinguish between the *nature* and the *focus* (or *scope*) of thinking. We define the scope of thinking as the *range* of subjects, areas, topics, ideas, *etc.*, which thinking actually covers. Over the years social scientists, especially anthropologists and psychologists (*e.g.*, Whorf 1947, Bernstein 1959, 1961, *etc.*), have been building up a case for the proposition that society is a most important determinant of thinking. The trouble is that these social sciences have not been sufficiently philosophical *i.e.*, formal, and the implication that social factors determine even the *nature* of thinking has haunted the work of many sociologists and anthropologists, as we have seen in Mannheim.

We must distinguish between "being mental" and "being social." They are quite different things. The former has a biological or, more exactly, an electrochemical basis, though "being mental" itself is not electrochemical. Society, on the other hand, though it may ultimately be of an instinctual origin, has only a very tenuous link with biology compared with the mind's relation to the brain. This does not mean that the mind and society have no relations or that they do not interact. The fact that we find minds *in* society forces the social scientist to consider and describe their mutual effects on each other and to give an account of how they interact, something which the behaviorists are unable or unwilling to do. Yet all this cannot and does not justify the claim that the be-all and end-all of thinking is social.

Thinking, we have seen in the preceding section, is possible only in terms of the proposition, which has nothing social about it, but is the *fact* (or situation) that thinking relates to mind, or as logicians put it, that the statement conveys. This is how we think, and socio-cultural factors do not touch it, though they determine the *focus* of our thought and restrict the scope of our thinking.

Now, because society ever changes, adapts itself, and evolves ceaselessly, so does the focus of the thinking of its members. Also, because societies differ from one another in so many respects but are also similar in many others, we find great dissimilarities as well as similarities in focus and scope of thought as we go from one society to another. Thus focus (or object) and scope of thought are variables, though thinking itself (in its essential character as a process) does not differ for any situation whatsoever.

We now shall briefly trace how society or culture determines the focus of thinking and go on to illustrate this process by concrete examples.

The Scope of Thought and Society

The view that society is the arena for the development of, and struggle between, specific interests, in the form of social classes, has been sufficiently analyzed by Marxists. For purposes of theory, the interactions between *demands* may be profitably regarded as the principal characteristic of society. Demands come in different shapes and forms but it is the disguised variety that is most prevalent. When, however, they can be made good, they become *rights*. And there are extreme as well as mild forms of disguises for social demands, as well as a whole range in between. The extreme types include *taboos, curses* and all forms of *sanctification*. Duty, privilege, value and the whole set of moralistic notions are all disguised demands, though of a slightly less extreme kind. In all these cases, if the social conventions are peeled off (whether taboo, privilege, duty, values, *etc.,*) what we are left with are straightforward historical events: simple demands.

In the more rigid forms of disguised demands, *e.g.,* taboo and sanctification, the disguise (or the whole rationale) for the demand is taken to be the *punishment* that visits upon the sacriligious. There is no reason for the observance of a taboo other than the retribution which follows fast upon breaking it. Thus through taboos, social groups or classes place their demands in suprasocial spheres. Two things are achieved: fear and ignorance are put into excellent use in social organization, and the mind is invited not to expend energy in attempts at understanding.

As we move over the range of social demands, we find that as the disguise becomes milder, as in systems of law for example, rationality comes in between the observance of the demand and the punishment. The latter is not the sole reason for the observance of the demand. There is now a separate justification, *e.g.,* some social goal. At the same time, however, demands by being rationalized lose their weird fascination; their hold on men's minds are weakened; and the punishment, no longer part and parcel of the demand, now gives a strong impression of superfluity.

It is in the motivational effect of the interplay of social forces that we must seek the mechanics of their influence on thinking. The sum total of human interactions in a society (including external influences)—the interactions and conflict of demands, the struggle between political forces, the impact of cultural and scientific ideas, the economic situation, the prevailing ideology — all these mix, combine, and react in one huge social chemistry. The resultant (in the sense that term is used in dynamics) of that chemistry at any given moment determines the *climate of thought.* This phrase encompasses the beliefs we hold, the ideas we emphasize, the interests we have, in short, the focus and scope of our thinking. And this, I maintain, is how society affects thought and the extent of its power. Thus, what we think is determined by our interests and social environment. Finally, what we think and how we think, as separate issues, are themselves quite distinct from the question of fact, which is settled neither by the way we think, nor by what society disposes us to think about, but simply by *what is the case.*

Tongan Society and Thinking

Though the specific influence of Tongan society on the minds of Tongans can be studied in different ways, we here consider the question from an ideological standpoint, *i.e.,* from the angle of how sets of general beliefs do affect the object and quality of their thinking. For this purpose, I will now consider how social changes (reaction to religion) are reflected in so-called primitive thought in the form of mythology, and how modern Tongans grade their interests (resulting in a system of values) under the influence of the powerful indoctrinating forces of church organization, socio-economic grouping, traditional customs, *etc.*

Mythology

We must recognize that myths proper are deliberate creations of the mind. They have an aesthetic form and so the name *oral literature* is quite apt. But they, at the same time, express a philosophy, a *Weltanschauung.* The insights of Vico (Vico, 1725), especially the recognition that the content of myths are of a *social origin* and that the psychological elements were later infusions, are of considerable usefulness for the understanding of mythology. But whereas the structuralist analysis tends to show up a socio-economic basis for myths, Vico's theory opens the way for a social theory of the origin of religion. In either case, the study of myths reveals that these traditional systems of thought (mythology and religion) are about the *interplay of demands in a social setting*.

Let me illustrate these points by discussing two Tongan myths. These myths are *complementary* because the great symbols employed cannot be understood without knowing them both. They are also what I call *ecological* myths, *i.e.*, they embody a view of the relation of man to his environment.

The Origin of the Coconut

Once upon a time there was a man and his wife. They had a most beautiful daughter whose name was Hina. They were very, very possessive of her and guarded her so jealously that she never set eyes on any human being other than her loving parents. She was strictly confined to within the boundaries of their home. Hina's days were filled with curious idleness disturbed only by the pleasant pastime of swimming in a pool near her house, an activity she indulged in every day. Now it so happened that an eel lived in the very same pool. He would lie in his hole and watch Hina go about her daily ablutions. At length the eel fell in love with the ravishingly beautiful young virgin. The eel's love deepened as the days passed, but being unable to relate to Hina in the humanly acceptable way, the poor love-sick eel resorted to sucking the piece of tapa cloth Hina used as a body scrub and left floating on the water every day after she had left the pool. This pattern of events persisted for some time and Hina became pregnant. When the parents found this out they were distraught with sorrow. When they asked Hina who was responsible for her pregnancy, she told them she had never known any man as she had never seen any others but them. But she told them about the eel in the pool. They were very sure then that it was the eel which was responsible for Hina's condition. They, at once, drained the pool, took out the eel and were going to kill it when it spoke to them thus: "Before you kill me I want to make a dying request to you. It is this," continued the eel, "after you have killed me, cut my head off and bury it near Hina's house and in time a plant will come out from my severed head. This plant will bear fruit which will be excellent food and drink for the child that Hina is bearing."

The parents did as the eel requested and in time a plant did grow up where they had buried the eel's head. It was a plant they had never seen before for it was the very first, the original coconut palm to have grown out of the earth. It is the most useful plant in Tonga. If the fibre is taken off from a mature fruit, a huge oval nut is left. On one end of this nut are impressions that so very strongly resemble the features of an eel.

The Rock Matahina

Once there lived near the beach of Keitahi a couple who had four children, three boys and one daughter, whose name was Hina. One day the father and the three boys were out fishing and they caught a baby shark which they did not kill but brought home and gave to Hina. She was overjoyed and had a pool for the shark dug on the beach near the water.

Hina would visit the pool every day to feed her pet and the relationship between them deepened as days passed until Hina almost literally lived at the poolside feeding the shark, stroking its head and talking to it. And the shark was growing fast. One day, however, a huge hurricane hit this part of the island and giant waves came from the sea and bounded on the beach at Keitahi, washing away everything to sea including Hina's shark.

When Hina discovered her loss, she was full of sorrows and begged her parents to take her out to sea to look for her pet. The parents did as she requested and they went far out into the sea in a canoe. Hina all this time was calling out to her shark to come back to her. At last when they were already half-way between Vava'u and Niue, Hina's shark swam up to them. After talking to it, Hina realized that the shark did not want to return to land but would remain in the deep, vast ocean.

Hina then told her parents to return to Vava'u without her for she had made up her mind to stay at sea with her pet shark. She then jumped into the churning waters and turned into a huge rock that comes out from the bottom of the sea and towers above the waves themselves. Her intention as she explained to her shark was for it to hide under the rock in safety during rough and stormy weather. And there stands to this day that huge rock, Mata-o-Hina, the "eyes of Hina" which is a haven for sharks of the seas. The fishing type known as *siu* in which people call out sharks from a canoe had its origins in this story.

Interpretation

We shall now look at the myths at three levels: the society-nature relationship, the ecological level and the idealogical level.

The Society-Nature Relation

Though Vico, as was noted above, focuses his study on the relationships between social groupings, *e.g.*, conflict between gods as signifying the struggles between plebeians and patricians *etc.*, and though Freud and the structuralists might emphasize revolt against custom, *e.g.*, the Oedipus Complex or father killing as sinning against social law (represented here by the father figure), the ecological myths of Tonga give a *social significance* to brute nature, *i.e.*, they give the environment a *role* in the creation of society.

Though man, in the course of normal activities, makes inroads into nature (Hina changing the physiognomy of the oceanic wastes by changing herself), nature establishes itself in man's society by giving it indispensable cultigens or cultivated plants. Thus we can regard the ecological myths as an improvement on those myths such as the Promethean corpus, where gods make gifts to man but man does not reciprocate. The great economic stays of society are located in physical nature which man knows so well because he is quite familiar with it. It is the *empiricism* of these myths that distinguishes them from those about god's bounty. The coconut palm, a plant of high sociability in Tongan culture, is given to man not by a god, but by an ordinary and humble animal, an eel. The dealings are those between equals. So if the myth of Prometheus is one about a minor god rebelling against higher ones, the ecological myths represent a revolution in thought in Tongan society—the refusal to give credit to gods for the development of that society.

But in both cases, whenever anything of permanent value is contributed, whether by man to nature or *vice versa,* a sacrifice is made. This means that all real gains made by man in building his society can only be done by unselfish effort or through serious enterprise. Hina must die to found a great and lasting tradition of fishing methods. In order to give society the coconut palm, Hina's "lover" the eel must be sacrificed, and it, too, is transformed into something else.

The Ecological Level

Viewed from an ecological standpoint, we see in these myths the assertion of a philosophy of continuity, a continuity between man and his environment. Interactions between man and environment are not limited but include the whole range of possibilities even the reproductive sphere. This is intensely symbolic, since reproduction in its sexual aspect is, in man's world, the supreme expression of a union which is at once physical as well as emotional. Thus these myths postulate a spiritual *unity* of man and nature. This oneness is expressed in terms of love (of the eel for Hina, and of Hina for her pet shark), the most powerful feeling man is capable of experiencing. And here the phrase "love conquers all" has a deeper significance, for amongst its conquests must be included the toppling of all barriers between man and his environment.

Also present in these myths is an element of wishful thinking. The goals, taken literally, are clearly unrealizable. But here the myth partakes of the character of the dream; it provides neurotic fulfillment of a wish. The myth therefore, like the dream, has therapeutic value as emotional release. The suspension of causality and the condition of indeterminacy (the combination of these two is what we mean by "the magical") in myth as well as the dream deepens the similarity. But the presence of *sequential* continuity (not always causal) in myth marks it out to be the work of the waking mind, that is, of the mind in attentive contact with the senses and with things. At any rate, it is quite possible that this *public dream* we call myth was "primitive" man's psychoanalysis.

The Ideological Level

As works of art, myths must reflect the society in which they arise, as well as the state of knowledge, public and private mores, political conditions and so on. And they must influence people's view of things, their morality and their beliefs, their attitudes to both men and things. And above all, myths restrict their *interests* to those areas of social activities that tend to foster accepted ideas and preserve the status quo. In other words, myths are tools for maintaining a *static society*. They are inimical to a dynamic and liberal society. If there is a subject that mythical thought cannot handle at all, it is *the inevitability of social change*.

What is remarkable in the ecological myths is the total absence of reference to the gods. They therefore represent a change from a theistic to a naturalistic or humanist view of things. Man has ceased to receive gifts through the condescension of gods (*e.g.*, fire was given to man by the demigod Maui) but instead develops his culture through direct transactions with the familiar things of his immediate surroundings. They are interdependent and they form a system, the ecosystem.

Somehow the symbols in these myths got distorted and vulgarised, and we now have the whole corpus of beliefs in spirits inhabiting every clump of trees, every niche in the land, every stretch of water at sea. Thus the shift from theism to humanism in mythology was responsible for the rise of *animism*. And it kept men's minds chained to thinking about spirits (which very soon got personified): how to avoid their wrath, how to propitiate them, and how to enlist their aid in time of need. And that was how the thinking of Tongans was directed, for centuries, to things which are simply non-existent. The important point to remember, however, is that this whole intellectual ferment is indicative of a breakdown of the religious sentiment in pre-history.

Identity of a Modern Tongan

The second illustration of the way society influences thought is taken from a study conducted by a lecturer and a social psychology class in 'Atenisi University in 1978 (Parr, 1981). The aim of the study was to determine the nature of modern Tongans' self-view, their conception of their own "identity."

For this project, the Twenty Statements Measurement Instrument first used by Kuhn and McPartland in 1952 (Kuhn and McPartland, 1954) was employed to measure self-concept. The instrument and questionnaire was prepared in both

English and Tongan; it was applied in thirteen educational institutions, encompassing 976 students and staff members. The age range of the respondents was nine to fifty-two with median and modal age both being seventeen.

The study statements were divided into consensual and non-consensual categories, and the responses were analyzed for content.

A preliminary question here is whether, indeed, such findings as those of this study provide insights as to the relationships of social factors to thinking. This cannot be settled by answers to the question, "what am I?" alone. For one thing, the field of reference of the responses is oneself and thus constitutes products of introspection, whereas we are interested in this paper in how social forces mold thought. For another, in analyzing the results of the study, the mere frequency of responses to any one type of question was assumed to be significant.

This can be maintained only on the basis of an assumption: that the *facility* with which people respond to questions or the ease with which they discuss issues, depends on their *familiarity* with the topics raised by the questions or issues. And, of course, we are familiar with situations, ideas, concepts through our participation in social activities, through playing our roles as members of social groups and at the same time getting molded, changed, and influenced ourselves by the very same activities and roles.

This *response-effect* of socialization is what is actually measured by the Twenty Statements Instrument. Therefore, even though the results do not yield a direct or clearcut answer to the question of social influence on thinking, they nevertheless provide *corroborative evidence* for the thesis of this paper.

The scope of Tongan social identity. As to the findings of the study, Parr writes, "The South Pacific way is not an emerging identity among the respondents of this research project. The scope of their identities is much more local and national than regional in nature, and there is very limited evidence of an encompassing pan-Pacific identity."

Table 1. Consensual Identity Statements

Type of Identity Statement	Number of Respondents Making at Least One Statement	Percent of Total Respondents (N = 1976)
Sexual Identity	728	74.6
Religious Identity	675	69.2
Occupational and Student Identity	591	60.6
Family Identity	424	43.4
Identity with an Educational Institution	388	39.4
Tongan National Identity	367	37.6
Identity with an Area of Residence	355	36.4
Age Identity	341	34.9
Identity as a Human Being ("I am a human being")	322	33.0
Identity with a Name ("My name is . . . .")	225	23.1
Racial Identity	147	15.1
Identity with Secondary Groups	140	14.3
Polynesian Identity	91	9.3
Identity with Primary Groups (Excluding Family)	79	8.1
Marital Status Identity	77	7.9
Other	80	8.2

At the local level, primary groups' identity is an important part of Tongan social identity. Forty-three percent of the respondents made family identity statements (Table 1).

Also at the local level, identity with a specific area of residence, such as the Nukuʻalofa area, is a moderately important part of Tongan social identity. Statements identifying with a specific area of residence were made by thirty-six percent of the residents (Table 1).

At the national level, identification with Tonga as a nation state is a moderately important part of Tongan social identity. Of all the respondents, thirty-eight percent made national identity statements (Table 1).

At the regional level, identification with the Polynesian region of the South Pacific is a minor component of Tongan social identity. Only nine percent of the respondents made statements of identification as Polynesians (Table 1).

Perhaps the most encompassing aspect of Tongan social identity is racial identification. This was manifested generally in the statement "I am brown," and fifteen percent of the respondents made statements of racial identification (Table 1).

The above conclusions are based on Table 1, which sets out the consensual identity statements in order of percentage frequency.

Granting now the abovementioned assumption that *facility* of discussion depends on *familiarity* with the questions discussed and that familiarity in turn depends on the focus of our socialization, we see a pattern emerging in the statistics of the study. This pattern is a *ranking* of the potent social forces which determine the content of our thoughts. Looked at in terms of those forces, we can write Table 1 as a ranking in the following manner:

1. Certain *socialized* biological divisions (in this instance, sex)
2. Christianity (religion)
3. Occupational identification
4. Family membership
5. School membership (education)
6. Nationality
7. Residential area
8. Age
9. Humanity
10. Name
11. Race
12. Secondary grouping
13. Polynesian identity
14. Primary grouping
15. Social contracts (marriage)
16. Other

Comparison with typical experience. Using my personal experience as a Tongan as a kind of check on the above ranking, I can certainly confirm the existence of a very high degree of correspondence between the study's findings and my personal experience as a Tongan. The following considerations are relevant to this observation.

The first three items in our list (certain social institutions, Christianity, and occupation) are the *most highly esteemed* departments of our culture. They are also the *most frequently discussed* and *most intensely* advertised (through *indoctrination*). It would be rare, indeed, to find a social situation, private or public, where these values are not openly discussed, promoted, praised, advertised or otherwise activated.

Extended family, nationality, community (residential area) and gerontocratic influence take middling positions and are not as important as the first three. The remaining identities concern the wider circles of a Tongan's relationships. They relate to matters that lie outside his immediate interests as he has been conditioned by environmental pressures. These include racial identity (Polynesian), membership in secondary groups, and Pacific identity. Therefore any identity with a global community, a sense of internationality, must be nonexistent in the consciousness of Tongans. What emerges is the general picture of a belief pattern, *a value system*. This implies that much the same picture would result if the question posed to respondents was not "what am I?" but "what are the most important things in life?" or a variant of it.

Thus when Kuhn and McPartland said the question "who am I?" is "one which might logically be expected to elicit statements about *one's identity*. . ." (Kuhn and McPartland, 1954, p. 72), they would have been talking much more to the point if they had said "to elicit statements about values."

Value mobility. The values revealed by the study can be regarded as being organized on an egoistic basis or principle. For convenience, they can be divided vertically into immediate, intermediate, remote, and non-existent values. Thus our findings show how a person views his relationships to other things, and he ranks these according to his perception of their *distance* to the self. This geometric conception of identity, I graphically represent in *Figure 1*.

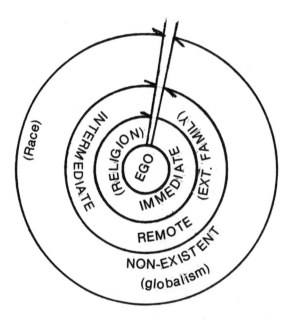

Figure 1

Mobility within these value sectors is entirely permissible and values can move up or down the scale according to how people fare in regard to social forces. It is revealing to see how the extended family, once the principal determinant of a Tongan's self-view, has depreciated quite markedly, and so is taken to be the breaking-point between immediate and intermediate values. The same can be said with regard to nationality and age. As a matter of fact, at one time in the past when Tongan society was still much more traditional, the whole intermediate sector constituted the immediate values of Tongan people. Thus the egoistic tendency shown by the study's results is indicative of a *materialistic-individualistic trend* in Tongan society.

These are, of course, signs of Westernization, a process originally set in motion by the early explorers and missionaries. It is now gathering tremendous momentum, though the Western ideas quickly attached themselves to existing social substructures modifying and transforming them at the same time.

CONCLUSION

The whole outcome of the foregoing general remarks is that we can, in fact, maintain — if only on logical grounds — that the distinction between *what* we think and *how* we think is a valid one. Meinong (Meinong, 1904), in fact, distinguished between the act, content, and object of thought. The act, as he defines it, would broadly correspond to what is referred to in this paper as "how we think," and content and object (variously) to "what we think." Russell (Russell, 1921) points out, however, that content and object, at times, are identical or, in certain thinking situations, there simply is no object of thought. In characterizing "how we think," I have maintained that thinking, in any of its forms, takes place by *taking something to be the case,* and, moreover, that this fundamental feature of thinking is a constant that persists in any thinking situation whatsoever.

The acounts of mythology and Tongans' self-view given above have indicated nothing to prejudice the said distinction. On the other hand, they show that men's minds are *conditioned* as to *focus* of thinking by social and environmental factors, especially the complex interplay of interests. They show, moreover, that this conditioning (also called socialization) takes place as *indoctrination*, which can be coercive or psychological, by furnishing people with *beliefs* (persuading them that certain states of affairs do exist). But the question of fact is absolutely immaterial. The whole issue is whether the beliefs or values instilled in people do promote certain interests or not. And, incidentally, this is tied up with the whole question of how society is maintained and kept intact. For to discuss interests in the form of social movement is to discuss politics. Here, however, we are in a domain where the ruling passion is not truth but utility, fashion, and relevance. Recognizing this and combining it with the pragmatic insight that we believe what we wish to take place, we can appreciate that the exercise and retention of power, or the ordering of society, must usually involve complete unscrupulousness. It may be an unpalatable idea but our conclusion forces us to this question: can society be kept under control on any bases other than irrationality and untruth?

REFERENCE NOTE

Parr, A. "Tongan Social Identity: an Emerging South Pacific Identity." Unpublished paper. 'Atenisi Institute, 1981.

REFERENCES

Bernstein, B. "Social Class and Linguistic Development: A Theory of Social Learning." In *Education, Economy and Society,* A.H. Halsey, J. Floud and A.

Anderson (Eds.). New York: Free Press, 1961.

Birch, H.G. "The Relation of Previous Experience to Insightful Problemsolving," *Journal of Comparative Psychology,* 1945, *38,* 367–383.

Eysenck, H.J. "Psychodiagnostics and Psychodynamics." *Experiments in Personality, Vol. 11.* London: Routledge and Kegan Paul, 1960.

Freud, S. *The Interpretation of Dreams.* New York: John Wiley & Sons, 1961.

Freud, S. *Totem and Taboo.* (Transl. J. Strachey). London: Routledge & Kegan Paul, 1960.

Harlow, H.F. "The Formation of Learning Sets," *Psychological Review,* 1949, *56,* 51–65.

Köhler, W. *The Mentality of Apes.* New York: Harcourt Brace, 1925.

Kuhn, M.H. and McPartland, T.S. "An Empirical Investigation of Self Attitudes," *American Sociological Review,* 1954, *19* (1), 68–76.

Levi-Strauss, C. *Structural Anthropology.* New York: Basic Books, 1963.

Mannheim, K. *Ideology and Utopia: An Introduction to the Sociology of Knowledge.* New York: Harcourt Brace, 1936.

Marx, K. and Engels, F. *Manifesto of the Communist Party.* New York: Labour News Company, 1948.

Meinong, A. von. "Concerning Objects of a Higher Order and Their Relationship to Inner Perception," *Journal for Psychology and Physiology of Sense Organs,* 1898.

Peirce, C.S. "The Fixation of Belief," *The Popular Science Monthly,* 1877–1878, *12* , 1–15.

Plato. *Meno.* (Transl. B. Jowett). New York: Doubleday and Co., 1960.

Plato. *Phaedo.* (Transl. B. Jowett). New York: Doubleday and Co., 1960.

Rex, J. "Nature Versus Nurture: the Significance of the Revised Debate." In *Race, Culture and Intelligence,* K. Richardson and D. Spears (Eds.). London: Penguin Books: 1972.

Russell, B. *The Problems of Philosophy.* Oxford: Oxford University Press, 1912.

Russell, B. *The Analysis of Mind.* London: George Allen & Unwin, 1933.

Thorndike, E.L. "Animal Intelligence." *Psychological Monographs,* 1898, *1,* (8).

Thorndike, E.L. *The Fundamentals of Learning.* New York: Columbia University Press, 1932.

Vico, G. *The New Science of Giambattista Vico.* (T.G. Bergin and M.H. Fisch, Transl.). New York: Cornell University Press, 1974.

SOCIAL STRUCTURE, SPEECH, AND SILENCE: FIJIAN REACTIONS TO THE PROBLEMS OF SOCIAL CHANGE[1]

Christopher M. Griffin

ABSTRACT

Adapting Bernstein (1971), the paper examines Fijian social structure and communication to argue that, in the context of change, Fijians lack the speech code requisite for the identification of new problems, and retain the inadequate social controls of the older code. Unable to think-out new roles, verbalize problems, and generate options, anxiety and frustration find outlets in expressive behaviour that is regarded as deviant.

This essay is about words; about the exchange and withholding of words as behavior patterns reflecting Fijian social organization, and about the form of social control embedded in those patterns. And because the display of both silence and words are means of expressing *thinking* about social relations, the paper is also an exercise in the sociology of knowledge.

Our problem quite simply stated is to explain the underachievement (or apparent failure) of Fijians relative to other ethnic categories in Fiji, notably Indians,[2] in formal education, private enterprise, and (in a somewhat different sense) before the courts of law, as their disproportionately greater number in prison attest. (Approximately seventy-five percent of the prison population is composed of Fijians; fifty years ago the prison population was almost entirely Indian.) This is a diagnosis of

---

C.M. Griffin is in the Sociology Department at The University of the South Pacific in Suva, Fiji.

1. The commentary throughout refers both to speech in the Fijian language and in English, which is spoken almost universally in urban Fiji. Though not a Fijian-speaker, the author draws upon the scholarship of anthropologists and others who are competent in the Fijian language. The analysis is checked against the author's own participant-observations and English conversations with a wide range of people in Suva over a period of seven years.

2. In 1976, Indians, most of them descendents of nineteenth century indentured laborers, accounted for 49.8 percent of Fiji's population. Fijians accounted for 44.2 percent.

failure shared by a wide consensus of local opinion, not least, amongst Fijians themselves.

To begin with, it is our basic contention that assuming the situation is indeed problematic from the Fijian viewpoint, or, for that matter, symptomatic of broader, more complex, social problems, then the analysis and resolution must involve talking it out. In other words, a greater use of public dialogue at both the individual and institutional levels, than is normal in Fijian culture is needed.

For almost a decade Fiji has witnessed a stream of rhetoric on the crisis of Fijian failure, and heard the recurring message to youth to look to its future in the land and in the customs-of-the-land enshrined in the political culture of the village. The message is unequivocal. The difficulty is that there is an equally common exhortation, incompatible with the first, which urges Fijians on to academic achievement and entrepreneurial success, and, in a more general guise, towards self-reliance. The overall communication is therefore ambiguous: stick to custom and change your ways. Fijians, especially those in towns like the capital of Suva, consequently face a dilemma. It is a dilemma of thinking or consciousness: a dilemma of *what* to think (content), *how* to think (process), and how to manage content in *talk* and *action* without loss of that community and cultural identity (which bestows a sense of social security) and comes essentially from the exchange of goods and ritual objects according to well-established conventions.

The difficulties and dilemma of Fijian values and structures in the face of a changing economy have been referred to at length by several commentators including Burns (1959), Fisk (1970), and, most notably, Oscar Spate (1959), who defined much of the problem in terms of the existing relations between leaders and followers (1965). Furthermore, a committee appointed by Government to look into emerging youth problems twenty years ago (1961), composed mainly of Fijian citizens, concurred with Spate, and even went so far as to urge an immediate transformation from communalism to individualism. Meanwhile, others have identified the root of Fijian problems of adjustment as lying more in the loss of flexible relations between chiefs and commoners, brought about by the policies of a British Colonial Administration (Belshaw, '1964; France, 1969; Nayacakalou, 1975). For, to quote the latter, a Fijian anthropologist:

> The Fijian Administration (therefore) came to rest on the 'communal system' or, to be more precise, on a certain model of it, always with the view it should develop into a fully modern institution,.... But it did not square with the facts of modern Fijian society and its processes; that is, there was a lack of structural adaptation in a situation of rapid change (p. 132).

The present, immediate task then, is not so much to demonstrate whether or not this situation continues, as to argue on the basis of such evidence that the newer social problems can only be understood in the context of Fijian social relations in general, and the relations of power and authority in particular, as these are epitomized in the nexus of chief and commoner, leader and led.

LEADERS AND LED

For brevity's sake, the Fijian social structure can be described as a hierarchical system of patrilineal descent groups, ranging from the extended family or *tokatoka* at base, through larger, encapsulating groups such as sub-clan (*mataqali*) and clan (*yavusa*), up to *vanua* (literally land or place) and possibly confederations (of *vanua*) known as *matanitu*. At each succeeding level, varieties of chiefs exercise greater degrees of authority as leaders, but with the exception of the Great Council of Chiefs, the physical location of this authority is principally the village, where seventy percent of ethnic Fijians reside.

The Great Council of Chiefs, comprising representatives from Fijian provincial councils, oversees all traditional Fijian interests and has representatives at the Senate. For an extensive discussion of the term "chief" see Walter (1978).

According to A.M. Hocart, who lived in the Lau Islands of eastern Fiji in the first decade of this century, Fijian leadership was not a matter of chiefs governing or ruling (1970, p. 129), nor was it a simple matter of power. The status of chief implied an obligation 'to face the land,' to receive the people's gifts and then to redistribute them.

In this, his essential role, the chief is a ritual specialist of the highest order, a demi-god and vehicle of communication between the people, their ancestors (*vu*), and ancestral gods (*kalou vu*). In this communion and sacrifice to a higher Being, a chief ensures that the land prospers, that the people fare well and that none is neglected.

As head of the body politic, and as a demi-god and symbol of the collectivity from which derives his sacredness, a chief is invariably shown deep respect (*vakarokoroko*). In fact, the concepts of respect (*vakarokoroko*) and shame (*madua*) are as integral to understanding Fijian organization as are the concepts honor (a somewhat different idea) and shame are essential to certain South-East Asian, Latin American, Mediterranean and even, to Micronesian societies. Respect is not only shown to chiefs *per se*, but to any authority figure (male in particular), including the father/husband who is always chief (*turaga*) of his own household — especially in the eyes of his sons. That respect is communicated primarily by deferential silence (*tiko lo*) and stillness, which in turn signifies good breeding. This emphasis upon stillness or silence as a token of respect is fundamental to any understanding of Fijian underachievement in fields demanding assertion and questioning.

In deriving authority from the group, the chief/commoner relationship is, normatively, not grossly unbalanced. Rather, it is reciprocal or mutually dependent, as contemporary Fijian national leaders still point out. Respect paid to chiefs is an exchange paid for the continued prosperity of the group. So while chiefs can exert power, and in the past often did so brutally, respect in the last analysis is earned. Ideally, dependency should resolve the problems of followers. However respect goes away when authority is no longer seen as serving the needs of those entrusted with it. Reciprocity and mutual dependency are seen to shift towards assymetrical relations, and those who feel deprived react.

This explains much of the present crisis in Fijian social order. Why there are, for example, sporadic cases of villagers refusing respect to their chief; why the urban young are increasingly disdainful of parental authority, of the school and its curriculum, and of the institutions of law and order.

Before the cession of Fiji to Britain in the mid-nineteenth century, constant warfare was frequently the result of dependents or allies shifting political allegiance or the result of chiefs being murdered by their sons, cousins, half-brothers, or uncles. For, as Scarr remarks, chiefs exerted their power with a "strong hand, *na liga qaqa*" (1980, p. 13). Nevertheless, as Clunie notes in his book on Fijian warfare:

> Too tyranical a rule could result in rebellion or desertion of vassals but more particularly tribute-paying vassals to a rival power; so chiefs had to be skilled politicians in order to retain their popularity with the bulk of their followers while having to punish offenders so as not to appear weak (1977, p. 5).

Here it is worth noting that in some cases the consecration of a high chief to power and authority—as in the case of the Tui Naceva (Lord of the Windward)—followed a period of probation in which he was the incumbent of a lesser title, and even afterwards he was put to the test of his chiefly qualities (Hocart, 1970, p. 134).

In broader terms, a culture is a collection of normative rules made to work for people in practice (even at the symbolic and ritual level) and, in so doing, it unites them. In order to work, a culture must undergo constant adaptation to the physical and social environment. When a culture fails for significant segments of the community, alternatives are sought. People may go to war, "drop out," form sub- or counter-cultures, retreat partially into alternative realities under the influence of alcohol or other drugs, or devise new forms of political or religious organizations. And over the past two centuries South Pacific societies, like Fiji, have seen many such movements, including Melanesian "cargo cults" (*i.e.,* millenarian movements in which followers oriented their activities towards the coming of "cargo" or Western economic goods, such as food and tools).

Today, in 1982, it is the acceleration in crimes of poverty and liquor offenses among ethnic Fijians, the spread of prostitution and of male and female homosexuality (none of which, of course, is confined to Fijians) that indicate new cultural adaptations, adaptations regarded as problematic. The fact remains that wherever a culture's formulae cease to provide for human needs, deviance may be expected to test that culture's authority and rules of socialization.

CULTURE AND SOCIALIZATION

A reason commonly given for Fijian delinquency and crime is the failure of parental upbringing (Grant, 1975). But observing the constantly growing rate of Fijian criminalization reflected in prison figures (seventy-five percent of the prison population is ethnic Fijian, who constitute forty-four percent of the total population), we are compelled to explain the phenomena not in psychological or moral terms, but in sociological terms.

The question of socialization is therefore not so much, "Why are parents negligent today compared with the past?" as "Why does contemporary socialization leave an increasing number of Fijians unfit for decent survival?" This demands an examination of both the *medium* (or *form*) and the *content* of socialization relative to a rapidly-changing environment.

There is also a more general, yet fundamental, question: Can the Fijians devise a culture which mentally equips them to cope with social problems arising from change, while simultaneously preserving the group structure which is the essence of Fijian custom or culture?

To change modes of thinking without radically altering traditional structures of exchange and authority, is a goal expounded by a number of writers on development. But whether this is feasible or not is debatable. Let us examine this idea with reference to Fiji where the concept of self-reliance—itself at odds with existing notions of dependency or reciprocity—is a prominent element of political rhetoric.

Firstly, development-cum-thinking, involving analytic ability in the subjective areas of culture, ideas, values, and relationships, is a process not easily acquired in social systems which lack opportunities for the reciprocal exchange of ideas, questioning, dialectic, and doubt. If, therefore, such skills are demanded (as by all accounts in Fiji they are), the task of teaching them ought to begin in the period of early socialization and not be left until it is too late.

Secondly, this development must inevitably involve not just psychological but sociological and cultural change as well: change in the way people *think about* others in general, and authority relations in particular; and changes in the way people communicate these thoughts, symbolically, in word and action. In this regard, the more flexible the social system is, the easier the change will be. Thus, for a Polynesian-influenced, political culture like Fiji's, with its multiple conventions of speech, silence, gesture, and etiquette, this will probably be harder to achieve than in, say, one of the more egalitarian societies of Melanesia.

In conclusion, if Fijian failure really *is* problematic, the reasons lie in Fijian social relations and the *expression* of these in such tightly-defined cultural idioms as the need to exchange property, to abide by and be with the group, and to communicate respect for custom and its human representatives. In addition, there are ample signs that the basic needs of a steadily increasing number of people are not being met by conventional, social relations. There is evidence of a quite dramatic (and in some cases sudden) shift of cultural norms to meet socio-economic changes in the presence of crime, heavy drinking, sexual promiscuity, school truancy, drop-outs, and marital break-down. Here the customs of respect are on the wane.

I would now like to examine this connection between culture and social structure in greater detail.

CULTURE AND STRUCTURE

Culture can be defined as the way people share ideas of thinking about their social and physical environment and the way they manifest this symbolic exchange in word and action. Where there is culture there is community, a community built on communication. The extent to which that communication occurs determines the nature of its border with other communities. Culture both reflects ideas about social relations and gives shape to them.

The heart of any culture lies in its language. This alone makes communication possible. Even non-verbal communication is modeled on a verbal prototype. Language (Saussure's *langue*) is the formal system of sounds man adapts in speech (Saussure's *parole*) to exchange thought. According to Saussure, language (*langue*) is a social institution and system of contractual values; it is, so to speak "language" minus speech. Speech (*parole*), in contrast, is the actualization of, and individual selection from, language.

Language makes thought itself possible by giving meaning or sense to a discovered world; sense precisely because it is meaning *shared* with others. In fact, both culture and sanity depend on the regular exchange of shared meaning, which explains why for Fijians, who are brought up to be highly dependent, being alone is a state to be pitied, avoided, or regarded with suspicion.

To speak and comprehend a language is to inhabit the world in a manner that separates Self from the Other who does not understand it. The Melanesian term *Wantok* (literally "one talk," people who share a language) captures this idea perfectly.

Language is less a part of culture as it is the matrix and code to culture. Or, as the linguist and anthropologist Edward Sapir once put it, "language is a symbolic guide to culture" (1970, p. 70). Without language there is no means of ordering, classifying, of making sense of the world. Language separates man from beast and makes culture out of nature. In the beginning of mankind was the word and the word was made flesh. Words make for world or, rather, for a particular conception of it—a culture.

To take up a new language is to enter a new world, to cross the bourne, to begin to think and see as others do. Conversely, to give up a language or lose some of its words is to give up the whole, or part, of a way of life. The late Ratu Lala Sukuna, a great Fijian statesman deeply loved by the Fijians and highly respected by Indians and others, has been aptly called a "Man of Two Worlds" (Scarr, 1980) because of this ability to communicate on equal terms with others, notably the British. Ratu Sir Kamisese Mara, the present Prime Minister, demonstrates similar skills. Significantly, both men were university-educated overseas.

Today the socialization of Pacific islanders for "two worlds" is, to varying degrees, being executed in schools, colleges, and the regional universities. In the process these secondary institutions, which are now as much part of Pacific culture as, say, the age-old obligations and ties of kinship, change attitudes towards primary customs and institutions. This change is both psychological and sociological. And those who complete the new rites of passage pass, culturally equipped, into the demands of adult roles in a changing environment. What, though, of those who do not? Here the evidence of Suva suggests that in its deviance and subculture, youth is already seeking new solutions to the problems of social and economic survival which the parent-culture has failed to provide. What is more, hundreds of adolescents are entering adulthood (or perhaps we should say, prolonging their adolescence) with children of their own; caring and controlling them only with the greatest of difficulty. For these people the codes and content of socialization are inadequate to their needs. The language of culture is impoverished. Why?

Before the advent of colonialism in the Fiji Islands, the authority of custom (culture or community) was taken for granted. Even the overthrow of a chief was done according to cultural rules. Custom coped with life's contingencies. Then the missions and British colonial administration brought respectively literacy and the greater formalization of both chieftanship and rules of land tenure.

Broadly speaking, literacy makes for detachment. Language that was formerly sound "in the round" acquires a sharper quality or, as the anthropologist Edmund Carpenter explains, the eye takes on a bigger part and thoughts become arranged seriously and serially (1976, p. 31). In other words, writing allows our thoughts to become objects arranged linearly. Thus writing is the very making of science, precisely because it allows thinking to be viewed critically, with detachment. Popper very appropriately refers to this as "World Three." Speech in literate civilizations has a similar, though less extensive, potential.

The more literate a person is, the greater is his capacity for articulating in written or spoken word new problems he wants to identify and solve. Greater literacy also increases a person's chances of generating new thoughts and discovering the range of options which evolve from dialogue. Without words or the right kind of language, none of this is possible and the result instead is anxiety or frustration, arising from a lack of detachment from the still-unarticulated problem.

Today, due to literacy, there are countless Fijians (many of them working in complex organizations) who possess the skills of analytic thinking required to deal with the intricate problems relating to change, but whose thoughts are rarely openly expressed because of cultural norms relating to communication in public and to respect. Underexercised, their thinking process fails to achieve optimum capacity. Unexpressed, thinking content is suppressed and reserved for private situations. The result is suffocation of creative talent and, I suspect, much personal frustration.

Apart from these people there is also a much larger body of individuals, usually less educated, who read and write little. They are constantly swamped by personal problems they cannot pinpoint and are baffled by connections they cannot see or put together. Quite literally, they can neither think out nor express what it is that bothers them. In the very absence of this ability, the culture has not developed listeners who can respond to or assist these people. In both these cases, the frustrated and the anxious substitute alcohol for achieving the need to get outside themselves. In brief, to use a phrase from Gluckman (1964), "closed systems and open minds do not go together." To elaborate on this we turn to the work of Basil Bernstein (1971).

SPEECH CODES

In his work on the problems of educability among British schoolchildren, Bernstein argues that patterns of speech communication vary directly according to social class. For example, working-class children from relatively close-knit social structures use a restricted code of speech, rich in metaphor but poor in precision. Meaning often derives not so much from what is said, as by how it is said. Where there is a relatively undifferentiated social structure with a system of well-defined, fairly unchanging role and status relations, the culture (or community) will be based on a body of common assumptions, background, and history. The result is that a great deal of knowledge can be taken for granted and go unspoken, or else be communicated in simple restricted speech. In such systems, social control is a function of one's position in society. This knowledge is acquired early in a child's life through the restricted and somewhat authoritarian code of parents. Social control in those cases is largely other-oriented control. Bernstein's working-class families and aristocratic families share similar characteristics. These societies we can call closed-systems.

In contrast, middle-class children use an elaborate code. In this sort of society, which finds its apogee in the university, relatively little can be taken for granted, as the division of labor undermines the stock of common assumptions and there is an extensive degree of social and physical mobility. In comparison with what Douglas (1970) calls the group structure of working-class society, interaction in a middle-class setting occurs on a grid basis. The social boundaries are generally open, but closed where it really matters, namely, around the nuclear family. Social control in these structures is a question of individuals learning collective general principles to apply, according to private judgment. It is not a matter of fearing community opprobrium as it is in closed-systems. Social control comes to mean self-control.

In social structures of the first kind, we can say that speech is geared to continuity and is community-assumed. In social structures of the second type, words are used for adaptation to change and are community-negotiated. In the first case, community boundaries are well-defined, but open to certain areas that matter, subject to an abiding by the language of its condensed symbols and ritual. In the other instance, community boundaries are vague but closed to most areas that matter, despite a paucity of condensed symbols (Douglas, 1970).

According to this model, Fijian society can be said to fit into the culture of the restricted code. Not only are history and assumptions shared, but so is blood; in fact, the word is often used to mean relative. Thus a stranger to a group is not usually introduced as it would be considered rude, for in the course of conversation a kin-tie with somebody or other present is bound to be discovered.

In order to belong or have a social identity in Fijian organization, a person must belong to a household which enjoys a recognized exchange with others, whether of goods, services, or (to take Levi-Strauss' point) people. In this regard, as Nation observes (1978, p. 3), there is a flexibility in Fijian social frontiers which demonstrates that membership results from horizontal accretion or adoption, as well as from principles of descent.

This openness of structure is, nevertheless, more than offset by the tightly de-fined rules of communication which govern relations between high chiefs and com-moners. In order for the chief to communicate with his people a special orator (*matanivanua*) exists whose ceremonial role splendidly demonstrates a chief's own dependency.

"*Sa sega ni vuka na kaka me biu toka na buina,*" runs an old proverb, "the par-rot leaves not its tail when it flies: the chief goes nowhere without his *matanivanua.*" (see Kikau, 1981.) The tail not only adds stature, it also lends balance. The *matanivanua* is at once spokesman for the chief and policeman for the community, punishing troublemakers when need-be, but acting as counsellor too, ready to admonish his chief if he seriously threatens the commonweal. Possibly, he is a chief's greatest rival (Hocart, 1970, p. 191). And rivalry is of the utmost significance to our general problem of failure, because it bears on the issue of motivation.

Pliant boundaries and strict rules for communication parallel another paradox in Fijian organization—the sense of hierarchy and sense of equality *within* ranks. John Nation has also already commented on this (1978, p. 23). From both these senses the most characteristic of all Fijian traits derives (especially in males), that of tension plus humor.

Egalitarianism pays its price in competition (Bailey, 1971, p. 19). People must compete to remain equal, particularly in cultures which emphasize gift-giving. Equally important, people ought not to appear to be superior to their peers ("*viavialevu*" as the Fijians call it, or "want to be"). That only brings gossip which consists of levelling words that scar reputations and distance the individual from his group—a situation uncomfortable for most Fijians. Gossip is central to Fijian ethics as Hocart and others (Thompson, 1940; Arno, 1974) have observed. And it pro-vides another explanation as to why, in formal education, a Fijian rarely exerts himself in front of others, preferring instead, to simply get by. Reputation-management among peers consequently involves a high degree of tension which, in turn, is partly reduced by joking or humor.

Aside from these horizontal considerations, to speak or act out is to risk en-dangering relations with authority, because where much is taken for granted, even an innocuous question may be regarded as shameful. Alternatively, to act or speak out of line—to innovate—and thus risk failure, is also to risk incurring the ridicule of superiors and equals alike. And this too has its effects on educational per-formance as a Fijian schoolmaster once explained in a personal conversation:

> Fijian parents of weak children do not turn up at the school on open days; they feel ashamed, boiling inside about their child. This will probably affect the child. Teachers can be blamed too: scolding in front of others kills the driving force of the child....Even at The University of the South Pacific the Fijian student doesn't talk. It's the chiefly system in us, one keeps quiet all the time. Silence comes from above, in front of an elder, chief, or father. This comes down to the children; it's a fear of the father embedded in our system. He is paramount. The emphasis is on "not." It's a negative attitude all the time. We were taught the negative not the positive. When you want to break away from negative thinking, it's a building process again.

The restricted code with its use of metaphor thus functions to conceal assertion and to keep information vague. It is better suited to what is old and understood than to what is new and not. Thus several Fijians have told me that their language is shady, meaning imprecise. Others have said that it is not so useful when one wants to talk about "change" (*vei sau*). All of which suggests that both the code and content easily fashion misunderstanding. One informant put it this way:

Our thinking is straight but when you speak...it is not very meaningful (*i.e.,* precise); it may have two edges, so what people say is changed very easily as it passes from one to another. The whole story changes.

Combined with what already has been said about anxiety, this might explain the marked lack of trust I detect among young urban Fijians (and which Suva-based psychologist Robert Stewart has also found [1980]). This characteristic imprecision of speech might also help explain the widespread accusations of malicious gossip (worse among young males than among females according to most informants), as well as the treachery and envy observers (*e.g.,* Williams, 1858, p. 128) in the last century reckoned to be common Fijian traits.

CONCLUSION

Although I have only briefly touched on the nature of the new problems in Fiji, I must emphasize by way of a conclusion, that many of these problems are tied to the fact that in a period of rapid change especially in urban settings where group controls are effectively reduced, the persistence of the restricted code has resulted (a) in inadequate socialization of children where individual self-control is lacking, (b) generation gaps of widening proportions, and (c) a generation—the children of these new, urbanized youth—who are probably even less equipped to mentally survive than are their young parents.

To speed sensible adaptations to the upheavals of change at a rate sufficient to forestall more serious problems, Fijian culture needs to change its existing processes and contents of communication, beginning with early socialization in the school and home. But such adaptation will only be achieved at the cost of certain changes in the overall existing structure of social ralations, which, of course, only the Fijian populus can decide upon.

Certainly, a more elaborate verbal code than the present one is needed to facilitate thinking about social problems. What Fijian culture desperately needs is a code which does not destroy respect for or eradicate the vitally important sense of mutual social and economic obligation which still exists. Instead, such a revised code must foster a reciprocal exchange of independent ideas which are respected precisely because *as* cultural content they can *generate* collective solutions to the problems of community identity and survival, albeit in a new form. In short, public dialogue within and between social strata must increase if further frustration and anxiety are to be prevented.

To this end, one traditional Fijian institution, which has so far gone unmentioned, could play a vital role, given its importance as a vehicle for community communication and democratic problem solving. I refer to the *kava* or *yaqona* bowl. *Yaqona* or *kava,* a non-alcoholic drink made from the pounded root of a pepper plant (*piper methysticum*), has a mild narcotic effect which promotes the social manufacture of fraternity and well-being. Taken in excess, however, it can lead to a loss of muscular control, especially in the lower limbs, and to a hangover the following morning. Continued heavy drinking (sometimes regarded as addictive) may, in the long run, result in the skin becoming dry and very scaly.

As a source of community with in-built social controls, the *tanoa* or kava bowl is unrivalled. By its special effects—social as much (if not more than) as pharmacological—speech is encouraged but also controlled. For, despite the strict protocol which forms an essential part of many types of *kava* ceremony, *yaqona* drinking has become, above all, an excuse for the informal social gathering of friends and neighbors, where an individual can express his troubles, listen to the opinion and related experiences of others and, possibly, reach some solution based on the collective wisdom of the group. To what extent it is successful in dealing with the novel and often highly complex problems associated with urbanization is something we barely understand, but in the absence of other forums for reasoned dialogue, its importance in Fijian society can hardly be underestimated.

REFERENCES

Arno, A. *Conflict Management in a Fijian Village.* Unpublished Ph.D. thesis: Harvard University, 1974.

Arno, A. "Joking, Avoidance, and Authority: Verbal Performance as an Object of Exchange." *Journal of Polynesian Society History,* 1976, *85*, 1, 71–86.

Bailey, F.G. *Gifts and Poison: The Politics of Reputation.* Oxford: Basil Blackwell, 1971.

Belshaw, C.S. *Under the Ivi Tree.* Berkeley and Los Angeles: University of California Press, 1964.

Bernstein, B. *Class, Codes, and Control.* London: Routledge and Kegan Paul, 1971.

Burns, A. *Report of the Commission of Enquiry into the Natural Resources and Population Trends of the Colony of Fiji, 1959.* Suva: Legislative Council Paper No. 1, 1960.

Carpenter, E. *Oh What a Blow that Phantom Gave Me.* St. Albans: Paladin, 1976.

Clunie, F. "Fijian Weapons and Warfare," *Fiji Museum Bulletin,* No. 2, 1977.

Doublas, M. *Natural Symbols: Explorations in Cosmology.* New York: Pantheon Books, 1970.

France, P. *The Charter of the Land: Custom and Colonization in Fiji.* Melbourne: Oxford University Press, 1969.

Fisk, F. *The Political Economy of Independent Fiji.* Wellington: Reed, 1970.

Gluckman, M. (Ed.) *Closed Systems and Open Minds: The Limits of Naivete in Social Anthropology.* Chicago: Aldine Publishing, 1964.

Grant, C. *Report of Royal Commission of Inquiry in Crime, 1975.* Suva: Government Printer, 1976.

Hocart, A.M. *Lau Islands, Fiji.* (Originally published 1929). New York: Bernice P. Bishop Museum, Bulletin 62, Kraus Reprint Co., 1971.

Hocart, A.M. *Kings and Councillors.* (Originally published 1936). Chicago: University of Chicago Press, 1970.

Kikau, Eli. *The Wisdom of Fiji.* Suva: The Institute of Pacific Studies, University of the South Pacific, 1981.

Nation, J. *Customs of Respect: The Traditional Basis of Fijian Communal Politics.* Canberra: Development Studies Centre Monograph No. 14, Australian National University, 1978.

Nayacakalou, R.R. *Leadership in Fiji.* Melbourne: Oxford University Press, 1975.

Sapir, E. "The State of Linguistics as a Science." In *Culture, Language, and Personality.* Ann Arbor, MI: The University of Michigan Press, 1970.

Scarr, D. *Ratu Sukuna: Soldier, Statesman, Man of Two Worlds.* London: Macmillan, 1980.

Spate, O.H.K. *The Fijian People: Economic Problems and Prospects.* Suva, Legislative Council Paper No. 13, 1959.

Spate, O.H.K. *Let Me Enjoy.* Canberra: Australian National University Press, 1965.

Stewart, R., Lui M.M., Mulipola and H. Laidlaw. "Beliefs about Human Nature Held by Adolescents in Fiji: Some Preliminary Ethnic and Sex Comparisons,"

Social Behavior and Personality. 1980, *1,* 125–128.

Thompson, L. *Fijian Frontier.* (Originally published 1940). New York: Octagon Books, 1972.

Walter, M.A.H.B. ''An Examination of Hierarchical Notions in Fijian Society: A Test Case of the Applicability of the Term Chief,'' *Oceania,* 1978, *XLIX,* 1, 1–19.

Williams, T. *Fiji and the Fijians. The Islands and Their Inhabitants,* Vol. 1, London: Alexander Heylin, 1858.

Youth Problems, *Report of Committee Appointed to Investigate.* Suva: Legislative Council Paper No. 39 of 1961.

BELIEFS ABOUT HUMAN NATURE
HELD BY YOUNG PEOPLE
IN THE SOUTH PACIFIC[1]

Robert A.C. Stewart

ABSTRACT

Beliefs in overall trustworthiness, rationality and complexity of others were investigated in studies of one hundred twenty-one adolescents from schools in Suva, Fiji; one hundred twenty university students in Fiji; and seventy-two adolescents from Honiara, Solomon Islands. Using Wrightsman's Children's Philosophies of Human Nature Scale, it was shown that Indo-Fijians and Europeans both had a higher level of belief in the trustworthiness of people than did indigenous Fijians. It was also shown that females had a higher level of belief in the trustworthiness of people and a lower level of belief in strength of will and rationality of others than males did. Additionally, Europeans were shown to see people in general as more complex than the Fijian and Indo-Fijian groups. The Solomon Island results show that people who are seen as "closer" are perceived as easier to understand and are more to be trusted than those seen as "distant;" this is particularly so for females. The three studies demonstrate how an inventory can illuminate an area of beliefs in human nature otherwise difficult to investigate. As in the multi-ethnic societies studied, it is important to understand objectively beliefs and perceptions such as these, as they are often the key to the way people behave toward one another.

Recent research in the social sciences (Rosenthal and Jacobson, 1968; Wrightsman, 1974) has underscored the significance of the beliefs and expectations we have about other people. Sometimes the belief itself can create the reality. For example, a person's acceptance of and openness to others could be very much in-

---

R.A.C. Stewart is Reader in Educational Psychology at The University of the South Pacific in Suva, Fiji, and international editor, *Social Behavior and Personality*.

1. Thanks are due for funding to The University of the South Pacific Research Committee. Thanks also to Sr. Malia Mulipola-Lui, Mrs. Helen Laidlaw, Mrs. Shankuntla Prasad, Mrs. Mary Stewart, and Mrs. Anita Naidu. Finally, acknowledgement is due to the subjects in the studies from Stella Maris Primary School, Suva Grammar School and Laucala Bay Demonstration School in Suva; King George VI School in Honiara; and The University of the South Pacific. Major results from the study are being communicated to all groups of subjects.

fluenced by belief in the trustworthiness of people. One tends to "see" confirmation of one's deeply-held beliefs. Thus, the person who believes that people are hostile to him will sooner or later find evidence to support the view (possibly by arousing counter-hostility in others as they react to this suspicious attitude). Erikson (1963) sees the development of a sense of basic trust as a central focus of the earliest months after birth. He defines basic trust as a "correspondence between one's needs and one's world, whereas basic mistrust is a readiness for danger or anticipation of discomfort." He, like Freud, sees early experiences as coloring much of the individual's later perspectives on other people and life in general.

Psychologists, surprisingly, have not devoted a great deal of effort to studying individual differences in "philosophies of human nature." Yet there is often an implicit recognition by psychologists of their importance in shaping the individual's perception of the world. Thus George Kelly, father of the Personal Construct[2] theory in psychology, suggests that we look at the world through "transparent patterns or templates" which we create and then attempt to fit over the realities of which the world is composed (Kelly, 1955, pp. 8-9). The degree to which what we "see" is a function of what we *want* to see has been long recognized in psychology. Thus the phenomenon of "selective perception" is seen in work such as that of Bruner and Goodwin (1947), who found for example that hungry subjects are more likely to identify "stk" as "steak."

Individuals do vary in the degree to which they believe in the trustworthiness of other people; they vary, too, in the degree to which they see people as "complex" as opposed to "simple." (Are people basically easy to understand or complicated and hard to understand?) Yet another dimension in an individual's beliefs about human nature is the degree to which others are seen as rational and possessing strength of will (as opposed to being irrational and lacking personal strength of will). Thus we have at least three dimensions of a philosophy of human nature, comprising beliefs in the *trustworthiness, complexity* and *rationality* of others.

Wrightsman (1974) suggests that philosophies of human nature are learned, just as other attitudes are. They are shaped by each individual's socialization experience—in the complex interplay of the individual with his social and cultural environment.

The South Pacific provides a rich laboratory for the study of the results of differences in social and cultural environments. In the eleven countries served by The University of the South Pacific, there are an estimated sixty different cultures and 300 languages, ranging across Melanesia, Polynesia and Micronesia. Bearing in mind that a person's basic beliefs about the nature of people are very significant in shaping his own perception of the world, these attitudes were investigated in two countries of the South Pacific Region, Fiji and the Solomon Islands.

Both Fiji and the Solomon Islands are members of the British Commonwealth. Fiji, independent since 1970, covers a land area of 18,300 sq. km. comprised of over 300 islands. With a population of over 612,000 (as of December 1978), it is a multiracial society composed of forty-four percent Fijians, fifty percent Indo-Fijians,[3] three percent Europeans and part Europeans, Chinese one percent and others two percent. The Solomon Islands, independent since 1978, cover a land area

---

2. The personal construct theory of George Kelly is a cognitive theory of personality which emphasizes how the individual perceives, interprets and conceptualizes events in his environment. The human being is viewed as a scientist who develops a theory or construct system to predict events.

3. Citizens of Fiji of Indian origin.

of 29,800 sq. km. and are comprised of six main islands. With a population of 196,823 as of the 1976 census, it is composed of ninety-three percent Melanesians, four percent Polynesians, one and one-half percent Micronesian and Others one and one-half percent.

Reported here are three studies dealing with the measurement of philosophies of human nature in groups of subjects from Fiji and the Solomon Islands. The first was a study of Fijian, Indo-Fijian, European and other adolescents from schools in Suva, Fiji; the second study tested students at the University of the South Pacific from these same ethnic groups. The last study used adolescents from a secondary school in Honiara, Solomon Islands.

Ritchie and Ritchie (1979) have described five characteristics of child rearing in Polynesia: many adult caretakers, early indulgence, early independence demands, peer socialization and a community context of child rearing. It has been suggested that these principles may well apply to Melanesia, as well as to Polynesia. In contrast to the indigenous Fijians, the Indo-Fijians are seen commonly as being more individually- than communally-oriented and possibly less trusting of others. These studies provide an opportunity to test some of these cross-ethnic perceptions in an objective manner. Study three in particular tests the hypothesis that for Melanesians with their strong communal orientation, there will be a substantially greater sense of trust for those perceived as "close" (extended family and village) than for people at a distance.

MEASUREMENT OF PHILOSOPHIES OF HUMAN NATURE

Wrightsman (1974) reports a considerable volume of research on assumptions about human nature, using the Philosophies of Human Nature Inventory (PHN) and the Children's version of the Philosophies of Human Nature Inventory (C-PHN). The PHN measures the dimensions of belief about human beings in the following categories: Trustworthiness, Strength of Will and Rationality, Altruism, Independence, Complexity, and Variability. The C-PHN focuses on three of these dimensions, namely beliefs in Trustworthiness, Strength of Will and Rationality, and Complexity.

In Study One (with Fijian adolescents) the results of a factor analysis reported in Wrightsman were used to collate fifteen key items which were shown to be most powerful in identifying the subject's views on the trustworthiness of people in general and the belief in how complicated people are on the whole. This is referred to as the Revised C-PHN Inventory. In the remaining two studies, the full thirty-six item questionnaire was used. Sample items from the C-PHN Inventory (and Revised C-PHN Inventory) are illustrated in *Table 1*.

RELIABILITY AND VALIDITY

Wrightsman (1974) reports quite extensive reliability and validity data mainly in the United States, on the closely related parent inventory PHN. For example, split-half reliability coefficients for the Trustworthiness and Complexity scales (Wrightsman, 1964) were respectively 0.89 and 0.76 for a sample of undergraduate men. A later study (O'Connor, 1971) found split-half reliabilities for 480 subjects as follows: Trustworthiness 0.78, and Complexity 0.69. Wrightsman cites as evidence for validity of the PHN the extensive research reported on the scale's relationships to behavior, consistent with the underlying theory of the PHN. Also, he suggests that the ability of the PHN to show differences in scale scores between men and women in predicted directions also supports the scale's validity. There appears to be face validity and reliability of the PHN and C-PHN in Fiji and the Solomon Islands. The results of these studies will contribute to an understanding of validity in Fiji, in terms of the scale's ability to distinguish between known groups.

Table 1. Sample Items from C-PHN Scale
(With Direction of Items on Trustworthiness, Strength of Will
and Rationality, and Complexity Scales Designated)

4.	(SWR +)	Most people who try hard do well in life.
*13.	(T −)	Most people will not keep a promise.
18.	(SWR +)	When people do things wrong, it is usually their own fault.
*20.	(C −)	It only takes a few minutes to get to know somebody.
*21.	(T −)	In a game, most people will cheat to win.
*25.	(T +)	Most people will do the right thing even if no one is watching them.
*26.	(C +)	Many people do the same thing for different reasons.
*27.	(T +)	If they could, most people would help a stranger who was in trouble.
*28.	(C −)	Most people are easy to understand.
30.	(SWR −)	Good people are luckier than bad people.
*34.	(C +)	You can't tell what a person is like by looking at him.
36.	(SWR −)	If a person is born poor, he will always stay poor.

*An asterisk indicates items included in the Revised C-PHN Inventory which was used in Study One. The remainder of the thirty-six items in the C-PHN Inventory are available (see Wrightsman, 1974), as are the complete fifteen items on the Revised C-PHN Inventory, in Stewart (1980).

SUBJECTS AND METHOD

Study One

Testing was conducted in three schools in the Suva, Fiji area: Stella Maris Primary School (sixty-four subjects), Suva Grammar School (thirty-one subjects) and Laucala Bay Demonstration School (twenty-six subjects). The 121 subjects ranged in age from thirteen to eighteen years, with a mean at fourteen point seven years (SD one point three years). There were sixty males and sixty-one females. In ethnic composition there were thirty-one Fijian, fifty Indo-Fijians and twenty-one Europeans, with nineteen classified as "other" ethnic group members. Using the fifteen-item C-PHN (Revised) Inventory, the subjects were told, "Each of the following statements represents something with which people probably agree and some disagree. There are no right or wrong answers. You will probably disagree with some statements and agree with others. We are interested in how much you agree or disagree with them." The subjects were asked to indicate their opinion by circling one of the following for each item: strongly agree (A), mildly agree (a), mildly disagree (b) and strongly disagree (B). Some examples were given and subjects cautioned, "The first answer you think about is usually the best one to mark." The tests were scored by the following method: items were scored A = 4, a = 3, b = 2, B = 1, if the item was positively related to the scale (*i.e.*, T + or C +). The scoring was reversed (*i.e.*, A = 1, a = 2, *etc.*,) if T− or C−. The scores were totaled to give the subject score.

Study Two

Testing was conducted at the University of the South Pacific with 120 students of Human Development (fifty-nine males and sixty-one females). The mean age was twenty-three years five months, with a standard deviation of six years four months. The group consisted of thirty-four Fijians, forty-six Indo-Fijian and forty from other island countries of the South Pacific. The main campus of The University of the South Pacific is based in Fiji, but it is also represented in, and serves, ten other countries and territories of the South Pacific. Including all programs, the University had an enrollment of 13,873 in 1982.

Using the thirty-six item C-PHN Inventory, students were asked to indicate their opinion by circling one of the following for each item: strongly agree (+ 3), somewhat agree (+ 2), slightly agree (+ 1), slightly disagree (−1), somewhat disagree (−2), and strongly disagree (−3). The full thirty-six item inventory (C-PHN) and description of scoring is available (Wrightsman, 1974 pp. 244–248).

Study Three

Testing was conducted at King George VI School in Honiara, Solomon Islands. A total of seventy-two students at the school took the thirty-six item C-PHN. One Form IV group (eighteen males and nine females, mean age sixteen years three months) took the test under standard conditions. They related the test to "people in general" (results in *Table 2*). The remainder of the Solomon Island subjects took the test twice. The first time they were instructed to think only of people "inside the *wantok*" and for the second time, only of people "outside the *wantok*." The term *wantok* is a Pidgin word referring to the immediate village, or group of people perceived as being close. Thus a comparison could be made of these attitudes to people inside and outside the *wantok*. The remainder of the subjects comprised another Form IV (eighteen males and eight females, mean age sixteen years seven months), and a Form VI (twelve males and seven females, mean age eighteen years six months (see Stewart, 1982).

The separate conditions for administration derived from the hypothesis mentioned earlier. This is the expectation that Melanesian subjects (indigenous Fijian

Table 2. Ethnic Comparisons between Fijian, Indo-Fijian and European Adolescents on Beliefs in Overall Trustworthiness and Complexity of Other People

	Trustworthiness Belief			Complexity Belief		
	N	$\overline{X}$	SD	N	$\overline{X}$	SD
Fijian	31	23.6***	3.0	31	13.9*	2.3
Indo-Fijian	50	26.1***	3.9	50	13.9*	2.4
European	21	25.7***	4.0	21	15.5*	2.3

* p < .05
*** p < .001

and Solomon Islanders) will trust substantially more those people perceived as being close (extended family and village), rather than people at a distance.

RESULTS

Study One: Adolescents in Suva, Fiji

As shown in *Table 2*, Europeans see people in general as more complex than both Fijians and Indo-Fijians in this study. This is significant statistically at the 0.05 level of significance ($t = 2.42$).

It should be noted also that both Indo-Fijians and Europeans have a significantly higher level of belief in the trustworthiness of people in general than Fijians. This is a very statistically significant finding at the 0.001 level of significance ($t = 3.91$).

As is shown in *Table 3*, females show a significantly higher level of belief in the trustworthiness of people in general than do males (level of significance 0.01, $t = 3.03$).

Table 3. Sex Comparisons on Beliefs by Adolescents in Fiji in Overall Trustworthiness and Complexity of Other People

	Trustworthiness Belief			Complexity Belief		
	N	$\overline{X}$	SD	N	$\overline{X}$	SD
Male	60	24.1**	3.2	60	14.4	2.1
Female	61	26.1**	4.0	61	14.1	2.1

** $p < 0.01$

Study Two: University Students

As with Study One and as shown in *Table 4*, the Indo-Fijians have a significantly higher level of belief in the trustworthiness of people in general than do Fijians

Table 4. Ethnic Comparisons Between Melanesian and Indo-Fijian University Students on Beliefs in Overall Trustworthiness, Strength of Will and Complexity of Others

	Trustworthiness Belief			Strength of Will and Rationality Belief			Complexity Belief		
	N	$\overline{X}$	SD	N	$\overline{X}$	SD	N	$\overline{X}$	SD
Melanesian (Fijian)	34	−0.3*	7.8	34	7.2	7.9	34	10.7**	8.8
Melanesian (Solomon Is)	27	1.2	9.9	27	7.1	5.9	27	5.3**	9.1
Indo-Fijian	46	3.2*	10.9	46	7.0	7.2	46	11.7**	10.9

** $p < 0.01$
* $p < 0.05$

(level of significance 0.05, t = 1.67). This confirms the same findings in Stewart *et al.* (1980) and Karotaua (1980). The other finding relates to the Complexity scale. The University students (both Indo-Fijians and Fijians) saw people in general as more complex than did the group of Solomon Islands Secondary School students (level of significance 0.01, t = 2.34). This difference in a predicted direction tends also to show validity of the Scale for this Study.

An interesting sex difference is shown in *Table 5*, also compatible with Study One results. Males are shown to see people in general as having more Strength of Will and Rationality than females (level of significance 0.01, t = 2.52). This seems to be in the direction of a traditional view of the sexes, with men seeing the world as more rational and people as stronger of will, than females.

Table 5. Sex Comparisons for Fijian and Indo-Fijian University Students for Beliefs in Overall Trustworthiness, Strength of Will and Complexity of Others

	Trustworthiness Belief			Strength of Will and Rationality Belief			Complexity Belief		
	N	$\overline{X}$	SD	N	$\overline{X}$	SD	N	$\overline{X}$	SD
Males	59	1.5	8.9	59	8.7**	7.1	59	1.0	9.1
Females	61	2.3	9.5	61	5.6**	6.4	61	2.0	9.8

** $p < 0.01$

Study Three: Adolescents in Honiara, Solomon Islands

Looking at *Table 6*, it is shown that people perceived as being close (inside the *wantok*) are *more* to be trusted ($p < 0.01$ t = 4.46) and *less complex* ($p < 0.05$ t = 1.78). Thus it appears that people closer to oneself are perceived quite differently than those at a distance (outside the *wantok*).

Tables 7 and 8 break down the attitudes of males and females to people "inside and outside the *wantok*." As shown in *Table 7*, there are no significant differences between the sexes in the way they view people *inside* the *wantok*.

Table 6. Solomon Islands Adolescents' Attitudes to Other People Either "Inside the Wantok" or "Outside the Wantok" (Beliefs in Their Overall Trustworthiness, Strength of Will and Complexity)

	Trustworthiness Belief			Strength of Will and Rationality Belief			Complexity Belief		
	N	$\overline{X}$	SD	N	$\overline{X}$	SD	N	$\overline{X}$	SD
"Outside the Wantok"	45	−4.1**	11.4	45	6.3	8.0	45	12.1*	10.8
"Inside the Wantok"	45	1.7**	8.9	45	7.9	6.7	45	8.0*	11.1

** $p < 0.01$
* $p < 0.05$

Table 7. Male and Female Adolescents' Attitudes to People "Inside the Wantok" (Beliefs in Their Overall Trustworthiness, Strength of Will and Complexity)

	Trustworthiness Belief			Strength of Will and Rationality Belief			Complexity Belief		
	N	$\overline{X}$	SD	N	$\overline{X}$	SD	N	$\overline{X}$	SD
Male	30	2.4	9.2	30	8.1	7.5	30	8.1	11.1
Female	15	0.3	8.2	15	7.3	5.2	15	7.7	11.2

Table 8. Male and Female Adolescents' Attitudes to People "Outside the Wantok" (Beliefs in Their Overall Trustworthiness, Strength of Will and Complexity)

	Trustworthiness Belief			Strength of Will and Rationality Belief			Complexity Belief		
	N	$\overline{X}$	SD	N	$\overline{X}$	SD	N	$\overline{X}$	SD
Male	30	−1.9*	9.8	30	7.2	7.5	30	10.9*	11.3
Female	15	−8.4*	12.6	15	4.5	8.3	15	16.4*	8.8

* $p < 0.05$

However in *Table 8*, it can be seen that males (compared to females) view people *outside* the *wantok* as *more* to be trusted ($p < 0.05$, $t = 1.75$) and less complex ($p < 0.05$, $t = 1.79$). This would be consistent with a view that adolescent males are allowed more freedom to associate with "outsiders." Perhaps they are then able to see "outsiders" as easier to understand and hence trust them more.

DISCUSSION AND CONCLUSIONS

Possibly the most remarkable finding emerging from Studies One and Two is the difference between the Fijian and Indo-Fijian groups on their belief in trustworthiness. This shows a more positive view of human nature held by the Indo-Fijian group, which runs against popular views. This was the clearest statistical finding of the studies. A subsequent study (Karotaua, 1980) used the standard thirty-six-item C-PHN Scale with 138 fifth-form boys at Marist Boys' High School in Suva. A significant difference also emerged between Fijians and Indo-Fijians in the same direction.

The remaining findings in Studies One and Two are supportive of validity of the measures in the South Pacific. Just as the ability of the scale to show differences in scores in predicted directions has been cited as lending support to the validity of the scale there, such a result in Fiji and the Solomon Islands is likewise supportive of validity here.

In Study One, females show a significantly higher level of belief in the trustworthiness of people in general than do males. In Study Two, females are shown to see people in general as having less Strength of Will and Rationality than do males. The other finding relates to the Complexity Scale. In Study One, Europeans see people as more complex in general than both Fijians and Indo-Fijians. These European subjects would have had familiarity with their own, probably more complex, developed and urbanized society. In Study Two, the University students (both Indo-Fijians and Fijians) saw people in general as more complex than did the adolescents from the Solomon Islands. With their more advanced educational background and experience, the tendency of the University students to see human nature as more complex is also in the predicted direction.

Looking at the results for Study Three, the Solomon Island results show that there are major differences, particularly for females, in attitudes toward people perceived as being close, rather than distant. People who are closer are seen as easier to understand and more to be trusted. Males are apparently more able to understand and trust "outsiders" than females. This suggests that it would be very useful to test this distinction with the indigenous Fijians. Here again, as hypothesized earlier, people perceived as close may be trusted substantially more than people at a distance.

These three studies have demonstrated how an inventory can be used to illuminate an area of beliefs (in Human Nature), otherwise difficult to investigate. The results of these investigations, based on subjects from a variety of cultures in a less intensively studied part of the world, reveal some significant sex and ethnic differences which in some cases represent unexpected findings. The beliefs which people hold about others tend to shape their subsequent actions. Their beliefs have shaped perceptions of the way others "are." In multi-ethnic societies it is important to understand more clearly these beliefs and perceptions, as these are often the key to the way people behave towards one another.

REFERENCE NOTES

Karotaua, Maara. "Adolescent Beliefs in Overall Trustworthiness, Complexity and Strength of Will and Rationality of Others." Unpublished paper, The University of the South Pacific, 1980.

O'Connor, J. "Multimethod Analysis of the Philosophies of Human Nature Scales." Unpublished paper, George Peabody College for Teachers, 1971.

REFERENCES

Bruner, J.S. and Goodwin, L.C. "Value and Need as Organizing Factors in Perception," *Journal of Abnormal and Social Psychology*, 1947, *42*, 33–44.

Erikson, E.H. *Childhood and Society*, 2nd rev. ed. New York: Norton, 1963.

Kelly, G.A. *The Psychology of Personal Constructs*. New York: Norton, 1955.

Ritchie, J. and Ritchie, J. *Growing up in Polynesia*. Sydney: George Allen & Unwin, 1979.

Rosenthal, R. and Jacobson, L. *Pygmalion in the Classroom: Teacher Expectations and Pupil's Intellectual Development*. New York: Holt Rinehart & Winston, 1968.

Stewart, R.A.C., Malia Mulipola-Lui and Helen Laidlaw. "Beliefs about Human Nature Held by Adolescents in Fiji: Some Preliminary Ethnic and Sex Comparisons," *Social Behavior and Personality*, 1980, *8* (1): 125–128.

Stewart, R.A.C. "Us and Them: Beliefs About Human Nature Held by Young

People in the South Pacific,'' *Social Behavior and Personality*, 1982, *10* (2), in press.

Wrightsman, L.S. ''Measurement of Philosophies of Human Nature.'' *Psychological Reports*, 1964, *14* : 743–51.

Wrightsman, L.S. *Assumptions about Human Nature: A Social-Psychological Approach*. Monterey, CA: Brooks Cole, 1974.

COGNITIVE MAPPING FEATURES OF MICRONESIAN NAVIGATION SYSTEMS[1]

Graham R. Davidson

ABSTRACT

Current research into cognitive mapping processes is used to study the cognitive mapping features of Micronesian navigation systems, said by Hage (1978) to be mnemonics for a large body of cultural myth and knowledge, rather than sea route-finding devices. This chapter discusses the definitional appropriateness of these systems as cognitive maps, their effectiveness as spoken versions of star courses, their role in navigational instruction, and their association with other aspects of Puluwatese voyaging.

The ancient art of navigation, once widely known and practiced throughout the Pacific, has been a source of curiosity among explorers, adventurers, and scholars. The research interests of the latter group are quite varied, although, at the most abstract level of analysis, they are all concerned in one way or another with locating the origins and possible migratory routes of the original Pacific Islanders. They include the construction of canoes and material conditions of canoe travel (*e.g.,* see Haddon and Hornell, 1936; Grimble, 1972), the performance and possible limitations of traditionally designed canoes under actual voyaging conditions (Lewis, 1978, pp. 180–200), and the possibility of undertaking particular voyages that are representative of those original ocean crossings (Sharp, 1963; Finney, 1976; Lewis, 1972).

In pursuit of these interests, navigation research in the Pacific has unearthed a vast body of indigenous information concerning the navigation aids and route-finding procedures used by Pacific Islanders. For example, it has uncovered information about the actual routes between specific islands and island groupings, and the methods and devices by which apprentices were taught this information as part of the art of navigation. These ancient skills are now barely remembered and almost never practiced in many parts of the Pacific. However the voyagers of

G.R. Davidson is affiliated with the Centre for Behavioral Studies in Education at the University of New England in Armidale, Australia.

1. The research in this paper was completed while the author was Visiting Senior Lecturer at The University of the South Pacific, and was funded by an Internal Research Grant from the University of New England.

Micronesia, particularly on the islands of Puluwat and Truk, still cling to ancient navigation systems, which include a knowledge of star paths and of natural environmental phenomena (Lewis, 1978). Here astronomical knowledge is embodied in a series of organised, complex schemata said to facilitate the learning and remembering of navigation paths or star courses (Lewis, 1978; Riesenberg, 1972).

Riesenberg (1976) described these schemata as "geographical arrangements based on as many metaphors" and "a path from place to place, real or mythical, in accordance with the schema of the metaphor" (p. 91). He distinguished between these schemata and sea life inventories described by Gladwin (1970). The schemata are separately owned by different schools for navigation which exhibit their knowledge on certain important social occasions. Riesenberg (1972) provided a comprehensive record of the schemata, describing in detail eleven of them and noting the existence of about seventy others.

PULUWATESE SCHEMATA AND MNEMONIC STRATEGIES

In a more recent article, Hage (1978) has argued that the navigation systems described by Riesenberg (1972) are less environmental maps or even memory devices for actual star courses, than they are memory devices for a broader body of cultural knowledge, including relationships with other parts of the social and spiritual worlds of the Puluwatese. He suggested that the systems or schemata, in and by themselves, constitute a large body of sea myths and magical formulae possessed by certain social groups within that society. Thus, points in the schemata, whether geographical or organismic, real, legendary, or imaginary, are links with a larger body of sea mythology and associated ritual; sometimes the schemata are themselves an actual part of that mythology and sometimes they act as a direct, concrete cue for retrieval of parts of it. Similarly, pathways between actual or imaginary locations are logico-cultural connections between interrelated parts of mythology. Thus, the systems have extra mnemonic value as logico-sequential orderings of cultural knowledge. The logico-cultural connections reflected in the geographical schemata may also represent relationships between these sea myths and other mythical traditions, and between social groupings in the islands of the Western Carolines.

To support his thesis, Hage has attempted to draw parallels between the form and role of these systems in Puluwat culture and similar mnemonic devices in Iatmul and Trobriand societies. In the latter case, myths were said to be geographically located or owned, such that their locations reflected a logico-temporal sequence in the Islands' oral tradition and in the relationship between associated social groupings such as clans and sub-clans (Harwood, 1976).

If we follow Hage's reasoning, it is possible to point to a number of other spatial tasks and spatial knowledge-systems found in Oceania that act as concrete cueing devices for the retrieval of myth and social knowledge. The simplest of these systems is the game of cat's cradling. Andersen (1969), in describing a number of Maori string figures, reported that there were certain figures whose names were geographical locations in Maori mythology. He also reported that the various parts of the figures had significance as mythological locations, environmental features or ancestral acts, and that the step-wise order in the construction of the cradles paralleled actual, logical steps in the unfolding of the related myths. The game of cat's cradling is widespread throughout Oceania (e.g., see Hornell, 1927; Maude and Maude, 1958; Firth and Maude, 1970).

Larger spatial orientation systems may also perform a similar function. Maude (1977, 1980) in describing the Gilbertese community building or *maneaba*, assigns *boti,* or clans, specific spatial locations within the building, with those locations reflecting mythical and ritual relationships between *boti.*

> Far more than a place of social festivities or hall of debate it was a tabernacle of ancestors in the male line; a sort of social map where a man's group or clan could be recognised the moment he took his seat, his totem and his ascendants known, and his ceremonial duties or privileges discovered (Grimble, cited in Maude, 1977, p. 11).

However, the *maneaba* also provided an opportunity for prospective navigators to acquire and rehearse their astronomical knowledge. The rafters and center beam divided the roof, said to be the heavens, into sixteen quadrants, eight on each side of the axis perpendicular to the centre beam. Star courses for the entire year were plotted within the divisions and thus learned by novices (Grimble, 1972). We may continue to speculate about the mnemonic value of these, and other, cultural activities in Oceania. For example *meke ni yaqona,* the action songs performed during the Fijian *kava* ceremony, recall the actual sequence and order of the ceremony, while *meke meke,* once sung often as an accompaniment to daily chores, contained a wide store of cultural information. Even the seating pattern of chiefs in the *yaqona* ceremony may reflect mythological ties between social groupings represented in the ceremony.[2] Nevertheless, the mnemonic value of any of these spatial schemata does not contradict nor detract from their other functions.

Hage's conclusion that these Puluwatese schemata are primarily mnemonic devices for a larger body of oral traditions was based on several observations: that place names were often imaginary rather than actual geographical locations; spatial sequences were "apparently arbitrary and unnecessarily fixed" (p. 81); they contained supposed "relative" positions of locations, which were often imprecise; and, finally, that there is a good deal of unnecessary redundancy in the seventy or so systems that Riesenberg (1972) had mentioned.

I will argue here that the above observations, in themselves, are not sufficient to discount those spatial systems as cognitive maps of actual geographic locations or star points. I will also argue that Hage (1978) has not given adequate consideration to the cognitive mapping features of these systems. This is not to dispute Hage's point that such systems have other mnemonic or ritual functions, but rather to suggest that such functions are not incompatable with a cognitive mapping function.

Puluwatese Schemata as Cognitive Maps

In order to test these bases for Hage's conclusion regarding Puluwatese navigation systems, attention needs to be focused on the mapping value of these systems. First it must be determined whether or not they may be considered by definition to be cognitive maps. Second, their actual role as teaching and learning devices needs to be defined clearly. Finally, their value as verbal systems of spatially-related information which can be translated into cartographic knowledge should be determined.

---

2. I am grateful to Ivan Williams of The University of the South Pacific for bringing these songs to my attention. It appears also that in Samoa, discrete sections of buildings including posts, panels and roofing supports have individual names which, like in other parts of Oceania, are passed on with construction specifications. However, the names of these sections, ordered from floor to ceiling, are said to be applied to various parts of dance performances, from the opening to the finale. My investigation of this link is not yet completed.

The Cognitive Map as a Theoretical Construct

The origin of the notion of a cognitive (mental) map is popularly attributed to the maze experiments of the psychologist, Tolman (1948). Although it has been suggested that the characteristic cognitive functions of these maps were never well defined by Tolman (Olton, 1979), generally within the context of his infra-human studies, the idea of a cognitive map was used to refer to the *search and spatial decision-making behavior* of animals, rather than to the physical assembly, or maze, in which the animals were placed. Human cognitive maps can also be said to possess those properties. Downs and Stea (1973) have described a cognitive map as "a series of physical transformations by which an individual acquires, codes, stores, recalls and decodes information about the relative locations and attributes of phenomena in his everyday spatial environment." These transformations, which may be about either a single, environmental feature in relation to the individual, or a number of such features in relation to one another, involve knowledge about the actual nature of the features, and their spatial properties of relative distance and direction, combined to form a personal view of the environment (Blaut, McCleary and Blaut, 1970). Expressed simply it is a "cognitive representation of spatial relations" (Foos, 1980).

Thus, in behavioral research with humans, as in Tolman's work, considerable care has been taken not to emphasize the cartographic form which maps may take (Hart and Moore, 1973), despite the obvious tendency to associate the form and function of cognitive maps with their real map equivalents. However, cognitive mapping research now also includes studies of spatial decision-making, which may involve cartographic knowledge often in the form of pen and paper representations, or drawn maps of those decisions (*e.g.,* see Blaut, McCleary, and Blaut, 1970; Robinson and Dicken, 1979). Beck and Wood (1976) have acknowledged this distinction when they describe the "map" as a system of "purely verbal terms where it functions in mnemonic form making long range migration possible" (p. 203).

Thus, we should view the cognitive mapping features of these navigation schemata as cognitive transformations of environmental information, but not as descriptions of conventional cartographic maps, as is implied in Hage's argument. He describes them as systems of "geographical locations of places in their ocean world" (p. 81) which have "a distressing lack of the precision and sharpness that we expect from a body of knowledge intended for practical use" (Riesenberg, cited by Hage, p. 81).

If the systems are not series of cartographic points, what, then, do they represent? Lewis (1978) and Gladwin (1970) state quite clearly that they are spoken versions of star courses between places. Thus, each new point in a schema may represent a new star course, either along the same dimension as the previous course (north-south or east-west) or along another dimension. Given that star courses themselves provide accurate sailing instructions and that any one star course is not just the path of a single star through the heavens but also it relationship with other stars in the same and in different quadrants, then the change points (each point in a schema) may provide relative, accurate estimates of distance and direction. In addition, to resort to Tolman's original notion of maps, these schemata should facilitate adaptive responding on the part of the navigator. That is, from any one star plot within his ken, the navigator should be able to outline a set of star courses to other points or places. This is ensured by the repetitive and reciprocal nature of the systems. The navigator, if he knows the system, has all possible useful star plots at hand and should, in theory, be able to enter the system at any point, digress at any point, or swap systems.

Cognitive Maps as Spoken Sentences

If these schemata are cognitive maps, based on sequences of star courses which are known (from tests under actual voyaging conditions) to provide accurate distance and direction coordinates, the issue then is how valuable they are both as mnemonic devices and as abbreviated, spoken versions of mapping decisions, based on star coordinates. It is important to bear in mind here that Gladwin (1970), Riesenberg (1972) and Lewis (1978) have emphasized the use of these systems for teaching star course navigation. Lewis wrote,

> A variety of memory aids makes the student's task possible. He may be asked, for exam-
> ple, to reach out with an imaginary *eyass* towards a particular star point and draw back all
> the islands that lie in that direction. Then, just as in the Gilberts, stories are woven round
> the stars wherein they figure as people. Piailug has a host of such tales and I have seen him
> have his pupils re-enact them by arranging them in a circle with each one representing a
> star point (Lewis, p. 134).

Thus, Hage is correct in suggesting that these schemata, in their spoken form, represent concrete cueing devices, but he fails to acknowledge their value as cueing devices in learning star-course knowledge. In this way, they are no different from concrete cueing systems, described by Grimble and Lewis in Kiribati.

A recent article by Foos (1980) may help us to evaluate their effectiveness as spoken, abbreviated versions of cognitive transformations based on star coordinates. Foos (1980) attempts to extend earlier research on the properties of simple, linear ordering of relationships between items, expressed in sentences to include the study of properties of spoken descriptions of one- and two-dimensional cartographic maps. The pertinent findings of his research for understanding these Puluwatese schema are as follows. Spoken descriptions of maps produced significantly better performance (map drawing based on short-term memory for sentences) when new items were connected in some way (matched) to previous items. Hence, *The church (a) is east of the hall (b). The hall (b) is east of the shop (c). The shop (c) is east of the park (d).*, or ab, bc, cd orders, resulted in better performance than *The church (a) is east of the hall (b). The shop (c) is east of the park (d). The park (d) is east of the church (a).*, or ab, cd, da orders. Complete orderings, *e.g.*, the ab bc order above, resulted in better performance than partial orders, *e.g.*,*The shop (a) is east of the hall (b). The park (c) is east of the hall (b).*, or a east b, c east b, where some relationships remain unclear.

Hage's analysis of four schemata recorded by Riesenberg reveals that all relation-ships are both matched (*e.g.*, in Figure 1a [p.83]1,2 2,3 3,2 2,4 4,2 2,5, *etc.*) and complete or unambiguous. Hence, the characteristics of these schemata which Hage labeled "unipathic" and "closed" may be an advantage, if they are indicative of matching, rather than a disadvantage in making sequences "unnecessarily fixed" (p. 81). Foos' examination of the effects of map type revealed no significant decrease in performance when there was an increase in the number of dimensions from one to two, say, from north to south (one-dimensional) versus north-south plus east-west progressions (two-dimensional), or in the number of end anchors. Hence the schemata shown in Hage's Figures 1a and 1b, which are two-dimensional and which have nine and eight end-anchors respectively, theoretically are no more difficult to remember and transform than the structure in Figure 1e, which is a single dimension with two end-anchors. Thus, all the systems Hage analyzed, ac-cording to Foos' findings, are plausible, useful mnemonic devices for constructing cognitive maps.

Foos did find, however, that performance decreased, as the number of items to be mapped increased. He used five and seven-item maps with his non-expert subjects. Thus, possibly, Hage's structure 1c, could be more difficult to remember and transform than structures 1a, 1b, 1e, with the latter three being more complex than 1d. If performance is adversely affected by the length of sequences, this may provide good reason for having a large number of shorter intersecting schemata, rather than a limited number of larger schemata, which Hage has advocated (p. 85). This would increase their revision value during the instruction of novices.

We can only speculate on the difficulty value of the systems: the number of items may be offset by using a limited number of culturally and situationally-appropriate item categories, e.g., islands and whales; neither Riesenberg nor Gladwin have presented information on the sequence in which they are introduced as instructional aids; and there is very little knowledge of the representational strategies that were involved in remembering the schemata or in transforming them into star courses. In relation to strategies, Foos has suggested that "imagers" perform better than "rehearsers," under certain mapping conditions. This may be relevant to the Puluwatese, whose actions, according to Gladwin (1970, p. 193) are characterised by "complex visual images of canoes, islands and stars." Thus the tremendous volume of star-course knowledge contained in these schemata may have been placed well within the memory capabilities of Puluwat navigators by the way in which relationships between points were matched and complete, the cueing value of the names selected to denote star-course changes, and the adoption of an appropriate cognitive strategy for transforming the schemata into maps.

The final characteristic of the schemata to consider is the use of "mythological phenomena and animate beings." If each name is viewed as a star-course change point, rather than as an actual geographic location, then Hage's hypothesis regarding the cueing salience of these particular names is appropriate also when their function in Puluwatese cognitive mapping structures is considered.

There is also another possible explanation that concerns the navigational concept of *etak* (Lewis, 1976). As described there by Lewis and also by Gladwin (1970) the theory of *etak* is an orientation system, based on the star-point location of reference islands (*etak*) chosen for their position away to one side of sea routes. Reference islands are said to "move." This means that, as the journey progresses, they pass beneath new star reference points. If lines are drawn through each new star point, corresponding to the new positions of the reference island, and the course being sailed, a number of intersection points occur along the course. These intersection points divide the voyage into a number of readily conceptualizable segments which aid in time and distance estimation. The theory, therefore, has benefits as a summary system but all the knowledge used in the identification of *etak* stages is derived from knowledge of star courses. In the mind of the navigator, these intersects (corresponding to the end of one *etak* stage and the start of another) have actual broad, though not easily recognizable, geographic locations. Such intersects therefore may be assigned mythical or imaginary names which are chosen for their cultural and visual imagery. Riesenberg (1972) has also suggested that these names may be used to differentiate *etak* stages.

Another possible use of non-geographical names, which is associated with *etak* theory, is the art of tacking. Gladwin (170, p. 191) illustrated pictorially the sequence of decisions to be made in tacking upwind, decisions that, like *etak*, are based on intersections of star points and the actual course that is being sailed. The points of intersection, in theory, may be sea-marked, as with *etak*. As tacking involves two-dimensional mapping, say north-south movement along an east-west axis, with the craft moving away from and then returning and passing through the latter axis, the actual route is similar to the two-dimensional systems which Hage has described as "unipathic" and which here are called matched. At a previous point in time, two-dimensional schemata may have been cognitive maps of known tacking routes.

Cognitive Maps as Complex Transformations

Recent cognitive mapping research has highlighted the variety of decisions and transformations that take place when an individual constructs a cognitive map, or when he decodes and acts on information presented in a conventional map. Blaut, McCleary and Blaut's (1970) description of mapping events involving decisions about actual features, distance and direction has already been mentioned. Kozlowski and Bryant (1977) in their study of differences between people who perceived themselves as having a good sense of direction, and those having a poor sense of direction, had individuals make directional, distance and time estimates of their movement within real and artificial environments. In the former environment, self-reported sense of direction was significantly correlated with directional and distance estimates, but in the latter it was correlated with directional estimates only. Decisions relating to what Blaut *et al.* call "cognitive salience of environmental features" involve the selection and subsequent use of landmarking. Allen, Kirasic, Siegel and Herman (1979) have suggested that landmarking is an important component of route learning, which is necessary for movement in large-scale environments. Such an environment, they suggest, seldom offers people an opportunity either to view it in its entirety or to view simultaneously the path to be traversed. Landmarking involves, first, learning to select environmental features of high, cognitive-perceptual valence to act as spatial cues and then relating these cues, in a tempero-spatial fashion.

The systems described by Riesenberg seem more to be concerned with direction-taking and landmarking in a broad sense than with distance and time estimation. This may not be strictly true if they are mnemonic systems for star courses, including *etak* intersects, as the latter theory provides relative time and distance estimates at any point within a journey. The systems, however, are represented in terms of series of seamarks, some apparently mythical, *e.g.*, " place of the whale with two tails," and some apparently unreliable, *e.g.*, "places of bird or porpoise sightings," but all having high cognitive valence as navigational aids (Riesenberg, 1976, p. 92). I am not suggesting that the places or things forming the systems are used as actual seamarks on a defined route, but rather that they are relevant as mnemonic cues for star courses and occasionally for direct action (see Riesenberg's account of critical decisions being based on coconut, bird or fish sightings [1976, pp. 126–127]).

As cognitive maps of routes governed by star courses, the schemata have a plausible function as directional systems on a broad scale, if their function is considered in relation to the wider body of Puluwatese navigation knowledge. The distinction here is between initial perspective taking or general direction finding, and subsequent accuracy judgment or directional fine-tuning. Hardwick, McIntyre and Pick (1976) have found that this two-part decision-process seems to be characteristic of adults' and childrens' perspective-taking behavior, when they are required to indicate the direction of a previously seen, but then unseen, object. Thus, the role of these navigational schemata may be one of providing initial directional information. Subsequent accuracy is achieved by combining star knowledge with other navigational knowledge in the form of bird, cloud and wave lore (Lewis, 1971). These latter systems, along with the phenomena of invisible land and deep phosphorescence, Lewis said, form a "screen" or "arc of landfall" which adequately compensates for small to moderate inaccuracies in star-course judgements. They also provide information about distance and timing, although the latter is greatly influenced by the conditions of sailing. The role of the star-course systems and these other lores (or broad directional systems for perspective giving and fine-tuning systems for navigational accuracy) are complementary. As Gladwin (1970) described it,

> ...the navigator (is required) to keep in his mind a great many things—estimates of rate, time, bearing, drift and some complex visual images of canoe, islands and stars. Of all these he can only see the canoe, the water and at night the stars (p. 193).

CONCLUSIONS

Hage (1978) therefore does not provide adequate reason for dismissing, or even minimizing, the cognitive mapping (albeit spatial mnemonic) function of the systems described by Riesenberg (1972). This does not mean that the schemata do not have a secondary function as mnemonic systems for other cultural information, as additional examples here demonstrate. These systems of geographical and metaphorical arrangements conform to widely accepted definitions of cognitive maps. Theoretically, they are effective, spoken, abbreviated systems of cognitive transformations, based on star-course knowledge. Their value lies in providing broad, directional guidelines for sea travel, not in calculating with absolute accuracy the direction of landfall; in cartographic terms they are star maps, not street directories.

Apart from their cueing value, imaginary or mythical locations may be associated with other decision systems, such as *etak*. The value of these navigational aids should be assessed in terms of their present function as instructional devices and in relation to representational strategies used by navigators to form cognitive maps of their voyages. We are told and, in fact, we know little about these two aspects of Puluwatese navigational tradition.

One possible way of assessing the cognitive mapping function of these mnemonic systems is to ask navigators to try to use them during actual voyages. If there is an association between star-course changes and real and imaginary place names, it may emerge from this type of inquiry. The difficulty here lies in knowing how to ask the questions in such a way that they tap the conceptual knowledge of the navigator and not our own cultural understandings of the navigational process (Hutchins, 1980). If we were to discover an association between star-course knowledge and these systems, and if we knew more about cognitive strategies for recalling and operationalizing that knowledge, then we may develop a better understanding of how the original navigators of Oceania have managed journeys over the centuries which we would have considered difficult, or maybe even impossible, without western navigational aids.

REFERENCES

Allen, G.L., Kirasic, K.C., Siegel, A.W. and Herman, J.F. "Developmental Issues in Cognitive Mapping: The Selection and Utilization of Environmental Landmarks," *Child Development*, 1979, *50*, 1062–1070.

Andersen, J.C. *Myths and Legends of the Polynesians*. Vermont: Charles E. Tuttle Company, 1969.

Beck, R.J. and Wood, D. "Cognitive Transformation of Information from Urban Geographic Fields to Mental Maps," *Environment and Behavior,* 1976. *8,* 199–238.

Blaut, J.M., McCleary, G.S. Jr., and Blaut, A.S. "Environmental Mapping in Young Children," *Environment and Behavior,* 1970, *2,* 335–349.

Downs, R.M. and Stea, D. (Eds.) *Image and Environment.* Chicago: Aldine, 1973.

Finney, B. (Ed.) *Pacific Navigation and Voyaging.* Wellington: Polynesian Society Memoir, No. 39, 1976.

Firth, R. and Maude, H.C. *Tikopia String Figures.* London: Royal Anthropological Institute of Great Britain and Ireland, 1970.

Foos, P.W. "Constructing Cognitive Maps from Sentences." *Journal of Experimental Psychology: Human Learning and Memory,* 1980, *6,* 25–38.

Gladwin, T. *East is a Big Bird.* Cambridge: Harvard University Press, 1970.

Grimble, A. "Astronomy and Navigation." In *Migration, Myth and Magic from the Gilbert Islands,* R. Grimble (Ed.), London: Routledge and Kegan Paul, 1972.

Haddon, A.C. and Hornell, J. *Canoes of Oceania.* Honolulu: Bernice P. Bishop Museum Bulletin No. 29, 1936.

Hage, P. "Speculations on Puluwatese Mnemonic Structure," *Oceania,* 1978, *49,* 81–95.

Hardwick, D.A., McIntyre, C.W. and Pick, H.L. Jr. *The Content and Manipulation of Cognitive Maps in Children and Adults.* Monographs of the Society for Research in Child Development, No. 166, 1976.

Hart, R.A. and Moore, G.T. "The Development of Spatial Cognition: A Review." In *Image and Environment,* R.M. Downs and D. Stea (Eds.), Chicago: Aldine, 1973.

Harwood, F. "Myth, Memory and the Oral Tradition: Cicero in the Trobriands," *American Anthropologist,* 1976, *78,* 783–796.

Hornell, J. *String Figures from Fiji and Western Polynesia.* Honolulu: Bernice P. Bishop Museum Bulletin No. 39, 1927.

Hutchins, E. *Conceptual Structures of Caroline Island Navigation.* University of California, San Diego: Centre for Human Information Processing, Report No. 93, 1980.

Kozlowski, L.T. and Bryant, K.J. "Sense of Direction, Spatial Orientation, and Cognitive Maps," *Journal of Experimental Psychology: Human Perception and Performance,* 1977, *3,* 590–598.

Lewis, D. "Expanding the Target in Indigenous Navigation," *Journal of Pacific History,* 1971, *6,* 83–95.

Lewis, D. *We, the Navigators.* Canberra: Australian National University Press, 1972.

Lewis, D. "A Return Voyage Between Puluwat and Saipan Using Micronesian Navigational Techniques." In *Polynesian Navigation and Voyaging,* B. Finney (Ed.), Wellington: Polynesian Society, No. 39, 1976.

Lewis, D. *The Voyaging Stars.* Sydney: Collins, 1978.

Maude, H.E. *The Evolution of the Gilbertese Boti.* Suva: Institute of Pacific Studies, The University of the South Pacific, 1977.

Maude, H.E. *The Gilbertese Maneaba.* Suva: Institute of Pacific Studies, The University of the South Pacific, 1980.

Maude, H.C. and Maude, H.E. *String Figures from the Gilbert Islands.* New Plymouth: Polynesian Society Memoir No. 13, 1958.

Olton, D.S. "Mazes, Maps and Memory," *American Psychologist,* 1979, *34,* 583–596.

Riesenberg, S.H. ''The Organization of Navigational Knowledge on Puluwat.''
    Journal of the Polynesian Society, 1972, *80*, 217–227.
Robinson, M.E. and Dicken, P. ''Cloze Procedure and Cognitive Mapping,''
    Environment and Behavior, 1979, *11*, 351–373.
Sharp, A. *Ancient Voyagers in Polynesia*. Sydney: Angus and Robinson, 1963.
Tolman, E.C. ''Cognitive Maps in Rats and Men,'' *Psychological Review*, 1948, *5*,
    189–208.

PART III.
TEACHING THINKING

Detail from Pieter Brueghel's "Children's Games"

INTRODUCTION

The teaching of thinking skills is at least as old as human language. Even the most "primitive" or preliterate societies illustrate this fact by the use of puns (plays on words), by the use of humor (seeing unexpected consequences in a chain of logic or expectations), by the use of language to illuminate paradoxes ("If I marry my half-brother's mother, then will my son be my uncle?"), and by the use of verbal connectors that imply complex relationships ("If...then..."), *etc*.

The teaching of thinking skills, historically, occurs very early in all societies by a host of other devices as well: puzzles, games, detective stories, long narratives requiring complex memory strategies and heuristics, *etc*. Yet, despite the cultural universality of the teaching of thinking skills, there is general agreement that all societies, without exception, today do a poor job of teaching problem-solving skills that are necessary to live in the modern world.

This more practical section of the book starts with Doris Crowell's description of a remarkably logical and successful language arts program at the Kamehameha School in Honolulu. The practical approach to the teaching of thinking skills continues with an essay by William Maxwell on "Games Children Play: Powerful Tools that Teach Some Thinking Skills." This essay describes several games, including Kalah which could be called "Abraham's Game," since Abraham probably played it as a child, given its probable origins in the land of Abraham's birth, but 3,500 years before his birth, in Sumer. The essay offers a classification system for children's games that would enable curriculum planners to integrate both classical and modern games into regular curricula, either with standard subjects or as a separate course.

Edward de Bono's 60-Lesson course in thinking, CoRT, has priority in modern times as a complete course in reasoning. Despite its widespread adoption (every school in Venezuela, for example, must teach his program) strangely, CoRT has not been systematically assessed by independent researchers until now. This section contains de Bono's own description and assessment, plus an assessment by two lecturers in science education at Australia's James Cook University. The Edwards and Baldauf paper provides a practical example of a research methodology in education that does not disrupt a school's regular program and that does not create two false groups: the control group and the experimental group. The Edwards and Baldauf study with high school science students provides strong evidence that de Bono's program has been a remarkable and powerful pioneering effort in the teaching of thinking.

R.A. Girle has been working for a number of years on developing a revolutionary new approach to teaching reasoning skills to university students. His paper describes his approach, which is gaining increased attention by lecturers in so-called logic courses in universities around the world. Simply put, Girle reverses the Aristotelian approach and adds several elements which offer university students a more balanced repertory of reasoning skills.

This section closes with the most difficult of all reasoning or thinking tasks—creativity. Delores Gallo describes a novel teacher training program based upon Torrence's study of creàtivity and her own creative efforts both to train teachers and to train teachers to train creativity in children.

All the papers in this section are remarkably different on the surface. Yet, you will find that all the papers in this section offer solid ground for optimism about teaching people to think more effectively than we are doing at present.

SYSTEMATIC DEVELOPMENT OF THINKING SKILLS THROUGH A LANGUAGE ARTS CURRICULUM

Doris C. Crowell

ABSTRACT

This paper describes an empirically developed scale of comprehension questions which serves as the basis for a language arts curriculum. Each question represents a different level of difficulty; each higher level requires cognitive processes not involved in answering questions at levels below. The scale has been validated and the curriculum used successfully with normal, urban, Polynesian children.

Normal children beginning elementary school have learned to understand and use language successfully in a variety of situations, such as following directions and conveying their needs within the family. Language development begins at birth and a remarkable level of competence in both verbal expression and in understanding spoken language is acquired by the time children enter school. However, they cannot, yet, be described as literate. The most noteworthy achievements during their next few years of cognitive development are the ability to read and write; hence the major components of the Kamehameha Language Arts System, described in this chapter, include the acquisition of precisely these skills. These skills, however, are only tools. The child must learn to use them at an automatic level and thus be free to develop more complex strategies for problem solving. The primary goal of the curriculum described in this chapter is to help the student understand new information, assess it critically, and express ideas effectively. These thinking skills are emphasized from the time the child first enters school.

While several papers in this collection focus on remediating poor thinking skills in older youth and adults, this program is aimed at preventing the habituation of faulty reasoning at the primary school level. The program is made up of the Kamehameha Reading Objective System (KROS) which provides the structure of the reading program (Crowell, Note 1) and the Kamehameha Writing Program (KWP) (Crowell, Note 2), both of which are designed for kindergarten through fourth grade. Initial tests of these curricula were made in laboratory classrooms at the Kamehameha Early Education Program which serves children of Hawaiian ancestry. These trials proved very successful. Subsequent tests of the materials have

D.C. Crowell is affiliated with the Kamehameha Educational Research Institute in Honolulu, Hawaii.

been made in both public and private schools and in both rural and urban settings serving multiethnic children from all socio-economic levels. The results of these trials were also highly satisfactory and will be discussed in greater detail later in this chapter.

In these curricula, carefully sequenced performance objectives and criterion-referenced exercises are included. The KROS emphasizes development of comprehension in both listening and reading. It builds on the language and listening skills young children have already acquired and helps to transfer these skills to material they learn to read. The KWP is concerned with helping children develop writing skills in order to express their own thoughts. Language is the medium for thinking that runs through both the reading and writing components.

Both programs share a common rationale and are based on several assumptions; the first is that the primary purpose of a language arts curriculum is to foster functional communication. The goal of reading is to understand the text; the goal of writing is to convey information effectively. Thus, in contrast to many traditional programs, comprehension in reading is emphasized over decoding skills and invention or composing one's own message is emphasized over the conventions of writing, even at the beginning levels.

The second assumption is that reading comprehension and written composition require many kinds of cognitive processes. For example, making sense of a passage requires that the reader combine this new information with relevant knowledge the reader already has. Selecting information to include in a written message and assembling it in logical sequence require judgments that are highly complex.

Another assumption is that although cognitive development in children proceeds in an orderly manner, there is a wide range of individual differences in most classrooms; thus, KROS and KWP are designed to accommodate these variations. Because the strands are made up of objectives set along a developmental continuum, a child can be placed at his own developmental level.

The final assumption is that children will learn best and will assume responsibility for their own progress when they know both what is required of them and how well they are meeting these requirements.

Looking more closely at the specific objectives that foster thinking skills, the comprehension questions in KROS are based on an empirically derived scale. Observations were made in primary classrooms over a semester to record comprehension questions used by teachers in their reading lessons. These questions were categorized by type and ordered according to how difficult children found them. Five prototype questions emerged, which operationally defined each level of difficulty on the scale; each higher level question requires cognitive processes not involved at levels below. These five questions scale from easy to difficult with coefficients of reproducibility ranging from .92 to .96 in a series of validity experiments (Crowell & Au 1979, 81a, 81b). *Figure 1* shows graphically the relative difficulty of the five questions for both the listening and the reading studies. In both cases, Questions 2 and 3 are similar in difficulty but are ordered appropriately. All other questions are significantly different from each other ($p < 0.05$) (Dunn-Rankin & King 1969).

Here is a description of the scale of questions:

1. *Association.* Questions at the lowest level are designed to elicit any detail of the story the child can recall. An answer is correct if it contains any information from the story.
2. *Classification.* Questions at Level 2 require a simple categorization of a story character or event. The child uses information from the story to justify his response.

3. *Seriation.* These questions deal with the interrelationships among details. Examples include questions that require understanding of cause and effect or that require the child to describe three events from the story in the order in which they occur.
4. *Integration.* This level requires the child to combine various elements of the story into a coherent structure. This would include, for example, abstracting a main idea, or stating the major problem in the story along with its solution, or, perhaps, combining information from the story into a single, reasonable framework.
5. *Extension.* At the highest level of the scale, the questions are intended to reveal whether the child can apply his understanding of the story beyond the confines of the immediate story structure. For example, the child may be asked to provide an alternate ending to the story or to compare this story with another he has recently read.

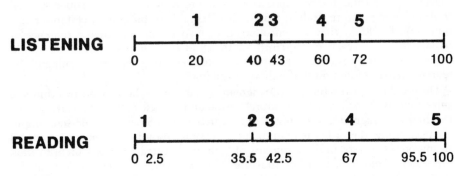

Figure 1. Relative Difficulty of Questions in the Scale for Listening and Reading Comprehension

By using the scale of questions to test children's listening and reading comprehension, the teacher is able to determine each child's progress through the various strands of the curriculum. Thus, the scale has the advantage of yielding direct implications for planning instruction. It also has been used as the basis for a study designed to improve comprehension of material received via television (Crowell, 1981).

The structure of KROS and the order in which these objectives are described reflect the relative importance accorded each strand. Comprehension, the major strand of KROS, is divided into three substrands. The first includes story material, expository passages, content area material and specific comprehension skills. Stories and passages are provided for listening tests at the earlier (kindergarten) levels and occur periodically throughout the system. Reading comprehension objectives occur from first grade on. The readability level (using the Harris-Jacobson formula [Harris and Sipay, 1975]) of these stories and expository passages is appropriate for the grade level where they occur. Teacher questioning, guided by the scale of questions described earlier, plays a major role in comprehension instruction. Criterion-referenced tests parallel each objective and are used to monitor the children's progress. These were also derived from the scale; they contain questions representative of each level of difficulty. At the higher grade levels, the proportion of questions from the more inferential levels is increased.

The second comprehension substrand is Information Retrieval. To maximize the emphasis on comprehension and thinking skills, a process-oriented approach has been taken in the development of reference and library skills. Learning how to seek information and find answers to questions efficiently can make a large pool of knowledge available to students. This process includes many of the same dictionary and encyclopedia tasks found in conventional reading programs, but KROS extends it to many situations that are part of everyday life. For example, in addition to the use of the usual reference books, tables of contents, and indices, KROS makes use of the telephone book, building or store directories, maps, tables and graphic materials. Many of these skills are combined with objectives in KWP to ensure that the child goes through the processes of selecting and organizing the information he finds.

The third substrand, Vocabulary Development, includes three formats: the meaning of words, analogies, and the use of context in identifying unknown words. The first is included to teach new words, especially in the content areas. The second, analogies, requires analytic thinking, abstracting a relationship or a principle and generalizing it to other concepts. Analogies provide a useful format for testing vocabulary, one that is used frequently in standardized testing procedures. Finally, the use of semantic and syntactic context is probably the most frequently used strategy among mature readers, making it a desirable technique for children to acquire. With KROS, they are encouraged to read to the end of the sentence or passage for clues. Teachers frequently ask the children to think of a word that would make sense in the position of the unknown word, ensuring that the meaning of the sentence remains foremost in the child's thinking.

During direct instruction, KROS demands that the teachers spend two thirds to three fourths of their time on comprehension and at least half of the seatwork the children are assigned also emphasizes comprehension. Since an understanding of the passage and the ability to manipulate and apply new information are considered so important, a very limited amount of time is allocated to Word Identification Strategies. Word Identification Strategies are also included somewhat later in this program than in more traditional reading curricula. In reading a passage, children are taught to rely initially on their sight vocabulary and to approach unknown words using a hierarchy of techniques. First, the unknown word is considered in the context of the passage; i.e., the child should attempt to put in a word that is meaningful and logical in that particular sentence. If more assistance is needed, the student is encouraged to look at the structure of the word and try to analyze its meaning from the parts. Phonics' rules are used relatively infrequently, usually to help a child find out whether an unknown word in printed text is really part of his speaking vocabulary.

In practice, classrooms using KROS are organized into from five to ten learning centers. Center 1 is used for the direct instruction of reading. Homogeneous groups of four or five children meet here for about twenty minutes daily. The other children are distributed at the other centers working on assignments related to KROS objectives. The reading lesson at Center 1 revolves around a passage or story, often from a standard reading textbook. The teacher typically initiates conversation to elicit from the children knowledge or experiences they have had that relate to elements of the story. This discussion prepares the children to integrate new information from the story they are about to read with what they already know. The teacher then sets a purpose for reading by asking a general question that can be considered using information from the story. A few, literal, level one- and two-type questions follow the silent reading period to stimulate participation. Most KROS teachers, however, concentrate on higher order questions designed to help the children manipulate the new information, integrate it with earlier experiences and form generalizations. These spirited discussions, when conducted on a regular basis, model thinking strategies that the children will find useful in other problem-solving activities.

RESULTS

KROS is now in its sixth year of application. It has been used in a variety of classrooms with large proportions of Polynesian children from both urban and rural backgrounds. *Table 1* includes summary scores for twenty-seven classrooms that have had comparison groups. These include the classes at the laboratory school which are made up of Hawaiian/part-Hawaiian children from low socio-economic families, and public school classes selected because they contained large proportions of Polynesian children and had low achievement scores on standardized reading tests. In every case, the KROS-taught classrooms have significantly higher scores on standardized tests than their controls.

Table 1. Percentile Ranks of Average Composite Score on the Gates-MacGinities Reading Achievement Test for Three Sites

	First Grade			Second Grade			Third Grade		
	1979	1980	1981	1979	1980	1981	1979	1980	1981
1. Laboratory School									
Experimental	41	37	69	41	49	41	47	44	45
Control	26	21	49	25	27	24	25	31	26
2. Field Site I									
Experimental	41			47					
Control	33			22					
3. Field Site II									
Experimental	43	51		40					42
Control	29	32		22					

In structure and organization, the Kamehameha Writing Program is similar to KROS. The major strand in KWP includes all original writing. The primary purpose is to enable the child to write for creative or imaginative expression, effective communication, and accurate recording of information. Although there is considerable overlapping among the three types of writing, they provide general categories that help the teacher define writing tasks for children. The first substrand includes creative written expression such as stories, essays, plays, poems or examples of humor the child writes for pleasure or for the entertainment of others.

The second substrand is functional writing, such as school assignments, reports, correspondence, and the recording of information such as note-taking, minutes and diaries. The child is exposed to a wide variety of situations that demand all of these tasks at increasing levels of difficulty.

To be able to write appropriately for a variety of situations requires the child to assess the demands of those situations. The same comprehension and problem-solving skills that are emphasized in KROS are a major part of KWP. The child's product must make sense in the context for which it is written. Writing that is truly creative provides maximum freedom in the choice of content and format. There is no limit to the new combinations of words and ideas the child can express, and originality is a highly valued characteristic. Functional writing, on the other hand, requires accurate assessment of each situation in order to result in relevant and effective written products. The child must perceive the situation, decide whether it is a classroom test, an assignment or a letter to be answered; he must select the information he needs from past experience or outside sources, and then generate a passage that is both appropriate and intelligible.

The mechanics of writing are included in the program but, in instruction and in practice, they are separated from invention. The child is encouraged to see these grammatical conventions as a courtesy to his reader and as a means of insuring that the message is, in fact, understood. Attention is given to editing or correcting only when the student has decided that the passage he has written is clear and complete.

Assessment is by criterion-referenced exercises. By periodically examining examples of a child's writing, it is possible to observe progress. Samples have been collected systematically and studies are underway to establish a scoring system that will evaluate written products in terms of complexity, originality and clarity. In evaluating the acquisition of the conventions of writing, examining writing samples gives a much better indication of the presence of these skills than formal test situations.

In summary, KROS seems to be effective because it places a heavy emphasis on comprehension and stresses the development, application, and generalization of thinking skills across a variety of reading materials. Children in the KROS program are expected to internalize a systematic strategy for seeking and understanding new information in text. Internalization of this strategy should enable them to deal effectively with content area reading, and to derive pleasure from recreational reading. The main feature distinguishing KROS from other curricula is its concentration on the understanding of what is read even at the earliest levels.

At the end of the first full year of field testing at the laboratory school, KWP promises to be an effective strategy to teach composition skills at the lower elementary level. Children who were taught using this program wrote passages with increasing complexity, accuracy and length throughout the year. Use of the conventions of writing also improved during the year, as the result of frequent practice, even though relatively little time was spent on those objectives. The KWP will continue to be revised as both the progress of the children and the reactions of the teachers are evaluated.

Both of these curricula are primarily concerned, at the broadest level, with the development of thinking and problem-solving skills, and in the more restricted sense, with reading and writing. The ultimate goal, however, is the receiving, processing and expressing of information using all modalities and a wide variety of media.

REFERENCE NOTES

1. Crowell, D.C. *Kamehameha Reading Objective System*. Revised edition. Honolulu: The Kamehameha Schools, 1981.
2. Crowell, D.C. *Kamehameha Writing Program*. Experimental edition. Honolulu: The Kamehameha Schools, 1981.

REFERENCES

Crowell, D.C. "Should We Teach Children How to Learn from Television?" *Educational Technology*, 1981, *XXI* (12), 18–22.

Crowell, D.C. and Au, K.H. "Using a Scale of Questions to Improve Listening

Comprehension.'' *Language Arts*, 1979, *56* (1), 33–43.

Crowell, D.C. and Au, K.H. ''A Hierarchy of Questions to Assess Reading Comprehension,'' *The Reading Teacher*, 1981, *34* (4), 389–393. (a)

Crowell, D.C. and Au, K.H. ''Developing Children's Comprehension in Listening, Reading, and Television Viewing,'' *Elementary School Journal*, 1981, *92* (2), 51–57. (b)

Dunn-Rankin, P. and King, F.J. ''Multiple Comparisons in a Simplified Rank Method of Scaling,'' *Educational and Psychological Measurement*, 1969, *29*, 315–29.

Harris, A.J. and Sipay, E.R. *How to Increase Reading Ability.* (6th ed.) New York: David McKay Co., Inc., 1975.

GAMES CHILDREN PLAY: POWERFUL TOOLS THAT TEACH SOME THINKING SKILLS[1]

William Maxwell

ABSTRACT

The paper argues that children's games often teach important thinking skills and may be structured to coincide with cognitive "sensitive moments." To support this view, tentative results of seventeen experiments with 424 Class I (five and one-half to six and one-half year old) children are reported. The author also discusses a sampling of children's games and proposes a classification system whereby some important games may be selected for school curricula.

How can we explain the apparently vast differences in the measured intelligence or thinking skills of any human population sample? Explanations designed to account for racial or socio-economic status differences essentially beg the question. Differences within racial or social class groups are greater than between groups.

Perhaps, as Gregory Bateson suggested, we need to reexamine the relationship between the human mind and nature. (See the Kobayashi paper in this volume.) One of the apparent aspects of nature which Bateson repeatedly called to our attention is experimentation. Experimentation in young humans, and sometimes in mature humans, often takes the form of play or games.

The possibility that all humans are potentially geniuses, at least at birth, is no longer a radical idea. It is the thesis of this paper that there might be a connection between high mental ability and play.

In support of this thesis I will offer eight propositions.

Proposition 1. High Mental Ability: In the Few or in All? There is much evidence that all humans are, potentially, geniuses.

Sir Francis Galton, the famous eugenicist, supported the view (1869) that genius runs in families; further, he argued that therefore genius is hereditary. The Galton

W. Maxwell is the Professor of Education at the University of the South Pacific in Suva, Fiji.

1. Similar but distinctly different versions of the thesis of this paper have appeared or will shortly appear in *Educational Leadership* and the *International Journal of Educational Development*. The author is grateful to David Perkins of Harvard and to Rex Dalzall of Palmerston North Teachers College, New Zealand, for helpful criticism on earlier drafts of this paper.

argument was genetically valid: those whom we designate as "geniuses" do inherit the neurological material to think creatively, as do their uncreative siblings and cousins. But here logic failed Galton and other eugenicists. That only a few humans manifest genius may be attributable to many factors, including family reading or health habits, or any number of possible contingencies that precede intellectual eminence.

An increasing number of thinkers reject the Galtonian view and prefer to assume that all humans are genetically or potentially geniuses at birth. The words of the French anthropologist Claude Levi-Strauss are often cited in support of the "genius proposition": all men are geniuses and "have been geniuses for at least a million years" (see Boyer and Walsh, 1968; Spitz, 1978).

That much of mankind does not appear to manifest that genius, such scholars argue, is a reflection more of our failure to understand how to nurture genius, than it is a reflection of nature's ability to create genius.

Are children born equal? Boyer and Walsh of the University of Hawaii (*Saturday Review*, October 19, 1968, pp. 61ff) observed that, "In societies where power and privilege are not equally distributed, it has always been consoling to those with favored positions to assume that Nature has caused this disparity."

Bateson (1979), in his *Mind and Nature: A Necessary Unity*, argued, "It is surely the case that the brain contains no material objects other than its own channels and switchways and its own metabolic supplies and that all this material hardware never enters the narratives of the mind...and in the mind there are no neurons, only ideas.... There is, therefore, a certain complementarity between the mind and the matters of its computation (Bantam edition, p. 209)."

Similarly, Chelton Pearce in his *Magical Child* (1977), reasoned that "barriers to intelligence have long since been winnowed out by nature because nature does not program for failure. Nature programs for success and has thus built a vast, an awesome program for success into our genes. What (Nature) cannot program is parental failure to nurture the infant child" (pp. 4–5).

Proposition 2. Is IQ From Genes or From Mastery of Environment? A child's IQ, or relative intelligence (problem-solving abilities), may relate to the number of games that the child mastered at the sensitive periods of his life.

This proposition must be treated as an hypothesis at this stage since the evidence is incomplete. However, some evidence for the statement has existed from as early as 1898, when a professor of pedagogy, Karl Groos, published his classic, *The Play of Man*. Groos argued that play is one of the ways that an individual mentally prepares for the future.

Groos' judgments as to games' importance was sanctioned by no less a person than Adler (1927) who wrote almost thirty years later:

> One of the fundamental tenets of individual psychology is that all psychic phenomena can be considered as preparation for a definite goal. There is in the child's life an important phenomenon which shows very clearly the process of preparation for the future. It is play. Games are not to be considered as haphazard ideas of parents or educators, but they are to be considered as educational aids and as stimuli for the spirit, for the fantasy, and for the life-technique of the child. *The preparation for the future can be seen in every game ....* The discovery of these facts which teach us that the play of children is to be considered as preparation for the future is due to Groos, a professor of pedagogy. (pp. 81–82, my italics.)

In looking at games, Bruner (1968) took us conceptually one step beyond Groos to the level of theory:

...a game is like a mathematical model, an artificial but powerful representation of reality. ...Games go a long way to getting children involved in understanding language,
social organization, and the rest; they also introduce...the idea of a theory to these
phenomenon (pp. 93, 95).

This remarkable statement, so far largely unresearched or untested insofar as I
know, served as a guiding hypothesis for seventeen of my students at The University
of the South Pacific who wanted to find out how much they could improve the
thinking abilities of young children (age five and a half to six and a half years) in
Suva, Fiji, via games and other devices. The students accepted IQ tests as the most
accurate current measure of thinking abilities. In effect, the students asked, ''How
much can we boost IQ scores through games or other measures?''

Each student, actually an in-service teacher with an average of fourteen years experience in the public school systems of Fiji, Tonga or the Solomon Islands, devised
a single strategy to improve a child's IQ. Two recent but essentially traditional types
of IQ tests (Maxwell's Child's Intellectual Progress Scale [CHIPS]; and Richmond's
and Kicklighter's Children's Adaptive Behavior Scale [CABS]) were administered
to 425 children in seventeen classrooms in the Suva, Fiji, area. Four of the children
in each classroom were then randomly selected to undergo the previously decided
treatment. The treatment took place over a six- to eight-week period. Another student researcher post-tested the classroom without knowing which of the pupils had
been in the experimental group of four children and which had been in the control
group, the balance.

The treatment methods selected by the student researchers ranged widely: improved diet, weekly physician visits, reading enrichment, mathematics tutoring and
daily exposure to traditional, and to some newer, educational games, among others.

The results were inconclusive but highly encouraging. Even in the limited time
available, about thirty minutes per day for six to eight weeks, significant IQ gains
occurred in most of the treatment groups. The IQ gains ranged from 5.25 points for
excursions to 19.78 points for a set of games developed by the author and patented
in Fiji under the name of INVENTIVE QUOTIENT. Details of the seventeen experiments are reported by Maxwell (1981).

The evidence from those experiments will not be compelling for some of the
usual reasons encountered in exploratory research: the data were gathered by inex-
perienced researchers; the experiments did not rigorously control for the Hawthorne
experimenter effect, nor for the usual fluctuations in children's IQ scores; the experiments have yet to be replicated by a disinterested set of researchers and the sample was restricted in size by time constraints, *i.e.*, the testing and treatment took
considerable time for each pupil. Nevertheless, the evidence is somewhat per-
suasive. The post-testing by a blind examiner (one who did not know which child
had undergone treatment) was conducted immediately after the treatment. Three
psychologists, a statistician and this author checked the data; we also conducted
statistical significance tests and controlled for the Pygmalion effect.

These data, however tentative, did suggest that for children ages five and a half
to six and a half, IQ increases of eight points or more (at least one-half of a deviation) can be expected from expert tutoring or expertly guided reading enrichment.
Of crucial importance to this paper was that at these ages, the greatest IQ gains may
come from several types of educational games, if the treatment averages about thirty minutes a day for four to six days per week, for at least six weeks. These findings
would not warrant the conclusion that play, and play alone, is superior to traditional cognitive-type lessons in language and mathematics for improving a child's
mental functioning. The findings do, however, support the proposition that the

play of some intellectually stimulating games may account for huge IQ differences within otherwise similar populations.

Proposition 3. Play or Experimentation? Children begin inventing games from birth to generate and test their theories of how the universe operates.

Recent observations of the newborn child suggest that we must revise our views of the infant's abilities to reason about its universe. *Newsweek* reported (January 12, 1981) that, "The child may recognize causality not because he learns it from experience or because he reasons it out by pure thought. Rather, he seems to use intuition: he can see only relationships that fit intuitive categories already in his mind (at birth). Causality is one of those categories."

The child apparently is "wired" to learn to experiment and hypothesize immediately from birth, and thus to seek causation for what it experiences. Is it this genetic "pre-wiring" to experiment, this search for causation, that compels all children to play?

One of the first games that the new infant seems ready to play with its mother is "Peek-a-Boo." The child apparently learns from the game of Peek-a-Boo the rule of bonding: the universe cares for, loves it, is aware of its existence. After Peek-a-Boo, we can observe the evolution of playful experimentation almost constantly manifest in children. Children will push, pull or manipulate objects in a large repertory of movements to try to discover the nature of the objects.

Pieter Bruegel brilliantly captured this cultural universal, the children's will to play, in his painting "Children's Games" (*Figure 1*). The painting hangs at the Kunnsthistoriches Museum, Vienna, and is widely reproduced; see for example, the *Encyclopedia Britannica,* Vol. IV, "Children's Sports and Games." Bruegel's painting contains at least seventy-eight children's games, thirty-two of which the *Encyclopedia Britannica* identifies, and nearly all of which have survived over the past 422 years.[2]

Bruegel was echoed in the twentieth century by a remarkably dissimilar personality type: physics Professor Richard Feynmann of the California Institute of Technology. Professor Feynmann reportedly attempts to disarm his 180 somewhat apprehensive first-year students—all of whom must be very bright to enter that elite institution—by indicating that they should not worry about learning physics since he himself learned ninety-five percent of his physics before he entered school. The students laugh since they assume he is joking. Is he?

If you look at the table of contents of Professor Feynmann's three-volume *Lectures in Physics,* you can count about 200 basic physics ideas. Then, in glancing at Bruegel's games and analyzing them, you will note that Feynmann was not joking at all. From the hoop, for example (and Bruegel offers us two in the foreground) children discover and reinforce in their minds the laws of inertia, momentum, centrifugal force, friction, gravity, equilibrium, *etc.* You may test this by giving a child a metal hoop one day, and letting the child play with it. If you then bend the hoop while the child is not watching, the next day, before he starts to play with the hoop, the child will correct the curvature. In correcting the shape of the hoop *before* he starts to play with it, the child will demonstrate that he learned in a few minutes of play a fundamental principle of physics: the efficiency of a wheel depends upon all radii being of equal length. No one will have lectured the child on this, nor given him the relevant mathematical theorems. He will have in-

---

2. Some of those identified by the *Encyclopedia Britannica* will be classified in a subsequent section of this paper.

Figure 1. "Children's Games." by Pieter Brueghel. This painting hangs in the Kunsthistoriches Museum in Vienna.

dependently arrived at this "law of the universe" by experimentation or, in a child's version of experimentation, in play.

Physics Professor Feynmann and artist Pieter Bruegel articulate the same law of children's learning: they learn about their universe in play.

Proposition 4. Limited or Limitless? There are an unlimited set of children's games in human cultures which teach one or more psycho-motor, social or intellectual skills.

No ethnographic study has reported an absence of children's games in any society. However, not all ethnographic studies have reported the presence of children's games.

A few examples might be instructive. Hocart (1909) describes two Fijian games but makes no mention of an older, more widespread and more mathematical Polynesian game, Four Coweries. Hocart did describe the games *Fitshin*, similar to Spilikins (wooden needles, the "pick-up-sticks" games) and *Veinbuka*, a running tag game. What he did not see (because, we might assume, he had no developed theory of games to guide his observations) was pedogogically much more important: Four Coweries, or "Shells." Fijians or other Polynesians or other Melanesians had long ago invented a simple children's game that teaches the two major branches of mathematics—numbers, or counting, or arithmetic and geometry. Four Coweries (Shells) is, as the name implies, played with four coweries. Two children alternate. The shells are tossed and if *all* four turn up, the player gains eight points; if *all* four turn down, the player gains four points. Then, using a finger the player flicks one with another and if a third is not touched or disturbed, the player gains one point. When more than one shell is disturbed, the turn passes to the other player. The first player to reach a designated goal wins.

It is fascinating to watch five- and six-year-old Fijian children playing the game. They will compute running scores as fast or faster than an adult, and they will demonstrate some consciousness of the geometry of "straight lines" and of "curved space."

Africa, India and China similarly offer a wealth of competitive games. Kalah (variously: *Wari,* or *Ayo* or *Wawo* in Africa; *Sung-ka* in the Philippines) is a very ancient game that has survived mainly in Africa and the Philippines, but which Haggerty (1979) says is 7,000 years old, and has been continuously played on three continents. Children and adults play the game from a very early age, sometimes three or four years. The game involves moving counters, usually forty-eight hard seeds, around twelve holes. The play is too complex to describe here. However, Haggerty argues that the game is "the best all-around teaching aid in the country," since it "develops intuitive decision making," "confirms and structures the habits of moving from left to right as in reading and writing," teaches all the basic mathematical operations, and involves "pure reason."

Proposition 5. Through Lectures or Games? An unlimited set of games have evolved in human cultures, and most teach an important intellectual skill.

Children around the world now are being taught in the middle or upper primary grades how to translate from one number system to another. For example, for base ten (the way most cultures normally count; that is, after reaching ten, we start over) to base four or the base two, or binary system of counting. But if we were to give a test, say, after six months, to those children who have studied the methods of translating from one system to another for two weeks, fewer than twenty-five percent will remember such methods. And even fewer will know why such skills and concepts are taught at all.

An ancient game solves that problem. Nim is an ancient game that helps to solve that problem. It is played in most parts of the world and is so old that its origins are lost. But Nim has one supreme virtue: with Nim, an eight-year-old child can learn how to translate painlessly, playfully from the decimal (base ten) system of counting to the binary system of counting. And after he will have learned how to win when the problem is easy, he will normally want to understand the "theory" behind the winning strategy so that he can always win, regardless of how large the number of objects is. Usually, that development takes place after a few minutes of play. When that natural curiosity matures to the stage where the child seeks a generalization or theory for what he has experienced, the theory behind winning at Nim can be taught in less than ten minutes.

The reader who is unfamiliar with Nim can easily understand the game. Nim is often played with matches or coins in parlors, bars, or tearooms. Matches, or any other counters, are arranged in two or more piles which may contain any number of the objects. The rules are very simple:

1. A player may remove one, two or more objects from one (and from *only* one) pile.
2. The players (traditionally, two players) alternate in taking one or more objects from any one pile. A player must take his turn.
3. The player removing the last object wins.

(Before proceeding further, readers are advised to find a partner, anyone over age six, to learn or to review the virtues of this game. Most people can master the basic game in less than ten minutes of play.)

The theory says that in order to win all the time (providing the opponent does not also know the theory) one useful strategy is to translate from the decimal (base ten) system of counting to the binary system of counting; and then to add. If you find a "1" in the total of the binary numbers, the array is "unsafe." You must then change the array so that only "2's" or "O's" appear in the total, so that the array will be "safe." Any unsafe array can be made safe; and any move of a safe array makes the array unsafe.

Six- to eight-year-old children, after playing the game a few times, will easily learn how to make the necessary translations:

Decimal		Binary
0	=	0
1	=	1
2	=	10
3	=	11
4	=	100
5	=	101
6	=	110
7	=	111
8	=	1000

For example, suppose the array consists of a pile containing three objects and a pile containing two objects. The player whose turn it is has a problem:

	Decimal		Binary	
Problem:	3	=	11	
	+ 2	=	10	
			21	(Unsafe! because a "1" appears in the total of the binary equivalent.)
Solution:	2	=	10	(The pile of 3 must become a pile of 2.)
	+ 2	=	+ 10	
			20	(Safe! because no "1" appears in the total of the binary equivalent.)

This very simple game prepares children for the higher mental skill of translating from one number system to another. Such skills enjoyably prepare children for the cybernetic age, the age of the computer, since all major computers use the binary system of counting and representation because of its simplicity and relative infallibility. (But for ordinary computation the binary system is much too cumbersome.)

There are two other interesting aspects of Nim: it was invented long before its practical uses in computers were discovered; and, the game is easily adapted to teaching translation from any one system of numeration to any other system.

Proposition 6. In Experiment or in Lectures; Via Play or Books? Many scientific, mathematical and social concepts can be taught more effectively in play and in games than in words.

In mathematics, the creation of new knowledge and new ideas is distilled into about 1,500 abstracted pages per year, or about six to eight essentially new ideas per school day. Yet students are fortunate if they learn one new (new to them) mathematical idea a day. At the current rate, then, the child will be further from the frontiers of mathematical knowledge when he leaves school than when he entered.

It is difficult to see how this problem can be resolved through additional class time, since all other disciplines are similarly advancing. In games, however, a way out of the problem can be found. Nim serves as one example. In seminars where I present the idea of Nim for the first time, even the brightest students and adults fail to grasp the rules, much less the idea and implications, from a single verbal explanation.

But when a demonstration occurs the idea is easily grasped. And it rarely takes more than five minutes for an average person to grasp the idea, *if* the learner actually *plays* the game. It takes about two to five times as long if the learner passively watches, and longer still if the learner *reads* the rules and theory.

Another example is a "game" I call Einsteinian Space (I am told that this "game" was invented by Isaac Asimov, the science and science-fiction writer). Imagine a rubber or elastic sheet, about ten by four feet, with parallel lines running lengthwise. Four children or players stretch the sheet by holding one corner each. The fifth player puts a heavy ball in the center, thus warping the sheet or space. The player now rolls a lighter ball down the sheet. If he can roll the ball the entire length of the playing surface of the sheet (about six inches from the end) without falling "out of space" and without falling into the "Black Hole" he continues to roll. The player making the most rolls wins.

The game is simple, easy, and, at certain ages and conditions, even fun. But the important thing is that a child who plays the game learns a considerable amount about Einstein's view of gravity or space. I know of no important scientific concept that cannot be taught via some sort of game. However, Bright and colleagues (1977) confessed that up until five years ago, the study of games as instruments of the learning process "had been neither thorough nor systematic."

But if we understand Bruner (1964) and accept his idea "that any subject can be taught to anybody at any age in some form that is honest" (p. 108), then we must rule out the typical university-type lecture as the preferred mode of teaching. For, demonstrably, in most disciplines, verbal instruction is less efficient than some of the forty or so methods of instruction identified by Henry (1960) from his analyses of cross-cultural ethnographic studies.

Bruner can be understood and implemented, then, in the Bateson sense that each mind is "wired" to comprehend what any other mind can comprehend, but not necessarily via the same method or in the same time periods. Each individual will have his own unique style of comprehending the universe. And of all the methods of comprehending, play is one of the most universal. Einstein used to invent playful analogies to teach himself about space. For example, to understand the speed of light, Einstein used to "race" trucks, in his imagination, across empty space, at the "speed limit." Not one of Einstein's "gedunken plays," as he called them, is beyond the comprehension of any child. Perhaps, however, if this proposition is accepted—that many scientific concepts can be taught in play—it will be necessary for educators and others to invent many new games.

Proposition 7. "Now or Never?" The Readiness Factor or the Sensitive Moment Factor operates to determine when a game should be introduced to a child.

Toy manufacturers discovered long ago that children are always ready for moving toys. But that fact often obscures a much more sensitive fact: children are ready for different toys or games at different developmental stages.

I once introduced *Kalah* to a six-year-old boy who thereafter refused to be separated from the game. But on another occasion we tried to introduce *Kalah* to an equally bright five and one-half-year-old. The latter child was not interested in the game. (If his older siblings had played the game, the story might have been different.)

It is nearly always difficult to predict exactly when a child will be ready for a particular intellectual experience. However, the difficulty of making that assessment must not obscure the critical need for a child to experience certain basic problems—social, psycho-motor, intellectual—at the appropriate, sensitive period.

If, for example, a child does not play with blocks (artificial bricks in Bruegel) before he is eight, that child is very unlikely to develop the three-dimensional, spatial relations comprehending and manipulating skills necessary to become a competent architect, engineer, builder, surgeon, or other professional where abilities to "see" and "feel" in three dimensions are important.

The factor of readiness has long been recognized by educators. However, the term has implied an irreversible stage from whence learning can take place at any time. But reasoning by P.P.G. Bateson (1969) and Thorpe (1961) appears to suggest that readiness is an imprecise term for certain abilities or experiences. Both suggested a more accurate term, "sensitive period," which was invented by the Dutch biologist DeVries and used in the same restricting manner by Montessori (Standing, 1962, p. 118).

P.P.G. Bateson, for example, writes, "One of the most striking features of imprinting is its apparent restriction to a sensitive period early in the life cycle.... What is more, the effects of most reinforcing stimuli are confined to limited periods which occur as a result of short-term fluctuations in the physiological state of the (being)" (p. 113).

And Bateson goes on, "It is reasonable to distinguish, as Thorpe has done, between periods of sensitivity occurring at many stages throughout the life cycle and periods that occur only once." And Standing wrote "...but the distinguishing feature of growth during a sensitive period is that an irresistible impulse urges the organism to select only certain elements in its environment, and for a definite and limited time" (Standing, p. 119). Montessori (1966, p. 38) states, "A sensitive period refers to a special sensibility which a creature acquires in its infantile state, while it is still in a process of evolution. It is a transient disposition..."

The implication that some sensitive periods occur many times or may be of great duration may explain why almost everyone masters his language; and the fact that some sensitive periods occur only once (and briefly) might explain the seemingly accidental advent of a Mozart or Einstein. Was one of Einstein's brief sensitive periods luckily synchronized with the gift of a compass? Was Newton's memory about the fortuitous fall of an apple a signal from his unconscious mind that certain questions are, in fact, triggered by seemingly trivial events, but events occurring at critically sensitive moments?

One might generalize and say that before age six no child is ready for a lecture, but every child is always ready to experiment, to play. Moreover, the assessment of sensitive period or readiness is non-threatening when presented in the form of games. In Bruegel's playground there are no borders; even the walls and fences are clearly open and encourage children to flow from one experience to another.

For certain types of geniuses it may well be that it is "now or never." And "now" may be a very brief period in the child's mental evolution.

Proposition 8. Not All Games are Equal. Nor do all games require equal time to master; nor do different games compete unduly for the learner's attention: the individual chooses freely.

Before we follow this proposition to its logical conclusion we need to define games. A helpful definition of games was provided by Jean Piaget (1962, p. 142ff) who stated that "games with rules rarely occur before stage II (age four to seven) and belong mainly to the third period (age seven to eleven years) of development;" he also said, "play is an end in itself" (p. 147–149); and, "A second criteria (of games) is that of spontaneity as opposed to compulsion, *i.e.,* voluntary;" "a third criterion is that of pleasure." Most writers (Bright, 1979; Huizinga, 1950, *etc.*) agree with these criteria and add others such as, "outside the sphere of necessity or material utility.... The play mood is of rapture..." (Huizinga, p. 132).

If the foregoing propositions have merit, perhaps children's games ought to be sequenced for the child's curriculum, especially in the period identified by Piaget, age seven to eleven years, when children seem to want to experience rules and the implications of rules.

Assuming that Bruegel's "list" of seventy-eight games was only a beginning, I sought some classification system that would help teachers, parents, and curriculum supervisors to ensure that each child has a "balanced diet" of games.

Harris (1971) had proposed a system of classifying certain kinds of games. But his system related to only one genre of games and therefore had to be discarded for any general utility. The "father" of the systematic study of chidren's games, Karl Groos (1901), had urged that the issue of classifying children's games merited serious attention. Yet in library searches I could find nowhere a system of classification that would help teachers and parents to make a kind of checklist of games that every child ought to know and that, perhaps, could enrich standard school curricula. Groos, for example, said, "While many have undertaken, by various methods, to classify human play satisfactorily, in no single case has the result been fortunate." Groos wrote that in 1898.

The other major writers who appear to have seriously contemplated the same need as Groos were Huizinga (1950) and Piaget (1962). Piaget discussed the history of the classification of games at length (p. 105ff); however, he virtually dismissed those who earlier had attempted to classify games (Stern, Buhler, *etc.*), since their categories were clearly too arbitrary or vague: "passive," "constructional," "collective," "functional," *etc.* But Piaget himself, while obviously aware of the value of children's games and consequently aware of the need to classify useful games, let the ball drop and apparently never picked it up again.

The logic of the above propositions passes on to educators the task of expanding our study of children's games, so that educators and other researchers, especially psychologists and anthropologists, might improve our understanding of children's needs and development by watching them play, and by classifying that basic activity, and then by developing theories from those systematic observations and classifications.

To initiate such a classificatory enterprise, and while keeping in mind the need for parsimony, I think only six questions need be asked initially:

1. At what age may play of the game begin? Or, by what age is the sensitive period for the particular intellectual skills taught by that game likely to occur?

2. Approximately how many minutes are necessary to learn and play the game to a reasonable consummation?
3. What would be the recommended frequency in, say, a year?
4. When should mastery be completed? Or, by what age may a child reasonably be expected to graduate from that particular game?
5. What is the priority of the particular game? How would a given game or play activity rate on a scale from highest (9) to lowest (0)?
6. And, in what domain is the game primarily placed? Psychomotor/perceptual? Social? Verbal? Mathematical? *Etc.*

Table 1. A Proposed Curriculum Code For Children's Games and Sports

First two digits:	Age in months when play of game may or should begin: (00–84)
Second two digits:	Recommended minutes per session: (01–30)
Third two digits:	Frequency approximately: 11 = 1 time per year, until mastery 12 = 1 time per season, 16 = 1 time per month, 17 = 1 time per week, 19 = 1 time per day, until mastery 21 = 2 times per year, 26 = twice per month, *etc.*
Fourth two digits:	Age in years when basic mastery should have been completed: (00–15) (Thereafter, play is for pure amusement, or for social purposes, *i.e.* not in the curriculum.)
Ninth digit:	Priority in the curriculum: 0 = not recommended, but may be useful 1 = low priority 9 = highest priority
Tenth digit:	Developmental domain: 0 = mainly perceptual or psych-motor 1 = mainly social 2 = mainly mental agility 3 = mainly verbal 4 = mainly arithmetical or mathematical 5 = mainly spatial or three-dimensional 6 = mainly clerical or commercial 7 = mainly scientific or technical 8 = mainly abstract reasoning or problem solving 9 = combination of two or more of above
Example: Nim:	66-06-17-08-94. 66 = Play should begin at about 66 months (5 ½ years). 06 = 6 minutes per day should be sufficient. 17 = About once per week until mastery is recommended. 08 = Age in years when mastery should have been attained. 9 = Highest priority in curriculum. 4 = Indicates the game is mainly mathematical.

Table 2. Classifying Some Classical Children's Games According to the Proposed Curriculum Code

Name of Game	More Information	Author's Estimate of: IQ Value	Social Value	Proposed Curriculum Code Classification
1. Backgammon	Scarne (1973)	high	med.	84-20-17-11-78
2. Base	Bruegel, Ency. Brit.	low	high	48-10-17-07-60
3. Blind Man's Buff	Bruegel, Ency. Brit.	med.	high	45-10-16-07-60
4. Bowling Hoops	Bruegel, Ency. Brit.	high	high	48-10-16-07-97
5. Building with Bricks	Bruegel, Ency. Brit.	high	high	18-10-19-12-97
6. Charades	Hindman (1956)	high	high	66-20-12-15-83
7. Checkers	Scarne (1973)	med.	med.	60-15-17-09-82
8. Chess	Scarne (1973)	high	low	60-15-17-15-98
9. Crack-the-Whip	Bruegel, Ency. Brit.	med.	high	54-10-16-09-70
10. Dominoes	Scarne (1973)	high	high	84-15-17-13-84
11. Four Cowries	This article	high	high	60-10-17-07-64
12. Go (Wei-chi)	Iwamoto (1972)	high	med.	72-15-17-15-88
13. Hide and Seek	Bruegel, Ency. Brit.	med.	high	42-10-16-07-90
14. King of the Mountain	Bruegel, Ency. Brit.	med.	med.	54-10-12-08-00
15. Kites	Hindman (1956)	high	med.	60-20-32-12-97
16. Leapfrog	Bruegel, Ency. Brit.	med.	med.	64-10-22-09-70
17. Marbles	Bruegel, Ency. Brit.	high	high	45-15-27-09-97
18. Nim	This article	high	high	66-06-17-08-94
19. Peek-a-Boo	(universal)	high	high	00-01-17-08-94
20. Playing Store	Bruegel, Ency. Brit.	high	high	54-15-27-15-96
21. Playing with Dolls	Bruegel, Ency. Brit.	high	high	30-15-27-09-91
22. Kalah	Haggerty (1979)	high	high	54-15-19-15-94
23. Tick-Tack-To	Hindman (1956)	med.	med.	60-10-16-07-88
24. Whipping Tops	Bruegel, Ency. Brit.	high	med.	40-15-32-09-97

From the answers to these six questions (which would probably be tentative for a very long time), it would then be easy to devise a classification system or curriculum code into which any children's game could fit. (See *Tables 1* and *2*.)

Children's games are so ubiquitous, so universal, so extraordinarily frequent that they have gone largely unobserved and unstudied by those who should have done so: educators, psychologists, anthropologists, *etc.* But our neglect is not total. Painters such as Bruegel, educators such as Groos, psychologists such as Piaget have urged us to look at children's games through the lens of intellect. When we do so, we find an incredibly rich display of creativity, and of thinking. It may be fortuitous that we have not disturbed this world of play by looking at it too analytically. On the other hand, perhaps it is time for us to employ pure pleasure to teach thinking. We have tried toil and it did not work very well. There is probably no harm in trying play to find out how much the pleasure of it can boost thinking skills.

REFERENCES

Adler, A. *Understanding Human Nature.* Greenwich, CT: Fawcett, 1927.
Almy, M., *et al. Young People's Thinking.* New York: Teachers College Press, 1966.
Bateson, G. *Mind and Nature: A Necessary Unity.* New York: E.P. Dutton, 1979.

Bateson, P.P.G. "Imprinting and the Development of Preferences." In *Stimulation in Early Infancy.* A. Ambrose (Ed.). London: Academic Press, 1969.

Boyer, W. A., and Walsh, P. "Are Children Born Equal?" *Saturday Review,* October 19, 1968.

Bright, G. W., *et al.* "Cognitive Effects of Games on Mathematics Learning" (Eric File No. 166–007, 1979). Revision of a paper presented at the National Council of Teachers of Mathematics, Cincinnati, 1977.

Encyclopedia Britannica, Volume 4, "Children's Sports and Games."

Bruner, J. S. *On Knowing: Essays for the Left Hand.* Cambridge, MA: Harvard University Press, 1964.

Bruner, J. S. *Toward a Theory of Instruction.* New York: W.W. Norton, 1968.

Groos, K. *The Play of Man.* New York: Appleton, 1901.

Haggerty, J. B. "Kalah—An Ancient Game of Mathematical Skill." In *Readings from the Arithmetic Teacher,* S. E. Smith, Jr. and C. A. Beckman (Eds.), Washington: National Council of Teachers of Mathematics, 1979.

Harris, Richard J. "An Interval Scale Classification System for all 2 × 2 Games" (Eric File Ed 055 114). Paper presented at the Annual Meeting of the American Psychological Association, Washington, 1971.

Henry, Jules. "A Cross-Cultural Outline of Education," *Current Anthropology,* 1960, *1,* (4).

Hindman, Darwin A. *Complete Book of Games and Stunts.* Englewood, NJ: Prentice-Hall, 1956.

Hocart, A.M. "Two Fijian Games," *Man,* 1909, 9, 184–5.

Huizinga, J. *Homo Ludens: A Study of the Play Element in Culture.* Boston: Beacon Press, 1950.

Iwamoto, Kaoru. *Go for Beginners.* New York: Pantheon, 1972.

Montessori, Marie. *The Secret of Childhood.* (M.J. Costelloe, S.J., Tr.) New York: Ballantine, 1972.

Maxwell, William (Ed.). *Experiments on Improving Mental Abilities in Children.* Suva, Fiji: School of Education, The University of the South Pacific, 1981.

Pearce, Chelton. *Magical Child.* New York: E.P. Dutton, 1977.

Piaget, Jean. *Play, Dreams and Imitations in Childhood.* (C. Gattegno and F.M. Hodgson, Trs.) New York: Norton Library, 1962.

Pinneau, Samuel R. *Changes in Intelligence Quotient.* Boston: Houghton Mifflin, 1961.

Scarne, John. *Encyclopedia of Games.* New York: Harper and Row, 1973.

Sutton-Smith, Brian. *Child's Play.* New York: John Wiley, 1971.

Spitz, Herman. "The Universal Nature of Human Intelligence: Evidence from Games," *Intelligence,* 1978, *2,* (4).

Standing, E.M. *Maria Montessori: Her Life and Work.* New York: New American Library, 1957.

Thorpe, W.H. "Sensitive Periods in the Behavior of Animals and Men: A Study of Imprinting with Special Reference to the Induction of Cyclic Behavior." In *Current Problems in Animal Behavior.* W.H. Thorpe and D.L. Zangwell (Eds.). Cambridge: Cambridge University Press, 1961.

THE COGNITIVE RESEARCH TRUST (CoRT) THINKING PROGRAM

Edward de Bono

ABSTRACT

This paper describes the Cognitive Research Trust (CoRT) Thinking Program which was developed by the author and which contains sixty relatively independent (non-hierarchical) lessons. The paper describes the theoretical basis, the methodologies employed, the structure of the program and discusses the major difficulties normally encountered in teaching thinking by this direct, process-oriented method. Some evaluations of the program are also examined briefly.

The Cognitive Research Trust (CoRT) Program has now been in use for over twelve years in a wide variety of schools. Much of this experience is described in my book, *Teaching Thinking* (de Bono, 1976). The program has been taught to more than 100,000 students, ranging from nine-year-old children to members of the boards of some of the world's largest corporations. For example, the University of Toronto School, which enrolls a large number of highly gifted children, has been using the lessons for some years now under the guidance of Norah Maier. At the other end of the scale the lessons have been used with children with IQ's as low as seventy-five. The age spread has been equally great. Sidney Tyler (1980) used the CoRT lessons with six-year-olds in the United States Armed Forces School Program. In Venezuela, the lessons are being used with nine-year-olds, with students at Technical Training Institutes, with adults in the public service and with the armed forces (at recruit and senior level) under the guidance of Margaretta Sanchez and Corinna Machado. In Israel, the material has been used to train teachers (Ronnie Shtarkshall). In New York, Michael Gleeson has been using the material with adult lay audiences. In England the processes were used by Sir Terence Beckett when he was chief executive officer of the Ford Motor Company. In Spain the materials are used in the teaching of English as a foreign language. The program is now in use in England, Eire, Canada, the United States, Venezuela, Australia, New Zealand, Israel, Malta, Germany and Spain.

It is important to mention this spread of experience for several reasons. Thinking is a subject area in which there are many theories and approaches and it is only too easy to sit down and produce a course based on a little experience in the actual teaching of thinking as a skill. Most of these programs will not survive the test of time. For example, it is easy to analyze the process of thinking into its apparent

---

E. de Bono is affiliated with the Cognitive Research Trust in Cambridge, England.

component parts or skills and then to attempt to teach each component skill directly. There is no reason why this approach should work. A practical thinking tool
need not be the same as a component produced by analysis. It has always been our
intention at the Cognitive Research Trust to encourage the use of the material with
applicability in a wide variety of situations. We believe that thinking is a basic process and that the same tools can be taught—and used—across a wide range of ages
and abilities. This has been born out by the experiences cited above: a nine-year-old
in the Venezuelan jungle learns substantially the same process as a senior executive
in a major corporation.

DESIGN FOR PRACTICALITY

Most teachers who have been teaching the CoRT Thinking lessons have not had
any formal training in their use. Training is an advantage but it is not essential. The
lessons are now in use in thousands of schools where the teacher has independently
developed the skill to use the program effectively. The format of the lessons has
been kept very simple with detailed instructions for precisely these sorts of reasons.
Complex programs which require extended teacher training are all too often limited
by their practicality. It has been our aim to make the lessons usable across a wide
range of teacher abilities. Since the CoRT lessons are meant to be a practical method
for the teaching of thinking, philosophical complexities have been excluded. In
Venezuela 100,000 teachers have now been trained under the guidance of
Margaretta Sanchez. The initial group of trainers were trained directly by Dr. Sanchez and, in turn, the trainers have trained other trainers—and so on through
several levels, until the final teachers have been trained. A viable program has to be
robust enough to survive this type of multiple-level transfer.

In the Dalton School in New York City the CoRT material was taught by a
sixteen-year-old pupil, Roxanne Anspach, to her fellow pupils. This illustrates
another benefit of a robust framework for the exercise of thinking skills.

For the reasons given above the program has been designed in a parallel, rather
than in a hierarchical fashion. In all there are sixty lessons; but any section of ten
lessons can be used on its own. If a teacher messes up one or other lesson, the remaining lessons can still work. This is not the case with an hierarchical design,
where the whole thing becomes confusing if the fundamental concepts are not
taught well enough. To claim that a curriculum program was teacher proof would
be both an insult and an absurdity, but there can be a range of demands made
upon a teacher, and the more practical the deliberate design of a program, the more
comfortable a teacher will be with it.

OBJECTIVES

Perhaps the most striking change noted in pupils who have been through part of
the CoRT course is the change in self-image. Before the course, pupils seemed to
have one of two self-images with regard to school: "I am intelligent" (good at
school work, good at pleasing the teacher and passing tests) or, "I am not intelligent" (uninterested in school or classroom work). After the CoRT course, both
these tended to change towards, "I am a thinker." That turns out to be a positive
and constructive image which allows a pupil to think about things, to listen to
ideas, to listen to others, to set out to think about things. It is an operating image,
as distinct from a value image. To achieve such a change in self-image is the primary
objective of the CoRT program.

The CoRT Thinking lessons provide a framework in which the emphasis is placed directly on thinking. This is in contrast to the absorption or sorting of knowledge that occurs elsewhere in education. The pupil is encouraged to think and is given credit for his own individual thinking. The pupil also gets the opportunity to think in groups: he has to put across his own ideas and also has to interact with the ideas of others.

The CoRT program offers a selection of specific and deliberate thinking skills. Pupils are encouraged to regard thinking as a skill that can be learned and practiced. They have an opportunity to practice these skills and to observe an improvement in them. The improvement is in confidence, focus, fluency and application. As a result, a youngster feels in control of his thinking, instead of drifting along from thought to thought in a sea of emotion and confusion.

All the effects mentioned above are quite separate from the learning of specific thinking tools which can then be transferred to other situations. This is another intention of the CoRT lessons.

In summary there are four levels of objectives:

1. That there is an area in the curriculum where thinking is treated directly in its own right.
2. That pupils should come to regard thinking as a skill that can be improved by attention, learning and practice.
3. That pupils should come to regard themselves as thinkers.
4. That pupils should acquire a set of transferrable thinking tools which they can carry to other situations.

TYPE OF THINKING

It is important to be very clear as to the type of thinking that is taught in the CoRT program. It is not concerned with solving puzzles or problems; it is not concerned with playing simulation games; it is not concerned directly with critical thinking; it is not concerned with the rules of logic. The CoRT program deals with the perceptual area of thinking.

In practical terms, most thinking takes place in the perceptual area. There are times when we have to solve a particular problem or win a particular argument, but on the whole most of our thinking takes place in the perceptual area: how we look at the world. In time, this area of thinking will come to take over almost all our thinking, since processing will be handed over to mathematics or computers.

I would define thinking as "the operating skill with which intelligence acts upon experience." Perception is the process of using our experience to find our way around the present situation. Imagine that you are in a room full of smoke. You have to find your way about by a process of reasoning: deducing the position of the furniture from what little you can see. If, however, the smoke clears, then you perceive everything clearly and can find your way about with ease.

Because of this emphasis on perception, we sometimes call the CoRT method the "spectacles method." If a person is short-sighted or has tunnel vision, we might seek to correct the problem by supplying spectacles which allow the person to see more broadly and more clearly. That is precisely the intention of the CoRT lessons. If the pupil can come to see more broadly and more clearly, then he can find his way around in the world more easily and purposefully. It should also be noted that this spectacles method does not seek to change values as such. A person still keeps his traditional values.

There are parts of the CoRT program which deal directly with creativity, argument, values and feeling and action—but in all cases the approach is a perceptual one. If you can see things clearly, then the reaction will be appropriate.

THEORETICAL BASE

The theoretical base for the CoRT program is very clear, but some people seem to have a hard time seeing it. This is largely because they are trying to fit it into an existing old-fashioned model. The theoretical base for the CoRT program is modelled after the nature of perceptual systems. In essence, this means the behavior of active information systems. In my book *The Mechanism of Mind* (de Bono, 1969), I describe how a self-organizing information system provides an environment in which experience organizes itself into patterns. This ability of the brain is quite marvellous and allows us to make sense of the environment, to use language and, generally, to carry on life. At the same time, patterning systems have certain drawbacks, such as the difficulty of scanning across patterns. There is also a need to create a new layer of patterns, that is, to direct our attention so that it does not just wander from point to point through our experience without direction. Point-to-point thinking is the major defect of ordinary perceptual thinking.

In summary, if we are dealing with a patterning system, we need ways of scanning across patterns and ways of directing attention. We may also need to create new patterned layers of "executive concepts."

METHODOLOGY

The major problem in the teaching of thinking has always been the difficulty of obtaining transfer. A pupil may show a high degree of thinking skill in playing a game, working through a simulation, devising a computer program or taking part in an argument. But these skills often do not seem to be generalized to other situations, unless they are very close indeed. In fact, skill in playing a game like chess may not even be generalized to another game.

This lack of transfer also seems to affect the discussion or case-study method. It is quite traditional to ask pupils to think about or discuss a particular situation. The teacher intervenes from time to time to guide the thinking or to point out errors. The same procedure is used in the case-study method, for example at the Harvard Business School.

Teachers and institutions using such case-study methods hope that these sorts of discussions will build up general thinking skills, which can be transferred to other situations. Again, this does not seem to happen.

ATTENTION-DIRECTING STRATEGIES

Mindful of this problem of transfer, the approach we have taken in the CoRT program is almost exactly the opposite. A number of attention-directing tools are created. For example, the very first lesson is the "P.M.I." which requires pupils to look first in the "Plus" or positive direction, then in the "Minus" or negative direction, and finally in the "Interesting" direction. In this way, they are forced to scan across the scene, instead of wandering from point to point. The P.M.I. is treated as a deliberate tool; it is practiced again and again, until it can be used fluently and at will. The practice items on which it is used are very short and contain very little information (*e.g.,* ''Should all cars be painted yellow?''; ''Should everyone wear a mask showing his or her mood?''). The P.M.I. is applied to the item for a very short period of time: typically two to three minutes. The tool is then practiced on another item for a similarly short period of time, and then on another. The purpose of this is to prevent interest from getting bogged down in the subject matter itself. Attention has to stay on the tool, rather than on the subject matter: on the process, not on the content.

The ''Plus-Minus-Interesting'' (P.M.I.) exercises are attention-directing tools. The intention is that the strategy embodied by the attention-directing tool gets embedded in the tool and this can then be carried to other situations. This is a much more direct approach than asking a pupil to abstract a principle from a general discussion and then to crystallize that principle and transfer it elsewhere.

A number of different attention-directing strategies are used in the CoRT program. For example, in a lesson on values, the pupils are asked to separate the values they find into High values and Low values. The effort to do this ensures that values, in general, get proper attention. That is the purpose of the exercise—not the splitting of values into two categories.

Some of the processes are given strange abbreviations (like PMI, CAF, OPV, EBS, ADI, *etc.*). This is deliberate. It is done to hold attention in that area and to create a specific tool of what might otherwise just have been a weak exhortation. (Contrast, ''do a PMI'' with, ''try to look at both sides of the question.'') These tools also create a meta-cognitive layer. Pupils can now see how well they—or their classmates—do a PMI, rather than just have a vague sense of how well they are thinking. The tools, in a way, objectify thinking and make it possible to think about thinking and to discuss it.

Experience is usually filled with descriptive concepts (chair, pen, room, game, etc.). The purpose of the CoRT method is to seed into our experience a number of executive or operator concepts which instruct us to do something. Instead of drifting from description to description, we can start inserting these executive concepts. For example, the OPV concept would encourage us to consider the Other Person's View and it should surface naturally in our description of a situation.

Throughout, the emphasis is on skill building through practice. Understanding the lesson takes only a few moments; the rest of the time is spent on practice. The practice should be clear and direct. Philosophical speculation reduces the impact of the lesson through encouraging confusion. The lessons need to be crisp, clear and focused.

PROCEDURE

A CoRT thinking lesson may be covered in one classroom period; or, a double period may be used. It is also possible to repeat the lesson in a subsequent period.

The theme of the lesson is clear to both teacher and pupil. It is outlined in the pupil's leaflet (or booklet). Attention must stay on that theme throughout the lesson. For example, if the lesson is OPV (Other People's Views) then the teacher must stick to that theme.

The teacher explains the theme of the lesson and gives some examples (from the teachers' handbook). The teacher then gives a practice item to the class and gets the pupils to work on it. The pupils' notes and the teacher's handbook contain a list of practice items for each lesson.

The pupils always work in groups of five, or six. The teacher sets the task and the time allowed. For example, the practice item may be the following: "A Father does not want his daughter to smoke: do an OPV on both father and daughter." Each group discusses the practice item and puts together its thoughts. There may be a spokesman for each group or the teacher can select anyone in the group to respond.

At the end of the allotted time, the teacher asks the groups for their output. He may ask one group for a complete OPV and then the other groups to add to this. Or, the teacher may ask one group for the father's view and a different group for the daughter's view. Or, he may take one point from each group (for each view in turn) going round the groups until no more are forthcoming. It is important to keep this feedback period as lively as possible.

The teacher then moves on to another practice item. For example: "There is a rise in basic food prices: list the people who might have an important view in this matter, then do an OPV." In this example, there are two stages: find the people concerned, then do the OPV. Three of four practice items would be covered in this fashion. Then the teacher would initiate a discussion on the OPV process itself: purpose, value, when it should be done, disadvantages, *etc.* Discussion points are given in both pupils' and teacher's notes. Finally a written project may be set for homework, if that is the custom in the school.

This, then, is the basic framework. Within it variations are possible. For example, a small role-playing scene might have been used in the OPV lesson. It is very important to realize, however, that such diversions should not preempt the main purpose of the lesson. In the pursuit of interest, it is quite possible to have a lesson that is very interesting but actually teaches nothing.

Guidance on the selection and changing of groups and on the mixing of abilities is given in the teacher handbook. Guidance is also given on the nature of the teacher's response. The teacher can offer his opinion alongside that of the pupils but the teacher is not there in a judgmental role. Nor is it the role of the teacher to guide pupils towards a particular answer. The teacher should comment on the suggestions in such a way as to emphasize their interest, how they link up with or contrast with other suggestions made, and so on. This type of response is no different from that which a teacher might make in any open-ended subject.

DIFFICULTIES

What sort of difficulties arise in the teaching of the CoRT Program? Teachers who have a direct, vigorous teaching style usually experience no problems in teaching this program. Teachers who are more used to teaching a knowledge subject and who require the security of a right or wrong answer may feel awkward in dealing in such an open-ended subject. The sense of focus is very important indeed. If the lessons become too discursive then the pupils lose the feeling of undergoing skill training and, after a few lessons will complain that all the lessons are the same. That is why it is so important to focus directly on the purpose of each lesson and to stick closely to it. Philosophical debate and discussion may seem interesting at the time, but such tangents only serve to confuse and to dilute the focus of the lessons. For example, in the "yellow car" example in a PMI lesson, one pupil said a plus point was that yellow cars would be kept cleaner. Another pupil said this was a minus point, as he "had to clean his dad's car and would therefore have to clean it more often." Both pupils were, of course, right.

There are review lessons from time to time and, in addition, the teacher can set a review lesson into which several of the attention tools are introduced. It would be wrong, however, to introduce other tools, except as a passing mention, into a lesson that was intended to focus on a particular new area. There is no need for the teacher to construct a hierarchical framework for the lessons, unless this is specifically recommended at a given point.

Teachers are often tempted to substitute practice items of their own for those given in the teachers notes. Experience would caution against this temptation. The practice items are chosen quite carefully, even though they may appear simple. They are chosen so as to make no demands on special knowledge and to be sufficiently lively and interesting. In inserting their own practice items, teachers are apt to be too solemn and to put in only heavy sociological problems, on the grounds that these are the only ones worth thinking about. This is a bad mistake. It is not advisable to attempt to develop thinking skills and to solve real problems at the same time. The thinking skills need to be developed first and this may require a mix of frivolous and remote problems (*e.g.*, what would the AGO—Aims, Goals and Objectives—be for the captain of an alien spaceship visiting the earth?).

On the other hand, while the subject or problem may not be real and should not be solemn, it is important that the teacher approach the subject with seriousness and deliberation. A tentative or hesitant approach can too easily give the pupils a sense of "messing around" and the subject will suffer. The program was designed to cover only one theme in a week. More themes than this are likely to cause confusion in the minds of the pupils.

With gifted children, there may at first be a reluctance to consider that any improvement could possibly be made in their thinking. Such pupils are also used to having their minds stretched by complex problems. They may, at first, resent the apparently simple structure of the CoRT lessons. It is up to the teacher to show them that they are not as good at this projective thinking, as they are at their more usual reactive thinking in which they react to what is put in front of them. A competitive approach can be used in which the output of one group is compared to that of another group. Gifted children are also often used to marks or grade, or some assessment of achievement. They may also want a written output from time to time (to show their individual ability as distinct from that of their group).

The Speed of Thinking in the CoRT Exercises

Perhaps the area where most teachers have difficulty at first is that of the short time allotted to the practice items. Teachers are used to having a lengthy and interesting discussion on some subject. The idea of spending only two, three or four intensely interesting minutes on an item and then moving on to the next one is contrary to their habits. Such teachers reason that if the discussion is going well and the pupils are interested, then the discussion should be allowed to continue. Unfortunately this attitude tends to destroy the whole basis of the CoRT method in which attention is to stay on the process, not on the content. The short time spans and rapid change of content must therefore be insisted upon. In a short while both teachers and pupils acquire the rapid-fire idiom and it is amazing how much can be thought in a short time span and how quickly thinking can be directed at will to a new area.

THE STRUCTURE OF THE CoRT PROGRAM

The CoRT Program is divided into six sections of ten lessons each. Each section covers one particular aspect of thinking. The sections can be used in any order although, in general, CoRT II should follow CoRT I. Some schools use CoRT I across a wide range of pupils. Others select CoRT I, IV and V.

CoRT I (Breadth)

The purpose of this section is to develop tools and habits for scanning widely around a thinking situation.

TREATMENT OF IDEAS: Plus-Minus-Interesting (PMI): deliberate examination of an idea for good, bad or interesting points, instead of immediate acceptance or rejection.

FACTORS INVOLVED: Considering All Factors (CAF): looking as widely as possible at all the factors involved in a situation instead of only the immediate ones.

RULES: the basic purposes and principles involved. Draws together the first two lessons.

CONSEQUENCES: Consequences and Sequel (C&S): consideration of the immediate, short, medium and long-term consequences.

OBJECTIVES: Aims, Goals, Objectives (AGO): picking out or defining objectives. Being clear about your own aims and understanding those of others.

PLANNING: the basic features and processes involved. Draws together the preceding two lessons.

PRIORITIES: First Important Priorities (FIP): choosing from a number of different possibilities and alternatives. Putting priorities in some order.

ALTERNATIVES: Alternatives, Possibilities and Choices (APC): generating new alternatives and choices, instead of feeling confined to the obvious ones.

DECISIONS: the different operations involved. Draws together the preceding two lessons.

VIEWPOINT: Other Point of View (OPV): moving out of your own viewpoint to consider the points of view of all others involved in any situation.

CoRT II (Organization)

This section is concerned with some basic thinking operations and their use.

RECOGNIZE: the deliberate effort to identify a situation in order to make it easier to understand or to deal with it.

ANALYZE: two types of analysis. Deliberate dividing up of a situation in order to think about it more effectively.

COMPARE: using comparison in order to understand a situation. Examining points of similarity and difference in offered comparisons.

SELECT: the deliberate effort to find something that fits the requirements. Selecting from among different possibilities.

FIND OTHER WAYS: the deliberate effort to find alternative ways of looking at things.

START: the practical business of starting to think about something. What is the first thing to do?

ORGANIZE: the practical business of organizing the way a situation is to be tackled.

FOCUS: looking at different aspects of a situation, but especially being clear as to what aspect is under consideration at the moment.

CONSOLIDATE: what has been achieved so far? Drawing together and being clear about what has been done and what has been left out.

CONCLUDE: arriving at a definite conclusion, even if that declares that no definite conclusion is possible.

CoRT III (Interaction)

This section is concerned with two or more party situations, with argument and discussion.

EXAMINE BOTH SIDES (EBS): deliberate practice in examining both sides of an argument instead of blindly supporting one side.

EVIDENCE: TYPE: the types of evidence put forward in an argument. Distinction between fact and opinion.

EVIDENCE: VALUE: not all evidence is of equal value. Practice in assessing the value of evidence.

EVIDENCE: STRUCTURE: examining evidence. Does it stand on its own, or is it dependent on other evidence, which in turn depends on something else?

AGREEMENT, DISAGREEMENT, IRRELEVANCE (ADI): mapping out these areas in order to increase areas of agreement and reduce areas of disagreement.

BEING RIGHT (1.): two of the main ways of being right. Examining the idea itself, its implications and effects. Referring to facts, authority, feelings.

BEING RIGHT (2.): the other two ways of being right. Use of names, labels, classifications. Judgement, including the use of value words.

BEING WRONG (1.): exaggeration—false generalizations, taking things to extremes. Basing conclusions on only part of the situation.

BEING WRONG (2.): the remaining two ways of being wrong.

OUTCOME: what has been achieved at the end of an argument? Seven possible levels of achievement, short of complete agreement.

CoRT IV (Creativity)

This section is concerned with creative thinking and contains some elements of lateral thinking.

YES, NO AND PO: 'PO' is a device for showing that an idea is being used creatively without any judgment or immediate evaluation.

STEPPING STONE: the use of ideas not for their own sake but because of other ideas they may lead to.

RANDOM INPUT: the input of random, unrelated ideas, into a situation as a stimulus for new lines of thought.

CONCEPT CHALLENGE: the testing of the uniqueness of concepts may lead to other ways of doing things. Use of "why."

DOMINANT IDEA: in most situations there is a dominant idea. For creativity to occur this must be identified in order to permit escape from it.

DEFINE THE PROBLEM: defining a problem exactly may make it easier to solve.

REMOVE THE FAULTS: the assessment of faults and their removal from an idea.

COMBINATION: by examining the attributes of seemingly unrelated items, new items may be created either by fusion or by combination.

REQUIREMENTS: an awareness of requirements may influence the creation of ideas.

EVALUATION: does an idea fit the requirements and what advantages and disadvantages are there?

CoRT V (Information and Feeling)

This section is concerned with the place of information and of feeling in thinking.

INFORMATION–IN—INFORMATION-OUT (FI-FO): the information that is available and the information that is seen to be absent.

FISHING QUESTION—SHOOTING QUESTION (FQ & SQ): skilled use of questions. The difference between shooting questions and fishing questions.

CLUES: clues, deduction and implication. Examination of clues separately and in combination.

CONTRADICTION: false jumps and false conclusions. Contradictions as distinct from false conclusions.

GUESSING: the use of guessing when information is incomplete. The degree of probability in a guess. Small guesses and big guesses.

BELIEF: beliefs based on our own experience and beliefs based on the experience of others. Credibility, proof, certainty, consensus and authority.

READY-MADES: use of pre-packaged ideas, either as a help to thinking or as a substitute for thinking. Stereotypes, cliches, prejudices, standard opinions, *etc.*

EMOTIONS AND EGO: the way emotions are involved in thinking. Usual emotions and ego-emotions (having to be right, face saving, power plays).

VALUES: values determine thinking and the acceptability of the outcome. Appreciation of the actual values involved in the situation rather than trying to change them or impose new ones.

SIMPLIFICATION AND CLARIFICATION: what does it boil down to? What is the situation? What is the thinking about?

CoRT VI (Action)

This section is an action plan or framework which can be used to draw all the previous lessons together into a stage-by-stage structure. Alternatively, it can be used on its own. There is a diagrammatic accompaniment to the thinking so that the structure can be expressed visually.

TARGET: the first step in thinking. Directing attention to the specific matter that is to be the subject of the thinking. The importance of picking out the thinking target in as definite and focused a manner as possible.

EXPAND: having picked out the target, the next step is to expand upon it: in depth, in breadth, in seeking alternatives.

CONTRACT: the third step is to narrow down the expanded thinking to something more tangible and more usable: main points, a summary, a conclusion, a choice or selection.

TARGET-EXPAND-CONTRACT (TEC): the use of all three preceding tools in one sequence. Practice in defining the target, exploring the subject and narrowing down to a usable outcome.

PURPOSE: being clear about the exact purpose of the thinking. With what does one want to end up: a decision, a solution to a problem, an action plan or an opinion? The general purpose of the thinking but also the specific objective.

INPUT: the situation, the scene, the setting, the information available, the factors, the people to be considered: the total input that goes into the thinking.

SOLUTIONS: alternative solutions including the most obvious, the traditional and the new ones. Methods for generating solutions and filling gaps.

CHOICE: the decision process. Choosing between the generated alternatives. Priorities and criteria of choice. Consequences and review of the decision.

OPERATION: implementation. Carrying through the results of the thinking. Setting up the specific action steps that will bring about the desired result. Putting the thinking into effect.

THE FIVE STAGES (TEC-PISCO): using the whole sequence of Purpose-Input-Solutions-Choice-Operation. Consolidation of the total procedure in which the first three tools are used to define and elaborate each of the five stages of the framework.

As mentioned at the beginning, the sections do not have to be used in the given order but it is advisable to start with CoRT I. In some cases, CoRT I can provide a simple basic thinking course on its own. Lessons should not be extracted from a section, since the choice of lessons in a particular section is intended to add up to a coherent whole (one lesson may add to or qualify the effect of another).

CONDUCT OF A CoRT THINKING LESSON

The comments given here refer to the general conduct of CoRT lessons. The detailed conduct varies from one section to another. There is a teachers' handbook for each of the six sections which gives the background for that section and notes on each of the ten lessons. Each pupil has a leaflet which carries a brief explanation of the lesson and the practice items.

EVALUATION

The Schools Council, the official United Kingdom government body for curriculum development, is in the middle of a three-year evaluation on the CoRT program. Ideally, I would like to see how a pupil who had been taught the CoRT materials reacted when faced with a real life situation that required thinking. I would like to see that person pause and then go through some of the scanning processes (PMI, CAF, APC, etc.) before coming to a decision. I would like to see that habit of mind persisting into adult life. Unfortunately, that sort of evaluation is almost impossible to obtain except on an anecdotal basis. We do get reports from teachers and parents regarding how youngsters, who have been exposed to the CoRT program, use the processes in making decisions for themselves (buying a camera, having long tresses cut off, acquiring a pony) and also for their parents. We have reports of nine-year-old children sitting their parents down around the kitchen table and putting them through the CoRT processes when a decision has to be made about buying a car, changing jobs or deciding the type of central heating to install.

Of equal importance is the general change in thinking behavior that is also reported back. For example, when the principal of a secondary school notes that all the pupils from one particular elementary school "seem different and more mature" and it turns out that the school has been using the thinking lessons. Brother Buhagiar in a personal communication from de la Salle College, Malta, reports, "Another case in point which shows the effect of such lessons on the boys is the change which took place in the organization of the various class competitions. Previously, boys would follow the dictates of the class master but for the past two years the boys themselves did all the work and the teacher has been put in the background as the moderator."

Sidney Tyler who was dealing with much younger children reports, "At first-grade level, where lessons are done two or three times each week, children willingly give up play sessions to do them and can be seen working right through recess and open time on a particular drawing or design."

David Lane at the Hungerford Guidance Center, United Kingdom, used the CoRT lessons with children with behavior problems and found an increase in the number of ideas generated; an increase in attention span, persistence when faced with a difficult problem; a longer response rate; generalization of thinking skills to other areas; and a general reduction in impulsive sensory-dominated behavior, both social and cognitive. These results seemed to be stable at three, twelve and, for some aspects, up to twenty-four months after the intervention. Ronnie Shtarkshall at the Hebrew University in Jerusalem reports in a personal communication that he found that the most striking feature when the CoRT lessons were used in teacher training, was the increase in the self-esteem of the teachers. Margaretta Sanchez in Venezuela also reports changes in the pupils' behavior.

In the end, this type of soft data may be the most significant data of all for they reflect thinking in an actual situation rather than in an artificial test. Unfortunately, such data are extremely difficult to measure or assess. Is the effect general or just anecdotal? How subjective is the observer's judgement? Is the difference really significant? What about the Hawthorne effect?

Because of these difficulties, we tend to prefer the convenience of objective tests in which differences can be assessed statistically. David Tripp (1980) points out the drawbacks of such tests which may simply be too insensitive to measure what is going on. We must be aware of the danger of limiting curriculum development through the inadequacy of available testing measures. It is perfectly possible to train pupils to perform better on objective tests, such as IQ tests, but the improved performance on such tests does not necessarily correlate with improved performance in most real-life situations.

I have not yet come across any formal test which adequately tests the skills that the CoRT material sets out to teach. There have been claims by several individuals that as a result of the lessons there has been improvement in IQ scores but I am not entirely happy with these data.

Performance tests seem more appropriate than abstract tests. A pupil who has been exposed to the CoRT material can be asked to perform a thinking task. Practical limitations usually mean that this is an essay-type answer (written or spoken) to some thinking demand. When the sheer production of ideas is measured, the CoRT-trained group in the majority of cases has produced more than the control group. For example, with thirty children in five schools in New Zealand Jack Shallcrass (1977) showed (using Zubin's t for proportional data) that the experimental group had a higher production in all cases (.01 significance level). Many such comparisons have been reported to us by teachers. Raw point scores do not necessarily reflect the use of the idea produced, though they do suggest a broader scan. David Tripp (1977) attempted quite a detailed analysis of discourse in an attempt to tackle this problem. The more detailed the method, however, the more the subjectivity of the judgement (e.g., the category into which a particular point is put) affects the outcome. It has been our policy to allow users of the CoRT material and actual teachers in the classroom to set up their own evaluation procedures. This has the disadvantage that they are sometimes primitive and rarely published in the educational literature. There are, however, compensating advantages because a gradual impression of the effect of the CoRT program builds up from a wide variety of sources. A tight experimental design, set up by the designers of a curriculum project, must always be suspect because of the ideal nature of the conditions, the inevitable bias, and the choice of test measures that have been directly trained. From our point of view, studies such as that by John Edwards and Richard Baldauf Jr. (1982) are of more value.

There is still a great deal to be done in this area of evaluation. For example the spread of skills to other areas (as suggested in the Edwards and Baldauf paper) needs further examination. The United Kingdom Schools Council evaluation now in progress will show whether there is any spread of reading and comprehension skills. Sidney Tyler (1980) claims to have shown that fifty-eight percent of her pupils were working above grade level at the end of the year.

There is a further aspect of evaluation which is too often forgotten. Can the material actually be taught in the classroom by average teachers? Specially trained teachers in a special experimental situation tell nothing about the generalizability of a program. The widespread use of the CoRT material in a variety of countries and cultures across a wide range of ages and abilities is perhaps the best proof of the feasibility of having thinking taught directly in the classroom. The majority of teachers have had little formal training in the material.

SUMMARY

The CoRT Thinking Lessons are designed for practical use in the classroom. The program has been used for several years in different countries across a wide range of ages and abilities. The design is parallel rather than hierarchical. The objective is to provide a curriculum area where thinking gets direct attention as a skill in its own right. The method is that of practicing attention-directing tools on a wide variety of practice items, so that attention stays on the tool, rather than on the subject matter. Skill is developed in the perceptual area of thinking so that a pupil sees more broadly and more clearly and can then react more appropriately. This can be called the spectacles method. An accumulation of observations and data from teachers in the field suggest that the lessons provide an effective framework for the practice of thinking skills.

REFERENCES

de Bono, E. *CoRT Thinking Lessons.* Oxford, U.K.: Pergamon Press.

de Bono, E. *Teaching Thinking.* London: Penguin Books, 1976.

de Bono, E. *The Mechanism of Mind.* London: Penguin Books, 1969.

Edwards, J., and Baldauf, R. Jr. "Teaching Thinking in Secondary Schools," in this volume.

Lane, D. *Teachers Using CoRT.* Cambridge, U.K.: Cognitive Research Trust, 1977.

Tripp, D. *Methods of Evaluation for CoRT Program.* Cambridge, U.K.: Cognitive Research Trust, 1977.

Tripp, D. *The Evaluation of the de Bono (CoRT) Thinking Project.* Cambridge, U.K.: Cognitive Research Trust, 1977.

Tyler, Sidney, Personal communication, 1980.

TEACHING THINKING
IN SECONDARY SCIENCE

John Edwards
Richard B. Baldauf, Jr.

ABSTRACT

There is increasing evidence that suggests that many students do not learn thinking skills through prolonged exposure to a discipline. A pilot study using de Bono's CoRT-1 Thinking Skills program with four grade-ten science classes produced significant learning of thinking skills. These thinking skills also appeared to generalize to the science content areas. These results highlight the potential benefits of the focused teaching of thinking in secondary schools.

Educators seem to assume that prolonged exposure to the study of an academic discipline somehow results in students inducing the underlying thinking skills of the discipline. Science students are expected to acquire "the scientific method," History students "the historical method," English students "the art of criticism," and so on. Exposure to the disciplines is commonly the only pathway offered to mainstream secondary school students for developing the systematic thinking skills they need for further education and for everyday living. A growing body of research in science education shows that this process is not working well.

Edward de Bono argues against our present approaches:

> Perhaps we teach a knowledge subject on the assumption that thinking skills will be developed in the course of our having to deal with the knowledge. If thinking skills are our objective then the by-product approach is not a very effective method, since knowledge has its own internal momentum which makes it difficult to pay attention to, or develop, thinking skills (1976, p. 14).

This paper reports on a pilot study using de Bono's CoRT Thinking Skills materials (Cognitive Research Trust, 1973) with a number of grade-ten secondary science classes. The purpose of the study was to investigate the effectiveness of a focused program for teaching thinking skills. The CoRT materials were introduced in an effort to broaden the thinking of a very able group of boys in a grade-ten secondary science program in Australia.

J. Edwards and R.B. Baldauf, Jr. are in the Department of Education at James Cook University in Australia.

THINKING SKILLS IN SCIENCE

A quick glance through the papers presented to the Australian Science Education Research Association over the past five years shows an increasing awareness of the effects on students of our present secondary science programs.

Typical of these studies is the work of Gunstone and White (1980). They investigated the knowledge of gravity possessed by 468 first-year physics students at Monash University. The results were depressing. While the students "knew a lot of physics," they could not relate it to the everyday world. They were unskilled in seeing which knowledge applied to specific situations. They showed an inability to explain a prediction, and they failed to resolve discrepancies between predictions and observations. Most of these students were the better secondary physics students in the state—the really successful minority. Their shortcomings are likely to be more widely manifest in the less successful majority of students.

Gunstone and White concluded:

> Certainly these first year university students did not show much evidence of some of the unfortunate characteristics observed in eleventh grade physics students in our preliminary study (Champagne, Gunstone and White, 1980), such as confusion of quantities, reification and animism. While this might indicate that the instruction in twelfth grade diminishes these shortcomings, the over-all performance of the participants in this large scale study remains a matter of concern (1980, p. 44).

These results were supported by the findings of Osborne and Gilbert (1980) with New Zealand elementary school students who found that:

> As students gain an understanding of the scientists' view of the world they occasionally get physical quantities confused; they frequently gain superficial knowledge with little or no real underlying understandings; and they sometimes acquire and retain in their language store what appear to be mutually contradictory views without concern (1980).

It was concerns such as these that led to this study. Very able grade eleven and twelve science students at the school involved in the study showed a disturbing lack of ability to apply their scientific knowledge and skills in even moderately novel situations. They showed a lack of confidence, and considerable confusion, and embarrassment when placed in such situations. This occurred despite their high ability levels and the successful completion of four years of what appeared to be a very thorough and well-taught junior secondary science program.

The studies cited above and others like them suggest that today's science students have learned the content of their disciplines reasonably well, but have failed to develop adequate thinking skills. The students in this study seemed to need a program to develop greater divergence of thought, self-confidence in thinking in unusual situations, and problem-attack skills. After reviewing the materials available in the area, de Bono's CoRT-1 materials were selected because they appeared to have the potential to develop these skills in the students.

METHODS

The CoRT-1 Materials

The CoRT-1 Thinking Lessons (Cognitive Research Trust, 1973) are designed to teach thinking skills directly and explicitly, regardless of the content that is used for the students to think about.

The CoRT-1 pack is the first section of a two-year course that has five further packs. Each of the packs focuses on an area of thinking which is covered in ten lessons that make up a term's work. The area covered in CoRT-1 is that of breadth or encouraging pupils to look more widely at a situation instead of in a narrow, egocentric fashion.

The ten lessons in the CoRT-1 pack are each presented on a separate sheet. A brief overview of each sheet is given in *Figure 1*.

Figure 1. CoRT-1 Thinking Lessons: A Brief Overview Adapted from the CoRT-1 Teachers Notes.

Sheet 1:   PMI (plus, minus, interest). This involves looking for the plus points (P), the minus points (M), and the interesting points (I) in any idea. The aim is to enlarge one's view of a situation and to provide a means of by-passing the natural emotional reaction to an idea.

Sheet 2:   CAF (consider all factors). This involves the exploration of a situation before coming up with an idea. The aim is to attempt to be as complete as possible in considering all the factors in any situation.

Sheet 3:   RULES—this provides an opportunity to practice PMI and CAF. PMI is used on an existing or proposed rule. CAF is used when making a rule.

Sheet 4:   C & S (consequence and sequel). This deals with what may happen after a decision is made. Short term (one to five years), medium term (five to twenty-five years) and long term (over twenty-five years) consequences are systematically explored.

Sheet 5:   AGO (aims, goals and objectives). This introduces and emphasizes the idea of purpose. Both aspects—"because" and "in order to"—are investigated.

Sheet 6:   PLANNING—this provides an opportunity to practice C & S and AGO, and to a lesser extent PMI and CAF.

Sheet 7:   FIP (first important priorities). This is a focusing device, directing attention to what is important. This is only done after using the earlier skills to generate as many ideas as possible.

Sheet 8:   APC (alternatives, possibilities and choices). This encourages the student to generate possibilities beyond the obvious and satisfactory ones. It is used as an antidote to emotional reaction or rigid thinking.

Sheet 9:   DECISIONS—this provides an opportunity to practice FIP and APC and, in a general way, the earlier skills.

Sheet 10: OPV (other point of view). This directs attention to other people's point of view. It is used to balance the focus in the earlier sheets on one's own point of view. The possible differences between viewpoints are emphasized.

In teaching each CoRT-1 lesson a general format was followed. First, the particular thinking skill was explained and discussed using an example. Then students attempted three or four practice items, working in small groups of three or four. After each of these activities, a brief whole-class feedback and discussion session was held. Full participation was actively encouraged and comments were made by the teacher on some student's thinking where necessary. A brief whole-class discussion of the particular thinking process followed. The lesson ended with the students choosing, from a list of five principles, the most important aspect of the particular thinking skill. This again led to a whole-class discussion of alternative viewpoints.

Subjects

This study was completed in a large independent school for Australian boys. One hundred and twenty-eight boys were put through the program in five classes (three of twenty-six, and two of twenty-five). There was no ability streaming in the classes, so they represent groups of mixed ability. Of the 128 boys, complete data were obtained for only seventy-two, and these make up the sample covered by the study. Incomplete results occurred because one of the five classes did not undergo equivalent evaluation procedures and because some students were absent at testing times.

Teaching Program

Boys in the grade-ten program were rotated consecutively through five different five-week units, each with a different teacher. The CoRT-1 thinking skills unit was one of these five units. The other four units in the program were introductions to senior chemistry, senior physics, senior biology, and senior geology. The remaining six weeks of the year involved a major science excursion and two short optional courses from a range of four offerings.

The actual teaching time for the CoRT-1 materials was approximately one month, in twenty consecutive science lessons. There were six, fifty-minute science lessons for every eight school days. The method of presentation of the materials was as follows:

Lesson 1:	Introduction to the CoRT-1 program
Lesson 2:	Pre-test
Lessons 3 – 17:	Ten CoRT-1 sheets covered over fifteen lessons (this involved one and a half, fifty-minute lessons for each CoRT-1 sheet, which provided about one hour of productive work-time per sheet)
Lesson 18:	Post-test
Lessons 19 – 20:	Discussion of the program and its application to science

Data Collection

For each of the seventy-two students the following data were gathered:
1. IQ as measured by the ACER Higher Test Form W (administered by the Commonwealth Education Department). The mean IQ score for the seventy-two sample students was 118.2, with a standard deviation of 10.5.
2. A pre-test consisting of two essays. Both topics were taken from the CoRT-1 teachers notes. One was on a familiar topic to the students: "Should pupils have

a say in making school rules?'' The other was on an unfamiliar topic: ''A man is found to have stolen a huge pile of left shoes. What do you think he is up to?''

3. A post-test consisting of the same two essays.
4. Each student was asked to make a brief, written comment on the thinking skills course. This was an optional requirement and was done immediately after the post-test.
5. The students submitted their homework which consisted of one essay topic on each CoRT sheet. These were chosen from the suggested project topics on the back of each CoRT sheet.
6. The grades the students obtained on their end-of-year science examination. A one-to-ten scale was used, with ten being the highest grade.

A standard science examination was used covering physics, chemistry, biology, and geology topics, consisting of seventeen multiple-choice questions, ten two-line answer questions, six five-line answers and three one-page essays. The questions were spread mainly across the three lower levels of Bloom's taxonomy: knowledge, comprehension and application. There were no specific questions on the thinking skills material, although the skills could have been directly applied on one of the optional essay questions.

Data Quantification

A major problem in this study was how to quantify the data in a meaningful way. As no comparable studies could be found in the literature which quantified CoRT results, it was necessary to develop a set of scales for the study.

For the pre- and post-test on ''school rules,'' three scales were used:
(a) *Number of discrete ideas.* These could be opinions or points raised to justify or support an opinion.
(b) *Quality of ideas.* This was rated on a five-point scale (1–5).
   5 –required both a revealed awareness of a range of views and convincing support or justification of the position taken;
   4 –required either one of the above (in 5);
   3 –required a limited awareness of alternative views and an attempt to support the position taken;
   2 –required either one of the above (in 3); and
   1 –required neither of the above.
(c) *Structure of response.* This was rated on a three-point scale (1–3).
   3 –required a sequenced, organized, tight, coherent, clear answer;
   2 –required some structure but some blemishes; and
   1 –was a poorly-structured, rambling, internally-inconsistent answer.

For the pre- and post-tests on ''left shoes'' two scales were used:
(a) *The number of discrete ideas.*
(b) *The novelty of the ideas.* These were rated on a three-point scale (1–3).
   3 –highly original, unusual ideas as a whole;
   2 –one or two moderately unusual ideas, mixed in with common ideas; and
   1 –very common ideas only, showing little imagination.

For the attitudes to the course two scales were used:
(a) *Overall attitude to the program,* rated on a seven-point scale (0–6).
   6 –very positive supported view;
   5 –positive, such as ''good course,'' ''helped me develop thinking skills;''
   4 –lukewarm, such as ''helped a bit,'' ''of some benefit,''

3 –above it all, such as "not really necessary for me," "reinforced what I already had;"

2 –cool, such as "wasn't a complete waste of time," "don't think it's that great," "hasn't done me much good;"

1 –negative such as "spoiled my thinking;" and

0 –no comment.

(b) *Attitude towards the effect of the course on their thinking,* rated on a seven-point scale (0–6).

6 –very positive supported view outlining real specific benefits, such as "in recent tests I think harder and faster;"

5 –positive but general, such as "expanded my thinking," "helped me to think differently;"

4 –lukewarm or neutral, such as "didn't make much difference;"

3 –above it all, such as "most people have these skills anyway;"

2 –cool, such as "you can't really teach people to think," "don't think it changed my thinking process;"

1 –negative, such as "I now think more illogically," "has interfered with my thinking;" and

0 –no comment.

The homework was assessed on two scales. First, it was assessed on the total number of pages submitted. Second, it was incorporated into an overall mark for the unit. This was arrived at using four of de Bono's criteria, as listed in the CoRT-1 teachers notes, together with a mark for class work. The percentage mark was arrived at as follows:

Twenty marks for comprehension:	have the main points been covered?
Twenty marks for organization:	is it well-structured and clear?
Twenty marks for interest:	for novel and interesting ideas that are relevant.
Twenty marks for opinion:	how convincingly is the point of view expressed?
Twenty marks for classwork:	quality of contributions in class throughout the unit.

RESULTS

An initial hypothesis was that group differences might exist because the design of the study meant that the different groups of students did the CoRT-1 unit sequentially. This created a differing time period between the completion of the unit and the end-of-year exam. An analysis of variance of final-exam results across the four groups found no significant trend for the four class groups on the end-of-year science exam. Further analyses revealed that the four classes of students did not differ significantly by IQ on the ACER Higher Test Form W, nor were there any significant differences between the four classes on their overall assessment on the CoRT-1 materials. The means and consequent F values (see *Table 1*) indicated that group differences were non-significant and could henceforth be ignored.

A second question was whether the CoRT-1 program had a positive effect on student thinking skills. The short-term nature of the treatment led to a concern that it would be difficult to pick up significant changes using general assessment measures. Five measures of change (outlined earlier) were available from the "school rules"

Table 1. Analysis of Variance by Class for Science Exam, CoRT and IQ Scores

Test	Means				
	Class 1	Class 2	Class 3	Class 4	F*
Science Exam	7.44	6.95	7.05	7.18	0.229
ACER IQ	120.4	116.4	116.9	119.5	0.596
CoRT Mark	68.4	66.4	62.6	66.6	1.746

* All F values (3 and 68 *df*) were non-significant

Note: Readers not familiar with the statistical procedures used in this study can refer to Huck, Cormier and Bounds (1974)

and "left shoes" pre- and post-tests. These were analyzed, using a repeated measures analysis of variance with groups used as a blocking variable. As *Table 2* indicates, all five measures indicated there had been a statistically significant change from pre- to post-test on thinking skills.

Table 2. Analysis of Variance[1] Results for Thinking Skills Five Measures

Change Measure	Pre $\overline{X}$	Pre SD	Post $\overline{X}$	Post SD	F
School Rules					
Number of Ideas	6.97	2.37	11.11	4.77	74.24*
Quality Rating	3.06	0.97	3.85	0.95	77.89*
Structure Rating	2.07	0.69	2.50	0.61	33.90*
Left Shoes					
Number of Ideas	4.07	2.52	9.63	5.68	84.67*
Novelty Rating	1.26	0.55	1.61	0.72	15.93*

*p < .001 (d.f. = 1,68)

1. See Veldman (1968, p.247ff.)

While there is no generally accepted criterion for deciding whether a gain is large enough to be considered educationally significant, with standardized tests Horst, Tallmadge, and Wood (1974, p. 69) suggest one-third of a standard deviation as a reasonable *rule of thumb* cut-off value. While these gains were not made on standardized tests, the size of the gains of between .50 and 2.20 of the pre-test standard deviation, certainly suggests that educationally significant learning has occurred. Anecdotal data from both science teachers and other subject teachers strongly supported this indication.

Another question investigated was the relationship between thinking skills and intelligence. Certainly from the comments some of the more intelligent students made (*e.g.,* "the course is not really necessary for me, but should be helpful for other pupils") it would appear that the students themselves believed there might be some relationship. However, while IQ correlated .39 (p < .01) with CoRT-1 unit results, the "left shoes" novelty measure (r = .30, p < .01) was the only gain score measure found to correlate significantly with IQ. These correlations suggest that there is either no relationship or a limited relationship, between IQ and the development of CoRT thinking skills, at least with above average IQ students.

The final question investigated was the relationship between achievement on the CoRT-1 materials and end-of-year science results, when student IQ is controlled. As *Table 3* indicates, there was a statistically significant relationship between CoRT unit results and end-of-year science results, even when these results were first controlled for IQ. Since the science results were based on a content and process-oriented science test, the covariance analysis suggests that students have learned some generalizable skills from the CoRT-1 unit.

Table 3. One Way Analysis of Covariance for Science Results

Source	SS	df	MS	F
CoRT Result	39.83	2	19.92	10.11*
Error	134.17	68	1.97	
Total	174.01	70		

*p < .001

CoRT Result		N	$\overline{X}_{IQ}$	Science Results $\overline{X}_{Obtained}$	$\overline{X}_{Adjusted}$
Low	50–61	25	114	5.88	6.12
Mid	62–69	26	117	7.27	7.33
High	70–86	21	125	8.48	8.12

DISCUSSION AND CONCLUSIONS

Student reaction to the CoRT-1 course was positive. Forty-eight of the fifty-nine respondents rated the course at four or better on the six-point scale. Thirty-four of the forty-two respondents rated the effect on their thinking as four or better on the six-point scale. These ratings were in keeping with the opinion of the teacher that the unit was effective. In particular, students showed greater self-confidence with their thinking, especially in less familiar situations. The other teachers taking the students in the units following the CoRT-1 course frequently commented on the great improvements in thinking resulting from the course. Teachers in other subject areas also commented favorably on the effect on certain students, particularly the less able and less organized students.

These anecdotal comments support the empirical results which show that the unit had a positive effect on student thinking and that the unit's effects were probably generalizable. The program was introduced to broaden students' thinking, which it did very successfully. While the effects, as measured, are short-term, the size and apparent scope of the gains is very impressive for such a short intervention.

These gains highlight a major problem of design in this study. The program was a pilot project to investigate the effectiveness of the CoRT-1 course, while causing as little disruption as possible to the usual grade-ten science program. This meant that it was not possible to set up an ideal experimental situation. Use of a control group and a delayed post-test would have helped to identify a range of other important factors, such as test-treatment interactions and differential effects of the CoRT-1 program and alternative science programs. It would have also allowed a closer study of effects on student thinking over time.

For many, the finding that IQ was not highly correlated with improvement would be surprising. It should be remembered, however, that this was an above average group of boys, so generalization from this finding would be unwarranted. Even so, it ought to be an encouraging finding for those who are considering general introduction of a program such as this.

Development and validation of reliable scales for quantifying achievement in programs such as these ought to be given high priority. The guidelines given in the CoRT teachers notes do not facilitate such quantification. Similarly, a search of the literature revealed no scales suitable for assessing the impact of such a program. It is hoped that the scales developed for this pilot study will point out this need and help towards developing some useful measures.

The strong correlation between CoRT-1 score and end-of-year examination result ($r = .62$, $p < .001$) suggests that the thinking skills, as taught by this CoRT-1 program, had a beneficial effect on science performance. This is made even more powerful by the lack of direct content overlap between the CoRT-1 program and the grade-ten science course as a whole, as reflected in the examination. This indication ought to be the basis for further research, but, again, it is a highly encouraging result for those seeing great potential in such programs.

In summary, a pilot study that taught CoRT-1 materials to seventy-two tenth-grade science students indicated that the program had improved students' thinking skills and that these skills seemed to generalize to overall science performance. While a lot more research in this area needs to be done, these results suggest it may be possible to help students develop the thinking skills they need to be scientific thinkers, and not just students who know science.

REFERENCES

Champagne, A.B., Gunstone, R.F. and White, R.T. *Knowledge of Basic Principles of Dynamics.* Clayton, Victoria, Australia: Monash University, 1980.

Cognitive Research Trust. *CoRT Thinking Lessons, CoRT-1.* Sydney: Direct Education Services Ltd., 1973.

de Bono, E. *Teaching Thinking.* London: Maurice Temple Smith, 1976.

Gunstone, R.F. and White, R.T. "A Matter of Gravity," *Research in Science Education,* 1980, *10,* 35–44.

Horst, D.P., Tallmadge, G.K. and Wood, C.T. *Measuring Achievement Gains in Educational Projects* (RMC Report UR-243, prepared for U.S.D.H.E.W.). Los Altos, CA: RMC Corporation, 1974.

Huck, S.W., Cormier, W.H. and Bounds, W.G. Jr. *Reading Statistics and Research.* New York: Harper and Row, 1974.

Osborne, R.J. and Gilbert, J.K. "A Technique for Exploring Students' Views of the World." Working paper: Learning in Science Project, University of Waikato, Hamilton, N.Z., 1980.

Veldman, D. *Fortran Programming for the Behavioral Sciences.* Englewood Cliffs, NJ: Holt, Rinehart and Winston, 1968.

A TOP-DOWN APPROACH TO THE TEACHING OF REASONING SKILLS

Roderic A. Girle

ABSTRACT

The usual approach in teaching reasoning skills to university and upper secondary school students concentrates on detail at the expense of context. This leads to a highly negative attitude to reasoning and argument. It is argued that a contextual approach, based on the notion of *dialogue* will be both positive and practical. A course is outlined.

INTRODUCTION

Several authors have told us of various kinds of shock we are likely to suffer—future shock, culture shock and the shock of the new—but I find myself suffering from a different kind of shock, especially after marking some thousands of logic and critical reasoning examination papers. It is a fallacy shock.

After searching the weeklies and the dailies for a long while, I find what seems to be a sensible, balanced, well-argued article or editorial (a rare gem) but when students see it, they act as if they had been presented with the ravings of a lunatic. The student manifests the worst case of spots (spot-the-fallacy) and feverishly utters all the "ad" phrases (see below). So the chosen article or editorial is accused of every known fallacy; and there are so many available. As Hamblin writes, they are:

> ...known as the *argumentum ad hominen,* the *argumentum ad verecundian, the argumentum ad misericordiam* and the *argumenta ad ignorantiam, populum, baculum, passiones, superstitionem, imaginationem, invidiam* (envy), *crumenam* (purse), *quietem* (repose, conservatism), *metum* (fear), *fidem* (faith), *socordiam* (weak-mindedness), *superbiam* (pride), *odium* (hatred), *amicitiam* (friendship), *ludicrum* (dramatics), *captandum vulgus* (playing to the gallery), *fulmen* (thunderbolt), *vertiginem* (dizziness) and *a carcere* (from prison). We feel like adding: *ad nauseam* (Hamblin, 1970. p. 41).

This student disease of spot-the-fallacy is, it seems to me, one manifestation of a malaise which lies at the heart of the present teaching of reasoning skills, and of

---

R.A. Girle is Head of the Department of Philosophy at the University of Queensland in St. Lucia, Australia.

many of the popular texts in logic and reasoning. Although there is a great deal of good material in these texts and in courses in reasoning, there is an unfortunate preoccupation with detail. There is a heavy emphasis on fine grain analysis and an absence of overall context.

We follow in the tradition of Aristotle. Like Aristotelians down the centuries, we first consider the fallacies of language, then the fallacies of relevance, then the formal fallacies. We begin with words and sentences, the finest-grained detail. We consider ambiguity of words and sentences, equivocation and accent. We look at definition—stipulative and reportive, ostensive and verbal—and so on. It is no wonder that students also begin by looking at details.

Then we consider the relevance of one proposition to another, generally in the framework of the logician's standard argument form: *Premises ∴ Conclusion.* Putting arguments into standard form also tends to dissect them, and isolate them from context.

Then, and often finally, we look at whether the standardized argument embodies a deductive or an inductive claim, and check out that claim. Even here, a valid argument can turn out to be unsound or question begging, an explanation vacuous, an analogy imperfect. Context is ignored.

The Bottom-up Spectrum

In this paper I will use the phrase "bottom-up" to indicate an approach which begins with detail and works up to more complex structures. It is my claim that most courses and texts in reasoning follow a bottom-up approach to the teaching of reasoning skills.

Overall, the students are taught to look at arguments in isolation and to distrust arguments because of detail. Most text books are in a bottom-up spectrum: they follow the Aristotelian tradition of moving from words up to standardized arguments. The examples used in most texts are oriented to standardized forms. There are short passages, short letters to the editor, ten-line summaries of extended arguments. If you consider that gold mine of problems for formal logic courses, Pospesel & Marans' *Arguments* (1979), you will find that nearly all the examples are condensed and out of context. Some texts try to distill arguments out of ads in newspapers or on television. These are all fine-grained, out-of-context cases. They are, of course, easier by far to find and present to students than longer arguments set out in context.

The irony is that out-of-context short arguments are very difficult to assess for the so-called informal fallacies. Yet, I sighted recently a book of 573 cases of out-of-context short arguments (Engel, 1980). Every one of these was claimed to be fallacious.

If you look at texts, you will see that most of them are in a spectrum which ranges from symbolic systems at one end, to systematic nonsymbolic analysis at the other end. Some people see this as a spectrum which goes from the formal to the informal. I prefer to describe it as a spectrum which goes from the pure to the applied. At the pure symbolic logic end we have texts like *Formal Logic: Its Scope and Limits* by R.C. Jeffrey (1967), or *The Logic Book* by Bergmann Moor and Nelson (1980), or *Natural Deduction* by Anderson and Johnson (1962). Fallacies of language and relevance are ignored. At the other end of the spectrum we have books like *An Introduction to Reasoning* by Toulmin, Ricke and Janik (1979), or *Reasoning* by Scriven (1976), or *Thinking about Thinking* by Flew (1975). In the middle of the spectrum we have *the* book of introductory books, Copi's *Introduction to Logic* (1972). Others in the center, as it were, are Carney and

Scheer (1980) and Baum (1981). In Copi, we have the three themes: fallacies of language, fallacies of relevance, and formal systems.

Within this spectrum we can argue about the merits of various texts, and of various areas *in* the spectrum. Some students love symbols and formalities; we know what texts are likely to interest them. Some students are symbol-haters, somewhere in their past is a traumatic two-times table; they must be protected from symbols. And so on.

PROBLEMS WITH THE BOTTOM-UP APPROACH

I want to question the whole spectrum of bottom-up analysis and instruction in reasoning, whether it is pure or applied, symbolic or nonsymbolic. Above all, I want to question the bottom-up approach, not simply because it's bottom-up, but because of its consequences and because of its pedagogic presuppositions, or lack of them.

The main worrying consequences, as I see them, are first the negative attitude to argument, and second the impracticality of the bottom-up approach. The negative attitude manifests itself in many ways. Two are worth noting. There is the whole spot-the-mistake syndrome, about which I have already had something to say. There is also a view that reasoned argument gets us nowhere, since we can always find a fallacy in the best of cases. This latter negative view of reasoned argument and sound reasoning has been analyzed in an excellent article, "Attitudes to Reasoning" by Tom Richards (1979). He writes:

> It seems to my observation that there is an attitude to reasoning that is the root of a great political and social malaise in our society. It is that the activity of critical reasoning ends when one has become clear about what others are saying and what their reasons are for saying it. From that point on there is no role for reasoning, since we are dealing with opinions and not with facts. Opinions are to be judged by whether they are sensitive, sympathetic, and based on a cultured interpretation of the background and lifestyle of their holders; in short by whether they issue from a heart informed by empathetic understanding. But opinions are not to be judged by their truth or falsity, correctness or incorrectness, their internal and external consistency, the resilience and strength of arguments in support and against, or the acceptability of their presuppositions (Richards, 1979, p. 2).

Richards points out that this empathetic approach to belief is most unfortunate because it denies the place of reasoning, but reasoning leads us towards the discovery of truth, even when the subject of discussion is an opinion. Reasoning should lead to the evaluation and creation of explanations, the forming of new concepts and the modifying of old ones. Reasoning should lead to the considered alteration of opinions in the light of truth and facts.

Unfortunately, if reasoning is not only seen in a negative way but also taught as a negative method, then it will be no surprise if people resort to irrational approaches to opinion.

The impracticality of the bottom-up approach becomes clear when we acknowledge that many, if not all, arguments are met in context. I have always found the most interesting and useful sections of Copi, and Carney and Scheer, to be those where there are the accounts of the development of explanations. I believe that the interest here is because the accounts are extended. The reality of what went on becomes clear; there is a context. Sometimes we see two rival explanations and hear how their respective merits were argued. Above all, we meet arguments in an interactive context.

In what follows I shall use the term *dialogue* to cover a wide range of interactive arguments and discussion ranging from head-on dispute, through the Socratic type of "leading-someone-on" dialogue, to the open, amicable discussion. The important practical point is that most reasoning is found in an interactive context. Even when someone develops an argument in the narrowest sense, it will be tried out on others to see what the response is. Even lengthy papers in academic journals are in a context, and part of an ongoing discussion. Too many logic text books disqualify themselves from the analysis of the to and fro of argument and discussion. A quote from one text reads: " By argument we do not mean verbal quarrels, even though this may be the first thing that comes to mind when we mention arguments" (Rennie and Girle, 1973, p. 3). At once, the analysis of much argument is divorced from the practical situation.

When we turn to look at the assumptions behind what is taught in reasoning courses, we often find a vast emptiness. There is no realistic assessment of student needs or abilities, or the goals for their work. If we are properly to consider the *teaching* of reasoning skills, we need to begin with a realistic assessment of where the students are, educationally, when they enter a logic or critical reasoning course. In the Australian scene, the vast bulk of students come to these courses in the upper level of secondary school, or at the tertiary level.

What are these students dealing with in other subjects? Well, they are not dealing with short arguments out of context. They deal with novels, histories, social science experiments and theories, mathematical proofs of up to a page or more, even Descartes' *Meditations*. Many of the arguments with which students deal are extended, very extended. But students are also involved in dialogue with other people, in tutorials, in the butcher shop, at home, and at parties. In these dialogues they discuss all these sorts of things. Students are constantly arguing, discussing, pooling ideas.

Remedial Reasoning

In this context we should, perhaps, be thinking in terms, not of critical reasoning, but of *remedial* reasoning. Remedial reasoning will involve not only the fine-grained particulars but also more general considerations such as paraphrasing, the study of questions and answers, detecting unspoken assumptions, detecting the implicit argument, and understanding the notion of onus of proof. Explanation, theory, analogy, and the use of typical cases will all have to be considered.

One important fact about most remedial reasoning courses for teenagers and adults is that there is little time. So decisions have to be made about how to spend the time. It is not possible in most courses to encompass the detailed study of both dialogue and fine-grained analysis.

Given the educational level of students in most reasoning classes, given also their actual intellectual activities and practical concerns, and given the very limited time available, I want to argue that reasoning should be taught in the framework of an analysis and understanding of dialogue. In that framework, fine-grain analysis has an appropriate place, but does not dominate. It might be the case that were reasoning to be taught a lot earlier in the educational process, that fine-grain analysis might be emphasized. Shorter arguments might be more appropriate to grades one, two and three. Even in the pure logics, things like truth-tables are more suited to primary school rather than to the University.

DIALOGUE AND FORMAL DIALECTIC

If we are to begin with the study of dialogue, then we will begin with context and work down to detail. This sort of approach can be called *top-down*. The theoretical background to much of my critique and the strategy I am advocating is to be found in the work of those logicians who have been looking at dialogue. The formal study is *Formal Dialectic;* one of the key texts is C.L. Hamblin's book *Fallacies* (1970).

Students should be taught not only how to operate with intuitive skill in the interactive context, but they should also learn how to analyze what is going on. They should be able to recognize the principal activities, and so on. This is especially so when it comes to dialogue. Dialogue is often held out as a way into reasoning and learning, but analysis of dialogue is mostly absent. For example, in their book, *Philosophy in the Classroom,* Lipman *et. al.* (1980) have a great deal to say about teaching, thinking and reasoning. I don't want to recapitulate what they say, much of which is excellent, but there is one interesting feature of the book. In the preface the authors set out a model for thinking and reasoning. The model is Socrates. They point to four things about Socrates which they heartily approve, even advocate. First, Socrates shows us how to think by doing it. Secondly, Socrates focuses our attention on the practical question of our own life. Thirdly, Socrates engages people in dialogue. Fourthly, by means of dialogue beliefs are tested. Although the authors go on to declare that "one of the best ways of stimulating people to think is to engage them in dialogue," (p. xv) and although they recount with enthusiasm some dialogues in which children were encouraged to reason out loud and to draw sound conclusions, the book does not really have any analysis of dialogue, or any material which would help children understand what goes on in dialogue. There is simply the unwritten hope that dialogue will be used effectively.

Indeed, one of the examples given in Lipman, Sharp and Oscanyan (1980, p. 70) can only be described as a case of a teacher manipulating a child into a corner. The child might have been in a better position to resist the manipulation had he known what was going on. The same might also be said of many of those who were led on by Socrates.

It is important, at this stage, to indicate some of the theoretical points which are made about dialogue in the formal study of it. In any dialogue there are at least five kinds of speech acts made by the participants. They are:

1. making a statement
2. withdrawing a statement
3. questioning whether a statement is true or not
4. challenging a statement (Why?)
5. asking for a resolution of some problem, or inconsistency.

The contrast between *1* and *2* indicates that dialogue leaves the participants open to a change of mind. Revising and changing opinions is a vital part of dialogue in every day life. The contrast between *3* and *4* is essentially the contrast between seeking clarification *3,* and asking for reasons *4.*

In any dialogue each participant has a *commitment store.* This is a set of beliefs or propositions to which that participant adheres. The store can be changed by drawing new conclusions, withdrawing propositions, making statements and resolving problems and inconsistencies.

The traditional approach to reasoning skills focuses most of its attention on answers to *4* only. The standard argument form gives us a proposition (conclusion) with the reasons for it (premises). We then look at the extent to which those premises give the claimed support for that conclusion.

If we take seriously these wider features of dialogue, features highlighted by theoretical study, then we will need to look carefully at topics such as the asking and answering of questions, the nature of inconsistency, and when to withdraw assertions, hypotheses and definitions.

It could also be noted that these theoretical points do not presuppose any particular form of dialogue. Although these points do apply to the adversary or courtroom dialogue, they also apply to any open discussion which involves the sharing of ideas, brainstorming or problem solving. (For a more detailed treatment of dialogue, see Girle, *et al.* [1978]).

TOWARDS A COURSE IN REASONING

Given the theoretical material about dialogue set out above, we can now turn to the practical question of teaching a reasoning course. In what follows, I will sketch out the sort of questions which a student would be advised to ask when faced with a dialogue. These questions will indicate the outlines of a course in reasoning.

In order to give some focus to the appraisal of a dialogue, it is best to begin with one contribution by one of the participants. At first, there should be the placing of that contribution in context. This should be followed by an assessment of the worth of the contribution to the dialogue. The first three questions will assist in placing the participant's contribution in context.

First: What is the general area of debate or argument?
There should not be too quick or narrow a focus at this point. Students should simply place the debate in some general area such as "the value of television" or "the philosophy of mind" or "politics" or "the dangers of smoking."

Second: What is the participant doing?
In terms of theory, is the participant asserting something, withdrawing (or qualifying) a statement, asking for clarification, asking for reasons, or posing some problem?
In general, we have here the two roles: the proponent role and the questioner role. In what follows, I will use the term "proponent" to refer to a participant in a dialogue who is asserting or contesting a point. The term "questioner" will be used to refer to a participant who is asking a question.

Third for a proponent: If the participant is a proponent, is the proponent withdrawing, contesting, or supporting a point?
If the proponent is withdrawing a point, to what is the withdrawal a response?
If the proponent is contesting a point, then the student should say who made that point earlier, or whether the proponent set it up to contest it, for example, by a locution such as "some people say."
If the proponent is supporting a point, is it a point made by someone else or by the proponent?

Third for a questioner: If the participant is a questioner, to whom is the question directed? What sort of a question is it? Is it for clarification or for reasons, or posing a problem case?
The next six questions are to be asked if the participant has been acting as a proponent. In a sense, these questions also help place the proponent's contributions in context, but they also give more detail about its content.

Fourth: How does the proponent contest or support the point?

This question can be given more detail by consideration of the following sub-questions concerning attack and support. Does the proponent attack (support):

  a. the credibility or authoritativeness of anyone?
  b. the truth or relevance of any general theory?
  c. the correctness or relevance of any evidence?
  d. the coherence of any views?
  e. the quality of any reasoning?
  f. the adequacy of any argument?

Fifth: Does the proponent have a view as to the onus of proof?

The matter of onus of proof is very important in the dialogue situation. There should be careful discussion with students of the whole notion of onus of proof. Use can be made of the typical courtroom situation. But it should also be noted how onus of proof can change in the course of a debate. Above all, it is important to assess what the proponent declares or assumes concerning onus of proof.

The first questions can be asked and answered without very much assessment on the way. The whole idea is to get an idea of the state of play, that is, the area of debate, the role of the participant or participants and the nature of their contribution to the dialogue. It may be necessary at this point to look at more than one participant in some detail.

At the next stage we go on to assessment. First, I will set out questions to be asked in assessing a proponent's contribution to a dialogue.

Sixth: What in particular does the proponent want to establish?

Here we need to establish both the main points being argued for and their nature. Are they theories, or simple negatives of what is being contested, or the contrary of what is being contested, or points of logic, or explanations, or what?

Seventh: Will these points do what was intended?

Will such points support or contest the points to be so addressed? At this stage it may be necessary to go back to the dialogue and look at some other proponent's contribution. One important subquestion will be: Is the debate to the point or at cross purposes?

The whole question of being at cross purposes is, like the question of onus of proof, quite vital in dialogue. Two of the traditional fallacies, the straw man and false contrast, are appropriate here.

Eighth: Ask about detail.

I think that here we come to the traditional questions of:

  a. clarification of the point at issue,
  b. whether the argument is inductive or deductive,
  c. does the argument establish its point in the appropriate way?

Finally: How would you have contested the point or supported the point?

The analysis and assessment of a proponent's contribution to a dialogue can be entirely negative. It is important to get students to produce contributions themselves. Otherwise we teach, not reasoning skills, but meta-reasoning skills.

If we are considering in detail what a questioner has asked, then the following are the questions which could be asked.

What sorts of answers would satisfy the question?

For some questions there is no reasonable answer. The so-called ''fallacy'' complex question is really one sort of unreasonable question. But there are others such as, ''Why do you believe you have a toothache?'' If we look at the sorts of answers which could be given, we will soon see whether or not the question is reasonable.

If the question is reasonable to answer, is it pertinent?
What, if any, would be a better question?

In asking these questions of either a proponent or a questioner, it is vital to refer back to the wider dialogue again and again. It will also become clear that some of the traditional informal fallacies can be made more sense of in this sort of dialogue analysis. But above all, students should be encouraged to construct contributions, either by way of question or statements, in order to gain a clearer understanding of how dialogue procedes.

CONCLUSION

The sketch that I have given indicates the content of a course in reasoning. The questions are the principal questions that students should ask when considering a debate or discussion. A good reasoning course will show students what answers are appropriate, and how to evaluate argument in the light of these questions and answers.

Such a course in reasoning, focusing as it does on discussion and argument, has two major advantages over the more usual bottom-up course. The first advantage is that students will be shown a way of looking at reasoning which is more closely related to practical realities. They should be able to see argument in a broad setting, and assess the several moves made by participants from the point of view of interaction, as well as in terms of the traditional notions of definition, validity and fallacy.

The second advantage is that this approach should lead to a more positive attitude to reasoning. Argument should be seen not in terms of just a set piece which is either valid or fallacious, but in terms of an ongoing process. Students can then see that it is in such an ongoing process that good argument can be vindicated, poor argument revealed, opinions changed, and the search for truth can proceed.

REFERENCES

Anderson, J.M. and Johnson, H.W. *Natural Deduction.* Belmont, CA: Wadsworth, Inc., 1962.

Aristotle. *Categories, On Interpretation, Prior Analytics.* H.P. Cooke and H. Tredennick (Tr.) London: Heinmann, 1973.

Baum, R. and Wieck, D.T. *Logic,* 2nd ed. New York: Holt, Rinehart and Winston, 1981.

Bergmann, M. Moor, J. and Nelson, J. *The Logic Book.* New York: Random House, Inc., 1980.

Carney, J.D. and Scheer, R.K. *Fundamentals of Logic,* 3rd ed. New York: Macmillan, Inc., 1980.

Copi, I. *Introduction to Logic,* 4th ed. New York: Macmillan, Inc., 1972.

Engel, S. Morris. *Analyzing Informal Fallacies.* Englewood Cliffs, NJ: Prentice-Hall, Inc., 1980.

Flew, A. *Thinking About Thinking.* Glasgow: Fontana, 1975.

Girle, R.A., Halpin, T.A., Miller, C.L. and Williams, G.H. *Inductive and Practical Reasoning.* East Brisbane, Queensland, Australia: Rotecoge, 1978.

Hamblin, C.L. *Fallacies.* New York: Methuen Inc., 1970.

Jeffrey, R.C. *Formal Logic: Its Scope and Limits.* New York: McGraw-Hill Inc., 1967.

Lipman, M., Sharp, A.M. and Oscanyan, F.S. *Philosophy in the Classroom,* 2nd ed. Philadelphia: Temple University Press, 1980.

MacKenzie, J. "Question Begging in Non-Cumulative Systems," *Journal of Philosophical Logic,* Vol. No. 8, 1979.

Pospesel, H. and Marans, D. *Arguments: Deductive Logic Exercises,* 2nd ed. Englewood Cliffs, NJ: Prentice-Hall, Inc., 1979.

Rennie, M.K. and Girle, R.A. *Logic: Theory and Practice.* St. Lucia, Australia: University of Queensland Press, 1973.

Richards, T.J. "Attitudes to Reasoning," *Australian Logic Teachers Journal,* 1979, *4* (1).

EDUCATING FOR CREATIVITY: A HOLISTIC APPROACH

Delores Gallo

ABSTRACT

Can the creative performance of teachers be increased? Can this increase be achieved through a single semester program? Will the program result in perceptible changes in the teachers' creative problem-solving, classroom practice? Will their students display increased creative performance? This paper begins with a brief review of the literature addressing these questions. It then focuses on my work with teachers in a program designed to enhance the creativity of their problem-solving and classroom practice.

In this last quarter of the twentieth century, we are confronted by innumerable and complex problems, problems that require not only rapid but imaginative solutions. Those who will invent the future solutions are now in our elementary and secondary schools. Clearly, the schools must allow the creative imaginations of their students to develop. But can and will the school environment permit and foster this creative growth?

Recent research, most notably that of Torrance (1965), and MacKinnon (1966), supports the traditional view that teachers with creative motivation—the conscious valuing of creative thinking and the drive to engage in it—do have a positive effect on the creative growth and productions of their students. In fact, the research indicates that the teacher, most importantly by the climate he ingenders and the attitude he projects, has a more significant influence on creative development than specific materials or methods do. Curriculum materials designed to foster creativity fail to achieve their objectives when used by teachers without creative motivation (Torrance, 1965). It is, therefore, discouraging to read Torrance's assessment of teacher behavior. He reported that as recently as the last decade, fewer than half of the teachers studied prossessed creative motivation. Furthermore, many of those who describe themselves as and believe themselves to be, creatively motivated (*e.g.*, who volunteer for in-service workshops on promoting creativity in the classroom), are unable to apply the principles of creative teaching to which they have been exposed.

D. Gallo is Co-Director of the Critical and Creative Thinking Graduate Program at the University of Massachùsetts in Boston.

It would seem then that schools are doomed to perpetuate dullness, unless we can help teachers to change. Teacher education must foster not only an awareness of creativity-related concepts and principles but an ability in teachers to incorporate those principles into their own personalities and behavior. Such an effort must consider all of the factors contributing to creative production and address the development of not only the cognitive skills but also the personality traits and attitudes relevant to creative performance.

We shall need an expanded conception of the creative process if this effort is to succeed. I shall begin by offering a holistic conception of the creative process. Then I shall describe the Critical and Creative Thinking Program at the University of Massachusetts at Boston, which is based on this conception, reporting briefly on its progress to date and directions for the future.

CREATIVE THINKING:
MOVING TOWARDS AN OPERATIONAL DEFINITION

Even if we conceive of creative thinking as a wholly cognitive act, the creative process poses serious problems for definition and study. Like almost all intellectual tasks, creative thinking involves a number of different cognitive processes. One prevalent view suggests that at least two processes are involved: divergent and convergent thinking. Convergent thinking is characterized by an ability to focus one's thoughts on factors relevant to the given situation; it moves toward a single, uniquely determined response, highly dependent upon the reproduction of the previously learned and upon the categorization of new experiences as examples of familiar ones. This process, also called logical problem solving, is the behavior evaluated by intelligence tests.

Divergent thinking is less direct and appears less directly measurable, although it is the process that tests of creativity purport to assess. Divergent thinking invokes the capacity to range flexibly in the search for factors relevant to a specific task; it leads to large numbers of varied responses and to the generation of new ideas and "logical possibilities."

The above descriptions are somewhat deceptive because they imply that "creative thinking" is the equivalent of divergent thinking and, is, therefore, the discrete opposite of rational thought. Guilford (1959) cautioned that although "we might arbitrarily define creative thinking as divergent thinking, it would be incorrect to say that divergent thinking accounts for all the intellective components of creative production" (p. 160).

The nature of the creative process may, therefore, be even more complex and subjective than other intellectual tasks. Barron notes (1969), "The creative process embodies an incessant dialectic between integration and diffusion, convergence and divergence, thesis and antithesis" (p. 112). This dialectical pattern in creative thinking makes it especially difficult to determine the proportion and interaction of the contributing processes.

Information-processing theory attempts to explain the substructure of these processes and interactions, based on a computer model analogy. It suggests that problem representations, goal states, and relevant rules and operations can all be sorted as either well-defined or ill-defined. A problem that is consistently ill-defined in all three aspects is one that requires more of the processes ascribed to creative activity; the problem that is well-defined in all three aspects is one that is solvable by the orderly search and retrieval of information that characterizes logical problem solving. While somewhat helpful, information-processing theory still stops with the cognitive contributions to problem solving. An important question remains: are cognitive processes the only types of processes involved in creative thinking?

CREATIVE THINKING: CONTRIBUTING FACTORS

A procedure that helps cognitive psychologists explain the behavior of creative people is one which sorts out the various ingredients that contribute to creative activities. When asked to name some creative people, the average individual complies by naming an array of people from a variety of fields and offers a creative product as the main evidence for the cited person's creativity—Joyce's *Ulysses,* Watson and Crick's discovery of the DNA molecule, Gödel's proof, Picasso's Guernica, Farrell's performance of Firebird, or Froebel's gifts. On the level of common sense, the definitive evidence that the creative process has occurred is the existence of an original and/or elegant product. I believe that this commonsense response is useful for an understanding of the creative process. Assume for a moment an objectivist position on product evaluation, that the creative product is one that is marked by originality, economy or summary power, and wholeness. We can then work backwards to identify the features of the activity that created these products, and this tracing can lead to the development of an adequate operational definition of the creative process, a definition on which educational programs can be founded.

It is obvious that cognitive processes play a significant role in the development of creative products. From various accounts—of eminent creators, empirical literature, and from my direct observation of and interviews with productive students and teachers—a pattern of factors emerges. Not surprisingly, the factors resemble those identified by Guilford (1959) as sensitivity to problems, fluency, flexibility, originality and elaboration.

Productive individuals are regularly observed and reported as being able to see things that need to be done, and to detect workable problems in situations others find chaotic. They see ways of beginning, methods of developing ideas, questions to ask. Often, they show unusual breadth in perceiving and defining problem space. These behaviors suggest the presence of a sensitivity to problems.

Productive people also show unusual playfulness in manipulating objects and concepts and unusual resourcefulness and risk-taking in the transformation of these items. They often generate many ideas and questions quickly, and fluently build on the responses of others; in addition, they categorize widely and transform elements with apparent ease. They regularly appear to alternate between high and low tolerances for error and disorder, being at times sustainedly open and persistent in exploration and at other times painstakingly attentive to fine detail, thus displaying cognitive flexibility. Often they outline the specific clarifying details and steps by which an appropriate plan or idea may be implemented, revealing skill in elaboration. Importantly, the productive individual's actions and responses, both verbal and nonverbal, are often novel in viewpoint or presentation, manifesting originality.

Given the prevalence of cognitive traits, we must still ask whether they are the *only* psychological factors or abilities needed to be creatively productive. We must also ask what other causal conditions are needed to precipitate the activation of these abilities? This second question is rarely asked.

In discussing experimental procedures and our ability to link a studied effect to a single cause or cluster of causes, John Stuart Mill (1892) distills the problem. He writes:

It is not true . . . that one effect must be connected with only one cause, or assemblage of conditions; that each phenomenon can be produced in only one way. There are often several independent modes in which the same phenomenon could have originated. One fact may be the consequent in several invariable sequences; it may follow, with equal uniformity, any one of several antecedents, or collection of antecedents. Many causes may produce mechanical motion: many causes may produce some kinds of sensations: many causes may produce death. A given effect may really be produced by a certain cause, and yet be perfectly capable of being produced without it (Mill, 1892, p. 256).

I believe creative activity is best accounted for by a plurality of causes. A definition of the creative process that focuses on only cognitive abilities is inadequate, since it isolates just one cluster of causal conditions and offers it as a sufficient explanation of creative activity. Cognitive factors are important, but they will not alone account for the realization of creative activity or of the creative product.

CREATIVE THINKING: THE CONTRIBUTION OF PERSONALITY

Three factors of attitude and temperament, often thought of as personality traits, appear at least equally crucial: dominance, openness and creative motivation. Creatively productive people are assertive. They demonstrate confidence, self-reliance, independence of judgment, initiative and leadership in a group. They ask questions and offer opinions with reasonable self-assurance; they defend their views, rather than withdraw when challenged; they often volunteer to assume responsibility in a group. Creative people appear open and flexible, projecting a balanced and realistic perspective of themselves, particularly under stress. They use humor to look beyond the immediacy of a situation, and often report accepting and using the nonrational within. They frequently demonstrate openness by offering and eliciting suggestions for new performances, by accepting constructive criticism, and by following through on some of the suggestions of others.

In addition, they reveal their creative motivation by expressing or implying a great and conscious valuing of creative activity and its products, placing it above more socially-prized items, such as wealth or peer approval. Related to this is their reported intrinsic need to engage in creative activities and to achieve at them. They express a penchant for and enjoyment of unusual, open-ended activities which elicit playful, fluent ideation and expression. They demonstrate sustained, dedicated involvement when engaging in such tasks, even in a flexible and undemanding environment. These common features of creative people suggest a broader conception of creativity than the merely cognitive: behind them are a variety of traits, attitudes, and dispositions that contribute to creative activity in conjunction with the cognitive skills involved.

Another cluster of apparently important dispositions that contribute to creative activity is the creative person's attitudes toward and use of environmental and cultural features and influences. (Environmental factors refer to those from the immediate physical and social environment; cultural factors refer to the accrued-over-time behavior and value patterns of a culture.) The behavior of productive individuals is marked by an eclectic and often critical attitude toward these features and influences. Overcoming environmental hindrances, creative people frequently produce solutions that go beyond the usual constraints of time, place, common materials and usual uses. Their social behavior may often be unconventional and original. They often exhibit choices that are free from the automatic and unquestioned adoption of cultural mandates or approved problem boundaries. Although not committed rebels, these creative people seem regularly to critique, select, and manipulate many features of the environment and culture; they report a sense of "creating their own destinies" (Barron, 1969, p. 112).

In summary, although cognitive processes play an indisputably important role in the creative process, they alone do not account for the manifestation of creative activity and for the development of creative products. Conditions of temperament, attitude, and posture *vis a vis* the environment and culture appear necessary to a sound causal explanation of creative activity in terms of inner psychological mechanisms. This is the conception of the creative process on which the Critical and Creative Thinking Program at the University of Massachusetts at Boston is founded.

THE CRITICAL AND CREATIVE THINKING PROGRAM: AN EXPERIMENTAL APPROACH

The educational practices developed in the Critical and Creative Thinking Program demonstrate the way this broad holistic conception of creative activity can both serve as a basis for an educational program and be tested for its viability. The Program is an interdisciplinary, team-taught Master of Arts program. The students in the program are primarily teachers from kindergarten to the community-college level. The program begins with a year-long introductory, core course; the first semester focuses on creative thinking; the second semester focuses on critical thinking. Course work in cognitive psychology, foundations of philosophical thought, a practicum, and a thesis all form part of the program. Each student selects a specialty area. There are now three specialty areas available: Creativity and Criticism in Literature and Art, Evidence and Discovery in Science, and Moral Education.

OBJECTIVES OF THE PROGRAM

Each course in the Program has three broad sets of objectives: to increase the students' own critical and creative thinking skills; to help students increase their knowledge about critical and creative thinking and its application to various content areas and curricula; and, finally, to help participants develop ways to enhance the critical and creative thinking skills of others, through a variety of strategies and in a variety of settings.

The introductory, interdisciplinary core course, Creative Thinking, bears a major responsibility for the intensive development of the relevant perceptual, cognitive and personality factors within a facilitating context, that is sensitive both to social and cultural influences. The course is based on two premises. The first is that potential for moderate creative activity is ubiquitous; the second is that creative performance is subject to positive influence. The course is founded on the holistic conception of creative activity described above and is also supported by the body of empirical research relevant to the development of that wide array of behaviors (Gallo, Note 1). I will briefly summarize it here.

There is substantial evidence in the empirical literature that attitude is the crucial element in programs designed to foster creative thinking, and that to nurture creativity, we must foster a positive attitude toward the creative enterprise and toward the individual as a source of competence and of worth. For this reason, the Creative Thinking course emphasizes climate factors over specific procedures and tasks, process over product. The leader's behavior is especially influential in developing this climate.

This influence is linked to several specific activities. The leader is needed to sustain a nonevaluative attitude during ideation (to discourage critical or stoical peer group response), to encourage and bolster confidence in the speculative approach, to urge the group to continue when fatigued, and to foster risk-taking. In addition, the leader serves as a model of an effective person who consciously values creative performance, as well as one who rewards it with respect, recognition, and delight.

In an effort to foster student confidence, self-acceptance and independence of judgment, the leader must try to establish a psychologically safe, nonauthoritarian, stimulating environment, which will provide opportunities and a request for the full expression of thoughts and feelings. He can achieve this climate of safety by being more idea-seeking than idea-giving and by using "democratic processes" for group decisions. The teacher should establish trust by "treating students as equals" and should respect (and make time for) students' questions and ideas, thus, showing valuing. The teacher can provide students with an opportunity to practice question generating and reward that act with recognition. An "error tolerant" atmosphere is urged, especially during idea-generating sessions. The leader should urge self-evaluation in order to engender what Rogers calls an "internal locus of evaluation" (1954).

To foster flexible ego-control and perception, as well as openness, the leader should establish a playful, spontaneous atmosphere by offering whimsical suggestions when it is his turn in the group and by suggesting that students bring in examples of humor for display. The focus on humor also elicits personal risk-taking, and, to some degree, cultural pattern-breaking, since most graduate courses are expected to be serious in tone.

One of the more difficult goals to achieve is a classroom climate that is both relaxed and unhurried, yet stimulating and exciting, one of genuine choice yet "expected" involvement. The leader should try to create an air of expectancy, an absorbing and exciting tone, by being enthusiastic about events, by communicating a sense of the importance of the task wordlessly, and by requesting but not demanding participation from the sluggish. Achieving the fragile balance between expectancy and subtle pressure, between an urging request and a thinly veiled demand is the most difficult aspect of the teaching.

Within this environment there should always be suggested activities, often a choice between two or three, but never a completely *laissez-faire* context. I have found that overly ambiguous environments produce not only frustration but high levels of anxiety in the students, which, in turn, increase their rigidity and fear and decrease their willingness to take risks. In addition, these environments produce mistrust for the teacher, since the students most often perceive complete directionlessness in a class setting as a violation of their expressed wishes. Thus, the environment the leader should foster is one that is unencumbering but not permissive.

In the Creative Thinking course, the team of teachers attempts to demonstrate each of the behaviors indicated. The three-hour class is generally divided into two sections; the first section often focuses on a review of relevant readings or study. There is a three-fold purpose to this portion of the class. The first is to increase the students' accurate knowledge about the creative process and about creative people by reviewing readings from relevant psychological, philosophical and imaginative literature. Second, it provides practice in analyzing, from an active, critical standpoint, large constellations of concepts and to begin to explore some applications of the useful ideas. Thirdly, it offers an opportunity to practice particularly important finite skills, such as question generating. Sometimes during this first part of the session, the class is divided into small discussion groups; each discusses the reading in terms of *self-generated* questions, intended to elicit a critical or a creative response to the readings. My colleague and I participate as resource persons and facilitators, not as discussion leaders. Occasionally we lecture briefly on particularly complex issues, such as the apparently paradoxical creative processes. The assessment of social, cultural, or perceptual blocks to creative functioning is often a focus of these sessions.

Sometimes during this first portion of the class, we will view and discuss films, curriculum materials, or guest panel presentations. Two panels are regularly included; the initial panel is one of creative people in the nonteaching professions: a creative scientist, a visual artist, a theatrical performer, a poet or a composer. Each describes the creative process, as it occurs within and the ways in which it is facilitated or blocked. Toward the end of the semester, there is a panel of creative teachers which includes teachers at the primary, secondary, and college level and sometimes educators from other institutional settings, such as museums. Each panelist addresses the above-stated question and talks about the specific ways in which he tries to enhance the creative thinking of his students. Both of these panels have been reported by the students as inspiring and highly insight-producing.

In all other class sessions, the second portion of the class is a work or activity period, designed to provide practice with problems requiring creative activity and with various facilitating techniques. In every class work period, some group activity precedes individual work, and the class "group experience" precedes the individual work done at home. Thus, practice is used in both of its senses: there is active participation (versus passive receiving), and there is unevaluated work preceding the expected product or assessment. A continuing focus is the deliberate manipulation of problem representation through various techniques, following the careful analysis of the problem statement, often from an information-processing perspective (the initial state, end state and relevant rules and operations).

Some techniques common to all work sessions are deferred judgment (brainstorming), extended effort (massed work), the use of direct instruction to promote innovative set, functional flexibility, the gathering of novel combinations, and the use of analogical thinking. Some sessions practice attribute listing, finding forced relationships, the use of visual imagery and Osborn's transformation techniques. A consistently offered, open-ended assigned problem is, "Select a problem in your real life, and use the technique(s) under study to develop new problem definitions, new alternative approaches, and/or new solutions." The real-life problems are offered after a brief practice on common exercises to develop the sub-skills of creative problem solving. Then the students are asked to apply the underlying heuristics to their self-identified "real-life" problems.

This use of real-life problems is an unusual feature among courses attempting to educate for creativity, and it has been adopted for several important reasons. First, from the study of both biographical and empirical materials, a pattern emerges: creatively productive people are most often attracted to complex problems that they consider to be real and important; they become engaged in problems of significant challenge. Textbook exercises are usually perceived by students to be trivial and unconnected to life; therefore, these are used briefly only to help the students identify the recommended or hindering techniques. The second reason emerges from our general knowledge about effective teaching for any kind of problem-solving skill. It appears that the generalized use of such skills is enhanced by practice on tasks that are, first, similar to those on which the skills need to be used in the future and on those tasks which learners perceive to be of practical importance in their lives. Cole and Means (1981) state, "Efforts to devise [thinking skills] training in such a way that general skill will be effectively transferred to other tasks *not* included in the training process are likely to encounter major obstacles" (1981, pp. 122–23). In addition, student work on real-life problems considered to be of both practical and continued importance in their lives, obviously benefits from a high degree of personal motivation and commitment.

The last two procedural characteristics common to all of the workshops are the questioning technique employed and the use of time. In relation to the readings and activity of each week, the students are urged to practice producing fluent and flexible responses by constructing and asking as many questions and as many kinds of questions as they can. They are also asked to combine the questions with transformations and hypothesizing, in order to build "what if" questions. In the classes, we make an effort to protect the time to probe deeply, to generate ideas, to evaluate extensively the subtle differences of outcomes, and to digress when appropriate.

Another goal of each practice period is to parallel the "natural" timing of creative experiences. The class is the preparation for the creative activity; it is designed to saturate, stimulate, and to start the thinking. This is followed by an untimed period for "incubation." The assignment sheets are distributed at the end of each class period, and the students are usually given a few minutes to think specifically about what they might do as a spin-off from the class activity, in order to begin the incubation, if it has not begun before. The students have a full week or as much time as they request individually to do the problem-solving assignments for each class.

Each of the classes has a three-part home assignment—the readings, a short paper (one to two pages) of applications of the class' ideas, and a task requiring creative thinking on either a figural or verbal activity. These assignments are founded on the belief that knowledge and information about the creative person and process do, contribute to growth in creative performance, that deliberate, active practice in finding real-world applications for the concepts and techniques is required, as are exploratory creative thinking exercises. As the empirical literature supports, all of the tasks are open-ended (have unpredictable outcomes), are aimed at eliciting both fluent and flexible ideation and evaluation against identified criteria, and all require active participation by the students. The tasks are designed to draw forth some "preconscious" fantasy materials or other ideas that are "real and important" to the students. At the idea-generating stages, the student is urged to be as "unusual, wild and silly" as he wishes; this helps elicit originality, risk-taking, and independence of judgment. Then the student is asked to practice evaluation and elaboration by selecting one or two responses or solutions to detail and "to make whole and complete." In each class, the process of the task is as important, if not more important, than the product.

Some examples of tasks are the following: generate cartoon captions; construct a real-life problem (as described above); write a short story using forced relationship techniques; develop an assessment tool for social creativity; develop a well-elaborated visual product from the in-class scribble drawings; or develop at least twenty-five uses for a common object. One especially popular and successful choice followed the reading of a freely chosen biography of a creative person. It asked the student to do the Lines Activity from the Torrance Test of Creative Thinking Figural Form A as the subject of the biography would have done it. The products were consistently bold and original. An analysis task is sometimes substituted for the application assignment; then the students are asked to analyze their home or work environment to identify hindrances to creativity to be eliminated.

EVALUATION

The Creative Thinking course was offered first in 1981. To date, no formal quantitative evaluation has been done. However, many specimens of student work and responses have been gathered to give an adequate qualitative picture. The results indicate a definite increase in observed behaviors and reported changes that relate to creative motivation, dominance, and openness.

Further, the students report their consistent use of the learned techniques in developing new problem representations on both exercise and real-life problems. Brainstorming, finding forced relationships, and Osborn's transformation techniques are reportedly the most frequently used. Weekly assignments reveal a substantial increase in fluency, flexibility, and elaboration, and some minor growth in originality. Student papers reflect an increasing awareness of applications of the learned processes suggesting, for example, new household tools or new resolutions to conflicts with adolescents at home and at school. Discussions make clear that the perception of the influence of social, cultural features on student problem solving has increased markedly, but demonstrated behavior changes (*e.g.* being less time-bound in the work place, adopting behaviors socially defined as androgynous, *etc.*) have not been widely reported or observed.

Given the successes in the crucial features of attitude change and demonstrated application of principles, it seems reasonable to conclude that the described procedures are fruitful ways of eliciting and developing creative activity, when it is holistically conceived. Test and survey data on participants in the program are now being gathered, and follow-up studies are being planned, so the reported conclusions must remain in part programmatic.

Important work remains to be done through both psychological and educational studies of creativity. How can we further define the abilities, traits and dispositions, their centrality to and specific functions in the creative process? What structural features do these display, and how do they interact causally in creative thinking? How can these causal factors best be brought about in an orderly way through the educational process? In its own way, The Critical and Creative Program at the University of Massachusetts at Boston is both a laboratory and a forum in which the faculty and students generate these kinds of questions and hope to stimulate others to join us in seeking answers.

REFERENCE NOTE

1. Gallo, Delores. *The Traits and Techniques of Creative Production.* Unpublished doctoral dissertation, Harvard University, 1973. Consult for a detailed review of the literature on which the specific strategies are based.

REFERENCES

Barron, F. *The Creative Person and Creative Process.* New York: Holt, Rinehart and Winston, 1969.

Cole, M., and Means, B. *Comparative Studies of How People Think: An Introduction.* Cambridge, MA: Harvard University Press, 1981.

Guilford, J.P. "Traits of Creativity." In *Creativity and Its Cultivation,* H. Anderson (Ed.). New York: Harper & Row, 1959.

MacKinnon, D.W. "What Makes a Person Creative?" *Theory into Practice,* 1966, 5, p. 152–156.

Mill, J.S. *System of Logic.* London: Routledge and Sons, 1892.

Rogers, C.R. "Towards a Theory of Creativity." In *Creativity,* P.E. Vernon (Ed.). Baltimore, MD: Penguin, 1970.

Torrance, E.P. *Rewarding Creative Behavior.* Englewood Cliffs, NJ: Prentice-Hall, 1965.

PART IV.

THINKING ABOUT
TEACHING THINKING

INTRODUCTION

If we wish to think about thinking where do we begin? If we wish to begin *teaching* thinking where do we begin?

None of the writers represented in this book would propose that there is one fixed perspective or point from which one must begin. One metaphor of thinking is that it is a large multi-faceted diamond, but shaped more like a sphere. From wherever one begins one finds brilliance. One begins from where one is. The important thing is to begin.

A modern beginner, or pioneer, in the development of new modes for the *teaching* of thinking is Edward de Bono. In 1966, North Carolina's educational "think tank," the Learning Institute of North Carolina, attempted to introduce his ideas to that state. Since then de Bono has promulgated his ideas with singular dedication and success. Yet, the serious literature in education, psychology, and philosophy has almost completely ignored de Bono's ideas.

Two of the papers in this book (Edwards' and Baldauf's, and McPeck's) complain about this absence of research studies or critical assessments of de Bono's methods. This section begins with John McPeck's highly critical appraisal of de Bono's theories. If you are coming to de Bono for the first time, you will be advised to recall the discussion of Hegel in the first section of this book. The search for Truth proceeds by a process that can be called a dialectic, a process akin to a dialogue or to a debate, or to continuous approximation. After reading McPeck, you may wish to re-read de Bono's own essay in Part III and to re-read Edwards' and Baldauf's paper, also in the same section. You may find yourself slightly confused. Good; sometimes thinking only occurs if you are puzzled.

John Carroll (1980) reminded us that "theory" and "theology" have the same etymological Greek roots. People resist giving up their faith in their theories or their theologies. Just as the ancient Greeks painfully resisted giving up their belief in polytheism, and as certain contemporary societies similarly resist giving up their belief in conflicting gods, so conflicting theories of intelligence attract fanatical adherents to all sides. But Perkins', Allen's and Hafner's essay reminds us that scientific theory must be based upon empirical research, sometimes in the form of experimentation. Perkins', Allen's and Hafner's study pioneers in another way the issue of everyday reasoning. They are developing a research method that promises practical results which can also inform theories of thinking. On reading Perkins, *et al.,* you may be reminded of John Dewey's assertion, "Nothing is more practical than theory."

Laura Jansson's paper attracted enormous interest from the world of competitive sports, as well as from people interested in the interplay of mind and muscle. A European diving champion, Jansson translated her interest in sports and her interest in psychology to contribute to a fascinating new field, sportspsychology. It promises results that transcend competitive sports and find application in rehabilitative therapy and more.

Kristina Macrae's paper does a de Bono "P.M.I." She briefly cites the adherents of the "pluses" and "minuses" of current psychometric testing practices to discuss a more "interesting" side. Under some conditions testing can teach, and, as she shows, even a "wrong" answer can reveal effective thinking and can suggest a diagnosis for defective thinking. The opponents of intelligence testing and psychometrics will profit from a close reading of Macrae's very interesting thesis.

As a careful reading of textbooks generally reveals, what is being taught today in schools and universities may often be twenty or more years out-of-date. For example, there has never been any scientific study that showed that IQ is fixed. Yet most people have the idea that it is (c.f., Pinneau, 1961). Commonly held beliefs or theories resist new beliefs or theories, as I said before. Sometimes they even resist common sense. ("And what else, besides IQ," I often ask my students, "in our universe is fixed?") Educational innovators and administrators must be sensitive to these facts of life. Here Arthur Costa raises a series of questions that anyone who wishes to introduce thinking as a school subject must consider. There will be theoretical objections to the teaching of thinking, which will appear almost theological. Costa's questions imply some strategies and tactics that share some aspects with religious or political revolutions. We will not deny that the reader may detect in this book a revolutionary enthusiasm. Taken collectively these essays may be a not very strident manifesto: "Let the thinkers arise!" Revolutions can be invigorating. All of these essays not only urge the teaching of thinking skills, they also offer optimistic arguments that doing so will provide entirely positive results.

REFERENCES

Carroll, J. *Skeptical Sociology.* London: Routledge & Kegan Paul, 1980.
Pinneau, S.R. *Changes in Intelligence Quotient.* Boston: Houghton, Mifflin, 1961.

A SECOND LOOK AT DE BONO'S HEURISTICS FOR THINKING[1]

John E. McPeck

ABSTRACT

Edward de Bono is one of very few writers whose programs for teaching people to think have enjoyed a wide international reputation. De Bono's *CoRT Thinking Lessons* and *Lateral Thinking* constitute part of the school curriculum in over twenty-five countries. It is therefore surprising that despite de Bono's popularity, his work has never been publicly scrutinized by philosophers or professional educators. The present essay attempts to rectify this situation by examining precisely what de Bono means by "thinking," and to assess the educational value of his programs. This paper argues that de Bono's view of thinking is systematically unclear, and that his teaching programs supplant the complex phenomena of thinking with superficial heuristic devices, which entertain more than educate.

THINKING

Edward de Bono's many books on teaching people how to think can be divided into two distinct programs: the CoRT (Cognitive Research Trust) thinking materials, and lateral thinking. I shall examine each of these programs in turn, but first I think it instructive to have some idea of what de Bono means by *thinking*. Insofar as thinking skills are the *raison d'etre* of de Bono's proposals, one would expect to find a fairly clear idea of what thinking *is* to emerge from all this. Instead, one finds many diverse definitions and descriptions of "thinking" spread throughout his work:

- What happens in the brain is information. And the way it happens is thinking (de Bono, 1971a, p. 18).
- Thinking is the flow of attention along the d-line pathways (de Bono, 1971a, p. 155).
- Thinking is a device to enlarge our perception (de Bono, 1976, p. 20).

J.E. McPeck is at The University of Western Ontario, London, Canada.

1. For permission to reprint material from *Critical Thinking and Education*, the editors would like to thank Martin Robertson & Company Ltd.

- In this book thinking will be regarded as a sort of internal vision which we direct at experience in order to explore, understand and enlarge (de Bono, 1976, p. 32).
- Thinking is the deliberate exploration of experience for a purpose (de Bono, 1976, p. 32).
- Thinking is the operating skill through which intelligence acts upon experience (de Bono, 1976, pp. 32–33).
- I would define thinking as "moving from idea to idea to achieve a purpose" (de Bono, 1974b, p. 6).

While suggestive, the definitions suffer from a lack of precision. For one thing, if thinking is a skill, as de Bono claims that it is, it is not at all clear how these vague descriptions, taken singularly or collectively, could be adequately distinguished from the rest of our mental processes. Perhaps the tacit recognition of this prompted de Bono (1976) to caution us:

> It is best not to have any preconceptions and to let the intangible subject of thinking gel into something definite and usable in the course of the book (p. 17).

But the caution not only effectively undermines his own definitions, it makes it practically impossible to determine whether de Bono (1976) ever makes good on his promise that: "This book is about a particular approach to the subject of thinking itself, and a practical approach to the teaching of thinking" (p. 17).

How could one determine whether one had taught thinking successfully, when it isn't clear what it is? There are two sources of de Bono's vagueness (and apparent duplicity) on this matter of teaching thinking. First, he assumes that thinking is a generalized skill; but second, he actually promotes a particular or specific *type* of thinking which differs considerably from what most people, and certainly educators, usually mean by "thinking."

That thinking is assumed to be a generalized skill is revealed in statements such as the following, "The aim is to produce a 'detached' thinking skill so that the thinker can use his skill in the most effective way" (de Bono, 1976, p. 50). And that this general skill is also considered capable of being directly taught is manifest in the way de Bono's materials are advertised:

> Can children be taught to think, not as a by-product of learning some other subject, but directly and deliberately in special "thinking" classes? If they can, does it really benefit them, in school and in the world outside? The answer this book gives both those questions is a clear Yes.[2]

De Bono, however, does not appear to recognize the logical connection between his view that thinking is a generalized and teachable skill, and his failure to provide an adequate definition of "thinking." His reluctance to settle upon a single definition of thinking stems from the tacit acknowledgement that there are many different types of thinking. It is a pity that he does not see that the wide variety of thinking skills, which defy accurate and singular definition, is also what implies that thinking is *not a generalized skill*. There are simply too many types of thinking, manifest in diverse skills, to infer a single generalized ability for their respective achievement. Just as a good builder of sand castles is not necessarily a good builder of everything, from mathematical models to utopian societies, so a good thinker in

2. From the widely reproduced dust-jacket of *Teaching Thinking*. London: Maurice Temple Smith, 1976.

one area does not possess a generalized skill applicable to all areas. To say that a person is a good thinker *simpliciter* is as vague and as meaningless as saying that a person is speedy: the first thing one asks is "at what?" Neither speed nor thinking ability are generalized skills which are true of people across any and *all* activities. We may have them for some things and not for others. My secretary is a speedy typist but very slow at jogging. The same holds for thinking.

The second source of de Bono's vagueness about teaching thinking stems from his confusion of a particular type of thinking (which he has in mind), with thinking in general. In *Teaching Thinking*, de Bono (1976), for example, promises a general method for teaching thinking *simpliciter*:

> The book is intended to deal in a practical and personal manner with the teaching of thinking. It is not philosophical speculation, but is based on what may well be the largest program anywhere in the world for the direct teaching of thinking as a skill and, quite apart from this, on considerable experience in the teaching of thinking to somewhat demanding pupils. Above all I should like the book to be of use to teachers who want to teach thinking directly as a skill (pp. 7–8).

However, what one in fact finds in *Teaching Thinking* (and, for that matter, his other books) are not methods for teaching thinking, but rather suggestions for how to generate different or unique hypotheses: what psychologists call "divergent thinking" or "generative thinking." (Divergent thinking, in contrast to convergent thinking, is that which permits more than one correct answer.) It is the type of thinking often associated with creativity, and de Bono often uses the terms interchangeably. But although this particular type of thinking is often useful and is sometimes important, it is a long way from capturing the diverse and polymorphous phenomena we call "thinking." More importantly, it is even farther away from the type of thinking teachers usually and properly see themselves as being concerned with. The reading teacher is properly not concerned with the student's ability to concoct an alternative alphabet, nor is the history teacher concerned with the ability to invent a different name for the Battle of Waterloo. The point here is not the relative merit of teaching divergent thinking or creativity, but that de Bono promotes it as something which it is not, *viz.* the generalized "teaching of thinking directly as a skill," as though one were to gain universal thinking competence from his instructions. This is not to say that de Bono's lessons and practice drills do not require thinking, but then Bingo and dishwashing require thinking too. It is to suggest that his materials do not come close to delivering the skill that is advertised on the package.

CoRT THINKING LESSONS

In recommending his specific proposals for teaching thinking, de Bono first criticizes some of the traditional methods used for getting students to think. Before turning to the CoRT materials directly, it is important to consider his criticism of logic (and its teaching) in particular, because it is the primary justification for the CoRT materials.

> It must be admitted that logic is a good way of teaching logic. It must also be admitted that most of the developments in the teaching of logic have been internal developments arising from the subject itself, and not from considerations of its practical applicability as a thinking tool. As has been discussed at various points in this book, logic is only part of thinking. The direct use of the deductive process forms only a very small part of ordinary

thinking. The emphasis upon it in education arises from the type of artificial problem that is so often used. In such problems all the information is given and some basic principles can be applied. In real life, information is very rarely complete and there may be no basic principles at all. The main deficiency of logic is the starting point. Where does one start? . . .

The rules of logic do matter, but unfortunately the perfection of the subject does not guarantee its usefulness as a practical way of teaching thinking (de Bono, 1976, pp. 103–104).

And elsewhere he correctly points out how unfortunate it is that:

When one sets out to teach thinking as a skill one finds that the "logic" concept has been so long established that it is at once assumed that one is trying to teach logic . . . In some cases . . . the term logic has been expanded to include anything that is to do with thinking and is correct and useful. This is a dangerous situation because the meaning of the term "logic" has come to embrace all of thinking, but the actual process remains confined to the rules of formal logic. This extreme type of "capture" occurs with many other long established concepts (de Bono, 1976, pp. 95–96).

Several similar criticisms of logic appear throughout de Bono's work and they can be summarized as follows: *1.* logic is often wrongly thought to be synonymous with effective thinking; *2.* formal logic requires that all the relevant information be given at the start, but most real problems are not like that; and *3.* logic cannot introduce new ideas, pose alternatives, nor cope with novel situations. Basically, I think de Bono correct on all three points. However, his solution to these deficiencies, that is, the CoRT Thinking materials, does have serious shortcomings.

The name of de Bono's thinking program "CoRT Thinking," derives from the initials of the *Co*gnitive *R*esearch *T*rust. The complete CoRT course is designed for the age range from nine-year-olds to sixteen-year-olds, and consists of a series of subject-neutral "operations," or exercises, from which the students are supposed to develop "tools" for transfer to any problem requiring thinking. The new focus here is that these operations are designed to improve thinking in what de Bono calls the "perceptual" phase of thinking, in contrast to the "processing" phase, where logic and other conventional strategies can be employed. How a person *perceives* a problem is every bit as important as how a person *resolves* it, once it is clearly seen. These different phases of problem solving have been labelled by others as "the context of discovery" and "the context of justification," respectively. De Bono is then properly focusing his attention on precisely that area of problem solving where logic is notably deficient—the context of discovery.

Most of practical thinking takes place in the perception stage and not the processing stage. People react to things as they see them and the way they see them determines the nature of the reaction. So the basic method could be called the "spectacles method"—that is to say, if you help pupils to see situations more clearly then their reactions will be more appropriate (de Bono, 1973b, p. 4).

De Bono's exercises, or "operations," constitute the so-called spectacles through which a student is taught to see a problem before venturing an answer or solution. The operations are intended to provide students with strategies for generating plausible ideas and hypotheses *before* they process an actual answer or solution.

The actual operations are so simple and straightforward that only a few of them need to be illustrated. The first CoRT operation is called PMI, (for *P*lus, *M*inus, and *I*nterest). The students are first given an artificial problem by the teacher, for example: consider the proposition, "All automobiles should be painted yellow." And the students are directed, either in small groups or individually, to spend five minutes considering the "Plus" factors for the proposal, five minutes considering the "Minus" factors, and then a few minutes considering "Interesting" points about the proposal. For the teacher, the point of this lesson is to get the students to understand and practice this PMI as a thinking *procedure*. Their answers are not the important part of the exercise, but rather the PMI thinking operation. The objective is to have this PMI thinking procedure become sufficiently crystallized in the child's mind, such that it can be transferred to other problem solving or thinking situations.

Another CoRT Thinking Operation is called "CAF" for "*Consider All Factors.*" Again, students are given a problem or proposition, and asked to generate as many factors as possible which might be relevant to the problem. With practice, they begin to construct progressively longer lists of factors than they could before training. The emphasis is upon extending the breadth of the student's consideration, and not upon getting right or wrong answers. De Bono considers the CAF lessons to be developing a generalized skill which is transferable to virtually any problem.

FIP, for "*First Important Priorities,*" is another of the dozen or more operations in the CoRT Thinking course:

> The FIP operation is of importance in such situations as making decisions or in planning. In both these situations, it may be a matter of balancing one thing against another and to do this one must decide the importance or priority of each of the things. For instance in choosing a job one may have to balance the pay that a certain job will offer against the enjoyment of that job.... The emphasis of the lesson is on deciding which things are important...(de Bono, 1974b, pp. 96–97).

The directives to teachers in this instance is to get students to internalize the following set of questions as a set drill, or thinking operation:

> What are the important things here?
> What are the priorities? (As before, the word priority should be introduced as much as possible rather than avoiding it.)
> Which of these things are the most important?
> Which thing matters most? (de Bono, 1974b, pp. 96–97).

Again, FIP is an operation which, according to de Bono, the student can apply to virtually any thinking situation which must issue in a decision or plan.

All of the CoRT Thinking operations are thus designed to emphasize the *process*, rather than the content, of thinking. The successful student should be able to use these crystallized skills on nearly all practical problems, according to de Bono. De Bono also refers to these operations (*i.e.,* PMI, CAF, FIP, *etc.*) as "attention-directors," meaning that once a student has mastered these operations they then serve to focus attention upon the many ways a problem can be fruitfully thought about or perceived. While de Bono makes any number of claims about the virtues of the CoRT Thinking operations, essentially they reduce to three: *1.* they constitute a set of "generalized thinking skills" that are independent of content and transferable to virtually all problem areas regardless of content; *2.* these skills can be likened to a set of "neutral spectacles" which enable students to "perceive" problems more clearly (*e.g.,* in the context of discovery); and *3.* nearly everyone can learn these operations, since they presuppose no prior knowledge or information. As de Bono says, "In the CoRT thinking lessons pupils can operate at once since the only resources used are already available within their heads." This last feature of this program requires our attention because it contains the key to some of the major problems with CoRT.

In his admonitions to potential teachers of CoRT, de Bono is at pains to point out how subject-matter content, such as the familiar teaching of mathematics, science, history and literature gets in the way, and actually hinders the development of thinking. If we want students to be aware of the *process* of thinking, de Bono argues, then it must be taught in isolation from content and information.

> "If a person is thinking about something then surely he is learning how to think."
> Unfortunately this is not true. A geography teacher would claim that in learning geography a pupil would be forced to think. A history teacher and a science teacher would make the same claim. All would be right. The question is whether thinking about something develops any transferable skill in thinking. In "content" subjects, the momentum of the subject is usually such that little attention can be paid to the actual process. Exhortations to "think about it" or to consider "what these things imply" merely ask the pupil to delve more deeply into his knowledge and find the right answer. In a content subject you cannot really think ahead of the content, because your speculation must always be inferior to the actual facts. There is comparatively little scope for thinking except of the hindsight variety: "Now you can see that this happened because of that and that..." This is no fault of the teacher. It is the nature of content subjects that is at fault (de Bono, 1976, p. 104).

It is not clear what de Bono means here by the ability "to think ahead of the content," nor whether it would be desirable to do so if one could, but it is plain that he regards traditional, content subjects as inferior instruments for developing the capacity to think. His major argument for this is that thinking *via* subjects is not conducive to transfer of skill, whereas CoRT, putatively, finds its *raison d'etre* here:

> Using thinking in particular situations develops thinking skill in those situations, but not a transferable skill in thinking. Skill has to be person-centred, not situation-centred. The dilemma is that it is usually possible to teach only situation-centred skills. You train a person to behave in a certain way in a certain situation. The way out of the dilemma is to create situations that are *themselves* transferable. We call such situations *tools*. A person is trained in the tool situation. He learns how to cope with the tool. The tool and his skill in using it can now be transfered to new situations (de Bono, 1976, p. 108).

The idea behind teaching CoRT, then, is to get away from content by creating artificial situations and problems so that the operations become transferable tools. This is why de Bono always uses hypothetical or fictitious examples like, "All automobiles should be painted yellow," *etc.*, and hundreds of similar problems which have few, if any, prerequisites of content.

It is ironic that de Bono's prescriptions for removing subject content, and creating artificial problems, are precisely the features of formal logic which he himself so aptly criticized. What was logic's vice turns out to be CoRT's virtue. The trouble with formal logic is:

> ...the deductive process forms only a very small part of ordinary thinking. The emphasis upon it in education arises from the type of artificial problem that is so often used. In such problems all the information is given and some basic principles can be applied (de Bono, 1976, pp. 103–104).

The only difference is that CoRT provides virtually no information, and no criteria for telling when its principles (*i.e.,* its operations) are being appropriately applied. De Bono is quite adamant that teachers should encourage *all* responses, and never say "that is wrong." At least logic has clear criteria for this.

With respect to skill transfer, which presumably is CoRT's greatest strength, there is no evidence whatever that the skills attained in the use of CoRT operations transfer to other types of problems which differ from those in the CoRT lessons. In de Bono's favorable reports of tests which he ran comparing CoRT-trained students with "untrained groups," three telling points should be noted: *1.* all of the problems are of the CoRT type, thus his results are anything but surprising; *2.* none of the questions are such that a wrong answer is even possible; and *3.* the *quality* of responses is never quantified, only the *quantity* of responses is recorded. These last two points about de Bono's scoring procedures are important because they reveal something more fundamental about the CoRT program as a whole.

In all of the CoRT exercises and operations, *truth* is never at issue: all that appears to matter is numbers of responses, and lists of more or less plausible suggestions. In general, the CoRT program subtly discredits the task of seeking truth in academic study, and in daily living as well. In most situations in life, and certainly in academic studies, the validity of one's thinking is far more important than the number of suggestions one can produce. In CoRT, the examples do not require knowledge and information, and being right or wrong is irrelevant. In his advocacy of so-called thinking skills, de Bono berates the schools for putting so much emphasis upon "mere knowledge and information." He seems to minimize just how difficult and complex it is to convey mere knowledge and information to adults, let alone children. A mere fact, or piece of information such as "the minister resigned because of political pressure from his constituency," or "gravitational forces cause tidal changes," may take a competent teacher weeks to convey. And it is no mean achievement. Moreover the type of thinking required for such understanding is what teachers and schools properly see as their responsibility.

There is a fundamental disagreement between de Bono and the advocates of traditional school subjects. Where de Bono thinks that content subjects hinder important thinking, others (including myself) would argue that the disciplines actually constitute it. Whichever way one decides the question, it is important to recognize that nothing short of an entire philosophy of the curriculum is at issue. Witness, for example:

> If children can already think so well at this age, then surely the long years of education must develop this ability to a high level. Not so. At the end of education there has been no improvement in the thinking ability of children—in fact there has actually been a deterioration. This opinion is based on experiments involving several thousand people, all of whom had benefited from higher education. It is an opinion which seems to be shared by others who have considered the matter. Why should education have this effect on thinking ability? (de Bono, 1972, p. 9).

On the other hand, most people believe, and not without foundation, that the traditional disciplinary modes of thinking are the most worthwhile in the long run. For all of their shortcomings, the disciplinary traditions do represent very powerful ways of thinking about, learning about, and viewing the world. They are not merely stagnant collections of information or content, as de Bono implies. They, too, are *ways of thinking.* However, de Bono believes that because disciplinary thinking is tied to content, it is inherently inferior to CoRT thinking, which is not so tied. We are led to believe, moreover, that content actually inhibits important thinking, and that there is a deterioration of children's thought as a result.

There is nothing wrong with suggesting radical revisions of existing school curricula, even when those revisions entail the rejection of long-standing intellectual traditions. But de Bono's proposals are not directly presented this way to teachers; nor is it clear that he sees such implications himself. Whether or not he is aware of this conflict, I believe it has its origin in two sources: *1.* his attempt to inject school subjects with novelty and originality; and *2.* his belief in the existence of "generalized thinking skills"—skills which are not dependent upon content. However, the price to be paid for novelty and/or originality is a proportionate de-emphasis on knowledge, or truth-seeking, as we have come to understand this through the disciplines. There is no inherent value in novelty or originality, if it does not result in some productive end. In the extreme, novelty for its own sake is chaos. With respect to generalized thinking skills of the kind de Bono envisages, I would argue that there is something incoherent about the very idea of such skills. There are instead, various *types of thinking skills* which are logically connected to various activities, subjects and tasks, but these are not generalizable.

Also, when anyone promises to change our perceptions by providing us with a new set of spectacles, a familiar claim in intellectual history, one should be aware that the intended changes are not mere additions to the *status quo. If,* and I stress *if*, the changes are in fact what they promise, then something presently valued must be given up. With regard to CoRT, de Bono explains that:

> ...the basic method could be called the "spectacles method"—that is to say, if you help pupils to see situations more clearly then their reactions will be more appropriate. Spectacles are neutral and in the CoRT lessons there is no attempt to impose or change values (though these may change as the result of better vision). In practice for "spectacles" we may read "methods for directing attention" (de Bono, 1973b, p. 4).

Effective spectacles, however, are not cognitively neutral. If spectacles produce changes in the way things are perceived, then knowledge has a different empirical foundation. The issue here is not about changing children's moral and political values, as de Bono intimates, but rather about changing *teachers'* educational values. It is about what kind of thinking teachers should regard as most worthwhile for a child's education. The issue is anything but neutral. Teachers already have "methods of directing attention," and a knowledge tradition worth directing attention towards. These are the values which de Bono's "neutral spectacles" would effectively change or undermine.

Let us consider whether the change in perception is worth the gambit. In the CoRT operation called CAF (for *Consider All Factors*), children are given a problem, and either alone or in groups, they are asked to list all the factors which bear upon the problem. But what *sorts* of factors should appear on the list? What is a factor? de Bono (1974b) replies:

> There should not be any philosophical attempt to decide exactly what a factor is and when something is a factor and when it is not. A factor is quite simply something that should be thought about in connection with the situation. If you like you could call it a consideration or something that has to be considered (p. 91).

Not only does this not answer the question, but it is not a philosophical definition of factor which was being sought—though that would be interesting! Quite simply, what is being sought by both the teacher and student is some kind of guidance as to what may be considered relevant to a given problem. And whereas CoRT simply backs off and "lets the student decide that," the traditional disciplines provide a broad range of relevant considerations.

Indeed, this is precisely why subjects like science and history, and the like are so valuable; they teach people what kinds of things are and are not relevant to a given problem—what a factor is. Contrary to de Bono's contention that content subjects are not the place to begin on a problem, I would argue that they at least limit the range of plausible hypotheses. Traditional content subjects likewise provide spectacles, but spectacles which have been ground by thousands of years of human experience. And competent teachers try to provide students with those spectacles so that they might *perceive* what factors are relevant.

In the CoRT operation called FIP (for *First Important Priorities*), the student is supposed to rank-order which elements of a problem should take precedence. As noted earlier, the student is supposed to ask himself the following questions:

- What are the important things here?
- What are the priorities? (As before the word priority should be introduced as much as possible rather than avoiding it).
- Which of these things are the most important?
- Which one of these two things is the most important?
- Which thing matters most? (de Bono, 1974b, p. 97).

To each of these questions, however, a student or teacher might legitimately reply, "Important for what? Are aesthetic priorities to take precedence over functional ones? Are moral priorities over legal ones?" De Bono (1974b) answers such questions with his characteristic simplicity, "In most situations the matters to be considered are already evident, and it is a question of assigning importance and priority" (p. 97). But this simply will not do. What is a priority in a given situation is highly contingent upon an agent's purpose. What is a priority for one person or task might not be so for the next. If it were literally true that, "In most situations the matters to be considered are already evident," then the whole point of the exercise is unclear. I suspect that de Bono's pedagogical warning that "the word Priority should be introduced as much as possible rather than avoiding it" unwittingly contains the only point to the exercise: to teach the meaning of the *word* "priority." But this hardly qualifies as a generalized thinking skill.

The CoRT operation called PMI (for *Plus*, *Minus* and *Interest*), which I outlined previously, suffers from the combined difficulties of CAF and FIP at once. Like CAF, this operation depends upon background knowledge and information in order to have some idea about what might be a plausible *plus* or *minus*. If knowledge is not required, as de Bono suggests, then there is no way to distinguish between good and poor suggestions. More importantly, there would be no way of distinguishing a *plus* from a *minus!* And like FIP, what is to count as a priority, or *plus* in this case, is highly contingent upon one's peculiar purposes. For example, given that "All automobiles should be painted yellow," in order to make *plausible* suggestions (in contrast to all the logically possible ones), a person would not only have to know something about the intended purpose of the suggestion but also the availability and cost of such a quantity of yellow paint—not to mention aesthetic and environmental considerations! It is not that a person would need precise information about any of these considerations, but one would need knowledge to understand that such things are relevant considerations. Without such knowledge, there is no way to distinguish the class of *plausible* suggestions from the class of logically *possible* ones; there is no way to distinguish a real plus from a real minus.

It, on the other hand, de Bono intends merely that students list their subjective likes and dislikes as pluses and minuses, then *a.* it is of limited use in contexts where truth matters, that is, in most academic studies and practical affairs; and *b.* it runs the risk of giving the false impression to students that productive thinking largely consists in being clear about one's subjective preferences—a view all to pervasive during the 1960's. Similar difficulties reside in the other CoRT operations such as C and S (*C*onsequence and *S*equelae), and AGO (*A*ims, *G*oals, *O*bjectives), but I shall not criticize them here. I wish only to give the reader some sense of the kind of spectacles de Bono offers teachers. For myself, I find the spectacles particularly opaque and much harder to see through than traditional methods for getting students to think.

There remains one final, general criticism of CoRT. Despite all of de Bono's advance warnings that CoRT is meant to improve "perceptions in the perceptual stage and not the processing stage," he has in fact confused and combined these two stages (*i.e.*, the context of *discovery* and the context of *justification*). The context of discovery refers to the generation of ideas or new ways of looking at things, and the context of justification refers to the judgment or proof of those ideas once generated.[3] However, many CoRT operations, in particular CAF (*Consider All Factors*) and PMI (*Plus, Minus and Interest*), clearly require *judgment* about the acceptability of ideas or proposals. Indeed in de Bono's (1974b) own discussion about the virtues of PMI it can be seen that people's *judgments* are supposed to be affected by PMI:

> If a random half of a group of people are asked to give their opinion on a situation then they will give a definite judgment. If the other half are asked to do a deliberate PMI and then give a judgment it is found that the judgment after the PMI is really rather different from the judgment before PMI. This means that a deliberate attempt to look at the good and bad points has actually changed the judgment of the group (p. 94).

However changing the judgment of the group has little to do with suggesting an idea in the perceptual stage, and a great deal to do with the *acceptability* of an idea in the processing stage. A similar criticism can be made of CAF. The reason it is desirable to consider all factors about X is to make an idea more *acceptable* as a judgment about X, but this is clearly processing an idea in the context of justification.

Perhaps the clearest indication of de Bono's confusion of the processing and perceptual stages of thinking can be found in his own misgivings about the use of the word "perception" for the CoRT operations.

> As will become apparent in this book, we also need a much better word than "perception" for the-way-we-look-at-things. Perception is too abstract, too psychological and too concerned with visual and other sensory perception to cope with the way the *mind* looks at things. One day I may find the right word for this, but I do not have one yet (de Bono, 1976, p. 9).

De Bono, of course, is correct. Perception is too psychological and too concerned with the visual. But if he were aware of the vast literature available on "the context of discovery" *vs.* "the context of justification," he would see that his distinction need not be so contaminated.[4] As it is, the word "perception" does capture the very real muddle that pervades the CoRT program. The program does collapse the distinction he wants to make between the two contexts, and that is why the word "perception" correctly strikes him as odd and unfortunate. Initial *perception* and final *judgment* are different things. Moreover, this is precisely why the CoRT operations, when abstracted from subject-content, are empty and superficial in the context of *discovery* , and would be absolutely useless as methods of *justification*.

LATERAL THINKING

Lateral thinking constitutes the final unit of the CoRT program, but de Bono (1971b, 1971c, 1973a, 1977) has also written four separate books about lateral thinking and considers it a distinct topic. Lateral thinking describes those methods of thinking which introduce new ideas, or the type of thinking we normally associate with inventiveness and creativity. It differs from the other CoRT opera-

---

3. I should like to make it clear that I am discussing CoRT operations which are *exclusive* of "lateral thinking."

4. This is a result of de Bono's admitted refusal to either read or footnote work done in his own field.

tions in that it does *not* purport to be a better way of thinking about normal problems, but is, rather specifically intended for generating new ideas and unorthodox solutions. Unfortunately, it is impossible to find a clear statement of what lateral thinking is that is free of de Bono's sales talk for it. He comes closest to defining what it is when insisting what it clearly is not.

> Lateral thinking is quite distinct from vertical thinking which is the traditional type of thinking. In vertical thinking one moves forward by sequential steps each of which must be justified. The distinction between the two sorts of thinking is sharp. For instance in lateral thinking one may have to be wrong at some stage in order to achieve a correct solution: in vertical thinking (logic or mathematics) this would be impossible. In lateral thinking one may deliberately seek out irrelevant information: in vertical thinking one selects out only what is relevant (de Bono, 1977, p. 11).

Elsewhere he summarizes the difference as follows,"vertical thinking [is] high probability, straight-ahead thinking, and lateral thinking [is] low-probability, sideways thinking" (de Bono, 1971b, p. 139). If and when a low-probability idea works, or leads to something, the payoff is far richer in terms of its usefulness than ideas whose implications are obvious. Often lateral thinking attempts to generate new ideas just for their own sake, and not necessarily for the solution of any known problem. Thus, lateral thinking might be described as an attempt to codify certain procedures and techniques which generate new ideas.

De Bono claims that lateral thinking is not intended to challenge or replace our conventional methods of vertical thinking, but rather to supplement them. But perhaps because lateral thinking is intended as a corrective for *a.* the known limitations of formal logic, and *b.* the tendency of people to pursue nonproductive lines of conventional thought, it is, unfortunately, *perceived* by the general public, and particularly educators, as being a replacement of conventional thinking. Moreover, despite his statements to the contrary, de Bono's own prefaces, dust-jacket blurbs, and occasional discussion do much to foster this misinterpretation of his work. He does not clarify sufficiently what the real intent of lateral thinking is, and what it is not.

The essence of lateral thinking is to avoid looking at familiar patterns, and to connect features of ideas or objects which are not normally associated. As de Bono says, "We want to move *across* tracks sometimes, not along them;" hence, the term "lateral thinking." He describes lateral thinking as composed of an attitude and a method for using information in unusual patterns. The attitude says, "Let's look at an idea to see where it gets us," because, he suggests, "the value of an idea is where it leads, not what it describes at the moment." The method consists in a series of different strategies and techniques for thinking about problems. These strategies range from familiar brainstorming techniques to de Bono's techniques of "concept challenge" and "random stimulation." Concept challenge, for example, involves taking some commonly held assumption, or a familiar object such as a walking stick, and trying to restructure either its parts, function or design into some new and potentially useful pattern. Random stimulation consists of taking virtually any arbitrarily selected object or word, such as a word picked from a dictionary, and working back from it through associations to some initial problem or situation. The selected word is called a "stepping-stone idea." The rationale here is that when one is bereft of solutions to a problem, the introduction of a strange word will carry associations and analogies of its own, and, in principle, any two ideas can be connected in some way. Very often, de Bono claims, these connections are productive of potential solutions, or at least ideas which might be of interest for their own sake.

"PO" is a quasi-word which de Bono introduces to render lateral thinking more accessible in practical situations. The word "PO" can be interjected into sentences in place of a noun, an adjective or a connective, and is intended to convey the same meaning as the words "possible" or "perhaps." Sample uses might be "PO planes land upside down," or "Penalties for PO crimes on Monday are double," *etc.* That "PO" itself is not a word, nor the resulting sentences always grammatical, is a virtue, according to de Bono, because where language leads to familiar thoughts and patterns, PO jars them and compels fresh and unusual associations. The most important characteristic of PO is that it always stands in contrast to "NO", which, according to de Bono (1977), is the operative word of logic and conventional thinking.

> Although both NO and PO function as language tools the operations they carry out are totally different. NO is a judgment device. PO is an anti-judgment device. NO works within the framework of reason. PO works outside that framework. PO may be used to produce arrangements of information that are unreasonable but they are not really unreasonable because lateral thinking functions in a different way from vertical thinking. [sic] Lateral thinking is not irrational but arational. Lateral thinking deals with the patterning of information not with the judgment of these patterns. Lateral thinking is prereason. PO is never a judgment device. PO is a construction device. PO is a patterning device. The patterning process may also involve depatterning and repatterning (p. 197).

Note the curious mix of explication and rhetorical persuasion which de Bono uses to promote his ideas. In this instance, to be critical of PO is like being critical of "constructiveness"—if that is possible.

In this instance, at least, de Bono does not confuse lateral thinking with the context of justification. It is clearly a thinking tool for the context of discovery. However, one must be wary of generalized prescriptions for thought within the context of discovery that are totally independent of subject areas. Of necessity, such prescriptions must disregard peculiarities of content and knowledge, which, in fact, provide ideas with their plausibility. Without some kind of content-dependent guidelines, lateral thinking could produce an infinitely large collection of literal nonsense. De Bono advises the lateral thinker to disregard normal clues and patterns so that the "traps" of conventional vertical thinking can be avoided. For this reason, a more accurate name for lateral thinking would be *lateral guessing*. De Bono should have no objection to such a change, except that it would lose much of its rhetorical punch. Educators, however, would be less apt to construe lateral thinking as something which it is not. They could better see how far it departs from what one would normally regard as thinking.

Even lateral guessing remains guessing. What is worse, it is uniformed guessing. De Bono frequently attempts to establish the usefulness of lateral thinking by suggesting that many famous scientists and inventors were tacitly using it, men such as Einstein, Edison, and Pascal, discovered too many things to attribute their good fortune to chance. Instead, de Bono (1971b) argues, they had the "habit of mind" to make the most of chance happenings, or accidental ways of looking at things, which is none other than lateral thinking in rudimentary form.

> Inventors and famous scientists usually produce a string of new ideas, not just one. This suggests that there is a capacity for generating new ideas that is better developed in some people than in others. This capacity does not seem to be related to sheer intelligence but more to a particular habit of mind, a particular way of thinking . . . (p. 20).

> With practice in looking at things in different ways the capacity to find a context for any given bit of information increases to a remarkable extent. As one gets better at lateral thinking, chance offering of information, chance conjunctions of ideas, come to be more and more useful. It is not that chance itself has changed, but simply that one gets better at harvesting it (p. 104).

The glaring deficiency with this explanation, however, is that it totally fails to consider the extent to which these men were steeped in the knowledge and information of their respective fields. They did not perceive their chance offerings in an informational vacuum. As Pascal himself once said, "Chance favours the prepared mind." What de Bono has failed to see is that this *preparation* does not consist in a peculiar habit of mind called lateral thinking, but in being thoroughly immersed in the knowledge and data in one's field. When one is in command of such information and data, then one is *prepared* to recognize chance offerings for what they are and to capitalize on them. Many people had isolated oxygen before the prepared mind of Lavoisier recognized it for what it was. And many people had seen molds grow on citrus fruit before the prepared mind of Fleming recognized its potential as an antibiotic. De Bono is correct is saying that such people can harvest the chance offering better than most people, but wrong in suggesting it is because of a special ability with lateral thinking. Theirs was a capacity for vertical thinking after being thoroughly prepared with the knowledge of their field. Such preparation is a prerequisite for discoveries of this magnitude, and lateral thinking offers no shortcut to significant discoveries.

Finally, there remains a serious methodological problem with the *use* of lateral thinking. Just as one would not conduct expensive experiments to find out something that is easily available in the nearest library, one would not use lateral thinking until one had first exhausted vertical thought. Vertical thought is by definition (as de Bono would admit) more direct and reliable. But learning *how* to use conventional vertical thought is a complex and time-consuming task; and learning when to use it in many instances often requires asking a lot of questions, or doing a lot of research. To be rational, all of this should be done first. One doesn't reach for the explosives until one has tried the latch on the door. Such considerations mitigate against the initial use of lateral thinking. In a practical context, there will always be a problem about when it is rational to use lateral thinking. Problems do not come marked "solvable" or "unsolvable." One finds this out through normal vertical means. This shows, as argued earlier, that normal vertical thinking is epistemically prior to lateral thinking. The schools, for all their faults, are correct in focusing upon this priority. Unfortunately, many teachers apparently feel (and I stress, *feel*) that de Bono's various thinking programs are providing their students with bright and shiny new thinking skills. They should be reminded that "all that glitters..."

REFERENCES

de Bono, E. *The Mechanism of Mind.* Harmondsworth: Penguin, 1971. (a)

de Bono, E. *The Use of Lateral Thinking.* Harmondsworth: Penguin, 1971. (b)

de Bono, E. *Lateral Thinking for Management.* New York: McGraw-Hill, 1971. (c)

de Bono, E. *Children Solve Problems.* Harmondsworth: Penguin, 1972.

de Bono, E. *PO: Beyond Yes and No.* Harmondsworth: Penguin, 1973. (a)

de Bono, E. "But How Do You Teach Thinking?" *Times Educational Supplement,* August 17, 1973, 4. (b)

de Bono, E. *CoRT Thinking Lesson.* Blandford Forum, Dorset: Direct Educational Services, 1974. (a)

de Bono, E. *Thinking Course for Juniors.* Blandford Forum, Dorset: Direct Educational Services, 1974. (b)

de Bono, E. *Teaching Thinking.* London: Maurice Temple Smith, 1976.

de Bono, E. *Lateral Thinking: A Textbook of Creativity.* Harmondsworth: Penguin, 1977.

DIFFICULTIES IN EVERYDAY REASONING[1]

D. N. Perkins
Richard Allen
James Hafner

ABSTRACT

We report data arguing that difficulties in everyday reasoning reflect superficial mental models of situations more than logical fallacies. The naive reasoner has a "makes-sense epistemology" whose truth test is whether propositions make superficial sense. The sophisticated reasoner has a "critical epistemology," including skills for challenging and elaborating models of situations. A critical epistemology can and should be taught.

REASONING

When one thinks of reasoning, it's natural to think of deduction. For those who have been thinking about deductive reasoning, it's not unnatural to think of some puzzle like this:

In a certain mythical community, politicians always lie, and nonpoliticians always tell the truth. A stranger meets three natives, and asks the first of them if he is a politician. The first native answers the question. The second native then reports that the first native denied being a politician. Then the third native asserts that the first native is really a politician. How many of these three natives are politicians? (Copi [1953], p. 16).

The philosopher Nelson Goodman invented the first truth-tellers-and-liars puzzle in 1931 (Goodman, 1972) and the many variants, including the one quoted here

D.N. Perkins, R. Allen, and J. Hafner are affiliated with the Graduate School of Education at Harvard University.

1. The research reported in this paper was conducted at Project Zero of the Harvard Graduate School of Education with support from the Spencer Foundation. The ideas expressed here do not necessarily reflect the positions or policies of the supporting agency. We thank Ray Nickerson, Jeff Pelletier, and Israel Scheffler for their suggestions on several points.

for its compactness, are problems in deduction. The information suffices, logically, to determine the answer. Of course, the charm of such problems lies in the seeming utter inadequacy of the information. We are not even told how the first native answered.

One of the ironies of reasoning is that in many everyday situations there seems to be a wealth of information. The man or woman on the street has had all sorts of practical experience with aspects of life such as raising children, buying cars, or voting for candidates for office. In the above puzzle there does not seem to be enough information, although there is; in everyday circumstances there *seems* to be a richness of information, but there is not. The everyday reasoner must wring whatever truth can be gotten from the knowledge at hand by weaving a kind of web of plausible conjectures that hangs together well enough to be worth believing in.

People are not very good at doing this, and that may matter a lot more than people not being very good at solving the above puzzle. Furthermore, it may be quite a different sort of activity. In the following pages, we will explore some possible differences between everyday reasoning and formal reasoning, provide some empirical evidence that those differences are not just plausible but actual, and then spend some time trying to characterize just what skillful informal reasoning involves.

A look at a hypothetical example will make a good beginning. One everyday issue used in a study of reasoning we are conducting was this: would a law requiring a five-cent deposit on bottles and cans reduce litter? A person carefully exploring the possible effects of such a law might reason as follows: (Indeed, each step below was mentioned by many subjects in our study, although no one subject explicitly reported all the steps.)

> The law wants people to return the bottles for the five cents, instead of littering them. But I don't think five cents is enough nowadays to get people to bother. But wait, it isn't just five cents at a blow, because people can accumulate cases of bottles or bags of cans in their basements and take them back all at once, so probably they would do that. Still, those probably aren't the bottles and cans that get littered anyway; it's the people out on picnics or kids hanging around the street and parks that litter bottles and cans, and they sure wouldn't bother to return them for a nickel. But someone else might — boy scout and girl scout troops and other community organizations very likely would collect the bottles and cans as a combined community service and fund-raising venture; I know they do that sort of thing. So litter would be reduced.

Now it does not matter for present purposes whether one agrees with the conclusion; the point lies in the structure of the reasoning. Each sentence amounts to a challenge to the sentence before. We have here a series of objections to the argument so far, which present a series of difficulties in everyday reasoning. What is the nature of these difficulties? In complaining about lapses which are neither of deduction nor of probabilistic inference, each objection amounts to a challenge of some premise lying *behind* the previous statement. For example, to the proposition that people will return bottles and cans for five cents, the objection is that five cents will not persuade people to bother. The objection could be rephrased, "The law assumes that five cents is sufficient to motivate people to return bottles. But five cents isn't enough." The objection to that, in turn, is that people need not return their bottles one at a time, but would do so in batches. It could be rephrased, "In saying five cents isn't enough, I'd be assuming that people are returning bottles one at a time. Instead, people would probably return them in batches."

Such challenges to premises are interesting in several ways. First of all, in contrast with reasoning as classically conceived, premises change and accumulate as the argument proceeds, rather than being given at the outset. Second, the premises are somewhat constructive, elaborating the reasoner's understanding of the situation rather than merely objecting. Third, these premises are very context specific. For instance, the judgment that five cents is or is not enough must take into account the reasoner's sense of how much of a nuisance returning a bottle is. Anyone will accede that people do many things for money — even minor amounts of money. But whether five cents is enough is to prompt most people to return bottles and cans cannot be decided by any such sweeping principle. Yet another curious feature is that these premises are not necessarily tightly held, although we usually think of premises being so. For instance, when it occurs to the reasoner that people might return their bottles and cans in groups, he quickly abandons the original image of people returning them one at a time.

In fact, at least in this made-up case, we might say that the reasoner is trying to construct a model of the phenomenon in question: the behavior of people if the deposit legislation were to be passed (Johnson-Laird, in press). As the reasoner proceeds, the model of the situation becomes more and more elaborated. Where the initial scenario has a faceless person returning a bottle for five cents, by the end we see household consumers of beverages accumulating their containers for return rather than discarding them. This of course, does not reduce litter since picnickers and kids are out in parks and on streets littering pretty much as usual. Boy scouts and other such groups are, however, collecting many of those bottles and cans. Perhaps to a considerable extent, difficulties in everyday reasoning are difficulties, not in the proper execution of inferences, but in the building up of an adequate model of the situation being reasoned about.

All this suggests a concept of sound reasoning very much at odds with sound reasoning as it has often been understood. The traditional study of logic and reasoning views premises as sacrosanct. They are the givens; proper reasoning is a matter of proper inference from those givens, and the adequacy of the givens is no proper concern of the study of reasoning. Matters are arguably nearly the reverse where everyday reasoning is concerned. Premises are not given — they must be generated by the reasoner. Proper reasoning, at least in the sense of effective reasoning, is very much a matter of adopting sound premises, and the adequacy of such premises certainly is a proper concern of the study of reasoning.

Reasonable as this may sound, it is a proposal that needs testing. Certainly there are other possibilities. Perhaps everyday arguments are riddled with cases of classical fallacies, to mention a few: affirming the consequent; arguing ad hominem; attributing collective properties of a group to its members individually; or contradicting oneself (Fearnside and Holther, 1959; Hamblin, 1970). Or perhaps the dominant difficulties concern errors of probabilistic inference, such as overgeneralizing from small sample sizes, or overweighting the significance of features supposedly representative of members of various classes (Tversky and Kahneman, 1971, 1974; Nisbett and Ross, 1980). What *sorts* of difficulties arise most often in everyday reasoning? This is an empirical question, a question to be answered by investigating such reasoning.

METHOD

With the need to look at the natural phenomenon in mind, we undertook an empirical investigation of everyday reasoning. There follows a brief description of the approach.

Subjects

There were six student subject groups and two nonstudent groups, each consisting of twenty males and twenty females. The student groups were drawn from local medium-to-top rated universities, and high schools. They ranged from ninth-graders to fourth-year doctoral students. One nonstudent group consisted of nonstudents with college degrees, the other of nonstudents without college degrees.

Procedure

Each subject participated in one session lasting over an hour. First, the subject was given an issue to think about, such as the deposit on bottles issue discussed earlier. After five minutes to ponder the issue and reach a tentative position if possible, the subject was asked to state the position and the reasoning behind it. Subjects who did not feel that they could reach a position were asked to explain the reasoning on both sides of the case that made this difficult. Then came a series of follow-up questions, focusing on some one reason the subject had mentioned, including such queries as, "How does your reason support your conclusion?" and "Can you think of any objections to your reason supporting your conclusion?" This entire process was then repeated for a second issue. Finally, each subject took a short form IQ test.

Issues

Four issues were used in the study: *1. Draft.* Would restoring the military draft significantly increase America's ability to influence world events? *2. Television violence.* Does violence on television significantly increase the likelihood of violence in real life? *3. Bottle bill.* Would a five-cent deposit on bottles and cans significantly reduce litter? *4. Art.* Is the stack of bricks (by minimalist sculptor Carl Andre in London's Tate gallery) really a work of art? Each issue was presented on a typewritten sheet that expanded on the brief statement here. These issues were chosen from several piloted issues as ones that drew a variety of arguments and many advocates on both sides. The four cannot, of course, be considered an adequate statistical sample of the universe of everyday arguments. Such a sample would have to involve many more issues and would have generated far too much data to cope with. Instead, we tried to choose a set of issues that had currency and complexity, and that seemed likely to be reasonably representative of the sorts of everyday reasoning tasks people deal with.

Scoring and Analysis

Using the data base described, we are investigating a number of questions: for instance, what sorts of reasoning do people use in everyday arguments? How do the kinds of arguments people make vary with education and IQ? And to what sorts of objections are everyday arguments subject? The latter, our operationalization of "difficulties in everyday reasoning," is the only one of concern here, and in the present paper we will only treat it in general, rather than in connection with different subject groups.

The objections analyzed came both from the subjects and the experimenters. First of all, each subject was asked to object to two aspects of his own argument during the follow-up questions for each issue. Second, depending on certain decision points in the interview, the experimenter often made an objection, a standardized one, if applicable, or else one conceived on the spot. Third, two investigators listened to a large sample of the tapes of the subjects' arguments and wrote down objections to the arguments they heard. This was a deliberately informal procedure. The investigators were not to try to impose any category system, but simply to respond in a natural manner of discourse, making whatever complaints seemed warranted.

Here a question arises: how can we be confident that the objections raised by the investigators are sound? The answer is that we cannot be fully confident of that. Indeed, we do not believe that the soundness of an objection to an informal argument can be defined in any more rigorous way than through the evaluation of other human judges, or through connoisseurship, so to speak. Nonetheless, there are grounds for proceeding. First of all, the investigators' objections are likely to be reasonably sound since the investigators were, by that point, much more familiar with the ins and outs of the issues than any subject. Second, we conjecture that the distribution of different kinds of objections is much the same for both sound and unsound ones. Third, during the further scoring, objections are being rated for their strength by an experimenter other than the one who generated them so it will be possible to compare distributions of high- and low-rated objections to determine whether any systematic differences occur.

The categorizing by two judges of a large sample of objections — about 2,000—is now in progress. A classification system with fifty-five categories in five major divisions is being used and an adequate, although not very high, rate of interjudge agreement is being maintained. The results we will report are based on those objections classified alike by the two judges, which are, of course, those objections that have the clearest character. In this short space, it is not practical to describe the category system or even its general organization, but mentioning a few of the more self-explanatory category labels may help to give the flavor of the system: contradiction, begging the question, equivocation, counterexample, neglected critical distinction, *reductio ad absurdum*, small sample size, and biased sample. We will describe fully those categories that account for most of the objections. Although scoring is not yet complete, at this point we can identify those categories that are dominant.

THE TROUBLEMAKERS

The scoring to date reveals that about eighty percent of the objections fall into only eight of the fifty-five categories. These categories individually account for from five percent to about twenty percent of the objections. No other category accounts for more than two percent. We will describe the eight "troublemakers" roughly in their order of frequency.

Contrary Consequent

An argument often is challenged by starting with the same situation — enactment of a draft, say — and reasoning to a "contrary consequent," or one inconsistent with the supposed consequent. For instance, someone might argue, "If we had the draft, this would strengthen the army and hence increase our influence on world events." People often object more or less as follows, "If we had the draft, people would resent being drafted and not serve well, so the army would not in fact become stronger." It's a requirement of the contrary consequent category that the objection not merely deny the original argument, but provide a substitute scenario, as in the above example.

Contrary Antecedent

This objection amounts to saying that the supposed consequent of the argument is not, or not necessarily, a consequent of the argument at all, but instead a consequent of something else. For example, subjects occasionally argue, "People are watching more and more television and violence is on the upswing, so television violence increases real-world violence." To this, there is the objection, "There are many other possible causes for increasing violence—for instance, a lax judicial system." Accordingly, there is no justification for reasoning backwards from supposed effect to television violence as the cause. Contrary antecedent objections can also apply to arguments in the forward direction, from cause to effect. For instance, subjects often assert that "more people in the army will make the army stronger." We find the objection, "It's not number of personnel *at all* nowadays that makes armies stronger, but high technology and number of nuclear weapons." This objection denies that numbers lead to strength and reassigns the antecedent role to high technology and nuclear weapons.

External Factor

Sometimes an objection holds that another intervening factor blocks or vitiates the inference, which is not denied as a general tendency, but denied in the case of concern, because of the external factor. For instance, people arguing the draft issue sometimes say,"We have a large population that would pull through in any military crisis." Objection: "A large population used to help, but today modern nuclear weapons can make short work even of a large population." Like contrary consequent objections, external factor objections aver that things will turn out otherwise than proposed in the target argument. Unlike contrary consequent objections, external factor objections identify an interferring factor not intrinsic to the hypothesized situation. Here, nuclear weapons are not caused by large populations, but, since they happen to be around, they can make short work of such populations.

Disconnection

Sometimes people make arguments where the reasons seem to have nothing to do, or not enough to do, with the conclusion. It's not that there is a specific objection, like an external factor or an alternative inferential chain leading to a contrary consequent. Rather, the reasons just do not bear sufficiently. For example, "The percentage of litter varies from place to place, therefore, I have no grounds for deciding whether the bottle bill would significantly reduce litter." Objection: "There's no apparent reason why variation of litter from place to place should eliminate all grounds for deciding on the effects of the bottle bill." For another example, "The United States already has a lot of influence on world events, so a stronger army wouldn't give it any more." Objection: "Having lots of something doesn't in general imply that you can't have more of it."

Scalar Insufficiency

Many arguments involve causal or other factors, and effects or other consequences, that are matters of degree. Sometimes the objection arises that there is an insufficient degree of a factor for the consequent to follow, or for it to follow to the expressed degree. For an example already mentioned, people often object to the anticipated effects of the bottle bill on the grounds that "five cents isn't enough for people to bother with."

Neglected Critical Distinction

The gist of this objection to an argument is as follows, "That may be true in general, but in this situation you're not distinguishing between certain relevant subclasses. In fact, the critical subclass is one you've overlooked, and it turns out contrary to the generalization." Such an objection often is used against the claim that people will return the bottle for five cents. It takes the form, "Many people may do so. But you have to distinguish between people consuming beverages in their homes and people on picnics, or bumming around the streets and parks. It's much less convenient for the latter to return the bottles, and they're the ones that do most of the littering anyway."

Counterexample

This category carries its familiar meaning. It should be added that classes of cases as well as individual cases are scored as counterexamples. The objection that "the people in my class" or "the people in my state" don't, in fact, do such and such would be scored as a counterexample. However, counterexamples must be empirically grounded. The objection that people "would not do such and such" is simply a prediction, and would not be scored as a counterexample.

Alternative Argument

This is a classification for a certain kind of objection to an objection. The new objection acknowledges the force of the original objection, but argues that the inference goes through on other grounds in any case. For instance, to the complaint that "Five cents isn't enough," people sometimes answer, "Probably not by itself. But a bottle bill and the associated publicity will make people more environmentally conscious, so they will be more careful about litter."

THE TROUBLE WITH REASONING

The eight categories discussed above describe the sorts of objections that everyday reasoning, at least as sampled in our study, invites most often. We should caution that we view these categories, for the most part, as constructs of the experimenters designed to sort a body of data. These constructs have no necessary reality as guiding schemata in the minds of skilled reasoners. Nonetheless, the general nature of the troublemakers illuminates the nature of the difficulties people encounter in everyday reasoning. Perhaps the most important point is this: most of the objections extend the reasoner's current model of the situation being reasoned about. Recall that our made-up soliloquy in the introduction emphasized such objections. There, the question was raised whether they played a large, even a dominant, role in difficulties in everyday reasoning. That question is answered here in the affirmative. Five categories — contrary antecedent, contrary consequent, external factor, neglected critical distinction, and alternative argument — all involve objections that introduce new causal chains or other major elements into the reasoner's model of the situation. Together, these account for nearly sixty percent of the objections categorized so far.

Scalar insufficiency is also a complaint about the reasoner's model, although a less revisionary one. Scalar insufficiency objects that a given model, while sound in principle, won't "run." For instance, the objection that "five cents is not enough" acknowledges that while, in principle, people might return their bottles for money, the five-cent reward isn't sufficient to set the scenario in motion. Such judgments, are, as discussed earlier, highly context-specific.

With the counterexample category, one might hope to get away from the context-specific considerations characteristic of the above categories. After all, counterexample is a favorite tactic of the philosopher and the mathematician in their dealings with highly abstract propositions. But nothing of the kind occurs. The sorts of counterexamples people offer tend to be finely tuned to the particulars of the reasoning situation. For instance, counterexamples are frequent in the art issue, where propositions that the stack of bricks is art because it is creative, or interesting to look at, or has symbolic significance, are met by complaints that much science is creative, construction sites are interesting to look at, and flags have symbolic significance, but none of these things is art.

The only frequent category of objections where rather general "logical" lapses appear is disconnection. For instance, there was the proposal that the United States could not get more influence via the draft because they already had a lot of influence. Such *non sequiturs* as these smack of failures to appreciate matters of meaning such as what "lots" does and does not entail. But the disconnection category accounts for only about ten percent of the objections so far scored. In summary, for the most part, objections in everyday reasoning involve elaborations of the model of the situation, scalar insufficiency judgments, and counterexamples, all rather context-specific. The picture is not one of lapses of deductive or inductive logic or probabilistic inference; rather the picture is one of a failure to use the context-specific knowledge people have to edit and evolve context-specific models that are not so subject to context-specific criticism.

ON CONVERSION

There is a natural reservation about this conclusion that needs to be met. What if many of the weaknesses in the arguments could be described *either* as classical fallacies or by raising some model-based point? Then it might be said that our results merely reflect the experimenters' bias toward making a model-based complaint, rather than citing a fallacy when both were available. The experimenters did not have such a policy, so any such bias was spontaneous. But more to the point, we want to argue that, when both are available, the model-based complaint is the right one to make. It is the one that most accurately reflects the psychology of how errors arise in everyday reasoning.

The case can be made by examining a common and classical error of reasoning: "conversion" or "affirming the consequent." This error has the following form: A implies B; B; therefore A. Arguments that can be cast into such a form were mentioned earlier. They are frequent in the art issue, where subjects reason from attributes of art to the conclusion that the bricks are art. To recall the earlier example, "Art is creative. The stack of bricks is creative. So the stack of bricks is art."

But we want a theory of how errors arise psychologically. Do such arguments reflect an actual psychological step of conversion? When a subject says something like the above, we do not know exactly what has occurred psychologically. For instance, as many have pointed out, English is often ambiguous concerning whether "is" means if-then or if-and-only-if. The arguer may have intended "Art if-and-only-if creative" in the first place, advancing a faulty premise rather than converting. There are other simple courses of thought that might yield the same surface argument too. So with just the surface argument to judge from, we cannot tell whether the appearance of a conversion reflects an actual conversion step in the reasoning process.

But we do know something else very important: whatever the course of reasoning, the argument, as stated, is subject to complaints like, "You've said that the bricks are art because they're creative. But many things that are creative are not art — innovative scientific theories for instance." In other words, such complaints have nothing to do with exactly what faulty step is to blame.

Furthermore, what if no such objection could be found? What if neither a critic nor the original arguer could think of things that we consider creative but do not consider art? Then the seeming conversion would be acceptable. It would have passed muster by the context-specific test of whether the conversion works in the world as it is. True, a critic could still complain, "Just because everything around that's creative is art, that doesn't mean that everything possible that's creative would be art. You still haven't shown logical necessity." But the original arguer might say, "Acknowledged. But, after all, conditions for art are not given in advance here, but are at issue here. What better move than to find conditions that seem to have some empirical soundness and project them?" Indeed, experiments suggest that people who appear to make conversion errors on syllogisms often are doing exactly that (Staudenmayer, 1975). They tend to convert just when the situation posed by the syllogism makes conversion a good practical bet.

Are we saying that conversion is a legitimate inference? Of course not. The original if-then premise is never *grounds* for the backwards inference, but is, at best, an occasion for considering whether the backwards inference might hold. Rather, the point is that often the backwards inference may be judged to hold, and that whether it can be so judged soundly is the real issue in contexts of everyday reasoning. A reasoner who actually did convert frequently, but then always checked the model being evolved for its match with world knowledge, would not reach unsound conclusions, unless the situation were a strictly formal one where new premises could not be added. Furthermore, such a reasoner might be better off simply in generating many conversions for editorial consideration. After all, conversions often are good practical bets, and the reasoner who never pondered them out of formal fastidiousness would be likely to end up with weaker models.

In summary, although a conversion step in itself is always an error, the practical question is whether the reasoner is a good editor, expunging conversions that have no justification beyond the inadequate justification of the original premise. Because such editing has the last word, we suggest that seeming conversions in nonformal arguments, whether there was an actual psychological conversion step or not, should be understood as failures to check the inference against a good context-specific model of the situation. Thus model-retrieving and model-building appear paramount in practical reasoning.

MAKES-SENSE EPISTEMOLOGY

In light of the foregoing, how should skilled reasoning be understood? What factors go into it? One such factor is a *large knowledge repertoire*. Clearly, the reasoner busily assembling cogent models of situations must have a repertoire of knowledge to draw upon. Such a repertoire would include what the reasoner believes are facts about the world, and also a variety of causal schemata and scripts that the reasoner could weave together to build models of unfamiliar situations (Nisbett and Ross, 1980; Schank and Abelson, 1977).

Another contributor to skilled reasoning might be called *efficient knowledge evocation*. Merely having a repertoire of knowledge does the reasoner little good unless that knowledge is brought to bear. The normal psychological processes of pattern recognition and everyday understanding figure here. Some reasoners, pondering a situation, may find that models of the situation suggest themselves, while other reasoners draw a blank. Some may find that complications in a model already conceived occur to them spontaneously, while other reasoners display no such critical alertness. Furthermore, efficiency of evocation might turn out to be a meaningful parameter of cognitive functioning. Westcott (1968), attempting an operationalization of the concept of intuition, demonstrated that individuals varied considerably in their ability to reach correct conclusions on the basis of minimal evidence.

However, there is some reason for dissatisfaction with large knowledge repertoire and efficient knowledge evocation as a complete explanation for effective reasoning. For those who believe that reasoning is a special skill, there is nothing specific to reasoning about these traits. They would serve numerous other cognitive endeavors besides deciding about the truth of propositions by constructing arguments. The two traits are resources of understanding in general. Indeed, most of the time a large knowledge repertoire and efficient evocation do not at all feed the sorts of extended deliberative processes we have in mind when we think of reasoning. They simply function reflexively. One sees or hears and understands.

Instead, it's plausible that effective reasoning depends not solely on sufficient knowledge and efficient spontaneous knowledge evocation, but on an active effort to interrogate one's knowledge base in order to construct arguments pro and con. With this in mind, it's useful to have an idealized characterization of what naive reasoners do wrong. Naive reasoners might be said to have a "makes-sense epistemology." Of course, this does not mean that they have an explicit philosophy about what grounds are necessary for belief. But it does mean something in terms of manifested behavior: such reasoners act as though the test of truth is that a proposition makes intuitive sense, sounds right, rings true. They see no need to criticize or revise accounts that do make sense — the intuitive feel of fit suffices.

A makes-sense epistemology gives a unified picture of a wide range of findings about faulty reasoning. Concerning model building, for example, the simple account of the effects of the bottle bill where people return the bottles for the deposit "makes sense." So does the complaint that people won't, because the deposit is not enough. And so on through the example we began with. At each stage along the way the latest version makes sense — until a complication is introduced that qualifies it and develops the model further.

The same test of making sense accounts for other pitfalls of reasoning. Concerning *ad hominem* argument, it makes sense to assume that reprehensible people's reasons are also reprehensible. For another example, why doubt that small samples are representative of the classes from which they are drawn since it makes sense that samples should be typical of their parent classes (Tversky and Kahneman, 1971). And so on.

There is another, more psychological, way of characterizing a makes-sense epistemologist. Such a person reasons so as to minimize cognitive load. Simon (1947) has written about the limited rationality of the human reasoner. In the makes-sense epistemologist, that trait appears in pure form. Anything that complicates the cognitive activity is shunned in favor of the simplest, most straightforward interpretation that seems to fit. Such a thinker's reasoning is dominated by a strategy of cognitive load minimization, rather than a strategy of truth-testing. Or perhaps it is careless to speak of a strategy. Perhaps this sort of behavior is simply a default condition.

It has to be understood that a makes-sense epistemology works rather well. It must, or there would be more environmental pressure on people to advance beyond it, and not so many people functioning as makes-sense epistemologists. In most situations, quick effortless understanding serves perfectly well. In situations not understood immediately, the first model we deliberately generate that makes sense often serves perfectly well. When it does not, and we are dealing with a situation in practical terms, we quickly discover that failing through experience. What matter if we could have found out the failing a little earlier through more careful thinking? The sort of probing, critical, comparative thinking that makes the very most of a person's knowledge resources is not usually needed. We value it for those occasions where it is.

CRITICAL EPISTEMOLOGY

The notion of a makes-sense epistemology that minimizes cognitive load at the expense of truth-testing shows how far, short of sound reasoning, a large knowledge repertoire and even efficient evocation of knowledge can leave a thinker. With a makes-sense epistemology, a thinker will not be cultivating available knowledge resources, but simply letting them grow willy nilly into all sorts of careless beliefs, some of which of course will be pruned by later experiences. It's useful to have a contrasting characterization of an idealized skilled reasoner. This reasoner could be said to have a "critical epistemology." Where the makes-sense epistemologist is not really much of an epistemologist at all — there is no explicit theory of grounds for belief and the tacit theory is unsound — the critical epistemologist not only has an explicit theory, but a sound one. A critical epistemology might be described as follows.

Espistemological Realism

First of all, there would be an understanding of the pitfalls of justification. A critical epistemology includes knowledge of how common superficial fits between models and data really are, and how frequently more than one model fits the same situation. It includes other characteristic problems of the relation between evidence and theory too. For example, that small samples cannot be relied upon to give an accurate picture of their parent classes; or that chains of inferences, each of which has a probability somewhat less than one, cannot be confidently made, even if the links in the chain are all rather high probability ones. Reasoners with such knowledge could be said to be epistemological realists. Knowing the score, they have higher standards for the sorts of justifications they take as adequate.

Dialectical Style and Skills

With a critical epistemology should also come practical tactics and skills for developing sound models of situations. One of the most powerful of these tactics is to ask the question, "What reasons are there why this model might fail" or, for short, "Why not?" (Perkins, in press). Asking "Why not?" runs absolutely contrary to the makes-sense epistemology, because it refuses to accept at face value what seems to be an adequate account. Instead of settling for the first decent fit, the "Why not?" tactic expects that a dialectical process of argument and counterargument will gradually evolve a more differentiated model. Of course, the "Why not?" question could lead to barren, nit-picking criticism. But it will not if the reasoner answers it in ways that improve the model, and so increase the reasoner's understanding of the situation.

Formal Repertoire

Also not to be neglected in a critical epistemology is what might be called a formal repertoire. This means a knowledge of logical and heuristic forms that can be applied to the practical business of reasoning. For example, there is the propositional calculus, something that may see some use in informal contexts, although not very commonly. There is a *modus tollens* and *reductio ad absurdum*, which certainly do see many uses in informal contexts. Elementary statistical knowledge about sufficient sample sizes can help to guard against unwarranted inferences and may sanction warranted ones, and such knowledge is applicable in many informal contexts. Several heuristics may be helpful in decision-making situations, where the justification for one or another course of action consists in weighing gains and risks — a mini-max strategy, cost-benefits analysis, or minimizing maximum regret as reviewed by Hayes (1981), for example.

Our aim in introducing makes-sense and critical epistemologies and epistemologists has been to try to capture a couple of points about everyday reasoning that seem apparent from the results of these and other studies. First of all, not only formal reasoning but even everyday reasoning is a genuinely distinct skill. It is more than a matter of general mental ability, as reflected in a large accumulation of knowledge and efficient evocation. Most of all, it is a matter of working with and through a critical epistemology, a combination of understanding, style, and tactics that makes the most of the knowledge and knowledge-evoking powers the individual has.

Second, formal reasoning, as it has often been studied, and everyday reasoning are two rather different matters. A look at the features of a critical epistemology makes this clear. Where a critical epistemology involves critical realism, a person skilled in formal reasoning might know little about, for instance, the risks of statistical inference, or might have little appreciation of the looseness of fit between casual everyday theories and the experiential data for them, and how readily that looseness of fit leads to unwarranted beliefs. Where a critical epistemology involves a dialectical style and skills, the "Why not?" question is not such a crucial one in formal reasoning contexts. True, it is often the mission of the mathematician to seek counterexamples if something cannot be proven. On the other hand, once something appears to have been proven, seeking counterexamples or any sort of contrary argument is beside the point. One solid deductive chain is sufficient to establish a theorem.

But informal reasoning is utterly different. New premises, grounded in knowledge or causal schemes not previously invoked, can always enter the scene to challenge old ones. Furthermore, inferences are often probabilistic rather than deductive in character. Therefore, one sound justification — as sound as justifications get in everyday situations — by no means makes it pointless to ask the "Why not?" question, which therefore takes on a much more crucial role. As to formal repertoire, the formal reasoner may have mastery of deductive forms, but heuristics such as minimizing maximum regret may be a worthwhile resource in everyday situations, where strict deduction is a rarity and the more esoteric syllogistic forms hardly ever appear.

A final point about a critical epistemology: if we are right in characterizing it as a matter of knowledge and know-how, it should be teachable. Teaching it would mean teaching something quite different from conventional logic or statistical inference, and also quite different from debate. To inculcate a critical epistemology would be to train people to build understandings of situations by interrogating their own knowledge, and playing off different sorts of knowledge and intuitions against one another in order to evolve sounder models. In short, it would be teaching an art and craft of understanding, a worthy enterprise if ever there was one.

REFERENCES

Copi, I.M. *Introduction to Logic.* New York: Macmillan, 1953.

Fearnside, W.W. and Holther, W.B. *Fallacy: The Counterfeit of Argument.* Englewood Cliffs, NJ: Prentice-Hall, 1959.

Goodman, N. "The Truth-tellers and the Liars." In *Problems and Projects.* Indianapolis, IN: Bobbs-Merrill Co., 1972.

Hamblin, C.L. *Fallacies.* London: Methuen & Co., Ltd., 1970.

Hayes, J.R. *The Complete Problem Solver.* Philadelphia: The Franklin Institute Press, 1981.

Johnson-Laird, P.N. "Logical Thinking: Does it Occur in Daily Life? Can it be Taught?" In *Thinking and Learning Skills, Volume 2: Current Research and Open Questions,* S.S. Chipman, J.W. Siegel, & R. Glaser (Eds.). Hillsdale, NJ: Lawrence Erlbaum, in press.

Nisbett, R. and Ross, L. *Human Inference: Strategies and Shortcomings of Social Judgment.* Englewood Cliffs, NJ: Prentice-Hall, 1980.

Perkins, D.N. "General Cognitive Skills: Why Not?" In *Thinking and Learning Skills, Volume 2: Current Research and Open Questions,* S.S. Chipman, J.W. Siegel, & R. Glaser (Eds.). Hillsdale, NJ: Lawrence Erlbaum, in press.

Schank, R., and Abelson, R.P. *Scripts, Plans, Goals and Understanding: An Inquiry Into Human Knowledge Structures.* Hillsdale, NJ: Lawrence Erlbaum, 1977.

Simon, H.A. *Administrative Behavior.* New York: Macmillan, 1947.

Staudenmayer, H. "Understanding Conditional Reasoning with Meaningful Propositions." In *Reasoning: Representation and Process in Children and Adults,* R. Falmagne (Ed.). Hillsdale, NJ: Lawrence Erlbaum, 1975.

Tversky, A., and Kahneman, D. "The Belief in the Law of Small Numbers," *Psychological Bulletin,* 1971, *76,* 105–110.

Tversky, A., and Kahneman, D. "Judgment Under Uncertainty: Heuristics and Biases," *Science,* 1974, *185,* 1124–31.

Westcott, M.R. *Toward a Contemporary Psychology of Intuition.* New York: Holt, Rinehart, & Winston, 1968.

MENTAL TRAINING:
THINKING REHEARSAL AND ITS USE

Laura H. Jansson

ABSTRACT

This paper discusses the practice of mental rehearsal used by elite athletes to increase learning speed and physical performance. Today increasing attention is being paid to the psychological aspects of coaching. Because the best athletes are all in top physical condition, psychological strength is often critical to winning. Mental rehearsal is only one of many methods of psyching up. In this paper, I will describe the physiological basis of the practice, review research data measuring its effectiveness, and present my own and other athletes' experience with it.

Attempts to separate mind from body have long been prominent in philosophical literature. It is common practice to believe that the mental or cognitive functions of the organism are what occur in the classroom, while physical responses pertain solely to the athletic field. From this point of view, the only way to improve skilled motor performance is through constant, overt practice of the specific task (Singer, 1975). Such a notion is, in fact, false. Cognitive and motor functions are very much interrelated. There is neurophysical evidence that when a person thinks about an action, or the movement of some part of the body, an increase in electromyographic recordings (*i.e.*, electrical activity of a muscle) occurs in the corresponding locations. When an action is imagined, impulses are produced which travel the nervous pathways associated with that action. This "Carpenter Effect" (Ulich, 1967) is the scientific basis for the practice of mental rehearsal.

Mental rehearsal consists of imagining a motion or series of motions and the situation in which they will be performed. When this is done in sufficient detail, the Carpenter Effect can facilitate neurological development which improves the coordination and efficiency of subsequent performance. Such improvement can occur even when the neural stimulation is not sufficient to cause observable actions (Fujita, 1973).

It is well recognized in sport that the mere execution of motions is only a partial determiner of success: perceptual processes are critical to effective timing; cognitive processes interact with motor execution when tactics and strategies are required.

L.H. Jansson is in the Sportpsychology Department of The Finnish Sports Academy, 19120 Vierumäki 2, Finland.

Now we see that to a certain extent athletic skills can be acquired or maintained with no overt physical practice (Singer, 1975). Of course mental rehearsal cannot completely replace active practice, but for skills involving a high degree of coordination, it has very nearly the same effect (Ulich, 1967).

It is important to make a technical distinction here. There is a difference between mental rehearsal and simple imagery. Rehearsal involves actively running through an image or series of images. By contrast, imagery simply involves the ability to develop an image without necessarily analyzing its content (Niedeffer, 1976). For instance, right now, without actually engaging in the movements, attempt to get both the image and the feelings associated with kicking a ball. Notice how, as you carefully attend to each movement, you begin to actually use the muscles involved. You do not use them in a way that increases their strength but rather in a way that helps your coordination and timing.

Rushall (1979) suggests that a word of warning is in order. The skills and behaviors that are rehearsed should be well-established conceptually. This is to insure that they are practiced consistently, so that the appropriate neurological pathways will be stimulated repeatedly. The athlete who has not learned a skill to an adequately high degree may make significant variations between repetitions; this can lead to erratic performance and an increase in errors.

Singer (1978) states that, as far back as 1899, the question was raised as to whether gymnastics movements could be learned through mental rehearsal, even when they were not practiced physically. Investigations of this type continued using terms such as mental rehearsal, self-verbalization, conceptualization, covert practice, and just plain mental practice. Most such studies concluded that mental practice benefited the acquisition of skills, in comparison to no practice at all.

However, in spite of the fairly common application of various types of mental rehearsal, relatively little has been done scientifically to examine its effects.

I will now examine the effect of mental rehearsal from two avenues: research data and documentation in sport. First I will review three scientific studies of mental rehearsal.

Experiment Number 1. Jessen, Medler and Volkamer in Germany (1971) studied running the 100m hurdles. Both the experimental group (EG) and the control group (CG) were Physical Education students. They were pre-tested by timing their running of the 100m hurdles. The experimental group was then taught to use thinking rehearsal; and asked to mentally practice running the 100m hurdles, ten times per day for two weeks. After a fortnight the runs were timed again. (The results are shown in *Table 1.*) The difference between the groups (about 3/10 sec.) is statistically significant in the five percent level.

Table 1

	Average improvement in seconds
EG	0.57
CG	0.24

Experiment Number 2. Verdelly Clark at Northern Illinois University (1960) examined basketball performance. He experimented with the effect of mental rehearsal on learning a specific basketball shot using varsity, junior varsity and novice high school students. The three groups were in turn divided in two each. For fourteen days, half of the subjects practiced the skill mentally, while the other half practiced physically. They all rehearsed thirty shots daily. (The results are shown in *Table 2*.) The varsity physical practice group improved sixteen percent, while the varsity mental practice group improved fifteen percent. The physical practice group of junior varsity performers improved twenty-four percent and the mental practice group of junior varsity improved twenty-three percent. The novice physical practice group increased forty-four percent, while the mental practice group improved twenty-six percent.

Table 2

	Experienced players (varsity)	Advanced players (jr. varsity)	Beginners (high school players)
Physical rehearsal group	16%	24%	44%
Mental rehearsal group	15%	23%	26%

These results show that mental rehearsal can be almost as effective as physical training, for those who already have sufficient skill. Notice that with experienced varsity players, it is not possible to improve the performance as much as with beginners: a player who shoots eight out of ten balls into the basket can improve his skill only twenty-five percent, whereas a beginner who shoots five out of ten balls can improve one hundred percent. Further analysis by Clark indicated a relationship between the subject's ability to visualize the motor skill and the amount of improvement experienced.

Experiment Number 3. M. Medler (1971) studied the effect of mental rehearsal in gymnastics. He used three experimental groups, each employing a different method for learning well-defined skills in gymnastics. Performance level was defined by judges in a competition, with a session before and after the experiment. (The results are shown in *Table 3*.)

Table 3

	Improvement
EG 1 (Mental rehearsal)	8.4%
EG 2 (Mental and physical rehearsal)	11.6%
EG 3 (Physical rehearsal)	10.9%
EG 4 (Control group, no rehearsal)	.8%

Performance level improved in all three groups. Combined mental and physical training was most effective. However, the difference between EG 2 and EG 3 is not significant at the one percent level.

Other experiments, such as The Finnish Sports Institute (Suonperä, 1980) study of the tennis forehand, have given results similar to those mentioned above. Volkamer (1976) got the best results when mental rehearsal was combined with physical practice. Jessen (1972) found that the effects of mental rehearsal depended on the intelligence level of the subject. Kanygin, V. and Kozlov, F. (1979) report successfully using mental rehearsal with weight lifters to control the psychological stresses of competition.

Another form of evidence for the effectiveness of mental rehearsal comes from statistics published by Unestål (1980) in his recent study of Swedish athletes in the Ottawa Congress of Sportspsychology (Canada). (His results are shown in *Table 4*.) Only one-half percent of all Swedish athletes used mental rehearsal. But thirty percent of all Swedish Champions used mental rehearsal and thirty-six percent of Swedes who won the European Championships used mental rehearsal.

Among the Swedish 1980 Olympic Team members, the results are even more dramatic: twenty-nine percent of the total team members used mental rehearsal as part of their training; fifty-eight percent of the Swedes who made it to the finals used mental rehearsal; sixty-seven percent of the Medalists used mental rehearsal and eighty-six percent of the Swedish Gold and Silver Medalists used mental rehearsal consistently.

These few studies summarize the general findings about mental rehearsal: first, repeated trials and sessions of mental rehearsal increase the performance levels of what is rehearsed. This means that it is possible to learn, or at least increase the efficiency of what is already learned, through mental practice (Prather, 1973). Second, the effect of mental rehearsal depends on the initial performance level. Most research has concerned the performance of short duration physical skills (for example, shooting a basket or throwing a ring). However, it has been shown that the mental rehearsal of complex and extended duration events also benefits the performance of what has been rehearsed (Prather, 1973 and Rushall, 1970). This means that it is helpful to rehearse whole races, set-plays to be performed in a game, downhill ski-runs, *etc.*

The famous French alpine skier Jean Claude Killy, conceded that after he physically practices a new ski slope, he mentally rehearses that same slope—with a stop watch! He concentrates on every turn and part of the slope, timing himself as he envisions his performance from start to finish. Killy states that the recorded time for his mental performance closely parallels the time he actually achieves in the competition that follows (Singer, 1975). Basketball player Pete Maravich has said that he mentally replays entire games in his head. During my active time in diving, I mentally rehearsed each dive several times before training sessions. This was a daily routine and part of practice. In competitions, like in the Olympic Games in Munich, 1972, I mentally rehearsed each dive. Mental rehearsal helped me to focus my attention on the dive to be performed and to forget the one already done. With mental rehearsal, I prepared both my mind for the coming dive and my body for the series of movements; mental rehearsal enabled me to forget everything else in the surroundings and in my mind.

Apart from learning motor skills in sports, mental rehearsal is beneficial for overcoming psychological problems associated with one's performance. One very common problem is failing to maintain effective concentration in the face of external disturbances. Through mental rehearsal, one learns to direct attention to those cues that are most important for his or her performance and at the same time to close his or her perceptive faculty to external stimuli.

Table 4. The Application of Mental Rehearsal Among Swedish Athletes (Unestål, 1980)

Percent of Mentally Rehearsed Athletes in Sweden 1980

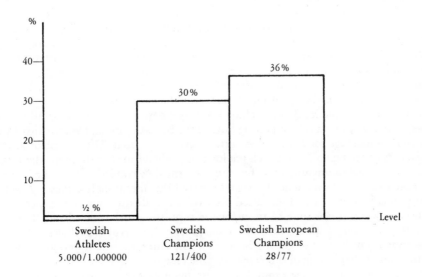

Percent of Mentally Rehearsed Athletes in the Swedish Olympic Team 1980

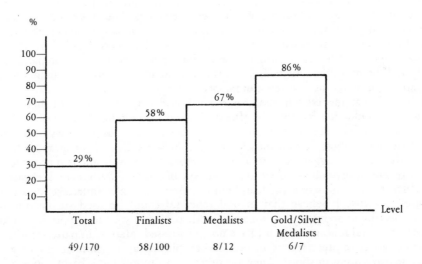

Other common psychological problems in sports include anxiety, tension, fear and stress, all of which can be brought under control with mental rehearsal. For instance, one learns to recognize feelings of muscle tension or learns to become aware of the relationships between one's bodily feelings and the actual performance. This means that one learns to control his or her level of arousal because the athlete is able to direct attention either toward or away from anxiety-inducing stimuli. In addition, one learns to deal with more complex situations because one is able to be more selective about what he or she attends to (Niedeffer, 1976). In my sport, for instance, divers respond to anxiety by running for the end of the board instead of taking a normal approach. Anxious bowlers and golfers find themselves pulling the ball or the club as they try to hurry through the activity. Mental rehearsal teaches these athletes to perceive their own anxiety and to learn to consciously slow down when feeling excited.

There is the story of a top skater who quite unexpectedly fell in practice and then continued falling in the same point in the back curve. His fear of falling—the mere thought—made him fall over and over again. Analyzing the whole situation with his coach, the skater learned the discriminative cues that he should be attending to when approaching the back curve. Rehearsing the situation mentally, he trained himself to focus his attention on the selected discriminative cues and, to his surprise, on the first subsequent attempt, he skated the back curve cleanly.

One more example for diving. When learning a new dive, for example off a 10m tower, there is always a fear of getting hurt in the first attempt and yet the first try is the most important for getting the correct form. My coach, Dick Kimball at the University of Michigan, used to tell me long beforehand to start thinking about the new dive. I tried to imagine myself performing the dive correctly. With the help of my coach and other experienced divers, I selected the discriminative cues typical for that particular dive. Then I rehearsed the dive mentally during a certain period of time, and when it was time to try it for the very first time, I was already familiar with the situation. With the help of mental rehearsal, I was able to direct my attention away from the fear of getting hurt (*i.e.*, the entry into the water) and instead focused on the beginning of the dive (*i.e.*, the take-off).

I have given only a few examples of the many positive experiences that elite athletes have had with mental rehearsal. Some have found the procedures extremely helpful, but others have not, complaining that they interfere with performance. It is thought that the failure of these athletes to benefit from the procedures may be due to inappropriate application. While everyone thinks about his or her own performance, not everyone does it systematically and consciously. One gets the most out of the method only when one is able to conceptualize every detail of the action being rehearsed. Correct systematic application of mental rehearsal prepares the body and the mind for activity and serves as the main mechanism for maintaining attention control on the task-relevant factors.

I believe that mental rehearsal has a much wider application than merely to athletes. It could, for example, be effectively used in the rehabilitation of injured patients. With mental rehearsal, one can stimulate the nervous pathways associated with the use of those certain muscles while they are still weak or incapacitated. Secondly, I would suggest the use of mental rehearsal to overcome fear or anxiety. Many people have phobias concerning some type of activity. With mental rehearsal, they can gradually overcome the fear, before having to actually undertake the activity itself. Finally, I believe that mental rehearsal could be used successfully in art—especially in acting and in music. Here it is easy to see the importance of an aspect of mental rehearsal which I have not yet stressed. Man is, in part, a spiritual creature; affective processes are involved when playing an instrument, a part in a play, or performing in sports. They are necessary to producing a harmonious outcome. The body performs, but the spirit tunes the instrument, and the instrument is both mind and body.

REFERENCES

Clark, C.V. "The Effect of Mental Practice on the Development of a Certain Motor Skill," *Research Quarterly*, 1960, *31*.

Fujita, A. "An Experimental Study on the Theoretical Basis of Mental Training." In *Proceedings of the Third World Congress of the International Society of Sports Psychology Abstracts.* Madrid: Instituto Nacional de Education Fisic y Deportes, 1973.

Kanygin, V. and Kozlov, E. "Psychological Stress in Weightlifting Competition," *Soviet Sports Review,* 1979, 14, *4,* 202.

Jessen, M. "Untersuchungen zum Zusammenghang und der Fähigkeit Mental zu Trainieren." In *Experimente in der Sportpsychologie,* Volkamer, M. (hrg.). Schorndorf: Verlag Karl Hofman, 1972.

Medler, M. "Untersuchungen zum Mentalen Training." In *Motivation im Sport,* Schorndorf: Verlag Karl Hofman, 1971.

Niedeffer, R.M. *The Inner Athlete.* New York: Thomas Y. Crowell Company, 1976.

Prather, D.C. "Prompted Mental Practice as a Flight Simulator," *Journal of Applied Psychology,* 1973, *57,* 353–355.

Rushall, B.S. *Psyching in Sport.* London: Pelham Books, Ltd., 1979.

Singer, R.N. *Myths and Truths in Sports Psychology.* New York: Harper and Row, 1975.

Suonperä, M. "Keskittymisen Taitoa Voidaan Oppia," *Valmennus-lehti,* 1980, *6,* 28–30.

Ulich, E. "Some Experiments of the Function of Mental Training in the Acquisition of Motor Skills," *Ergonomics,* 1967, *10,* 411–419.

Unestal, L.E. "Mental Training Among Swedish Athletes," Congress of Sports Psychology, Ottawa, Canada, 1981.

Volkamer, M., Jessen, K. and Medler, M. "Formen und Möglichkeiten des Mentalen Training," *Leistungs-sport,* 1971, *1,* 50–56.

THE ANALYSIS OF PROBLEM-SOLVING STRATEGIES: IMPLICATIONS FOR PSYCHOMETRIC TESTING[1]

Kristina Macrae

ABSTRACT

Psychometrics has been traditionally concerned with statistical techniques for determining the properties of test parameters, rather than the psychological process underlying their performance. However, studies analyzing actual strategies of item solution challenge the validity of the fundamental assumptions of test theory, and hence the statistical techniques applied to test data.

THINKING

Psychometric testing has become increasingly contentious in recent years; this is amply demonstrated in the October 1981 issue of the *American Psychologist,* which is wholly devoted to the debate of test theory and practice. It is the hiatus between theory and practice that is often seen to characterize disputes over testing. Scarr (1981) for example states that "proponents of tests cite their exemplary statistical virtues; opponents strike at their role in perpetuating social and economic injustice" (p. 1159). For many authors (*e.g.*, Glaser, 1981; Gordon & Terrell, 1981; Scarr, 1981) a chief source of injustice stems from the use of tests as selection rather than as diagnostic instruments. The emphasis on selection, once prevalent in western educational systems, is now giving way to the desire for every individual to succeed to the limit of his educational opportunities (Glaser, 1981). According to Gordon and Terrell (1981), "current testing practices . . . all but preclude attention to the diagnostic and prescriptive functions of assessment that are so essential to effective intervention" (p. 1170). Hence it has been claimed that psychometric testing yields little information of direct relevance to educators.

Why is it that tests are so lacking in diagnostic virtues? There are at least two reasons for this. One is our limited knowledge of the cognitive processes underlying test performance; the other, the untenable assumptions entailed in psychometric theory. The two are not distinct: unwarranted statistical assumptions about test-

---

K. Macrae is in the Psychology Department of La Trobe University, Bundoora, Australia 3083.

taking behavior can only be rectified through a clearer understanding of what these behaviors are. McNemar in 1964 was critical of the failure of differential psychologists to "come to grips with the *process* or operation by which a given organism achieves an intellectual response" (p. 881). Now, nearly twenty years later, the same criticism is still being levelled (Garcia, 1981; Glaser, 1981; Gordon and Terrell, 1981). This lack of progress in delineating processes and operations promotes injustice for low-scoring groups in particular. If we are to accept the construct validity claimed for a test, we know what the low-scoring individual *can't* do; but we do not know what he does instead, and why, nor whether it can be or even ought to be remedied. Glaser (1981) regards investigation of the misconceptions that lead to errors in test items as one of the crucial areas of future testing research. He suggests that error responses may represent a "complex and logical thought process toward which teaching can be directed" (p. 926).

If to date there has been slow development in this kind of research, it is perhaps understandable that psychometric theory has also been accused of progressing very little (*e.g.,* Hunt, Lunneborg and Lewis, 1975; Lumsden, 1976). The aim of what follows is to use two psychometric issues, test score changes and item-scoring formulas, to illustrate the failure of psychometricians to support statistical models with adequate empirical evidence or theoretical justification.

A central feature of classical test theory is the true-error model of test scores, which defines an individual's observed score as the sum of a true and an error component (Lord and Novick, 1968). A number of assumptions are associated with the model, the two chief ones being that the true score is assumed to be constant across repeated testing, and that the expected error score is zero. For the model to be applicable, it follows that the means of observed scores should be equal across testing occasions. Ng (1974) tested this proposition with three administrations of Raven's Progressive Matrices. His results indicated that one or the other, or both of the assumptions stated above, is false. He further claimed that "some or all of the postulates concerning distribution properties of errors are not tenable" (p. 4). While Ng cautions against generalizing these results to other tests and other samples, he argues for the importance of routine examining of the applicability of the model.

Ng's results are not unexpected, as systematic changes (typically gains) in ability test scores have been observed and discussed for many years in the literature. Alexander (1947) and Hoffman (1963) developed models attempting to account for systematic changes in test scores. Alexander attributes such changes to systematic errors, while Hoffman regards them as systematic changes in true scores. Alexander's model implies that improvement in test scores is essentially spurious, and reflects no real change in the ability measured by the test. Under Hoffman's model, score gains reflect the individual's capacity to profit from past experience, and hence his "ability." Various authors have discussed this issue from a theoretical perspective (for example, Anastasi, 1981; Guilford, 1967; Heim and Wallace, 1949, 1950; Vernon, 1938, 1960; Woodrow, 1939). However, nowhere in the literature is there any empirical evidence that would allow one to choose between an interpretation of systematic changes in test score as "true" or "error" variation. In my view, this can only be determined by investigation of the psychological processes underlying test performance. While statistical analysis may demonstrate the existence of systematic changes in test performance, it provides no clue as to the nature of these changes or their explanation.

A separate issue concerns the item-scoring formulas by which indices of test performance are obtained. The most widely used scoring system is the dichotomous distinction between correct and incorrect responses to test items. This relies on the assumption that if the subject is wrong, then he is "completely ignorant . . . and has no basis for choosing among the possible responses'' (Lord and Novick, 1968, p. 309). All incorrect responses are considered equally likely to occur and hence receive equal weight.

The assumption stated above is clearly empirically false. Lord and Novick point out that the distribution of error responses to multiple-choice test items is never rectangular in practice. The notion of random guessing may also be theoretically untenable; it is quite feasible that an individual could justify the choice of one incorrect alternative over others. Dressel and Schmid (1953) investigated the degree of certainty of correctness experienced by subjects in selecting response alternatives to test items. Random guessing accounted for only ten percent of response choices, and Dressel and Schmid concluded that individuals experience high levels of certainty even when incorrect.

A number of authors (for example, Bock, 1972; Chernoff, 1962; de Finetti, 1965) have developed scoring models which embrace the notion that testees may prefer some incorrect alternatives over others. The models generate various ways of differentially weighting error responses. However Lumsden (1976) states that there have been no serious attempts to evaluate the relative merits of different scoring systems. Response alternatives may vary in the extent to which they represent the use of the processes intended to be measured by the test. Some error alternatives may represent the use of strategies which deviate only slightly from the ''ideal'' strategy, leading to correct solution of an item. Such response choices might be considered less erroneous than those founded in strategies showing more severe distortions of the thinking required to solve the item correctly. Response alternatives could then be weighted according to degree of departure from the ideal strategy.

In the alternative scoring models referred to above, weightings for response alternatives are derived from either distribution of error choices (*e.g.*, Chernoff, 1962), or personal probabilities (de Finetti, 1965). However, neither the most frequently occurring error choice, nor the alternative assigned the highest probability, necessarily reflects the quality of the strategy underlying it. Statistical criteria for weighting response alternatives do not guarantee that a scoring system will be psychologically meaningful.

To conclude this overview of psychometric testing, it is being argued that there is a need for greater understanding of the processes underlying performance on psychometric tests. Knowledge of the problem-solving strategies that individuals adopt in solving test items, and knowledge of the way in which these change over repeated testing, would provide a basis for developing psychometric models with some theoretical substance to them. The aim of the present study was fourfold: first, to generate a multiple-choice test whose response alternatives represented the use of uniquely specifiable problem-solving strategies; second, to rank order error alternatives, according to degree of departure from the ideal strategy; third, to investigate patterns of response choices occurring within and between item sets; and fourth, to identify the types of changes in response choice occurring on a second testing occasion using a parallel form.

EXPERIMENT 1

The first stage of this experiment involved the construction of a test of twelve items. These were similar in format to Raven's Progressive Matrices, except that each item consisted only of the item stem (that is, the matrix) and contained no response alternatives. The test comprised three sets of four items. Within each set the matrices were structurally equivalent but varied in content; the logical form of the matrix was expressed in number, letter, pictorial and figural form. The three-item sets differed in structure, and using mathematical criteria, were ranked in order of complexity (see Thorburn, 1977). Item Set 1 denoted the set of items with the least, and Item Set 3, that with the most complex structure.

The length of the test was limited to twelve items, as each subject would be required to give a detailed description of the strategy employed in solving each item, and it was anticipated that this would take up to one and a half hours.

The purpose of Experiment 1 was to derive from subjects' protocols, a set of six response alternatives for each item. A further objective was to rank order the strategies underlying the alternatives in terms of departure from the "ideal" strategy.

Subjects

The subjects were fifty male and forty-eight female undergraduate psychology students. Mean ages were 19.1 and 20.2 years for males and females respectively, with standard deviations of 3.95 years for males and 5.85 years for females.

Procedure

Subjects were administered the test in groups of two to five. Each subject was given a booklet of the test items, a sheet printed with standard instructions, and a pile of loose sheets of blank paper. The test items were presented in random orders. The experimenter read aloud the instructions, asking subjects to follow their printed instruction sheets. Subjects were instructed to write down in as much detail as possible, all stages of their thinking from first beginning work on an item until they had generated a solution. They were asked to do the items in the order in which they appeared in the booklet. Subjects were not compelled to express their strategies verbally; they were free to use words, pictures, diagrams or symbols.

Selection of Multiple-Choice Alternatives

The testing procedure generated for each item ninety-eight solutions and for each solution, an accompanying strategy. Solutions chosen to function as multiple-choice alternatives met the following criteria:

1. One was the correct solution.
2. Each error solution represented the use of a unique strategy; that is, the solution had been obtained by different subjects using formally equivalent strategies. Strategies were regarded as formally equivalent if they were of the same logical form, even though some subjects may have expressed them in words and others in diagrams. If any solution had been obtained by different subjects using non-equivalent strategies, it was excluded from consideration. That is, for any solution to be a candidate for inclusion in the set of multiple-choice alternatives, it was necessary that there be a one-to-one relationship between solution and underlying strategy.
3. Error solutions were relatively frequent. However, while each item would subsequently contain five error alternatives, it was not necessarily the case that these were the five most frequent solutions generated. Selection of multiple-choice alternatives was further constrained by the next criterion.

4. Each error solution and its associated strategy, when expressed in logical form, occurred relatively frequently across all structurally-equivalent items.

Using these criteria, we generated a set of six response alternatives for each item. Within a set of structurally equivalent items, every error alternative to a given item appeared in a strategically-equivalent form in the other three items in the set.

In determining a rank ordering of strategies from "best" to "worst," two factors were considered: power and consistency. More powerful strategies were those that used more of the relevant information contained in the item stem. Less powerful strategies used irrelevant information, or failed to use all the relevant information. Consistency meant that, given the information and set of rules predicated in the strategy, the latter were applied to the former without resulting in internal contradictions. Analysis of the strategies underlying the response alternatives generated a rank-ordering of the alternatives. While strategies varied in two respects, power and consistency, the single term "efficiency" was chosen to denote the dimension along which the alternatives were ranked. The most efficient error strategy was considered to constitute the least departure from the ideal strategy leading to correct solution; the least efficient error strategy constituted the greatest departure from the ideal strategy. See Thorburn (1977) for detailed information on the selection and ranking of the multiple-choice alternatives.

EXPERIMENT 2

The initial step in the second experiment was the construction of a parallel form of the multiple-choice test devised in Experiment 1. The parallel form was based on exactly the same item structures as those of the original test, again expressed in number, letter, pictorial and figural content. The changes were in the specific elements depicted in the items; for example, where an item in the first test contained pictures of animals, the structurally equivalent pictorial item in the parallel test had articles of clothing. Similarly, the response alternatives retained their strategic properties but were translated into the new content of the parallel item.

In this experiment, the aim was to confirm that a different group of subjects administered either the first multiple-choice test or the parallel form, would rely on the same strategies as those that had generated the response alternatives in Experiment 1.

Subjects

There were eighteen male and twenty-two female subjects with mean ages 19.7 and 20.9 years respectively. The standard deviation of their ages was 2.88 years for males and 4.09 for females. All subjects were undergraduate psychology students.

Procedure

Testing procedure was the same as in Experiment 1, with the following differences. Half the males and females were administered the first test, and the other half the parallel form. Instead of creating their own solutions, subjects were required to select from the set of multiple-choice alternatives. They were instructed to give detailed descriptions of the strategies underlying response choices.

Results

The strategies underlying choice of incorrect alternatives were classified according to whether or not they corresponded to the strategies by which the alternatives were generated in Experiment 1. Correct responses were examined to determine whether they resulted from use of the correct strategy. The results of this analysis appear in *Table 1* below. The numbering of the item sets is according to increasing complexity of item structure.

Table 1. Proportion of Incorrect Responses Based on Strategies Generated in Experiment 1, and Proportion of Correct Responses Based on Erroneous Strategies

Item set	Proportion of incorrect strategies corresponding to Experiment 1 strategies	Proportion of correct responses obtained by incorrect strategies
1	.71	.00
2	.86	.12
3	.75	.04

No item in the least complex item set was correctly solved with an incorrect strategy. The proportion of incorrectly based correct responses is low in the two more complex item sets. For each item set, at least seventy percent of incorrect responses relied on the same strategies as those which had generated the responses in Experiment 1. In general then, it appears that given the response to any item, one can fairly confidently predict the problem-solving behavior underlying the response choice.

EXPERIMENT 3

Experiment 1 demonstrates that it is possible to construct a multiple-choice psychometric test so that error alternatives denote psychologically meaningful processes which are discriminable quantitatively. It is evident that this method of test construction entails more time and effort than the traditional approach, where incorrect response alternatives are intended to function merely as "distractors," to draw less able testees away from the correct alternative (Horst, 1966: Thorndike & Hagen, 1969). However, it is also evident that the former approach provides more information about test-taking behavior, as long as the response alternatives function reliably. The results of Experiment 2 suggest that this can be achieved with reasonable success.

The third experiment investigated two further issues. The first was whether the distribution of error responses varied systematically, according to item complexity. It may be that with an increase in complexity of item structure, the items become more difficult to solve and there is a greater incidence of less efficient processing. The second issue related to the nature of score changes on a second testing occasion. A working hypothesis was that greater improvement would occur in less complex, compared to more complex items. If items of lower complexity are easier to solve, then it might be reasonable to expect greater gains in score as assessed by number of correct responses. As a corollary, it might also be expected that incorrect strategies would shift towards greater efficiency on a second testing occasion, and that this shift might be greater in the less complex items.

Subjects

There were 258 subjects in total; eighty-six year-nine secondary students, eighty-six year-eleven secondary students, and eighty-six first-year undergraduate psychology students. There were equal numbers of each sex in each of the three groups above. The mean and standard deviation of the ages of each group is given in *Table 2* below.

Table 2. Mean and Standard Deviation of Ages of Experiment 3 Subjects

		MALE			FEMALE		
		Year 9	Year 11	Undergrad.	Year 9	Year 11	Undergrad.
Age in Years	Mean	14.46	16.53	20.61	14.42	16.52	19.74
	S.D.	.42	.41	2.82	.38	.63	2.10

Procedure

Subjects were tested in groups of fifteen to thirty-five, in two sessions approximately three months apart. The test constructed in Experiment 1 was administered on the first occasion, and the parallel form on the second occasion. Standard instructions were used. Subjects were required only to select a response alternative to each item, and were not asked to describe their problem-solving strategies.

Results

This section gives, for each item set, summary data which have been pooled across all items within the set, and pooled across all subjects. The statistical analysis of the data was performed on each item separately, and where there was sufficient data, within each group of subjects of the same sex and educational level. For the sake of brevity, details of these data and statistical analyses are not given here, but are available (see Thorburn, 1977).

The proportion of correct responses, averaged across items within an item set, is shown in *Table 3* for each of the two testing occasions.

On testing occasion 1, the least complex items (Item Set 1) have a higher pass rate than the two more complex item sets which have similar pass rates. This difference was statistically significant for five out of the six subject groups, when the number of correct items was analyzed by a Friedman one-way analysis of variance. On the second testing occasion, the most complex items (Item Set 3) have a lower pass rate than the two less complex item sets which have similar pass rates. This difference was statistically significant in four of the six subject groups, when tested by the Friedman analysis.

Inspecting change in pass rate from the first to the second testing occasion, there is no improvement in Item Set 1, but a twenty-three percent and sixteen percent gain respectively in Item Sets 2 and 3. Individual subjects were classified according to whether they had shown a gain, no change, or a loss in number of structurally-equivalent items correct on each testing occasion. Analysis of the distribution within each item set by X^2 analysis demonstrated that the improvement in the two more complex item sets was statistically significant. In Item Set 1, the implication of the analysis was that subjects were equally likely to show a gain, no change or loss in score.

Table 3. Pass Rates for Each Item Set, Averaged Across Structurally-Equivalent Items

Item Set	Testing Occasion	
	1	2
1	.64	.64
2	.40	.63
3	.38	.54

The distribution of error choices on each item set, for each testing occasion, appears in *Table 4.* The response alternatives are ranked such that Alternative 1 represents the most efficient, and Alternative 5 the least efficient error strategy. The data are given in terms of percentage frequency of choice, and are averaged across items within an item set.

Table 4. Percentage Frequency of Choice of Incorrect Alternatives for Each Item Set, Averaged Across Structurally-Equivalent Items

Item Set	Testing Occasion	Response Alternative				
		1	2	3	4	5
1	1	23.8	19.5	36.0	11.8	8.8
	2	21.8	28.0	14.8	22.8	12.5
2	1	19.0	16.3	18.8 ·	15.0	30.3
	2	23.0	18.3	17.0	14.0	27.8
3	1	8.0	20.0	25.3	12.3	34.0
	2	12.0	19.0	13.8	32.0	23.0

The distribution of responses was analyzed separately for each item on each testing occasion, using a X^2 analysis to test the hypothesis of equiprobability of choice of error alternative. This hypothesis was rejected for every item of the first testing occasion. On the second occasion, the hypothesis was rejected in three out of four items in Item Set 1, two of four in Item Set 2, and all items in Item Set 3. In general then, there is statistical evidence that some error choices are more popular than others.

On the first testing occasion, the most popular choice in Item Set 1 is the third most efficient error alternative, while in both Item Sets 2 and 3 the most frequent choice is the least efficient alternative.

On the second testing occasion, the most frequent response in Item Set 1 is the second most efficient alternative, in Item Set 2 it remains the least efficient, but in

Item Set 3 is the second least efficient. Ostensibly, there is a trend for some items to show a shift towards more efficient (albeit, incorrect) strategies on the second testing occasion. However, these averages ignore the way in which individuals, rather than a group as a whole, shift their error choices from the first to the second occasion. For each item, individuals were classified according to whether their error choice on the second occasion represented a change to a more efficient strategy, a less efficient strategy, or no strategic change. The distribution for each item was analyzed by X^2 to test the hypothesis that the three forms of response were equiprobable. In all but two of the twelve items this hypothesis was accepted. In general, then, there is no statistical evidence that subjects show systematic change in choice of error alternatives on the second testing occasion.

DISCUSSION

The hypothesis that items of greater complexity would be more difficult to solve has been supported. Although the difference in pass rate between item sets changes on the second testing occasion, the trend on both occasions shows a decrease in pass rate with an increase in item complexity. The implication of this finding for classical test theory is that item difficulty may be defined independently of test performance, in terms of stimulus complexity. Psychometric conceptualizations of item difficulty are notably lacking any theoretical basis for specifying what properties of the test item make it more or less discriminating or difficult. Like most psychometric concepts, item discrimination and difficulty are defined in terms of response characteristics rather than with respect to *a priori* properties of the stimulus (*e.g.*, Lazarsfeld, 1961; Rasch, 1966; Samejima, 1974). The present study demonstrates the possibility of explaining the relationship between pass rates and item difficulty without circularity.

The results also suggest that item complexity affects the choice of error alternatives, in the direction predicted. On both testing occasions, there is a trend for increasing complexity of item structure to be associated with greater popularity of response alternatives representing less efficient strategies. These findings imply that existing psychometric approaches to item scoring do not lead to effective discrimination between individuals making error responses. From a theoretical point of view, the score assigned to an individual should reflect his capacity for processing the information contained in a test item. This, in turn, should reflect the ability being measured by the test. Hence, if two error strategies vary in efficiency, it would be reasonable to weight the solution generated by the more efficient strategy more heavily than that arising from the less efficient. In the context of the present experiment, Alternative 1 in Item Set 3 should therefore be weighted more than Alternative 5. Yet the item-scoring formulas in the psychometric literature would undoubtedly lead to a greater weighting for Alternative 5; under Chernoff's (1962) model because it is the most frequent choice, under de Finetti's (1965) model because it is likely to be that assigned the highest personal probability. As with the question of item difficulty, psychometric solutions to the problem of item scoring have no *a priori* or theoretical justification.

The hypothesis that gains in score would be greater in less complex items has received no support, as the results show the reverse. There were substantial gains in the two more complex sets of items, but no increase in pass rate at all in the least complex item set. There is no ready explanation for this. It may be that on a second testing occasion, the simpler items are recognizably similar to those encountered in the first test, and that subjects recall their original responses. However, this seems inconsistent with the finding that individuals are no more likely to get the same number of items correct on Item Set 1 than they are to either increase or decrease in score. Why this occurs and why individuals show significant improvement in more complex items requires further investigation. What is of importance to psychometrics is that score gains are not uniform across the item domain, but vary systematically as a function of item complexity. If some types of item are subject to greater gains than others, it is vital to the interpretation of "true" and "error" scores to determine the relationships between the stimulus characteristics of test items, and concepts such as "learning," "memory" and "insight."

When the response choices of individuals who had solved an item incorrectly on both testing occasions were examined, there was no support for the hypothesis that subjects would select more efficient strategies on the second occasion. In conjunction with the findings about score gains, this suggests that subjects only show systematic improvement in an all-or-none sense, by switching from an error strategy of whatever level of efficiency, directly to the correct strategy. Perhaps these subjects experience an "aha" insight on the second testing occasion. Whatever the explanation, the finding that systematic improvement shows up in test scores, but not in error strategies, has implications for psychometric models of test scores. How the observed score is partitioned, and what assumptions are entailed, depends on the theoretical interpretation of systematic changes in test performance.

In conclusion, then, there is a wealth of information contained in incorrect responses to multiple-choice psychometric tests, information which has in the past been virtually ignored by psychometricians. Some of the potential benefits of utilizing this information are: more accurate and more sensitive discrimination between individuals and groups; more effective use of tests as diagnostic instruments; and a stronger theoretical basis for psychometric concepts. When an individual is administered a psychometric test purporting to measure "intelligence" or any other ability, he must engage in problem-solving behavior. And "if we are to understand human problem-solving behavior, we must get a grip on the strategies that underlie that behavior, and we must avoid blending together in a statistical stew quite diverse problem-solving behavior whose real significance is lost in the averaging process" (Simon, 1975, p. 288). It does not follow from this that the psychometric approach to cognition must henceforth be abandoned. Rather, what is indicated is a serious commitment to the task of integrating statistical and psychological models of behavior.

REFERENCES

Alexander, H.W. "The Estimation of Reliability When Several Trials are Available," *Psychometrika*, 1947, *12*, 79–99.

Anastasi, A. "Coaching, Test Sophistication and Developed Abilities," *American Psychologist*, 1981, *36*, 1086–1093.

Bock, R.D. "Estimating Item Parameters and Latent Ability when Responses are Scored in Two or More Nominal Categories," *Psychometrika*, 1972, *37*, 39–51.

Chernoff, H. "The Scoring of Multiple-Choice Questionnaires," *Annals of Mathematical Statistics*, 1962, *33*, 375–393.

de Finetti, B. "Methods for Discriminating Levels of Partial Knowledge Concerning at Test Item," *British Journal of Mathematical Statistics*, 1965, *18*, 87–123.

Dressel, P.L. and Schmid, P. "Some Modifications of the Multiple-choice Item," *Educational and Psychological Measurement*, 1953, *13*, 574–595.

Garcia, J. "The Logic and Limits of Mental Aptitude Testing," *American Psychologist*, 1981, *36*, 1172–1180.

Glaser, R. "The Future of Testing: A Research Agenda for Cognitive Psychology and Psychometrics," *American Psychologist*, 1981, *36*, 923–936.

Gordon, E.W. and Terrell, M.D. "The Changed Social Context of Testing," *American Psychologist*, 1981, *36*, 1167–1171.

Guilford, J.P. *The Nature of Human Intelligence*. New York: McGraw-Hill, 1967.

Heim, A. and Wallace, J. "The Effects of Repeatedly Retesting the Same Group on the Same Intelligence Test: I. Normal Adults," *Quarterly Journal of Experimental Psychology*, 1949, *1*, 151–159.

Heim, A. and Wallace, J. "The Effects of Repeatedly Retesting the Same Group on the Same Intelligence Test: II. High Grade Mental Defectives," *Quarterly Journal of Experimental Psychology*, 1950, *2*, 19–32.

Hoffman, P.J. "Test Reliability and Practice Effects," *Psychometrika*, 1963, *28*, 273–288.

Horst, P. *Psychological Measurement and Prediction*. Belmont, CA: Wadsworth, 1966.

Hunt, E., Lunneborg, C. and Lewis, J. "What Does It Mean to Be High Verbal?" *Cognitive Psychology*, 1975, *7*, 194–227.

Lazarsfeld, P.F. "The Algebra of Dichotomous Scoring Systems." In *Studies in Item Analysis and Prediction*, H. Solomon (Ed.). Stanford: Stanford University Press, 1961.

Lord, F.M. and Novick, M.R. *Statistical Theories of Mental Test Scores*. Reading, MA: Addison-Wesley, 1968.

Lumsden, J. "Test Theory," *Annual Review of Psychology*, 1976, *27*, 251–280.

McNemar, Q. "Lost: Our Intelligence? Why?" *American Psychologist*, 1964, *19*, 871–882.

Ng, Kim T. "Applicability of Classical Test Score Model to Repeated Performance on the Same Test," *Australian Journal of Psychology*, 1974, *26*, 1–8.

Rasch, G. "An Item Analysis which Takes Individual Differences into Account," *British Journal of Mathematical and Statistical Psychology*, 1966, *19*, 49–57.

Samejima, F. "Normal Ogive Model on the Continuous Response Level in the Multidimensional Latent Space," *Psychometrika*, 1974, *39*(1), 111–121.

Scarr, S. "Testing for Children: Assessment and the Many Determinants of Intellectual Competence," *American Psychologist*, 1981, *36*, 1159–1166.

Simon, H.A. "The Functional Equivalence of Problem-Solving Skills," *Cognitive Psychology*, 1975, *7*, 268–288.

Thorburn, K.S. (now Macrae, K.S.) *Problem Solving Performance as a Function of Task Content and Structure*. Unpublished doctoral dissertation, La Trobe University, 1977.

Thorndike, R.L. and Hagen, E.P. *Measurement and Evaluation in Psychology and Education*, 3rd ed. New York: Wiley, 1969.

Vernon, P.E. "Intelligence Test Sophistication," *British Journal of Educational Psychology*, 1938, *8*, 237–244.

Vernon, P.E. *Intelligence and Attainment Tests*. London: University of London Press, 1960.

Woodrow, H. "The Relation of Verbal Ability to Improvement with Practice in Verbal Tests," *Journal of Educational Psychology*, 1939, *30*, 179–186.

TEACHING TOWARD INTELLIGENT BEHAVIOR

Arthur L. Costa

ABSTRACT

The process of curriculum change is complicated and multifaceted. Simplistic, piecemeal attempts to change one aspect at a time have proven ineffective. If schools want to install intelligent behavior as a learning outcome, there are numerous conditions which must be provided and coordinated. In this article, fourteen organizational, curricular and instructional concerns, with supporting research, are presented. Educators will need to resolve these concerns if intelligent behavior is to become a valid educational goal.

Education's role in developing intelligence will best be realized when an integrated curriculum system is installed, with the component parts tuned to work harmoniously to produce desired results. There are numerous interrelated domains of the curriculum: the ideal, the formal, the instructional, the operational, and the experiential (Klein, Tye & Wright, 1979). An historical view of curriculum change demonstrates the ineffectiveness of efforts when these components are not in sync. Recent school-effectiveness studies demonstrate what can happen when they are (Cohen, 1981). Decision makers in each of these domains must act harmoniously to generate momentum for the "back-to-complexities" movement.

Following are fourteen suggested questions, intended to stimulate inquiry into curriculum and instructional conditions necessary to develop intelligent behaviors. Some of the conditions are based on assumption; others on hard data. The questions are not intended to be a complete and handy check list; they may, however, provide some cues to accelerate the dialogue.

1. Are intelligent behaviors valued as a goal of education?

Community values play an important role in influencing what is taught. In turn, teachers usually perform in a manner consistent with how they are valued. One basic condition for teaching towards intelligent behavior is that teachers, parents,

---

A.L. Costa is affiliated with the School of Education at California State University in Sacramento.

211

administrators and board members adopt it as a basic goal of education. The demonstration of such a community-wide emphasis would be exhibited in several ways:

- Instructional materials will be developed and adopted to enhance thinking.
- Administrators will be trained in how to recognize and evaluate teachers on how well they produce intelligent behavior.
- Staff development will be provided on how to describe, teach and measure thinking.
- Problem solving will be heard as the subject of discussion and debate in faculty, parent and board meetings.
- Monies will be allocated to increase cognitive education.
- Community groups will complain that we're not doing enough of it.
- A system will be developed and installed for monitoring and assessing students' growth in thinking.
- Parent-education will be provided to foster and support thinking at home.
- Incentives and rewards will be given to teachers, students and administrators who excel in intelligent behaviors.

2. Do we believe that human intellectual capacity can be enhanced?

Teacher expectations and preconceptions of student abilities are correlated with achievement (Cohen, 1981; Good & Brophy, 1971). These preconceptions are generated and communicated with such labels as "learning disabled," "retarded," "below grade level," "deprived," "gifted," *etc.*

These preconceptions are further aggravated with the myth of a static and unchanging I.Q. Many educators still believe and act as if the score on a test is an accurate prediction of ability. Our expectations of students are influenced when magical numbers of 70 and 132 are mentioned.

A prerequisite to teaching toward intelligent behavior is the belief that *all* human beings have the capacity for learning; that the ability to use intelligent behavior is never fully developed; and that the capacity for a more highly developed intellect continues throughout life. There are, of course, certain environmental, psychological or physiological factors present in a child's life which may contribute to intellectual underdevelopment. The teaching act, therefore, becomes one of compensating for those handicaps.

With the adoption of such a faith, we will alter some of our stereotyping practices such as ability grouping, watering down the curriculum so that "slower" learners work at a "slower" pace on content with which they have already failed; or giving more of the same material faster to "gifted" students who already know how to do it well.

3. Is there consensus on a model of human intellectual behavior?

While there are numerous models of human intellectual functioning, it is probably more beneficial to spend time and energy understanding one or more of them, rather than deciding which model and exactly whose terminology is correct.

An examination of several models yields more similarities than differences. Most authors distinguish *three* basic thought clusters (Smith and Tyler, 1945). These are: an *input* of data from the senses and from memory; the *processing* of those data into meaningful relationships; and the *output* or application of those relationships to novel situations. A comparison of several authors' constructs are shown in *Table 1*.

Table 1.

DATA INPUT PHASE	PROCESSING PHASE	OUTPUT PHASE	SOURCE
Internal and External Input	Central Processing	Output	Atkinson & Shiffrin, 1968
Participation and Awareness	Internalization	Dissemination	Bell & Steinaker, 1979
Knowledge	Comprehension Analysis Synthesis	Application Evaluation	Bloom, 1956
Descriptive	Interpretive	Evaluative	Eisner, 1979, pp. 203–213
Input	Elaboration	Output	Feuerstein, 1980, pp. 71–103
Fluency	Manipulation	Persistence	Foshay, 1979 pp. 93–113
Cognition and Memory	Evaluation	Convergent and Divergent Production	Guilford, 1967
Fact	Concept	Value	Harmin, 1973
Receiving	Responding Valuing Organizing	Characterizing	Krathwohl, 1964
Alertness	Information Processing	Action	Restak, 1979, p. 44
Learning	Integrating	Applying	Sexton & Poling, 1973, p. 7
Intuitive	Awareness	Function	Strasser, 1972, pp. 46–47
Intake Storage	Mediation	Action	Suchman, 1966, pp. 177–187
Concept Formation	Interpretation and Inference	Application of Principles	Taba, 1964, pp. 30–38
Detailed Observation Recall of Previous Knowledge	Comparison	Rule Generation Auto Criticism	Whimbey, 1976, pp. 116–138
Romance	Precision	Generalization	Whitehead, 1929, p. 29

Figure 1, which omits such important concepts as affect, motivation and perceptual abilities, is a simplified attempt to synthesize the commonalities of Table 1 into a simple yet dynamic model of human intellectual functioning which could serve as a basis for curriculum and instruction.

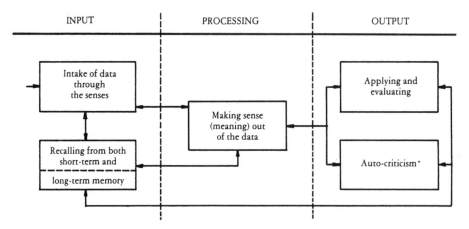

*Auto-criticism is explored in 12 below.

Figure 1.

Another purpose of teaching towards intelligent behavior would be to develop each of these functions. A description of some of the capacities in each phase of input, processing and output follows: (These rely heavily on Feuerstein's *Instrumental Enrichment* with adaptations from Bloom and Broder, 1950.)

I. Gathering Information (Input)

A. Using the senses (listening, smelling, observing, tasting, feeling) to gather clear and complete information (perceiving clearly).
B. Using a system or plan to collect all relevant information, rather than having to repeat observations (exploring systematically).
C. Naming the objects, conditions and events observed and experienced so that they can be remembered and talked about (labeling).
D. Describing objects, conditions and events in terms of where and when they occur (perceiving temporal and spatial relationships).
E. Identifying which characteristics of an object, event or condition stay the same even when changes take place (conserving constancy).
F. Considering more than one variable at a time as a basis for organizing and reorganizing the information gathered (using more than one frame of reference).
G. Being precise and accurate.

II. Making Sense Out of the Information Gathered (Processing)

A. Defining what the problem is, what is needed to resolve the problem and what must be done to figure it out (analyzing discrepancies).

B. Discriminating among information gathered that which is relevant and applicable and that which is not (perceiving relevance).

C. Having a picture (image) in mind of what to look for and what must be done (interiorizing).

D. Making a plan or strategy which includes the steps needed to reach the goal (systematic planning).

E. Remembering the various pieces of information needed (broadening the mental field).

F. Searching for relationships among disparate objects, conditions, events, and past experiences (projecting relationships).

G. Finding similarities and differences among objects, conditions and events (comparing).

H. Finding the class or set to which a new object, condition or event belongs (categorizing).

I. Exploring alternative solutions and projecting what would happen if one or another were chosen (hypothesizing).

J. Defending an opinion with logical evidence.

K. Having a repertoire of problem-solving strategies so that another can be used when one does not produce results (flexibility).

III. Applying and Evaluating Actions in Novel Situations (Output)

A. Communicating accurately and precisely (using precise language).

B. Expressing another person's ideas, point of view and feelings accurately (overcoming egocentrism).

C. Thinking through a solution or answer, rather than making mistakes and having to repeat (overcoming trial and error).

D. Pausing to formulate an idea, rather than blurting out the first answer that comes to mind (restraining impulsivity).

E. Having alternative strategies of finding answers when they are not immediately apparent, rather than giving up in panic or despair (overcoming blocking).

F. Checking to see if the results of the strategy (product) matches the intended outcome (image) (checking for accuracy).

Applying this model, we shall now consider the types of teacher behaviors which facilitate the development of these intellectual behaviors.

4. Do students realize it is an objective?

> Teacher: "Why do you think Carl Sandburg repeated the last line of this verse?"
> Student: (no response)
> Teacher: (After a long pause) "Well, what feelings did *you* have as you read the poem?"
> Student: "Why don't you just tell us the answer?" (Wassermann, 1978).

Students expend great amounts of energy trying to figure out the teacher's intentions. Because some students come from previous contexts in which intelligent behaviors were not valued, they are often dismayed by and resistant to a teacher's invitation to think. Such resistance and reluctance to respond should be taken as an indication that a program to develop intellectual skills is needed.

Teachers must emphasize to students that the goal of instruction is thinking; that the responsibility for thinking is theirs; that it is desirable to have more than one solution; that it is commendable when they take time to plan and to think; and that an answer can be changed with additional information.

Regardless of how often teachers make the objectives of thinking explicit, several other implicit teacher behaviors will communicate this goal even more effectively.

5. Does the teacher's language invite it?

Based on the model in 3 above, information taken in is constantly interpreted in terms of what is already known. If new information can be easily understood with familiar knowledge, no problem or challenge exists (assimilation). If, however, the new information cannot be explained or resolved with the knowledge in short- or long-term memory, a discrepancy is perceived. The information must be processed, action taken to gather more information to resolve the discrepancy and the ultimate resolution tested for its ''fit'' with reality (accommodation). Thus, a problem may be defined as a stimulus or challenge to which the response is not readily apparent.

The teacher, crucial as a mediator of intelligent behavior, calls attention to discrepancies and poses problems intended to invite more than a memory-type response. Embedded in the teacher's questions and other statements are the cues for student's cognitive performance (Davis and Tinsley, 1967; Andre, 1979; Lowery, 1980). Teachers' questions can cause a lifting from one level of cognition to a higher level (Taba, Levine and Elzey, 1964).

Thus, with a model of intellectual functioning in mind, the teacher can manipulate the syntactical structure of questions and statements to invite the student to intake information, to compare that information with what is in memory, to draw meaningful relationships, and to apply or transfer those relationships to hypothetical situations.

6. Are instructional activities arranged sequentially?

''A child learns first to recognize a rectangle by abstracting the features of many particular rectangles and then applying this knowledge to future situations'' (Restak, 1979, p. 229).

Bloom, Taba, Bruner, Piaget and others have helped us see that these levels of thinking are cumulative. It may be counterproductive for the teacher to invite processing or output thinking tasks without providing adequate time and experience at the levels of input and data accumulation. If the student has had inadequate input from memory, experience or sensory stimulation, there will be inadequate data with which to perceive discrepancies and, therefore, to function at the processing level. If those data are not processed and integrated by comparing, exploring causal relationships, sequencing, etc., the higher levels of thinking will be performed with little quality or substantive content.

This model can be used as a diagnostic tool to observe and analyze student's thinking performance. If a teacher's question, statement or problem-focus indeed produces cognition at the level intended, there is a match. If, however, the level of student's thinking elicited is inconsistent with the teacher's intended level of intellectual functioning, or if no discrepancy in the problem is perceived, there is a mismatch. Noting this, the teacher can adjust the level and complexity of the cognitive task to one more appropriate to the student's current level of intellectual functioning and remain at that level until enough data are gathered or the data are processed sufficiently before moving to higher levels productively.

7. Do teachers' responsive behaviors enhance and extend intelligent behavior?

Much of students' cueing comes *not* from the question or statement but rather from the teacher's response behaviors. How students anticipate the teacher will respond to their answers may exert greater influence on their answers than the question which the teacher asked. If a teacher reacts to a student's answer with a response that signals conformity—praise (Brophy, 1979), corrective feedback, criticism or other value judgments (Rowe, 1974)—students will soon realize that their individual thinking is not valued as much as correctly guessing what the teacher had in mind.

Responsive behaviors which seem to facilitate intellectual functioning are the following: silence after having asked a question or after a student responds (Rowe, 1974); accepting, building upon, integrating and extending student's ideas (Flanders, 1969); clarifying (Klevin, 1958); and providing additional information (Andre, 1979 and Suchman, 1966). Such behaviors seem to create a stress-free, cooperative classroom condition where experimental ideas can be risked, alternative hypotheses explored, and answers changed with additional data. In this classroom more value is placed on creative problem-solving strategies rather than on conformity to "right" answers.

8. Do the materials of instruction support it?

Because the "medium is the message," our materials of instruction communicate educational values. If materials are designed to be read, memorized and tested, then this is the concept of schooling which students will derive. If, however, materials are organized and articulated through the grades and across content areas with common and recurring intellectual goals, they can, over time, convince the learner that thinking is valued.

The development and adoption of instructional materials, therefore, must be made because of their contribution to and development of those intellectual skills described in the model of intellectual functioning. The range of available instructional materials runs the gamut from those that make hopeful claims that intelligent behaviors will result from their use through those that utilize a content vehicle, such as math (*e.g.*, Curriculum Development Associates, Inc.), science (*e.g.*, Science Curriculum Improvement Study) or social studies (*e.g.*, Curriculum Development Associates' *Man: A Course of Study*, Holt's *Data Bank*) to experience and apply the behaviors; to those that are expressly designed to focus on and deliberately develop one or more of the cognitive skills, (*e.g.*, Benefic Press' *Thinking Skills Development Program*, Innovative Science Institute's *THINK*, and Feuerstein's *Instrumental Enrichment* from Curriculum Development Associates, Inc.)

9. Is adequate instructional time devoted to developing thinking?

While much research has demonstrated that achievement (in basic skills at certain grade levels as measured by standardized tests) correlates highly with the amount of time students are successfully engaged in learning (Borg, 1980), this same proposition would undoubtedly hold true for teaching intelligent behaviors as well.

The way we use our time is a reflection of our value system. If the development of intelligent behaviors is to achieve a high value in our schools, high priority and substantial time must be allocated. The intellect, much like the musculature, needs constant exercise over extended periods of time, to perform with efficiency, synergy and fluid grace.

10. Does instruction provide for differences in modality strengths?

"I hear and I forget; I see and I remember; I do and I understand" (Old Chinese Proverb). Because some students are *visiles,* and some are *audiles* (Barbe and Swassig, 1979; Dunn and Dunn, 1978), we realize that the input, processing and output phases of thinking must also incorporate the student's modality preference. When a teacher asks a question, it is usually posed orally and is responded to verbally by one student at a time. Anderson and Faust (1973, Ch. 6) contend, however, that a question will not have an instructional effect unless a student actually makes a response. The response may be overt or covert. Thus, teachers' questions may appeal and be responded to by mainly auditory learners. Some students will need to intake and process the data, then apply those relationships experientially, others visually, some auditorily, and for some, in all three modalities.

Furthermore, some students respond better in group settings, others individually or one-to-one. Posing questions and problems for small-group resolution causes a positive friction against other minds when students must examine various points of view, achieve consensus and compare and evaluate alternative decisions.

Thus, by providing alternative grouping practices, by providing a visually-, auditorily- and experientially-stimulating environment (input), by providing manipulatives and discussion (processing) and alternative modes of expression (output) (*e.g.,* visual, dramatization, construction), opportunities increase for more students to become involved in exercising their intellectual capacities.

11. Are modalities sequenced according to developmental theory?

Psychobiologists have found strong support for Piagetian theories of cognitive development. New information is processed on the right side of the brain and begins with action and perception. As the information becomes familiar, it is then processed on the left side of the brain and proceeds to words and concepts (Restak, 1979, p. 217 and pp. 255–264). Too often, educational practice ignores or reverses this sequence of learning. Probably the true cause of failure (according to Piaget) in formal education is that we begin with language rather than with real and material action.

Again, the teacher's role as mediator of this sequence is crucial in providing direct, concrete experiences first, then mediating that experience by inviting students to think about what they see and do, and then by inviting them to talk about what they saw and did.

12. Do students and teachers discuss their thinking?

When children enter the concrete-operational stage, they develop a conscious awareness of self interacting with a real, objectively verifiable world. During this stage, they develop inner language. As they enter the formal-logical stage, another uniquely human capacity emerges; the ability to stand away from, reflect on and evaluate one's own behavior. Binet referred to this as "auto-criticism" (Whimbey, 1976, pp. 116–138).

Much evidence suggests that causing students to talk about their thinking processes and strategies of problem solving during (introspection) and after (retrospection) enhances their ability to think. Evidently thinking and talking about thinking, begets thinking (Strasser, 1972, pp. 63–65; Link, 1980; Whimbey, 1980; Bloom and Broder, 1950).

13. Do evaluation measures assess intelligent behavior?

Most learning is evaluated with paper and pencil criterion-referenced or norm-referenced test of what has been stored in short- or long-term memory. While it is easy to construct good test items to measure lower level cognitive skills, it is much more difficult to design items that measure higher-order mental processes (Metfessel and Michael, 1973). Because of this difficulty and because of the format (mostly multiple choice) of standardized achievement tests, intelligent behaviors are often not measured (Eisner, 1979, p. 181).

Probably the main problem that has plagued educational assessment is that it has not separated the effect of instruction covered in a lesson from the concepts, meanings and intellectual functions *not* covered in a lesson (Andre, 1979). Thus, the focus has been on learning *of* the objectives, not learning *from* the objectives.

If growth in intellectual behavior is to be evaluated, we must reconceptualize our approach to assessment: the testing situations, instruments, processes, products and interpretations. Individual cognitive maps displaying deficiencies and peaks in intellectual capacities would replace test scores. Teacher-observers would interact with the student to diagnose his abilities. The test itself would be a learning experience, starting with real and concrete problems and advancing to more abstract complex tasks. Longitudinal studies would seek evidence of the student's increased spontaneous and autonomous use of the behaviors, cited in *3* above. Thus, the product of assessment would *not* be what answers the student knows but how the student behaves when he *doesn't* know. We would search for indicators of a shift from the attitude that reasoning has little value, that an answer is either known or it is not, that the first idea that comes to mind is as good as any other, to the view of problems as challenging, of finding fun in reasoning thus doing it voluntarily. For example, see *Table 2*.

14. Do significant adults model intelligent behaviors?

With imitation being a most basic form of learning, teacher's, parent's and administrator's modeling of desired intellectual behaviors is requisite to student performance (Bandura, 1962; Belcher, 1975). Thus, in day-to-day events and when problems arise in schools and classrooms, students must see adults employing the same types of behaviors identified in *Table 2*.

O.J. Harvey (1966) describes personalities in a sequence of categories (similar to Piaget's) ranging from what he called "concrete functioning behaviors" to "abstract functioning behaviors." The University of California at Berkeley Education Research and Applications program found that abstract functioning teachers seem to be most suited to the profession of teaching, while concrete functioning teachers seem to be detrimental to effective teaching (Lowery, 1981).

Table 2.

FROM	TO
INPUT (Example: Exploring Systematically)	
Exhibits difficulty in ascertaining what is required. Gives inadequate attention to directions and is careless with details and haphazard with approach to solution. If unable to solve a problem, gives up in despair.	Demonstrates a systematic plan of attack. Takes time and makes directed effort. If unable to solve problem as a whole, perseveres with such strategies as breaking problem into parts.
PROCESSING (Example: Perceiving Relevance)	
Is unable to bring forth relevant information and knowledge to bear on problem solution; perceives no relationship between present and previous problem situations.	Commands the basic information necessary for the solution, as well as the ability to bring this knowledge forth in attacking the problem.
OUTPUT (Example: Overcoming Egocentrism)	
Introduces personal considerations into problem solving. Is unable to extract subjective feelings and opinions from problem solution.	Reasons systematically and provides evidence with logic. Expresses confidence in problem solution.

Some classroom examples of abstract teacher behaviors consistent with successful intellectual functioning might be those shown in *Table 3*. It is believed that this concept has great implications for teacher selection, training, evaluation and staff development.

Table 3.

INPUT	(Perceiving Clearly)	Being sensitive to subtle clues in student behaviors.
	(Systematic Planning)	Planning for instruction.
PROCESSING	(Flexibility)	Considering alternative teaching strategies.
	(Logical Evidence)	Using information and expertise as guidelines for beliefs and judgments, rather than using power, rewards and punishment.
OUTPUT	(Overcoming Egocentrism)	Taking a student's point of view.
	(Restraining Impulsivity)	Using reason and patience in dealing with discipline problems.

SUMMARY

This list of fourteen questions is double the number of variables with which the typical human brain is capable of dealing at any given time (Miller, 1956, pp. 81–97). Curriculum leaders are invited to consider these, to relate them to their own experience, to explore the meaning and consequences of each and to apply and evaluate them in their own situation. Perhaps this can contribute to a more intelligent approach to curriculum change.

REFERENCES

Anderson, R.C. and Faust, G.W. *Educational Psychology*. New York: Dodd Mead, 1973.

Andre, T. "Does Answering Higher-level Questions While Reading Facilitate Productive Learning?" *Review of Educational Research*, 1979, *49*, 280–318.

Atkinson, R.C. and Shiffren, R.M. "Human Memory: A Proposed Systems and its Control Process." In *The Psychology of Learning and Motivation*, Spence, K.W. & Spence, J.T. (Eds.). New York: Academic Press, 1968, 90–195.

Bandura, A. "Social Learning Through Imitation." In *Nebraska Symposium on Motivation*, Jones, M.R. (Ed.). Lincoln: University of Nebraska Press, 1962, 211–269.

Barbe, W. and Swassing, R. *Teaching Through Modality Strengths: Concepts and Practices*. Columbus: Zaner-Bloser, Inc., 1979.

Belcher, T. "Modeling Original Divergent Responses: an Initial Investigation," *Journal of Educational Research*, 1975, *67*, 351–358.

Bell, M. and Steinaker, N. *The Experiental Taxonomy: a New Approach to Teaching and Learning*. New York: Academic Press, 1979.

Bloom, B.S. and Broder, L.J. *Problem-Solving Processes of College Students*. Chicago: University of Chicago Press, 1950.

Bloom, B.S., Engelhart, M.D., Furst, E.J., Hill, W.H. and Krathwohl, D.R. *Taxonomy of Educational Objectives: Handbook I: Cognitive Domain*. New York: David McKay, 1956.

Borg, V.R. "Time and School Learning." In *Time to Learn*, Denham, C. and Lieberman, A. (Eds.). Washington, D.C.: National Institute of Education, 1980, 43–72.

Brophy, J.E. *Teacher Praise: a Functional Analysis*. East Lansing: Michigan State University Institute for Research on Teaching, Occasional Paper No. 28, October, 1979.

Bruner, J., Goodnow, J.J. and Austin, G.A. *A Study of Thinking*. New York: Wiley, 1956.

Cohen, M. "Effective Schools: What the Research Says," *Today's Education*, 1981, *70*, (2), April-May, 44–47.

Coker, H., Medley, D. and Soar, R. "How Valid are Expert Opinions About Effective Teaching?" *Phi Delta Kappan*, 1980, *62*, (2) 131–135.

Davis, O. and Tinsley, D.C. "Cognitive Objectives Revealed by Classroom Questions Asked by Social Studies Teachers," *Peabody Journal of Education*, 1967, *45*, (1) 21–26.

Dunne, R. and Dunne, K. *Teaching Students Through Their Individual Learning Styles*. Reston: Reston Publishing Co., 1978.

Eisner, E. *The Educational Imagination*. New York: Macmillan Co., 1979.

Feuerstein, R. *Instrumental Enrichment*. Baltimore: University Park Press, 1980.

Flanders, N.A. Quoted in "Teacher Effectiveness," *Encyclopedia of Education Research,* 4th Ed., Ebel, R. (Ed.). New York: Macmillan Co., 1969, 1426–1429.

Foshay, A.W. "Toward a Humane Curriculum." In *Education in Flux: Implications for Curriculum Development,* Jelenek, J.J. (Ed.). Tempe: University of Arizona Press, 1979, 93–113.

Good, T. and Brophy, J. "The Self-fulfilling Prophecy," *Today's Education,* April, 1971, 52–53.

Guilford, J.P. *The Nature of Human Intelligence.* New York: McGraw-Hill, 1967.

Harmin, M., Kirschenbaum, H. and Simon, S. *Clarifying Values Through Subject Matter.* Minneapolis: Winston Press, Inc., 1973.

Harvey, O.J. "System Structure, Flexibility and Creativity." In *Experience, Structure and Adaptability,* O.J. Harvey (Ed.). New York: Springer, 1966, 39–65.

Klein, F., Tye, K. and Wright, J. "A Study of Schooling: Curriculum," *Phi Delta Kappan,* 1979, 244–248.

Klevin, A. *An Investigation of a Methodology for Value Clarification: Its Relationship to Consistency of Thinking, Purposefulness, and Human Relations.* Unpublished doctoral dissertation. New York University, 1958.

Krathwohl, D., Bloom, B.S. and Masia, B.B. *Taxonomy of Educational Objectives Handbook II: Affective Domain.* New York: David McKay Co., Inc., 1964.

Link, F.R. "Instrumental Enrichment: the Classroom Perspective," *Educational Forum,* 1980, *XLIV,* (4), 425–428.

Lowery, L. and Marshall, H. *Learning about Instruction: Teacher-Initiated Statements and Questions.* Berkeley: University of California, 1980.

Lowery, L. *Screening.* Unpublished Manuscript. Berkeley: University of California, Educational Research and Applications Program, 1981.

Metfessel, N.S. and Michael, W.B. "A Paradigm Involving Multiple Criterion Measures for the Evaluation of the Effectiveness of School Programs." In *Educational Evaluation: Theory and Practice,* Worthen, B.R. & Sanders, J.R. Belmont: Wadsworth Publ. Co., 1973, 269–289.

Miller, G.A. "The Magical Number Seven, Plus or Minus Two: Some Limits in our Capacity for Processing Information," *Psychological Review,* 1956, *63,* 81–97.

Restak, R. *The Brain: the Last Frontier.* New York: Warner Books, 1979.

Rowe, M.B. "Wait Time and Rewards as Instructional Variables: Their Influence on Language, Logic, and Fate Control," *Journal of Research in Science Teaching,* 1974, *11,* 81–94.

Sexton, T.G. and Poling, D.R. *Can Intelligence Be Taught?* Bloomington: Phi Delta Kappa Educational Foundation Fastback Series #29, 1973.

Smith, E.R. and Tyler, R.W. *Appraising and Recording Student Progress.* New York: Harper, 1942.

Strasser, B.B., *et al. Teaching Toward Inquiry.* Washington, D.C.: National Education Association, 1972.

Suchman, J.R. "A Model for the Analysis of Inquiry." In *Analyses of Concept Learning.* New York: Academic Press, Inc., Ch. 11, 1966, 177–187.

Taba, H., Levine, S. and Elzey, F. *Thinking in Elementary School Children.* Cooperative Research Project. No. 1574. San Francisco State College, 1964.

Wassermann, S. *Put Some Thinking in Your Classroom.* Chicago: Benefic Press, 1978.

Whimbey, A. *Intelligence Can be Taught.* New York: Bantam Books, 1976.

Whimbey, A. "Students Can Learn to be Better Problem Solvers," *Educational Leadership,* 1980, 37, 7, 560–565.

Winne, P.H. "Experiments Relating Teacher's Use of Higher Cognitive Questions to Student Achievement," *Review of Educational Research.* 1979, 49, (1), 13–50.

PART V.

ARTIFICIAL INTELLIGENCE

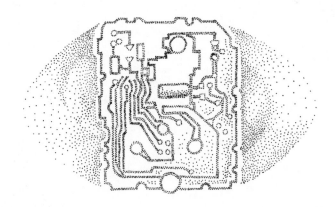

INTRODUCTION

Can computers think? How would one know if a computer were thinking? There is the classical Turing Test: suppose two humans were on opposite sides of a wall and they were conversing via some sort of teletypewriters. Then suppose, midway in the conversation, an intelligent computer replaced one of the humans. If the other human were unaware of the substitution and the intelligent conversation continued, a third observer would have to grant that both man and machine were intelligent. Alan M. Turing, a British mathematician, devised his now famous test in 1950. Since then both hardware (computer components, especially "chips") and software (computer programs) have advanced at such a rate that the Turing Test can now be reasonably invoked for a large number of computer programs. Thus, artificial intelligence is not science fiction or a futuristic dream—or nightmare. It is a present reality. For recent discussions of the Turing Test see Boden (1977) and Hofstader and Dennett (1981).

No book on thinking would be complete today without some discussion of artificial thinking or of those processes of solving problems and proving theorems or hypotheses that simulate, or that can substitute for, processes that humans use to solve problems or to establish a reasonable path toward some goal.

We are very pleased that we are able to include in this volume two outstanding essays on artificial intelligence: one describes an heuristic theorem prover that might well be one of the most powerful developed so far. (The claim that the authors make is a very serious one, and their professional status demands that we give their claim some attention.) Pelletier's and Wilson's paper, "Heuristics Theorem Proving," describes a computer program they have developed. If you are unfamiliar with any of the various languages used in programming or with formal academic logic, you may have some difficulty, initially, in reading Pelletier and Wilson. These difficulties are easily remedied.

Early in their article, Pelletier and Wilson refer to an abstract system of logic developed by Church (1956). (Church is generally acknowledged to be one of this century's most distinguished mathematical logicians.) Church, in effect, proposed that we play a series of logical games. One game is played with a string of symbols, and has ultimate starting points: any string of symbols of the form (p > (q>p)) will be an admissable starting point. Then, there are rules about where we can go from our starting point. If you are unfamiliar with such literature, it will not take long to understand such games and symbols if you refer to Church (1956) or to Boden (1977) or to Hofstader and Dennet (1981) or to some of the other references listed by Pelletier and Wilson or Boden.

Margaret Boden is a well-known authority in both Piagetian developmental psychology and artificial intelligence. Her books are standard treatments of both subjects. But for this volume she wisely elected to explain to teachers and educational theorists the pedagogical virtues of artificial intelligence (AI). Her essay here is one of the best introductions to the subject we know of.

Both papers in this section are somewhat sharply focused, one on a particular theorem prover program and the other on AI in the classroom. If you should desire a more complete treatment of AI, you will find Boden's reference list a most helpful guide. And, as we hasten to point out, since the area of artificial intelligence appears to be one of the most exciting new fields in human thinking, no one who will live or who will prepare children to live into the twenty-first century can afford any longer to ignore this important new domain.

REFERENCES

Boden, M.A. *Artificial Intelligence and Natural Man.* New York: Basic Books, 1977.

Church, A. *An Introduction to Mathematical Logic.* Princeton: Princeton University Press, 1956.

Hofstadter, D.R. and Dennett, D.C. *The Mind's I.* New York: Basic Books, 1981.

EDUCATIONAL IMPLICATIONS OF ARTIFICIAL INTELLIGENCE[1]

Margaret A. Boden

ABSTRACT

Artificial Intelligence (AI) can help us to understand and improve thinking. Given its influence on cognitive and developmental psychology, it promises to illuminate the procedural complexities of thought. Applied in the classroom, it can foster autonomy and self-confidence in normal and handicapped children. It can also provide tutorial aids significantly more flexible than those of traditional Computer Assisted Instruction (CAI). Through nonspecialist courses in higher education, AI can encourage the judicious computer literacy that modern societies will need.

The volcanic peaks of Fiji, described by Rupert Brooke as the most fantastically shaped mountains in the world, remind me of the well-known reason for climbing Everest: "Because it is there." This reply may be adequate justification of the mountaineer's obsession, but it would not explain why people involved in education should be interested in Artificial Intelligence (AI). AI is the attempt to write programs enabling computers to do things that would involve intelligence if done by people (Boden, 1977). Like every human activity, it has its own peculiar fascination. But there are more pressing reasons why AI is educationally relevant, reasons both theoretical and practical.

Many cognitive psychologists today look to AI for help in understanding problem solving, learning, and intelligence. Even creativity might be illuminated by AI-related ideas. Psychological theory can be expected to influence pedagogical practice, and relevant recommendations have already been drawn from the AI way of thinking about thinking. The entry of AI into the classroom in the form of AI-based automatic tutors calls for an appreciation of the differences between this approach and the traditional view of computer-assisted instruction. Current work with

M. A. Boden is Professor of Philosophy and Psychology at the University of Sussex in Brighton, England.

1. I am grateful to the British Council (Committee for International Cooperation in Higher Education) and the Commonwealth Foundation for sponsoring my visit to the University of the South Pacific for which this paper was written.

handicapped children suggests that AI ideas can help these children to realize their intellectual and emotional potential. And the increasing use of computers in schools and universities prompts people to ask whether social life will be impoverished by the widespread introduction of "intelligent" programs in educational institutions. For these various reasons, then, educators might be expected to take an informed interest in AI.

Educational psychology and pedagogical practice alike are unavoidably (if often implicitly) influenced by general psychology. Today, theoretical psychologists increasingly draw concepts from AI and computer science in asking questions about thinking. According to the computational approach, thinking is a structured, interpretative process. Given this view, AI is in accord with many non-behaviorist psychologists — such as Piaget. Indeed, AI agrees with Piaget in a number of ways, including its commitment to formalism and cybernetics, and the insight that psychology (being concerned with meaning and symbol-manipulation) is semiotic rather than causal. However, Piaget gave only vague answers to his questions about thinking and its development; he also failed to make his questions about these matters sufficiently detailed: his vocabulary of "disturbance," "regulation," and "compensation" is inadequate to express the procedural complexity involved (Boden, 1979; in press, b). Nor is Piaget alone in this. Non-computational psychologists, in general, tend to underemphasize mental process, taking it for granted as unproblematic rather than inquiring into it. This is hardly surprising, since computational concepts are needed to express the content, structure, construction, comparison, transformation, function, and development of differing representations and information-processes. A central lesson of AI, then, is that our theoretical aim should be to specify the procedural complexity of thinking.

One way of attempting to do this is to write computer programs that achieve an intellectual task that human thinkers can manage. Because programmed procedures must be explicitly and rigorously defined, this exercise may provide ideas as to what psychological processes might be involved — and it will certainly help to locate lacunae in current psychological theory. However, the way in which a program does something may bear very little relation to the way in which human minds do it. We need to make careful comparisons between the various levels of the program and psychological data, to assess the degree of match between the artificial and the natural systems. In many cases, the relevant data are not available. Often, there are methodological difficulties in deciding just which aspects of the program might be worth testing empirically (some aspects are included merely in order to produce a program which will run, and have no psychological interest). And many psychologists are not sufficiently interested in the activity of programming to want to spend their time in writing complex programs. For these reasons — not to mention a positive commitment to working with human subjects — many psychologists sympathetic to AI do not desert empirical research for the computer console. Instead, they try to plan their experiments with computational questions in mind, their studies being more closely focused on the procedural details of thinking than is usual.

In developmental psychology, for instance, the computational influence has been largely responsible for the increasing interest in microdevelopmental research, which studies the dialectical interplay between action-sequences and changing cognitive representations (theories, models, heuristics, choice-criteria . . .). The emphasis of microdevelopmental studies differs from more traditional approaches in emphasizing the specifics of action, on the assumption that the procedural detail of performance (not only its overall structure) gives clues to underlying competence. Admittedly, Piaget was one who took seriously details of action which others had ignored as trivialities. But the degree of detail aimed at in microdevelopmental research is greater — and that which would be needed to specify an adequate computational theory of these matters is greater still.

For example, a microdevelopmental study of children's learning to balance blocks found that a non-balanced block may at first be ignored as an apparently irrelevant anomaly, and only later be accepted as a genuine counterexample challenging (and prompting an improvement of) the child's current theory (Karmiloff-Smith and Inhelder, 1975). This fact is not predicted, still less is it explained, by generalized talk of "accommodation." The experimenters suggested that time is needed for "consolidation" of any theory — but they did not ask just what consolidation is, and how it is effected. These questions would need to be answered if "consolidation" is to be accepted within a computational theory of cognitive change (Boden, in press, a).

In another example, microdevelopmental work has cast doubt on the common assumption that the classificatory power of five- and ten-year-olds is very similar (Thornton, 1982). This view relies on the fact that the *product* of classification may be identical between these two age-groups, but it ignores the fact that the *activity* of sorting is significantly different. Thornton's experimental design highlights many procedural differences, and she interprets her observations in broadly computational terms. She suggests that children of ten treat the whole classification as a single unit composed of interrelated classes, that at five they proceed as though each class were independent of the others, and that seven-year-olds attend to the relations between classes so as spontaneously to effect the transition by organizing their initially "juxtaposed" procedures into more coherent systems. She admits that the procedural content of concepts like these needs to be clarified if cognitive development is to be understood, and is currently attempting such a clarification with the help of AI-ideas. (With reference to bugs and creativity, both discussed below, one should note that Thornton takes her work to show that cognitive change need not be failure-driven. This conclusion is supported by the comparable finding that a child asked to draw maps may spontaneously construct a more powerful map, even though the current one has always succeeded [Karmiloff-Smith, 1979].)

The educational potential of AI has been explicitly recognized by a number of workers in the field. One of these is Seymour Papert (1980), an ex-colleague of Piaget who has been deeply influenced by Piaget's ideas about autonomous constructive learning and the epistemological relevance of the structure (not only of knowing but also) of what is known. Papert's ideas are likely to be influential, not least because in November 1981 he was invited by President Mitterand of France to advise on a new Paris computer research center (with a budget of £20 million a year) devoted to the development of a low-cost, pocket-sized computer that will be available on a mass scale throughout the world. In a recent book, Papert (1980) explores the promise of the nascent "computer culture," focusing not on the many uses people will find for computers, but rather on the power of computational environments to affect the way people think and learn — and, crucially, the way they think about themselves.

Papert reminds us that psychological theories of thinking usually affect educational practice not *via* detailed hypotheses, but *via* relatively general ideas, and he identifies a number of "powerful ideas" that enable us to think more confidently and effectively. An important example is the notion of "bugs" in thinking. This concept originated in computer programming, wherein one soon discovers the ubiquity of bugs. Bugs are mistakes, but not just any mistakes: a false factual assumption is not a bug, nor is a momentary slip in executing some procedure, nor the choice of a procedure that is wholly inappropriate to the goal. A bug is a precisely definable and relatively systematic, erroneous variation of a correct procedure.

Several AI workers have attempted to classify bugs. Sussman (1975) distinguished several types in terms of general teleological notions such as goal, brother-goals, and prerequisite; he wrote a self-modifying learning program that diagnosed its bugs so as to criticize and repair its self-programming accordingly. More recently, O'Shea and Young (1978) have analyzed a large sample of children's subtraction errors in terms of the deletion or overgeneral application of individual rules, such as the "borrowing" rule. Brown and VanLehn (1980) and Burton (1981) have also studied subtraction, and their programs BUGGY and DEBUGGY provide a notation for precisely describing bugs, as well as a diagnostic tool for identifying errors in students' work. They are developing a "generative theory of bugs," a set of formal principles that can be applied to a particular (correct) procedural skill to generate all the bugs actually observed in the data, and no others. They expect their theory to predict the bugs that occur during the learning of arithmetic, algebra, and calculus (and, possibly, operating computer systems or controlling air traffic).

Their central idea is that many bugs are "patches" (a term drawn from computer programming) that arise from the attempt to repair a procedure that has encountered an impasse while solving a particular problem. The theory defines various repair heuristics and critics (procedures for finding mistakes in a strategy) and the way in which a repair will be attempted is theoretically independent of the reason why the procedure was incorrect in the first place. This enables the authors to explain "bug-migration," wherein a subject has a different bug on two tests given only a few days apart. Using their diagnostic system, they find that only certain bugs migrate into each other, and that they seem to travel both ways. For instance, "Stops-Borrow-At-Zero" migrates into "Borrow-Across-Zero," and *vice-versa*. The hypothesis is that bugs will migrate into each other if (as in this example) they can be derived by different repairs from the same impasse. Repair theory thus makes empirical predictions about the detailed pattern of errors observed when people are learning skills of thinking.

Despite its emphasis on error, "bug" is an optimistic rather than a defeatist notion. For it implies that elements of the correct procedure or skill are already possessed by the thinker, and that what is wrong is a precisely definable error that can be identified and fixed. In this it differs from the broader notions of "anomaly" and "counterexample," the educational value of which has been stressed for instance in the Piagetian tradition (Groen, 1978). As Papert puts it, the concept of bug helps one to think about thinking in "mind-sized bites." These insights led Papert to develop the LOGO programming language (usable even by six-year-olds), in the conviction that AI in the classroom could lead children to a fruitful insight about their own thinking abilities. There is some evidence that the experience of LOGO-programming does indeed encourage children to replace the passively defeatist, "I'm no good at this" with the more constructive, "How can I make myself better at it?" (Papert, 1980; Howe *et al.*, 1979).

Thus Papert stresses the educational value of the activity of programming itself. But AI can enter the classroom in another way, namely, in the form of tutorial programs. Automatic teaching aids, of a sort, have long been with us. B.F. Skinner's "teaching machines," and their descendants in Computer Assisted Instruction (CAI), can vary their response to a limited degree with the student's level of understanding, by means of branched programs with predefined choice-points. But the flexibility of tutorial programs based in AI is much greater because they incorporate complex computational models of students' reasoning that enable them to respond in more subtly adaptive ways. A number of such programs already exist that are useful in limited domains, and several groups around the world are working on these issues (Sleeman & Brown, 1981). Only if a clear articulation of the knowledge involved in the chosen domain has been achieved can it be embodied in an instructional program — though before this embodiment it might be usable by a human teacher in an instructional program. DEBUGGY, for instance, is as good as or better than human diagnosticians at discovering the nearly one hundred bugs that explain a student's subtraction errors. In the hands of a specially primed teacher, it can be put to use in the classroom. It has not yet been incorporated within a remedial program, with which students can interact to improve their subtraction skill; nor has it yet been presented so as to be a diagnostic aid for a mathematics teacher. But these educational developments are in the forefront of the authors' minds; one of Brown's aims has been to develop diagnostic and remedial principles that can be used by tutors — whether human or automatic — to help people learn (Brown & Burton, 1975). (Some practice with DEBUGGY might profitably be provided in teacher-training courses, even though it cannot yet be adopted as a classroom tool.)

We have seen that AI helps to foster a constructive rather than a defeatist attitude to our mistakes. But to emphasize the creative potential of bugs is not to say that all creative thinking is a reactive response to failure (Boden, in press, a). On the contrary, it often appears to be grounded in a spontaneous exploratory urge. This much is recognized by psychological accounts of creativity in terms of "competence," "adaptation-level," "functional assimilation," and "play." However, creativity cannot be understood by way of these concepts, nor by any other structurally undifferentiated, quasi-quantitative, notions of novelty and familiarity. For such concepts enable us to say little or nothing about precisely how individual creative achievements come about. A theory of creative thinking should be able to explain how *these* or *those* novel thoughts are generated, how promising pathways are recognized in preference to probable dead ends, and how potentially interesting ideas are distinguished from novel banalities.

The idea that AI might help answer these questions strikes many people as paradoxical. It is commonly assumed that, because of its programming provenance, AI must be fundamentally incapable of modelling creativity. Were this so, its educational relevance would be gravely limited, for a prime aim of education is to encourage creativity. However, unless it is either random or essentially mysterious, creativity must be grounded in some systematic, generative principles. From the viewpoint of theoretical psychology, which assumes thinking itself to be food for scientific thought, to regard creativity as essentially mysterious is to be intellectually defeatist. That creativity cannot be a random process (though there is sometimes a random aspect to it) is recognized by all who scorn the idea that a barrowload of monkeys with typewriters could produce *Hamlet*. Rules or generative principles there must then be, and since AI is specifically concerned with transformations in generative structures, we may expect it to be relevant.

Although most AI studies do not attempt to model systems in which genuinely novel ideas arise or in which radical constraints are relaxed, some relevant work has been done. For instance, Lenat's (1977a; 1977b) "Automatic Mathematician" starts off with some elementary concepts of set-theory and a collection of heuristics (rules for combining, transforming, and comparing concepts), and sets out to explore their potential in an open-ended way to discover new mathematical concepts. Significantly, the program does not merely churn out new ideas, but focuses on some heuristic pathways as more likely to be promising than others, and on some novel ideas as more interesting than others. Thus, having discovered the natural numbers and decided to explore this path, it then discovers and dubs "interesting" concepts such as prime numbers, square roots, and maximally divisible numbers (with respect to which the last program developed two minor new results in number theory).

Granted that the heuristics were thought up by Lenat (1977b) rather than by the program, it is significant — and surprising to many people — that this sort of fruitful exploratory thinking can be formally represented at all. The degree of creativity evinced by the program is, however, difficult to assess. The concept of creativity is itself so unclear that it is not obvious just what would count as "discovering," or "creating," natural number theory (or anything else). Critics (Hanna and Ritchie, 1981) have remarked that Lenat (1977b) does not list all the concepts regarded by the program as interesting: perhaps a high proportion were mathematically trivial. It is not clear from the published accounts whether some crucial "discoveries" were made possible only by the use of unacceptably *ad hoc* heuristics, nor is it easy to draw the line between an acceptably specialized expert heuristic and a disingenuous programming trick. Certainly, many of the heuristics are highly domain-specific, relevant only to set theory. But it is a prime theoretical claim of Lenat's (1977b) that intelligence depends heavily on expert knowledge, as opposed to general skills.

Lenat's view that special-purpose heuristics are necessary to creative thinking is consonant with the view of intelligence now held by many people in AI. In the early days of AI research, it was a common assumption that very general thinking procedures suffice to solve most problems. This faith was reflected in the title of one of the most famous early programs, the "*General* Problem Solver" (Newell and Simon, 1963), and it motivated much of the early work in "theorem-proving." Since then, it has become increasingly apparent that, while there are some relatively general strategies (such as depth-first or breadth-first search, for instance), the intelligent deployment of knowledge also involves large numbers of domain-specific heuristics suited to the structure of the subject matter concerned.

Like the notion of "buggy thinking," this view of intelligence contradicts the all-too-common idea that intelligence is a monolithic ability, which one either has or lacks. If more ammunition against so-called "intelligence tests" were needed, there is a full arsenal here: the AI approach highlights the absurdity of trying to assess people's intelligence by deliberately *preventing* them from using any of their acquired expertise (Gregory, 1981, pp. 295–333).

Since intelligence is the deployment of many special-purpose skills, learning and microdevelopment must involve the gradual acquisition of a myriad of domain-specific facts and heuristics. Many of these are presumably picked up during the initial immersion in a problem domain, when the unskilled person may appear to be merely thrashing around. Just how they are picked up is, however, obscure. Microdevelopmental studies thus need to focus on precisely what information is being attended to by the child at a given time, and what micro-strategies he is using to deploy it, with what results.

The case for asking these informational questions, with reference to distinct procedural rules, has been argued in the context of an AI model of children's seriation behavior. Young (1976) showed that qualitative behavioral differences can result from the addition or deletion of one simply definable Condition-Action rule. Moreover, the use of a rule, once acquired, depends on tests related to its appropriateness in a particular context of information. For example, even adults will use a trial-and-error seriation strategy if given a large number of blocks, differing only slightly in length. Piaget explained this in terms of regression from the formal to the concrete-operational stage, implying that the subject chooses a sub-optimal method over an optimal one. However, the informational demands here differ from those where there are only a few blocks, of obviously differing lengths. The perceptual judgment of which block is the largest (or smallest) cannot be made instantly, since the information from so many blocks cannot be handled all at once. Consequently, the optimal informational strategy is to compare the blocks one by one. Young's study of seriation (1976) is in the microdevelopmental rather than the macrodevelopmental category, not only because he is able to explain minute details of behavior (such as the stretching out of the hand towards a block that is not then picked up), but because of his AI-based view that intelligent behavior is better described in terms of many independent rules than it is in terms of holistic structures.

Handicapped children can benefit greatly from an AI-based computational environment (Weir, 1981; Weir and Emanuel, 1976). I have in mind here not the use of computers as gadgetry (controlling typewriters and the like), practically important though these are. Rather, I am thinking of recent research showing how AI can help encourage a variety of intellectual and emotional abilities; AI can be used not only to study the mind of a handicapped person, but also to liberate and develop it. Weir, a psychiatrist with a mastery of AI techniques, has worked with a number of different handicaps and has started a long-term project with the sponsorship of the Massachusetts Institute of Technology. Commenting on the varied examples she describes, Weir points out that we have as yet only scratched the surface of what is possible.

For example, her work with a severely autistic child suggests that a sense of autonomous control (over oneself and others) may develop for the first time as a result of the experience of interactive (LOGO) programming. The immediacy of results and the non-human context (in which the threat of personal rejection or adverse judgment is removed) combine to provide an inducement for the emotionally withdrawn child to venture into a world not only of action, but of interaction. Interaction with human beings follows, apparently facilitated by the computational experience.

Another example is our wish to build and improve the spatial intelligence of severely palsied children. Since they lack normal sensorimotor experience, we might expect them to suffer from generalized disabilities of spatial cognition. But manipulative tests are clearly of little value in assessing just what abilities a palsied child has or lacks. The use of computer graphics (for which LOGO was developed) provides a window onto the intelligence of these children, one that allows diagnosis of their specific difficulties in understanding spatial concepts. Weir's aim is not just to understand their minds but to help change them; she has the satisfaction of reporting considerable advances in the children's intellectual achievement and general self-confidence.

Linguistic defects, too, may be bypassed in assessments based on computer graphics. For instance, a grossly dyslexic boy was found by Weir to have superior spatial intelligence, involving highly developed metaknowledge (knowledge *about* knowledge) in the spatial domain. The dissociation between linguistic and spatial knowledge is, of course, consonant with the AI view of intelligence discussed above. Much as I suggested that DEBUGGY might be useful for teacher training even though it is not ready as a classroom tool, so ideas from Weir's LOGO projects might be useful in training teachers for the handicapped. But since it is a prime claim of her approach that the experience of interaction with a LOGO machine is itself highly therapeutic, she would recommend increased availability of computers for use by handicapped people.

This raises an aspect of the "computer culture" awaiting our children that has not yet been mentioned, namely, the enormous increase in the number of computers used in society. By 1980 there were already two million personal computers in use in the United States (Levin and Kareev, 1980), and the market is expanding; and there is an increasing use of programs by institutions (governmental, medical, educational, and commercial). In their discussion of "the future with microelectronics," Barron and Curnow (1979) point out that, as well as vocational training and adult retraining, we shall need contextual education to ensure that everyone is aware of the technology and its possible consequences. As users get less expert, there will be an increasingly urgent need for relevant nonspecialist courses in higher education. They conclude that, "It should perhaps be a target that every graduate has the capability to use computer systems and a thorough understanding of their potential [and, I would add, of their limitations]" (p. 231).

Several universities already have courses with these aims in mind, and some people are already doing comparable work with school pupils. For instance, we at the University of Sussex have found that one can alert naive (and non-numerate) users on their first day of programming experience to the facts that even an "intelligent" program is incapable of doing many things we might *prima facie* expect it to do, and that even a nonspecialist may modify the program so as to make it less limited. A conversational or visual program, for example, is initially impressive, but the user soon realizes that apparently obvious inferences about the meaning of the input words or pictures are not actually being made by it. The beginner student can then attempt to supply the missing rule so that the unmade inference can now be drawn. Since they themselves are altering these complex systems, students gain confidence in the activity of programming. More important, they realize that programs, however impressive they may be, are neither godlike nor unalterable.

These insights would not readily be communicated merely by teaching students to program — in FORTRAN, for example, or BASIC. They are best conveyed by prepared teaching demonstrations which make use of AI techniques. (Ours owe a great debt to the late Max Clowes, whose imaginative vision of student-friendly computing environments inspired us all.) Educational projects such as these are socially important, since for most people the ability to write usable programs will be less important than the ability to use — and to avoid misusing — programs written by others. This sort of computer literacy will be necessary if people are to be able to take advantage of this new technology rather than being taken advantage of by it.

Widespread access to computing environments, especially in primary or middle schools, may have significant social-psychological effects. The computer junkie, or "hacker" (Weizenbaum, 1976, pp. 115–126) has already appeared in infantile form — so much so that a brochure for a children's computer camp reassured parents that their offspring would not be allowed to remain at the terminal all day, that they would be *forced* to ride, swim, or play tennis. Whether this presents a threat to normal social development is not yet known. Research on the impact of such environments on young children's play patterns is currently being planned (Robert Hughes, National Playing-Fields Association: personal communication), in the hope that any unwelcome changes in play behavior could be forestalled.

We should not assume, however, that any changes in social interaction would necessarily be unwelcome. For instance, there is evidence in the LOGO projects that the greater self-confidence, induced by a child's experience of computing, can lead to less antisocial behavior. Moreover, programming contexts are in some ways less threatening or oppressive than interpersonal ones, and so have a liberating potential that could be useful in education. This potential has already been mentioned with respect to the autistic child who was led to interact with people after the safer experimentation in a computational environment; it has also been observed in the context of medical interviewing (Card *et al.*, 1974). A computer system is something to which (not to whom) one can direct remarks that do not carry the usual social consequences (Pateman, 1981). Interaction with the system thus avoids the sort of face-saving maneuvers which, in interpersonal contexts, can inhibit the creative exploration of ideas: "I wonder what it will do if I say this?" is significantly less threatening than "I wonder what she will think of me if I say that?"

In sum, AI has much to offer to people involved in the theory and practice of education. It can help both in the understanding and the improvement of thinking. Through its influence on cognitive and developmental psychology, AI promises to deepen our insight into the procedural complexities of thought. Through its applications in the classroom, AI's view of intelligence as a self-corrective, constructive activity can foster personal autonomy and self-confidence. This is so with respect to normal and handicapped students, children and adults. Used as the basis of intelligent tutorial programs, AI can offer greater aid and challenge to both student and teacher than the more familiar forms of computer-assisted instruction. Last but not least, AI ideas can be used to convey a deeper understanding of the potential and the limitations of programs, in societies where computer literacy will be an increasingly important aspect of the communal good. The satisfactions of viewing AI are not those of scaling Tomaniivi or the Namosi Peaks. But AI, too, is there: let us not fail to explore it.

REFERENCES

Barron, R. and Curnow, I. *The Future With Microelectronics: Forecasting the Effects of Information Technology.* Milton Keynes: Open University Press, 1979.

Boden, M.A. *Artificial Intelligence and Natural Man.* New York: Basic Books, 1977.

Boden, M.A. *Piaget.* London: Fontana, 1979.

Boden, M.A. "Failure is Not the Spur." In *Adaptive Control in Ill-Defined Systems* (NATO Workshop, 1981), M. Arbib, O. Selfridge, and E. Rissler (Eds.). In press (a).

Boden, M.A. "Is Equilibration Important? — A View from Artificial Intelligence," *Brit. J. Psychology* (Piaget Memorial Issue, 1982), in press (b).

Brown, J.S. and Vanlehn, K. "Repair Theory: A Generative Theory of Bugs in Procedural Skills," *Cognitive Science,* 1980, *4,* 379–426.

Brown, J.S. and Burton, R.R. "Multiple Representations of Knowledge for Tutorial Reasoning." In *Representation and Understanding: Studies in Cognitive Science,* D.G. Bobrow and A. Collins (Eds.). New York: Academic Press, 1975.

Burton, R.R. "DEBUGGY: Diagnosis of Errors in Basic Mathematical Skills." In *Intelligent Tutoring Systems,* D. Sleeman and J.S. Brown (Eds.). London: Academic Press, 1981.

Card, W.I., *et al.* "A Comparison of Doctor and Computer Interrogation of Patients," *Int. J. Bio-Medical Computing,* 1974, *5,* 175–187.

Gregory, R.L. *Mind in Science: A History of Explanations in Psychology and Physics.* London: Weidenfeld and Nicolson, 1981.

Groen, G. "The Theoretical Ideas of Piaget and Educational Practice." In *The Impact of Research on Education,* P. Suppes (Ed.). Washington: National Academy of Education, 1978.

Hanna, F.K. and Ritchie, G.D. *AM: A Case Study of AI Methodology.* Electronics Lab., Univ. of Kent, 1981.

Howe, J.M., *et al.* "Teaching Maths Through LOGO Programming: An Evaluation Study," *Proc. IFIP Working Conference on CAI,* London, 1979.

Karmiloff-Smith, A. "Micro- and Macro-Developmental Changes in Language Acquisition and Other Representational Systems," *Cognitive Science,* 1979, *3,* 81–118.

Karmiloff-Smith, A. and Inhelder, B. "If You Want to Get Ahead, Get a Theory," *Cognition,* 1975, *3,* 195–212.

Lenat, D.B. "The Ubiquity of Discovery," *Artificial Intelligence,* 1977, *9,* 257–286. (a)

Lenat, D.B. "Automated Theory Formation in Mathematics." *Proc. Fifth Int. Joint Conf. Artificial Intelligence,* Cambridge, MA, 1977, 833–842. (b)

Levin, J.A. and Kareev, Y. *Personal Computers and Education: The Challenge to Schools,* Univ. Calif, San Diego, Chip Report 98, 1980.

Newell, A. and Simon, H. "GPS — A Program that Simulates Human Thought." In *Computers and Thought,* E.A. Feigenbaum and J. Feldman (Eds.). New York: McGraw-Hill, 1963.

O'Shea, T. and Young, R.M. "A Production Rules Account of Errors in Children's Subtraction." *Proc. AISB Conference,* Hamburg, 1978, 229–237.

Papert, S. *Mindstorms: Children, Computers, and Powerful Ideas.* Brighton, Sussex: Harvester Press, 1980.

Pateman, T. "Communicating With Computer Programs," *Language and Communication,* 1981, *1,* 3–12.

Sleeman, D.H. and Brown, J.S. *Intelligent Tutoring Systems.* London: Academic Press, 1981.

Sussman, G.J. *A Computer Model of Skill Acquisition.* New York: American Elsevier, 1975.

Thornton, S. "Challenging 'Early Competence': A Process Oriented Analysis of Children's Classifying," *Cognitive Science,* 1982, (in press).

Weir, S. "LOGO as an Information Prosthetic for Communication and Control." *Seventh Int. Joint Conf. Artificial Intelligence.* 1981, 970–974.

Weir, S. and Emanuel, R. *Using LOGO to Catalyze Communication in an Autistic Child.* D.A.I. Research Report 15. Dept. A.I., Univ. Edinburgh, 1976.

Weizenbaum, J. *Computer Power and Human Reason: From Judgment to Calculation.* San Francisco: W.H. Freeman and Co., 1976.

Young, R.M. *Seriation by Children: An Artificial Intelligence Analysis of a Piagetian Task.* Basel: Birkhauser, 1976.

HEURISTIC THEOREM PROVING[1]

Francis Jeffry Pelletier
Dan C. Wilson

Francis Jeffry Pelletier
Dan C. Wilson

ABSTRACT

Many people view the essential difference between computer output and human thinking as "blindly following an algorithm versus heuristically using and altering strategies." A computer program which invokes heuristics is discussed and applied to the problem of producing proofs in ordinary logic. The conclusion is twofold: our computer program performs significantly better than existing algorithmetic methods, and it performs in a manner indistinguishable from the heuristics that humans use.

THEOREM PROVING AND THINKING

In the last twenty years it has been common to mark off human performance from computer performance in terms of heuristics versus algorithms. A computer, so it is claimed, blindly follows a humanly devised algorithm and therefore cannot be counted rational, no matter what its performance. Humans, on the other hand, have a variety of heuristics or strategies at their disposal and engage in goal-directed thought by employing these strategies, so long as they appear to be leading toward the goal; they switch to another strategy when the previous one appears not to be succeeding. Now, the distinction between blind algorithms and heuristic strategies seems to us not to be very sharp and clear; we think that they merge into one another, and that the real difference between them is a subjective impression of unsureness of success in the case of heuristics. But we shall not argue that here. Instead, we shall accept the perceived distinction and display a program which uses exclusively what everyone would recognize as heuristic strategies.

The area where we intend to employ our heuristics is in theorem proving. We should perhaps indicate why we think this is a good and important testing place in

F.J. Pelletier is in the Department of Philosophy at the University of Alberta, Canada. D.C. Wilson is with A.G.S. Computers, Inc., in Mountainside, New Jersey.

1. We wish to thank Lenhart K. Schubert for his support of this project, both in terms of computer time and information. We also thank Jeffrey Sampson for encouraging us to develop our system in the first place. Dave Sharp supplied us with lists of "tricky" theorems to test THINKER with.

which to use heuristic techniques. The first reason is simply that logic has, since Aristotle, been considered one of the crucial areas that define rationality and thinking. Secondly, there are a variety of models of theorem proving (*i.e.,* systems of logic) available for use and their abstract properties are well-known. Thirdly, there are a variety of computer-based theorem provers around to which we may compare ours. Finally, and most importantly, the current state of artificial intelligence invokes theorem proving in a wide range of tasks which are taken to simulate thinking. For example, natural-language-understanding systems—including data-base retrieval and question-answering systems—all require a theorem prover to go from "what is literally said" to "what is meant by the speaker."

It is well known that to understand a normal speaker, a lot of "inferencing" is required to take into account background information, mutually known intentions, and what is likely to be meant in the current situation. The currently believed best way to handle this is to have a theorem prover take what is literally said, add it to this knowledge base, and construct likely conclusions about what was meant on this occasion. Also, current models of planning and action use theorem provers. Thus a robot is ordered to move Box A to Location Z. To do so, our robot first tries to prove that A is already at Z. When this proof fails, it inspects the proof to determine the simplest position, Y, it could be in which (together with one of its primitive movements) will allow it to prove that A is at Z. It then tries to prove that it is in position Y. When this proof fails, it inspects the new proof to determine what is required to prove Y. This is continued until it can prove that some series of primitive movements will get A to Z. And then it performs that series of movements.

The claim in artificial intelligence is that some similar procedure occurs when humans are planning actions and understanding language. Thus it would seem to be of paramount importance for research into thinking to be able to have a theorem prover which operates in a manner akin to human theorem proving. And, as we indicated earlier, we think that heuristic-based theorem proving provides the most likely hope in this regard.

The subject of what theorems can be proved in classical logic was pretty thoroughly canvassed by Whitehead and Russell in 1910–1912; and while various new and interesting theorems were discovered in the decades since, the truly exciting work in logic has been done at the model-theoretic level, and not *within* the logic itself. We therefore wish to emphasize that the present study of theorem proving is done with an eye toward discovering how people in general, when working with abstract matters of logic, actually proceed in formulating a proof (and not an investigation hoping to prove new theorems). We have another eye toward implementing such a theorem prover within natural-language-understanding systems and within robotic-planning systems. In this regard, Feigenbaum and Feldman (1963, p. 107) say:

> The fascination with mechanical theorem proving...lies less with the end (the production of theorems, perhaps new and important) than with the means (a thorough understanding of the organization of information processing activity in mathematical discovery). It is felt that understanding these problem-solving processes is an important step toward the programming of more complex, more general problem-solving processes for a variety of intellectual tasks.

SYSTEMS OF LOGIC

In the abstract, systems of logic can be divided into three sorts: axiomatic, "semantic," and natural deduction. We wish to justify our choice of natural deduction as appropriate, especially in light of the facts that the earliest theorem prover was based on an axiomatic system and that almost all present theorem provers are "semantic" in nature. To this end, we shall describe the three types in this section, and in the next section point out what we take to be flaws in the first two types when it comes to computer theorem proving.

An axiomatic system of logic takes certain formulae as "given" (in the sense of requiring no other justification), gives a set of "rules of inference" (methods of transforming one or more formulae into another), and defines a *proof* as an ordered (finite) set of formulae, each one of which is an axiom or follows from previous (in the ordering) formulae by a rule of inference.

To give an example of a proof in a typical propositional axiomatic system, consider the system P1 of Church (1956). Included in the axioms are A1: $(p{\rightarrow}(q{\rightarrow}p))$, A2: $((s{\rightarrow}(p{\rightarrow}q)){\rightarrow}((s{\rightarrow}p){\rightarrow}(s{\rightarrow}q)))$; and the two rules of inference, MP: from $(A{\rightarrow}B)$ and A, infer B; and Sub: from A, if b is a propositional variable in A, infer the result of replacing all occurrences of b in A by a formula B. A proof of the theorem $(p{\rightarrow}p)$ in this system would be

1.	$((s{\rightarrow}(p{\rightarrow}q)){\rightarrow}((s{\rightarrow}p){\rightarrow}(s{\rightarrow}q)))$	A2
2.	$((s{\rightarrow}(r{\rightarrow}q)){\rightarrow}((s{\rightarrow}r){\rightarrow}(s{\rightarrow}q)))$	1, Sub (r for p)
3.	$((s{\rightarrow}(r{\rightarrow}p)){\rightarrow}((s{\rightarrow}r){\rightarrow}(s{\rightarrow}p)))$	2, Sub (p for q)
4.	$((p{\rightarrow}(r{\rightarrow}p)){\rightarrow}((p{\rightarrow}r){\rightarrow}(p{\rightarrow}p)))$	3, Sub (p for s)
5.	$((p{\rightarrow}(q{\rightarrow}p)){\rightarrow}((p{\rightarrow}q){\rightarrow}(p{\rightarrow}p)))$	4, Sub (q for r)
6.	$(p{\rightarrow}(q{\rightarrow}p))$	A1
7.	$((p{\rightarrow}q){\rightarrow}(p{\rightarrow}p))$	5, 6MP
8.	$((p{\rightarrow}(q{\rightarrow}p)){\rightarrow}(p{\rightarrow}p))$	7, Sub $((q{\rightarrow}p)$ for q)
9.	$(p{\rightarrow}p)$	6, 8MP

The extension of the axiomatic method to the predicate calculus is accomplished by adding further axioms and rules of inference.

"Semantic" systems of logic are so-called because they attempt to mirror the intended semantical interpretation into the system of logic itself. For the propositional logic, this intended semantical interpretation is just the truth table, and consequently, to prove whether a formula A is a theorem or not, it is customary in these systems to introduce devices which enable us to find out whether the assumption that A is *not* a theorem would also require that some atomic sentence and its negation both be assigned True. This is normally done by "breaking down" the formula ¬A into simpler and simpler components. Many of these methods can easily be represented by trees. Jeffrey (1967) has the following system of rules for tree construction:

where the intuitive idea behind a rule is that we are interested in "ways the complex formula might be true." The definition of a proof of conclusion C is: *1.* ¬C is the root node, 2. if a rule of inference is applied to a formula B which occupies a node of the tree, the result of the rule of inference is represented in every "uncancelled" branch that B dominates, 3. any branch which contains an atomic formula and also its negation is "cancelled" by putting an "x" at the bottom of the branch, 4. C is a theorem if and only if every branch is cancelled. The proof of the formula (p→p) is very simple in this system. We put ¬(p→p) as the root node and use the rule for ¬(A→B):

$$
\begin{array}{c}
\neg\,(p{\rightarrow}p) \\
| \\
p \\
\neg\,p \\
x
\end{array}
$$

A somewhat more interesting theorem is DeMorgan's (¬ (p→q) ↔ (p & ¬ q)), which is proved:

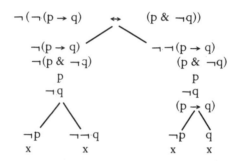

It is quite clear here (as opposed to the axiomatic system) what the strategy is: we assume the (alleged) theorem to be false, and break it down into simpler and simpler components by the truth-preserving rules (the branched formula is true if, and only if, at least one of its sub-branches is true). Since the resulting formulae get shorter and shorter, the method (in the propositional calculus) is guaranteed to halt.

In computerized theorem proving, the most commonly used method is "resolution"—a variant of the semantic methods. Here (in the propositional logic case) we negate the formula to be proved and represent it by its equivalent "clause form" in which the formula is converted to a conjunction of disjunctions of "literals" (=atomic formulae or their negations), and each conjunct is called a *clause*. Each clause (which is itself in disjunctive normal form) is written on a separate line and the one rule of inference, "resolution," is used. The rule is (in its simplest statement):

$$
\begin{array}{l}
A1 \lor B1 \lor \ldots \lor P1 \lor \ldots \lor Z1 \\
A2 \lor B2 \lor \ldots \lor \neg P1 \lor \ldots \lor Z2 \\
\hline
\\
A1 \lor B1 \lor \ldots \lor Z1 \lor A2 \lor B2 \lor \ldots \lor Z2
\end{array}
$$

where: each of the lines is in clause form and the conclusion (a new clause) has no mention of P1 or its negation (it has been "resolved out"). If the original formula was a theorem, then eventually the method will yield a *null resolvent*—the "empty formula," a formula with no subformulae. (The rule is usually generalized to apply to an arbitrary number of premises at one swoop.) Clearly the resolution method is semantic in nature: we are trying to discover whether the purported statement is necessarily true by looking at ways its negation might be true. If none are found (null resolvent), the negation can't be true and so the original statement must be.

These semantic methods can be extended to the (non-decidable) predicate calculus in various ways. Jeffrey (1967) adds branching rules for quantifiers, but these rules are not effective in the sense that they needn't ever be used again. Another way would be to convert the formula into a Skolem normal form by *1.* getting the prenex normal form (all quantifiers have widest scope); *2.* having every variable bound by an existential quantifier which is *a.* not in the scope of a universal quantifier is replaced by a name, *b.* in the scope of a universal quantifier is replaced by a (Skolem) function of the variable(s) mentioned by the universal quantifier(s); and *3.* dropping universal quantifiers. The resulting (non-quantified) formula can now be treated in various ways. We could apply the tree method of above, or we could continue to use the resolution procedure by introducing a special understanding of what variables can resolve against which and generate the null resolvent. Even in the complex case of quantifiers, it should be clear that the strategy is *semantic*: quantifiers are interpreted—existential quantifiers not in the scope of a universal are replaced by a name (the thing in the model that the sentence asserts the existence of), existential quantifiers in the scope of a universal quantifier are replaced by a function of the things named in the model by the universal quantifiers, and so on. Finally, we merely look to the possible co-truth of the atomic formulae.

A natural deduction system is like the semantic systems and unlike the axiomatic systems both because it has no unjustified statements (axioms) and because it has a large number of rules of inference; however, it is unlike the semantic systems in that it does not attempt to "break formulae down" into simple components and evaluate their possible co-truth. Rather, the rules of inference are supposed to correspond to psychologically plausible modes of reasoning. A proof is a method of breaking down a formula into "what you can assume" and "what still needs to be proved," together with methods to actually do some of the "proving." There are a number of these natural deduction systems in the literature; we shall here present (and later employ) the one found in Kalish & Montague (1964). For the propositional logic, the *rules of inference* are:

$$\frac{A}{A} \text{ (R)}; \quad \frac{A}{\neg\neg A} \text{ and } \frac{\neg\neg A}{A} \text{ (DN)}; \quad \frac{(A \,\&\, B)}{A} \text{ and } \frac{(A \,\&\, B)}{B} \text{ (S)};$$

$$\frac{A}{(A \lor B)} \text{ and } \frac{A}{(B \lor A)} \text{ (Add)} \quad \frac{(A \to B)}{B} \text{ (MP)}; \quad \frac{(A \to B)}{\neg A} \text{ (MT)}; \quad \frac{A}{(A \,\&\, B)} \text{ (Adj)};$$

$$\frac{(A \lor B)}{B} \text{ and } \frac{(A \lor B)}{A} \text{ (MTP)}; \quad \frac{(A \to B)}{(B \leftrightarrow A)} \text{ (CB)}; \quad \frac{(A \leftrightarrow B)}{(A \to B)} \text{ and } \frac{(A \leftrightarrow B)}{(B \to A)} \text{ (BC)}$$

which abbreviations stand for, respectively R: Repetition, DN: Double Negation, MP: Modus Ponens, MT: Modus Tollens, S: Simplification, ADj: Adjunction, Add: Addition, MTP: Modul Tollendo Ponens, BC: Biconditional to Conditional, CB: Conditionals to Biconditional. These are all taken to be psychologically plausible modes of reasoning. An *antecedent line* is defined as a line which is earlier in the proof and neither boxed nor containing an uncancelled "show" (both defined below). A *proof* is defined as:

1. If A is a formula, then "Show A" can occur as a line. (The "show" is *uncancelled.* Intuitively we are setting the task of proving A.)
2a. If "Show A" occurs as a line then ¬A can occur as the next line ("assume the negation").
2b. If "Show ¬ A" occurs as a line, then A can occur as the next line.
2c. If "Show (A→B)" occurs as a line, then A can occur as the next line ("assume the antecedent").
3. If C follows from antecedent lines by a rule of inference, then C may be entered as the next line.
4. If the proof has a subpart which looks like
    Show A
     X1

     .

     .

     .

     Xn

and *a.* there are no uncancelled "Show" among X1...Xn, and *b.* either A occurs unboxed (defined below) among X1...Xn, or else both C and ¬C occur unboxed among X1...Xn, then

     Show A
     X1
     .
     .
     .
     Xn

can be the next step in the proof (X1...Xn are now *boxed* — and thus are no longer antecedent, and the "Show" line is *cancelled* and now antecedent (intuitively, the lines in the box constitute a proof of A).

5. If the proof has a subpart which looks like
    Show (A→B)
     X1

     .

     .

     .

     Xn

and *a.* there are no uncancelled "Show" among X1...Xn, and *b.* B occurs unboxed among X1...Xn, then

     Show (A→B)
     X1
     .
     .
     .
     Xn

may occur as the next step to the proof.

6. The formula A is proved if it occurs unboxed in a proof and there are no uncancelled "Show" in the proof. (The method can be extended to arguments with premises by allowing a premise to be entered anywhere in the proof.)

This natural-deduction system is extended to the predicate calculus by adding rules for Existential Instantiation, Universal Instantiation, Existential Generalization, and another method of boxing and cancelling called universal derivation. The system we shall exhibit below is of the full predicate calculus, and hence uses these other quantifier rules also. We close this section with two short proofs to give a feeling for how theorems might be proved using this system. First, the theorem ((p→q) → (¬q→ ¬p)), which was the longest proof completed by the Logic Theorist (to be described below).

1.   *Show ((p→q) → (¬q→ ¬p))
2.   (p→q)   Assumption
3.   *Show (¬q→ ¬p)
4.   ¬q   Assumption
5.   ¬p   2,4MT

Second, the theorem (p ∨ ¬ ¬ ¬ p) of which it has been proved that the Logic Theorist cannot prove it.

1.   *Show (p ∨ ¬ ¬ ¬ p)
2.   ¬(p ∨ ¬ ¬ ¬ p)   Assumption
3.   *Show ¬p
4.   p   Assumption
5.   (p ∨ ¬ ¬ ¬ p) 4,Add
6.   ¬ (p ∨ ¬ ¬ ¬ p) 2,R
7.   ¬ ¬ ¬p   3,DN
8.   (p ∨ ¬ ¬ ¬p)   7,Add

SOME REMARKS ABOUT PREVIOUS THEOREM PROVERS

The first theorem prover was the Logic Theorist of Newell, Simon, and Shaw (1957; its latest incarnation is in Newell and Simon, 1972). It employed the axiomatic system of Whitehead and Russell and was heuristic-based in the sense that it made use of such procedures as "Is there an axiom, the consequent of which is a substitution instance of what we're trying to prove? Yes — try to prove the axiom's antecedent;" ("backward chaining"), or "Are any of our current lines a substitution instance of the antecedent of an axiom? Yes — use MP"; ("forward chaining"), and so on. However, the Logic Theorist was not very successful in proving theorems. We have already indicated above that it could not prove (p ∨ ¬ ¬ ¬p) and that, in fact, the longest theorem it could prove was the simple ((p→ q) → (¬ q→¬ p)). Furthermore, its proofs, of the few it could prove, tended to be extraordinarily inelegant. Part of the problem was the machine being used—it had limited storage and these strategies required a very large amount of storage of possible "substitution instances" of axioms and previously proved lines. We shall show below how we have solved this storage problem.

Another part of the problem was that the strategies employed were just too simplistic to be taken seriously. But another, more important, part of the problem is that the Logic Theorist used an *axiomatic* system. Almost every person (professional logician or student) finds axiomatic systems very difficult. If we want to mirror actual logical abilities, we would do better to look at how we learn one of the other versions of logic. Therefore, both on the grounds of its technical difficulties and the grounds of its implausibility as a model of thinking, we reject axiomatic systems.

We also reject the semantic systems. We have three reasons for this. The first is the abstract, theoretical consideration that semantics just isn't really logic, and it is people's logical abilities we are concerned with. On this issue we quote from Georgacarakos and Smith (1978: xiv):

> In keeping with our aim of theoretical soundness, we have sharply distinguished be-tween the semantical and the syntactical correlates of the logical concepts we study throughout the text. We introduce the technique of tree construction as a semantical device, the aim of which is to discover counterinterpretations for invalid argument forms. Many authors regard trees as syntactical devices and of course in a sense they are (they involve manipulation of symbols). However, the correct purpose of tree construc-tion is semantical in that it is to be used as a device to find possible counterinterpreta-tions.

The second reason is that the use of the semantical logics lends itself too easily to methods which are beyond the ken of reasoning people (*viz.*, resolution pro-cedures). We wish to stick strictly to what ordinary people can actually know and use. It is the unanimous voice of resolution theorists that their techniques are too complex and time consuming for people to use. (Many writers claim this, but see Chang and Lee 1973.) The third reason we reject semantic methods is technical. The method used is, when not augmented by any heuristic search control, very inef-ficient, time consuming, and storage consuming. We quote here from Kowalski (1979, p. 163):

> The search space determined by unrestricted application of the resolution rule is highly redundant. Redundancy can be avoided, at the cost of flexibility, by restricting resolu-tion to top-down or bottom up inference.

One might have to live with this unhappy state of affairs presented by these semantic, resolution provers if there weren't any better method. One way to make the method better is to control the search by certain heuristics. The mechanical theorem-proving literature is rife with suggestions, such as "set of support," "unit preference," "purity," *etc.*, but it must be admitted that these improvements in performance are at the expense of even what tenuous link resolution provers may have to human theorem proving. Two of these techniques ought to be mentioned here, nonetheless, since it is our aim to show that our program performs better than the best resolution prover (which uses one of these methods), and it does so because it more fully implements some of the ideas and techniques in the other.

Kowalski (1974, 1979) is the most fully described "connection-graph" theorem prover. The idea behind a connection-graph strategy is to first, prior to trying to prove anything by resolution, lay out the possible "resolvings out" as a graph. Thus suppose our clauses are:

$$p1 \lor p2 \lor p3$$
$$\neg p3 \lor p4$$
$$\neg p4 \lor \neg p1$$

We draw connections between the literals which might resolve out, thus:

Any clause which contains a literal that is unconnected cannot possibly lead to the derivation of the null clause, and so is deleted, along with any of its connections. So, in the above example, we delete the first clause and its connections, leaving:

$$\neg p3 \lor p4$$

$$\neg p4 \lor \neg p1$$

But these too now have unconnected literals and thus are to be deleted. If there were no other clauses, we would know prior to starting the resolution portion of an attempted proof that it is not a theorem and hence we would not start. Using this technique, we get a theorem prover which, in a large number of cases, performs better than the usual resolution provers. The most advanced resolution prover we know of uses this connection-graph technique: it is that of J. Siekmann and his associates at the Universität Karlsruhe. However, even it is unable to show the following (predicate logic) argument as valid. (These remarks and the following argument are due to Len K. Schubert who presented this argument to Siekmann in 1978. We do not know the present status of the Karlsruhe theorem prover.)

> Every animal either likes to eat all plants or all animals much smaller than itself that like to eat some plants. Wolves, foxes, birds, caterpillars, and snails are animals, and there are some of each of them. Also there are some grains, and grains are plants. Caterpillars and snails are much smaller than birds, which are much smaller than foxes, which are in turn much smaller than wolves. Wolves do not like to eat foxes or grains, while birds like to eat caterpillars but not snails. Caterpillars and snails like to eat some plants. Therefore there is an animal that likes to eat a grain-eating animal.

(In passing here, we might point out that resolution provers require input in clause form — skolem normal form and the result in conjunctive normal form. As the above example demonstrates, it is not always a trivial task to transform ordinary language argumentation into clause form; yet when resolution theorists talk about the efficiency of their programs, they rarely mention the added effort required to massage the natural data into suitable input. Our theorem prover will accept any well-formed formula of first-order predicate logic.)

Bledsoe (1971) took what we think was a giant step forward in mechanical theorem proving when he introduced "splitting and reduction" techniques. These techniques are the basis for a human-like natural deduction system: they give overall strategies for proving theorems, which strategies depend upon the "main connective" of the formula to be proved. Thus for example, the strategy for proving a conjunction is to prove each of its conjuncts separately (rather than a resolution procedure's attempt to prove that the disjunction of the negations of each conjunct leads to the null resolvent). The strategy for proving a biconditional is to prove each conditional separately; the strategy for proving a conditional is to assume the antecedent true and attempt to prove the consequent — and so on. In 1971, Bledsoe used some of these techniques to "simplify" the formula to be proved, but then the final step for each subproblem was to do a resolution proof. We think, as in Bledsoe *et al* (1972), that this takes away a lot of the "human qualities" from the theorem prover. In this latter article, the resolution subsection was replaced by a procedure called IMPLY which used "forward chaining" and "backward chaining," in addition to some of the more usual resolution techniques. We have already mentioned above that we think forward and backward chaining by themselves are not very likely candidates for theorem proving because they require an immense amount of storage. We find furthermore that the mixture of resolution procedures still with it takes us away from human-oriented theorem proving. Finally, it appears that the 1972 system cannot prove that:

$$((p \& (q \rightarrow r)) \rightarrow s)$$

is equivalent to:

$$((\neg p \lor (q \lor s)) \& (\neg p \lor (\neg r \lor s)))$$

which ours does, easily.

We think that the flaw with the Bledsoe systems is that the heuristic techniques were not followed far enough. We have found, with the complete use of the heuristics described below, that we could prove all theorems of the propositional logic and first-order predicate logic (without function symbols other than constants and without identify — two areas we have not yet tried to implement) found in Kalish and Montague (1964) and Thomason (1972). In addition, we can prove some theorems which are not in them, but which have cropped up in the mechanical theorem proving literature — such as $(p \lor \neg \neg \neg p)$ from the Logic Theorist, the Schubert argument from connection-graph resolution, and the example just given from Bledsoe.

THINKER: A HEURISTIC-BASED THEOREM PROVER

We wish now to describe THINKER. We can divide the description into two components: the heuristics employed and the implementation of them. We shall skip lightly over the latter, for we think it of little interest to know that, *e.g.*, a doubly-linked circular list of all antecedent formulae with a '$\rightarrow$' as main connective was kept. But there are some features of the implementation which deserve to be mentioned, since they show how we have solved some of the problems of earlier theorem provers. First among these is that we used a version of SNOBOL (namely SPITBOL) rather than the more usual LISP-based languages. SNOBOL's basic operation is pattern matching, where these patterns can be as complex as one can describe (*e.g.*, recursive patterns). We are thus able to directly compare, for example, whether formula A is the negation of formula B by simply asking:

A ('$\neg$' B)

The blank after A is "match the pattern following" (which is what is in the parentheses) and the blank inside the parentheses indicates that one is to pre-concatenate a '$\neg$' to the pattern B. This is both *a.* in keeping with our syntactic view of logic as manipulation of symbols rather than with semantic structures, and *b.* in accordance with our intuitive psychological position that people attend to these patterns when constructing logical proofs.

As a side benefit, we get to store our formulae as strings, and this is less consuming than storing tree-like structures, as other provers usually do. (We could expand further on this, especially point *b.*, indicating how our patterns are essentially akin to human thought: "Ignore everything except to notice that the formula is a conditional that is universally quantified. Ignore the particular variable of quantification and only attend to the rest of the structure of the antecedent to see whether any other line has this same structure when its variable is similarly ignored. *Etc.*" But we will not dwell on this here.)

Another feature of SNOBOL is that it has a primitive data structure called a TABLE, which is like an ARRAY, except we can access any element by using a string rather than an integer as an index. Thus, if we wish to know whether a certain formula is an antecedent line, we merely use that formula as an index and check directly. Again, this is much more efficient than the usual sequential search, even when the latter is augmented by graph-theoretic features; and it allows us to cut down our storage requirements.

One final feature should be mentioned here, and that is our use of TEMPLATES. When a line is added to the proof (when it becomes an antecedent line) we store information as to what type of line it is. If, for example, it is the conditional $(A \rightarrow B)$, we store these two pieces of information: *1.* it is a conditional with antecedent A; *2.* it is a conditional with consequent B. These are stored as the strings $(A \rightarrow @)$ and $(@ \rightarrow B)$, where @ is a kind of metavariable indicating "some subformula or other." Since these are strings, we can use all the apparatus mentioned above about TABLES to access these "metaformulae." As an example, if we are trying to prove B, we might look to this TEMPLATE table, directly accessing by means of the string '$(@ \rightarrow B)$', to see if there is such a formula type in the antecedent lines. The information in this table is what formula @ is; and we therefore know exactly what this conditional in the Antecedent Lines TABLE (this table is called ANTELINES) is; so we can directly see whether the formula @ is also in ANTELINES. If it is, we perform a MP and add B to the ANTELINES, which constitutes a proof of the formula to be shown. It is easy to see that all this direct accessing solves the problems which have plagued the earlier theorem provers from the time of the Logic Theorist. Indeed, we think this breakthrough is one of the most important innovations of THINKER.

Having said that much about the implementation of THINKER, let us now turn to the heuristics involved. In fact, the heuristics are extremely simple and can be quickly described. What is surprising is that these simple heuristics, together with the implementation described above, will prove all that it does.

A Kalish and Montague proof has two structurally distinct parts to it. First is a stack of goals (formulae to be proved: the "show" lines detailed above) and second is a sequence of antecedent lines. We are always working at proving the most recently added goal, by adding more and more ANTELINES. When that goal is proved, it becomes an ANTELINE (= "cancelled") and all lines which had been added to ANTELINE after the goal was added to the goal stack get deleted (= "boxed"). When the first-to-be-added goal becomes antecedent, the proof is finished. So, when a theorem to be proved is entered, it becomes the first goal; since there are no ANTELINES to work with, it cannot be proved yet. THINKER then, on the basis of the theorem's main connective, decides what to do. Its choices are *a.* make an assumption (which becomes an ANTELINE), or *b.* add other goals. If the main connective is '&', '↔', or a universal quantifier, it will add a more simple goal and recursively call the whole set of heuristics on this new goal. When this simpler goal is proved, it uses it to prove the original goal. (These are Bledsoe's "splitting heuristics.") Otherwise it makes an assumption: if the main connective is '→', it assumes the antecedent; otherwise it assumes the negation. (Some of these are embodiments of Bledsoe's "reduction heuristics.") This is how proofs get started. From this point on, it uses the following heuristics.

1. If there are no antecedent lines (see *b* of last paragraph), it reapplies the "splitting and reduction" procedure.

2. ONESTEP(X) checks whether there is a rule of inference which uses X (some particular antecedent line), one application of which will prove the most recent goal. This is rather simple to implement, since there are but a small number of rules of inference, and their working depends only on the structure of X and the most recent goal. Every time we add an ANTELINE to the proof, we call ONESTEP(X); if it succeeds, we "cancel" the most recent goal and "box."

3. SIMPLEPROOF(X) checks whether there are any two ANTELINES which, if one rule of inference were applied to them, would allow us to be able to add X (a particular formula we want to have, but not necessarily the most recent goal) as an ANTELINE. This is simple to do, since the "one application of a rule" applied to ANTELINES to yield X makes a rather limited search.

4. TRYRULES is a "blind" procedure which attempts to apply the propositional rules of inference and existential instantiation to ANTELINES. Each time a line X is added by this, ONESTEP(X) is called, which is one way to terminate TRYRULES. Another way to terminate it is if an ANTELINE is added to which heuristic 5 is applicable. Of course, TRYRULES and SIMPLEPROOF add lines to which TRYRULES is again applicable.

5. TRYNEGFLA is a rather clever strategy which — when more direct approaches fail — will search ANTELINES for an occurrence of the negation of a conditional and add the unnegated conditional to the goals. (It also looks for negations of disjunctions and adds one of the disjuncts to the goals; for negations of biconditionals, and negations of conjunctions. It then adds appropriate goals.) If this is successfully proved, the resulting contradiction will allow us to "cancel" the most recent goal.

6. TRYCHAINING: When other strategies fail, we look for a conditional in ANTELINES for which we do not have the consequent. We add, as a goal, the antecedent of the conditional. (If successful, we can perform a MP we couldn't before, so we can again TRYRULES). If this fails, and the negation of the antecedent isn't in ANTELINES, we try to add the negation of the consequent as a goal (to do a MT). A similar strategy applies to disjunctions and MTP.

7. HELP. When THINKER fails, either because the formula to be proved is not a theorem or because its heuristics are inadequate to prove it, it displays the proof as thus far constructed and requests the user to enter another line (either an ANTELINE or a new goal). It adds this to the proof with an appropriate annotation, and once again attempts the proof.

8. PROOF is the overall monitor of these other heuristics. It adds goals, calls the lower level heuristics as necessary, and recursively calls itself as new goals are added.

AN EXAMPLE

We give here a moderately simple, propositional calculus example which illustrates how THINKER works.

The example is to show the equivalence between disjunction and the conditional: $((PvQ) \leftrightarrow (\neg P \rightarrow Q))$. This is put on the goal stack. Since it is a biconditional, PROOF adds a conditional to the goals: $((PvQ) \rightarrow (\neg P \rightarrow Q))$, and calls itself recursively. Since this is a conditional, it assumes '(PvQ)' and asks whether ONESTEP('(PvQ)') will prove the most recent goal. The answer is no, so it asks whether SIMPLEPROOF('$(\neg P \rightarrow Q)$'). Again no, so it adds '$(\neg P \rightarrow Q)$' as a goal, recursively calls itself, and assumes '$\neg P$'. It now calls ONESTEP('$\neg P$') to see whether '$(\neg P \rightarrow Q)$' is derivable from the ANTELINES. The answer is no, so it calls

SIMPLEPROOF('Q'). This succeeds (from the ANTELINES '(PvQ)' and ' ¬ P' by
MTP) and so it adds 'Q' to ANTELINES, and then notices it can cancel the
(¬P→Q) goal. So it does (and deletes the ' ¬ P' ANTELINE), thus ending that
recursive PROOF call. But this makes ((PvQ)→(¬P→Q)) be proved, so it cancels
that goal (and deletes the (PvQ) ANTELINE). PROOF then decides that to prove
the original goal, it needs to prove ((¬P→Q)→(PvQ)), so this is added to the
goals. PROOF is recursively called and assumes (¬P→Q). ONESTEP('(¬P→Q)')
fails, as does SIMPLEPROOF('(PvQ)'). So '(PvQ)' is added to the goals, and
PROOF called recursively. It assumes '¬(PvQ)'. At this stage the proof looks like:

1.	Show $((P \lor Q) \leftrightarrow (\neg P \to Q))$	
2.	*Show $((P \lor Q) \to (\neg P \to Q))$	
3.	(P $\lor$ Q)	Assume
4.	*Show $(\neg P \to Q)$	
5.	¬P	Assume
6.	Q	3, 5MTP
7.	Show $((\neg P \to Q) \to (P \lor Q))$	
8.	$(\neg P \to Q)$	Assume
9.	Show (P $\lor$ Q)	
10.	¬(P $\lor$ Q)	Assume

No rules of inference apply to our three ANTELINES (#2, 8, 10). PROOF notices
that line 10 is the negation of a disjunction and so calls TRYNEGFLA, which adds
'P' as a goal and calls PROOF recursively, ' ¬P' is assumed, and a MP is performed
with the lines 8 and 12, yielding 'Q'. ONESTEP('Q') is called and succeeds, since
by doing ADD on it, we generate a contradiction and hence can cancel our most recent goal. Having proved P and thus adding it to ANTELINES, PROOF notes that
ONESTEP('P') allows us to prove the most recent goal (by ADD). But this most recent goal, '(PvQ)', was the consequent of the previous goal, and so that goal too is
proved. We are now on the topmost recursion, trying to prove line 1, and we have
two ANTELINES (#2, 7). We apply the rule CB to give us the final line #17, which
allows us to cancel line 1, finish and print out the proof:

1.	*Show $((P \lor Q) \leftrightarrow (\neg P \to Q))$	
2.	*Show $((P \lor Q) \to (\neg P \to Q))$	
3.	(P $\lor$ Q)	Assume
4.	*Show $(\neg P \to Q)$	
5.	¬ P	Assume
6.	Q	3, 5MTP
7.	*Show $((\neg P \to Q) \to (P \lor Q))$	
8.	$(\neg P \to Q)$	Assume
9.	*Show (P $\lor$ Q)	
10.	¬(P $\lor$ Q)	Assume
11.	*Show P	
12.	¬P	Assume
13.	Q	8, 12MP
14.	(P $\lor$ Q)	13, Add
15.	¬(P $\lor$ Q)	10, R
16.	(P $\lor$ Q)	11, Add
17.	$((P \lor Q) \leftrightarrow (\neg P \lor Q))$	2, 7CB

CONCLUSION

While this example proof is rather simple, the heuristics employed are powerful. We think it surprising that with this meager set of heuristics, THINKER performs its task so well. Its success should encourage others to build natural-language-understanding systems and robotic-planning systems which incorporate similar heuristics. We hope that THINKER's success doesn't merely make critics say that heuristic theorem proving isn't "real" thinking, or that these aren't "real" heuristics. Anyone who tends in this direction might consider whether they think people do this any differently.

REFERENCES

Bledsoe, W.W. "Splitting and Reduction Heuristics in Automatic Theorem Proving," *Artificial Intelligence*, 1971, *2*, 55–77.

Bledsoe, W.W. "Non Resolution Theorem Proving," *Artificial Intelligence*, 1977, *9*, 1–35.

Bledsoe, W.W., Boyer, R.S. and Henneman, W.H. "Computer Proofs of Limit Theorems," *Artificial Intelligence*, 1972, *3*, 27–60.

Chang, C.L. and Lee, R.C.T. *Symbolic Logic and Mechanical Theorem Proving*. New York: Academic Press, 1973.

Church, A. *An Introduction to Mathematical Logic*. Princeton: Princeton University Press, 1956.

Feigenbaum, J. and Feldman, J.A. *Computers and Thought*. New York: McGraw Hill, 1963.

Georgacarakos, G.M. and Smith, R. *Elementary Formal Logic*. New York: McGraw Hill, 1978.

Jeffrey, R. *Formal Logic: Its Scope and Limits*. Englewood Cliffs, NJ: Prentice-Hall, 1967.

Kalish, D. and Montague, R. *Logic: Techniques of Formal Reasoning*. New York: Harcourt, Brace, Jovanovich, 1964.

Kowalski, R. "A Proof Procedure Using Connection Graphs," *Journal of the Association for Computing Machinery*, 1974, *22*, 572–595.

Kowalski, R. *Logic for Problem Solving*. New York: Elsevier North Holland, 1979.

Newell, A., Shaw, J.C., and Simon, H.A. "Empirical Explorations with the Logic Theory Machine: A Case Study in Heuristics." 1957; reprinted as pp. 109–133 of Feigenbaum and Feldman 1963 (page references to reprint).

Newell, A. and Simon, J.C. *Human Problem Solving*. Englewood Cliffs, NJ: Prentice-Hall, 1972.

Thomason, R. *Symbolic Logic*. New York: Macmillan, 1972.

PART VI.

THE SYMPOSIUM ON GREGORY BATESON'S *MIND AND NATURE: A NECESSARY UNITY*

INTRODUCTION

When Professor Victor Kobayashi of the University of Hawaii's College of Education heard of our proposed Conference on Thinking, he suggested that a symposium on Bateson's last work might provide a theme, and one large enough to unify some of the major papers from a variety of disciplines. The organizing committee readily agreed. The result was a most stimulating and challenging symposium. The first paper published here is Professor Kobayashi's own formal paper prepared for the Symposium, a paper which both summarizes Bateson's problem and problem-analysis and offers us a personal glimpse of that gifted and versatile researcher and teacher. Bateson's problem, briefly, was what is the relationship between man and nature? When man violates nature does man violate himself?

The second paper is by Patrick Pentony of the Australian National University who has made a detailed study of all of Bateson's work and who unfortunately was prevented from attending the Conference. In this paper Pentony looks closely at one central aspect of Bateson's theory of nature, the cybernetic. The papers by Professor Gregson and Dr. Maas take highly contrasting views of Bateson, and almost form a debate. The last "paper" is Professor Kobayashi's summary of that symposium, which was a plenary session of the Conference and which drew a large and keenly interested audience. For those for whom this is a first introduction to Bateson, we wish to welcome you in your acquaintance with one of the most original academic minds of this century. Professor Kobayashi's summary of the symposium is offered to whet your appetite to read more of Bateson, especially his last book, *Mind and Nature: A Necessary Unity*.

With this symposium, the conference and this book come full circle. Man may have been given dominion over Nature, if we interpret the Pentateuch. And that dominion implies a responsibility for care and benevolence. Who wishes to rule over that which has been profaned and corrupted? Can a pure mind (or pure reason) exist independent of a sacred bough from which it draws its images and its own nurture?

MIND AND NATURE:
TEACHING AND THINKING

Victor N. Kobayashi

ABSTRACT

As an introduction to the Symposium on Bateson's *Mind and Nature: A Necessary Unity*, some major concerns are presented, especially Bateson's view that the way we usually think is in profound error, and that this error is reflected in the multitude of problems relating to the health of the global ecosystem and to the sanity of human beings. Bateson challenges us to reconsider science, to make its unifying premises and epistemology more compatible with the way healthy living systems work.

One of Gregory Bateson's major concerns was the need to make our thinking congruent with nature. By that he meant that the way we think, the concepts and maps we use, should be supportive of and not destructive of the complex living system of which human beings are a part. Because destruction of the natural environment is reaching proportions that might trigger the collapse of the world ecological system, and because there is so much degradation of the quality of human life, Bateson believed that our usual ways of perceiving and thinking are in profound error. His book, *Mind and Nature*, attempts to set forth some of the tools of thought he felt would help us dispel the pathologies of our thinking (Bateson, 1980). Bateson believed that what had gone wrong in the environment was intimately connected to the insanity of our thinking.

Nature is not perceived directly, but through the lens of the human mind, as influenced and shaped by our purposes and our cultures. When it is apparent that the environment is deteriorating to the extent of severely endangering future generations, apparent that alienation has become widespread in human life, and that many of these conditions are due to the actions of modern man, then the images and metaphors we use to approach nature need to be re-examined and changed. Thus Bateson criticized the mis-use of models from Newtonian science in both the biological and social sciences. Notions such as lineal causality are inappropriate to the world of living organisms which adapt and learn, rather than merely react according to Newton's physical laws.

V.N. Kobayashi is with the Department of Educational Foundations at the University of Hawaii at Manoa.

Aristotelian formal logic was also an area of concern because Bateson considered it an inappropriate model for the way living systems work. The hypothetical, "if, then" logical statement is not the same as the "if, then" statement of cause and effect, since the latter involves time. Working within time, living systems often operate such that an event might lead to a chain of consequences that might loop back and change the original event, leading to a negation of the statement that described the original event (Bateson, 1980, p. 64). With the idea of time, ordinary logic would thus yield self-contradictions that would be intolerable by logic's own rules.

Bateson viewed these "contradictions" as paradoxes, and using ideas from both cybernetics and Bertrand Russell's theory of logical types, he constructed models of thinking that were in better harmony with the way biological processes are structured (Bateson, 1980, pp. 127–142). The contradictions and paradoxes found application in the double-bind theory of schizophrenia and in his study of humor, mammalian learning, cultural character structure, climax ecosystems, Zen paradoxes, and alcoholism (Bateson, 1972).

The discovery of circular, causal models with features such as recursiveness, feedback looping, and self-regulation was, for Bateson, a major advance, since circuit structure modeled nature more accurately than the then-current linear models of causality. These models came from the cybernetic movement, led by Norbert Wiener, and they provided the basic foundations for the science of ecology. Bateson enlarged them to include not only living systems, but the realm of mental phenomena, art and religion as well.

As someone who had profound faith in such perennial philosophical ideas as wisdom, love, beauty, and truth, Bateson felt that these ideas were based in the network of the cybernetic structure of feedback loops and recursive circuits that made up mind and nature. They were embedded in a system of several layers of meta-circuits, several logical types deep. Bateson's speculation here is important for the vulgar world of today, where spiritual and aesthetic values are trivialized in the name of intellectual clarity or positivism, and where concerns for political and economic power dominate the landscape. He suggests that some of the ideals cherished by the great religious teachers, philosophers and artists have a place in the new, more rigorous science he foresees as both possible and necessary, and which would be more congruent with nature. These ideas are complex and difficult to describe in a system of feedback loops and layers of meta-loops, but the new science cannot reject these ideas merely because nature is so complex, or because these ideas would be so difficult to verify empirically within a brief timespan. As a scientist, Bateson was not interested in complex explanations for complexity's sake. On the contrary, he considered it ". . . the task of every scientist to find the simplest, more economical, and (usually) most elegant explanation that will cover the known data. Beyond this, reductionism becomes a vice if it is accompanied by an overly strong insistence that the simplest explanation is the only explanation" (Bateson, 1980, p. 252). He warned, however, that an extreme search for simplicity could have disastrous consequences for all life.

In the new science, Bateson proposed that we focus on relationships, rather than on the material entities, the "relata," as the basic building blocks of thought. Preoccupation with objective matter ignores or masks the fact that an observer is in relationship with what is being observed (Bateson, 1980, pp. 67–68). Material data themselves are never raw data; they are inevitably and always "cooked." What we perceive as an entity is actually based on an act of selection, an aesthetic judgment, on the part of the perceiving subject:

Kant, in the *Critique of Judgement*—if I understand him correctly—asserts that the most elementary aesthetic act is the selection of a fact. He argues that in a piece of chalk there are an infinite number of potential facts. The *Ding an sich*, the piece of chalk, can never enter into communication or mental process because of this infinitude. The sensory receptors cannot accept it; they filter it out. What they do is select certain *facts* out of the piece of chalk, which then become, in modern terminology, information (Bateson, 1972, p. 453).

All living systems are interconnected in an interacting structure comprising the biosphere. Ecosystems evolve; interacting species co-evolve. Man is a part of that larger unitary network. The kind of thinking that separates man from the universe (of which man is a part) is the mental equivalent of the world ecological crisis. Bateson was critical of the fragmentation of knowledge and of ideas antithetical to a more holistic view of man and nature. The human being is a complex ecological entity itself: physiologically, psychologically, socially, and anatomically. Although unable to perceive the details of each cybernetic loop and connection, either within itself and in relationship to the external world, the human being, by virtue of being a sub-network, a universe unto itself, is able to sense intuitively that it is an analogue to the larger system of which it constitutes a part. This complementary sense of being a part is stuff for the basic religious experience, and the sense of empathy for other forms of life, from oak trees to Lady Macbeth, is a basis for art. Bateson even suggests that the role of art in the evolution of culture is not due to its use as magic, but its place as a corrective to the disruptive tendencies, caused by man's discovery of technology, on the ecosystem. Although cavemen hunted reindeer with tools, their cave paintings communicated a sense of empathy, of a respectful relationship between man and animal:

> Consider the case of the man who goes to the blackboard—or to the side of his cave—and draws, freehand, a perfect reindeer in its posture of threat. He cannot *tell* you about the drawing of the reindeer ("If he could, there would be no point in drawing it"). "Do you know that his perfect way of seeing—and drawing—a reindeer exists as a human potentiality?" The consummate skill of the draftsman validates the artist's message about his relationship to the animal—his empathy (Bateson, 1972, p. 144).

Art always entered Bateson's thinking because, for him, there was always the possibility that the work of a poet or an artist was a better analogue to the way nature thinks, and was more in keeping with holism, the sense of multiple levels of relationships that Bateson's new science had to preserve.

The very description of living systems, which is, after all, the primary task of biology and of the social sciences, itself has to model what is being described, so the thinking involved is both clear and internally congruent:

> If our explanations or our understanding of the universe is in some sense to match the universe, or model it, and if the universe is recursive, then our explanations and our logics must also be fundamentally recursive (Bateson, 1977 [a], p. 242).

Bateson's view of art and nature provides a clue as to why his prose often lapsed into the poetic, and why he loved writing "metalogues" that involved a conversation between a father (himself) and his pre-adolescent daughter, who was acutely concerned about an idea. The conversation was about a problem in thinking and its structure was an analogue to what the conversation referred, *i.e.* it was recursive.

> Notably, the history of evolutionary theory is inevitably a metalogue between man and nature, in which the creation and interaction of ideas must necessarily exemplify evolutionary process (Bateson, 1972, p. 2).

Finally, his view of art and nature provides clues to his approach to the teaching of thinking, an endeavor which he took seriously. Although Bateson was sometimes criticized by students for his seemingly elliptical, abstruse, pedagogical style, he also attracted students who found him gentle and compassionate, and who cared deeply about his relationships with them, while also maintaining a deep commitment to intellectual clarity. He gave much of his time to students. Conversations with Bateson always had the potential of reaching a higher, more edifying level of thinking, whether the original starting point was the spiral of a snail shell, the structure of American corporations, or the reason why the British lecturers seemed so arrogant to American audiences. He often introduced the latter topic, since he himself was of British upper middle-class origins, speaking in an American classroom; it was always important for participants to keep in the back of their minds, the context of the discussions they were involved in. The context was also a message.

Often he shared his lunch with students, as if to affirm the sacramental nature of breaking bread with each other. Conversations seemed to become more dialogical as a result. He often observed that most college students had not really learned to think, despite their years of schooling. He occasionally lectured, but oftentimes he sat and listened to students, noting perhaps simultaneously the interaction patterns, the feel of the discussion, the different personalities that made up the group. Usually, he engaged in conversations with the students.

His classroom was often very crowded at the start of the sessions, but by the second or third class, it would shrink to about half to two-thirds its original size, whereupon, he once remarked, "Now we can discuss," as if to indicate that student participation in class was a kind of selective, stochastic process, a part of the natural order of things of the evolutionary process that was under discussion.

He was most pleased when the classroom, with him included, evolved into a "thinking group." In his discussions, he often quoted Wordsworth or his favorite poet, William Blake. In these discussions one often felt a part of an ecological system in the process of evolution into a more complex pattern. (And, of course, one *was.*) Thinking, to Bateson, was an aspect of human evolution, and illustrative of evolution, as it not only included conscious reflection and effort and practice, but it included also, and overwhelmingly, the unconscious processes.

The whole ecology of one's being was involved in thinking. Bateson often described a mathematical genius who twirled his hair when he worked on his theorems, and Konrad Lorenz, who while lecturing on animals would take on the stance and visage of the animals he was describing. When the unconscious intuitive aspects of one's mind were in full play, one felt as if one were on a tiny island in the midst of a great ocean, which would be swept once in a while by a miraculous tide, bringing us into the spirit of a Great Dialogue, a Hermann Hesse Glass-Bead Game, only to ebb again, quite leisurely. New ideas needed to be examined and reexamined, integrated, and handled with a sense of craftsmanship, although their emergence often seemed sudden:

> ...The adoption of any invention becomes irreversible very quickly. It becomes built deeply, irreversibly, into the physiology of our society within very few years of invention. There is no barrier between immediate adaptation and pickling the change into society.
>
> For this reason, more than any other, I distrust consciousness as a gimmick added to the evolutionary scene. Conscious cerebration is much too fast. It doesn't give any time for growth into the new state of affairs. There is no trial and error or tentative assimilation which would slowly flow, hesitate and flow, hesitate and flow, into new patterns (Bateson, 1977 [b], p. 154).

He wasn't, therefore, interested in immediate pragmatic applications of what was thought out. Perhaps, too, the process of engagement in thought and dialogue had its own aesthetic validity, ephemeral though that moment might be.

Bateson often spoke in a slow, thoughtful manner, spinning ideas, never afraid to repeat tales that embodied important ideas. The repetitions were never really repetitions since, often, a new facet or twist would be revealed to the student (or to Bateson) that came from the same anecdote. His manner of speaking—speaking fondly of his own moments of intellectual insight sometimes accompanied by a tear, seemed to say that the excited, agitated, adrenalin-laden, virtuoso style of teaching that frequently appealed to American students was not conducive to thinking—inspiring or entertaining as it might be. Bateson shared the view of the ancient Chinese sages who sought the quelling of anxiety because anxiety was inappropriate to the comtemplation of nature. The mind, after all, works best when it mirrors nature.

REFERENCES

Bateson, G. *Steps to an Ecology of Mind.* New York: Ballantine Books, 1972.

Bateson, G. "Afterword." In *About Bateson,* John Brockman (Ed.) New York: E.P. Dutton, 1977, 242(a).

Bateson, G. "The Thing of It Is." In *Earth's Answer,* Katz, Marsh, and Thompson, (Eds.) New York: Harper and Row, 1977, 154 (b).

Bateson, G. *Mind and Nature.* New York: Bantam, 1980.

GREGORY BATESON AND CYBERNETICS

Patrick Pentony

ABSTRACT

Gregory Bateson devoted most of his life to the development of an "epistemology of cybernetics" and its application to the explanation of mammalian behavior. Before he heard of the concept of feedback, he had arrived at the essential ingredients of his later position. This chapter outlines how he related these ingredients—time, circular causation and hierarchical order—to each other and showed their relevance for such issues as learning and evolution.

It is not possible here to do more than touch upon Gregory Bateson's thinking, with its wide-ranging implications for behavioral science and the human situation. I will confine myself to a brief statement on his interest in cybernetics.

It can be said of him that he was a cyberneticist before he heard of cybernetics. He had already arrived independently at the three essential elements of what he came to call an epistemology of cybernetics, before Warren McCulloch and Julian Bigelow introduced him to the concept of feedback at a Macy Foundation conference in 1942.

These three elements are *time, circular causation* and *hierarchical order*. In *Naven*, published in 1936, he was concerned with time and change and stressed the importance of seeing behavior in a sequential context. It is not enough to speak of stimulus and response, for the response acts back on the stimulus source and affects the next output. This emphasis on the sequential nature of interaction between behavior and environment led to the notion of circular causation and the concept of schismogenesis, which we would now formulate in terms of deviation amplifying feedback. A few years later in a paper on deutero learning (first published in 1942) he discussed the principles of levels of abstraction in learning and related communicational processes, which he came to speak of as logical typing.

It is hardly surprising, therefore, that the concept of feedback struck a responsive chord in him. He took the first opportunity provided by the Macy Foundation Conferences after the Second World War to extend his understanding of cybernetics. These conferences had a profound impact on him and, to use his own words, shaped everything he did subsequently. That "everything" involved the application of cybernetic thinking to the explanation of mammalian behavior, ranging

---

P. Pentony is with the Psychology Department at the Australian National University in Canberra.

across a broad spectrum from the communication of schizophrenics to the play of otters and the training of porpoises. The fruits of his endeavors are to be found in his final work, *Mind and Nature: A Necessary Unity.*

CIRCULAR CAUSATION

Circular causation is a relatively new concept. As Bateson points out, Reichenbach (1956) denied circular causation less than thirty years ago. Reichenbach had kindered spirits among philosophers and logicians from the time of the Greeks for whom circular reasoning was anathema. Nevertheless, over the last two hundred years, beginning with the invention of Watt's centrifugal governor for a steam engine, and culminating in the development of weapon-control systems and computers during the Second World War, there have been applications of circular causation not only in mechanical devices, but also in the explanation of evolution by Wallace, of bodily functioning by Cannon and of social process by Hegel and Marx.

By circular causation he means a sequence of cause-effect relationships which curve back in a circular manner, such that each event around the circle can be seen as the consequence of the event preceding it and the cause of the event following it, with the starting point in the circular sequence remaining a matter for arbitrary decision. That is to say, no single element in the sequence controls the operation of the sequence as a whole, for it is itself governed by the operation of the other elements in the system. The thermostat that governs the temperature of the room is governed by the temperature it controls. A human governor in a political system is constrained by the activities of the other elements in the system which his decisions and actions in turn determine.

With these general remarks we can now return to our initial point that there are three essential elements in Bateson's epistemology—time, circular causation and hierarchical order. Their relationship can be illustrated by considering Clerk Maxwell's solution to the problems posed for him by the inventors of steam-engine governors.

The function of the governor of a steam engine is to ensure that the engine runs at a constant rate, even though the load on it may vary. The governor achieves this by varying the fuel supply, increasing it when the load increases and decreasing it when the load decreases. We can use Bateson's model (1980, pp. 115-116) with four components: *1.* a flywheel; *2.* a governor which is a mechanical device so designed that as the flywheel speeds up, it changes to reduce the fuel supply (and conversely changes to increase fuel supply as the flywheel slows down); *3.* a fuel input; *4.* a cylinder with a piston that drives the flywheel.

The inventors of these governors were practical men who were competent in constructing such devices, but who lacked a mathematical theory of how their inventions worked. In practice the inventions often worked badly, so that the engine speeded up until something broke or slowed down until it stopped. Sometimes there were wild oscillations with the engine speeding up for a time and then slowing down almost to a stop before gradually speeding up again and repeating the cycle. Sometimes there were oscillations in the oscillations.

Unable to solve their problems, the inventors sought the help of Clerk Maxwell. He went around the circle, working out the equations of the relations between the component parts at each step in the sequence. Then he combined these equations and found, as the engineers had found, that this did not solve the problem. Then he saw what was wrong. The inventors had ignored time.

TIME

In the operation of the system, a change in the speed of the flywheel produces a change in the governor, designed to bring the flywheel back to the standard rate. The governor does this by changing the fuel supply which, in turn, changes the piston stroke which, in its turn, changes the speed of the flywheel. But all these changes take time and while they are working their way around the circle, the speed of the flywheel is continuing to change. So while the change required at time T_1 when the flywheel first deviates from the standard is, let us say, D, by the time the changes have worked their way around the circuit and back to the flywheel, at time T_2, the change required is no longer D but D + a.

This time lag is a feature of all feedback loops. Mathematicians such as Maxwell and Norbert Wiener have provided the basis for dampening down the oscillatory effects. Even so, some perturbation remains, though for practical purposes it is negligible.

HIERARCHY

The interesting feature, from Bateson's point of view, in Maxwell's analysis is the emergence of hierachy as a consequence of the role of time. Note that when we talk about the system as if we were within it, we talk of change. We say that change in the speed of the flywheel causes change in the governor, and change in the governor causes change in the fuel supply and so on. But when, like Maxwell, we stand back and look at the system as a whole as if we were outside it, we talk of change in change. We say that the *change* which was required at time T_1, when the speed of the flywheel began to deviate from the standard, *had changed* by the time the correction had worked its way around the circle and back to the flywheel at time T_2.

Change in change is of a different order from simple change. If we regard velocity as rate of change in the position of an object, then acceleration, which is rate of change in velocity, is an example of change in change. It is change of a higher order.

We see here the link between time, circular causation and hierarchical order with which Bateson was grappling before he heard of feedback or cybernetics. What it means is that whenever we consider a feedback loop, we find, since time is involved, that in dealing with the loop as a whole, we are dealing with a higher order of events than that which applies to the interaction between the component elements that participate in the feedback loop. Furthermore, if we have a situation such as that envisaged by Miller, Galanter and Pribram (1960) in which sequences of feedback loops occur within the operational phase of a more comprehensive feedback loop, then events occurring at the level of the superordinate loop will be of a higher order than those occurring at the level of any of the subsidiary loops. Hierarchy is thus an inevitable feature of circular causation.

CAUSATION AND LOGIC

Bateson perceived in the dimension of time a significance which had been largely overlooked in behavioral science. This significance becomes more evident when we consider the difference between causation and logic. While *circular causation* has opened up new vistas in pure and applied science, *circular reasoning* is vacuous. We may therefore ask about the relationship between causation and logic.

Bateson (1980) noted that logic and causation sequences are expressed in the same language. He tells us, we say in logic, "*If* Euclid's definitions and postulates are accepted, *then* two triangles having three sides of the one equal to three sides of the other are equal each to each," and we say in causation, "*If* the temperature falls below 0°C, *then* the water begins to become ice" (p. 70).

But there is a difference between the "*if ... then*" of logic and the "*if ... then*" of causation. Computers work by cause and effect with transistors triggering other transistors. These sequences of cause and effect are used to *simulate* logic. In the early days of computers, a question often asked was whether a computer can simulate *all* processes of logic. The answer proved to be yes. However, as Bateson points out (1980)," ... the question was surely wrong. We should have asked: Can logic simulate all sequences of cause and effect? And the answer would have been no" (p. 70).

His point is that if we try to map circular cause-and-effect sequences onto timeless logic, we arrive at self-contradictory statements. The paradoxes that are generated in this way can be illustrated by an ordinary buzzer (or a make-and-break) circuit which is essentially similar to countless cases of homeostasis found in the biological realm.

The essential components of a buzzer circuit are a spring-loaded armature, which makes contact with an electrode to complete a circuit that includes a coil, which activates an electromagnet, when the current flows through it. These components are so arranged that when the current flows and the electromagnet is activated, it will attract the armature away from the electrode, thereby breaking the circuit. The current will then cease to flow, the electromagnet will become inactive and cease to attract the armature, which, under pressure from the spring, will return to make contact with the electrode and the cycle will be repeated.

As Bateson points out, we can spell this out as follows:

"If contact is made at A [the electrode], then the magnet is activated.
If the magnet is activated, then contact at A is broken.
If contact at A is broken, then the magnet is inactivated.
If magnet is inactivated, then contact is made" (1980, pp. 70-71).

But although this sequence is valid as long as if "the...then" junctures are causal, we would generate a paradox, if we were to understand them as they are used in logic. In such a case we would, in Bateson's words, be saying:

"If the contact is made, then the contact is broken.
If P, then not P."

And he goes on:

"The *if ... then* of causality contains *time*, but the *if ... then* of logic is timeless. It follows that logic is an incomplete model of causality" (p. 71).

The timelessness of logic—its lack of time—thus becomes a matter of some significance when we are dealing with circular or reflexive processes. We can note two aspects in which there are important implications for behavioral scientists. The first concerns the relation between explanation as formulated at the level of physical events and explanation as proposed at the mental level. The second concerns those manifestations of inconsistency, such as perceptual illusions and verbal paradoxes, which exercise cognitive theorists.

In respect to the difference between explanation at the level of physical as contrasted with mental events, we can note that the nervous system, observed objectively, acts causally with neurons triggering other neurons. On the other hand, the mental correlates of the neuronal activity function in terms of logic. In the psychological realm it is consistency, not causation, that is relevant. Although psychological explanation, as in Freud's deterministic account, may seem to invoke causation, in fact it is consistency that is at issue. This is manifest in the recourse to such concepts as conflict, dissonance and incongruence to account for behavior. Logic in its various forms, from the conventional thinking of the ordinary person to the rigorous formulations of the mathematician, is an application of the principle of consistency.

In the matter of cognitive inconsistency, Bateson (1978) has noted the relevance of time, "There is no contradiction between: 'If this message is true, then it's untrue. If it's untrue then it's true,' if the word 'then' contains time. The 'then' in logic contains no time. . .and if you're not in timeless logic but are in essentially a causal system, the 'then' is causal and not logical, then you oscillate. This is one of the very early points that Norbert Wiener made a long, long time ago" (p. 226).

In other words, in causation, which incorporates time, the illusion of synchronous contradiction, which logic is subject to, does not occur.

While the dimension of time provides a basis for distinguishing between causation and logic, the precise nature of the relationship between these two concepts remains to be explicated. Bateson has been exercised by this question over the years. While noting that explanation in science consists of the mapping of causal sequences onto formal logical models, he has sought to formulate the nature of the relation between the map (the logical model) and the territory (the objective data). Toward this end, he has invoked the concept of "logical typing" which he has borrowed from Whitehead and Russell (1910). It is, however, beyond the scope of this paper to develop his use of this concept.

I want to go on from these rather abstract issues to consider two areas in which time, circularity and hierarchy figure prominently and in which Bateson was deeply interested throughout his life. These are the interrelated areas of learning and evolution.

For Bateson these are stochastic processes. As he points out, the term stochastic comes from the Greek "stochazein," which means to shoot at a target with a bow and arrow. It involves the occurrence of events in a random way such that some of the events achieve a preferred outcome and are selected for recurrence. So "if a sequence of events combines a random component with a selective process so that only certain outcomes of the random are allowed to endure, that sequence is said to be *stochastic*" (1980, p. 245).

Consider learning. In his 1942 paper, Bateson drew attention to a phenomenon with such varied labels as transfer of learning, generalization, set learning, learning to learn, and the like. These refer to the observation that learners who are given a series of problems, similar in type and of equivalent difficulty, perform better on problems later in the series—that is solve them more rapidly or with fewer errors—than on problems earlier in the series. Bateson was distinguishing between learning to solve a particular problem and learning how to go about solving problems of a given class or type. The former he called "proto" learning and the latter "deutero" learning.

As he pointed out, this distinction between the two levels of learning had been noted by Frank (1926) and Maier (1940); it was later to be noted by Harlow (1949). However, Bateson gave the issue a different theoretical significance from that of the others and he continued to develop the theme of a hierarchy of learning types to the point where he proposed (1972, pp. 279-308) a series of levels ranging from Learning Zero, characterized by specificity of response that is not subject to change, to

Learning IV in which a new pattern of response occurs through genetic change. While these are the extreme points in his learning hierarchy, he is not dogmatic about the number of intervening levels.

For psychologists and other behavioral scientists, the most interesting levels are Learning I and Learning II, which he originally called proto learning and deutero learning, respectively. Learning I is *"change in specificity of response* by correction of errors of choice within a set of alternatives,"* while Learning II is *"change in the set of alternatives from which choice is made"* (1972, p. 293).

There are two points to note:

1. Learning consists of a process of change and must be distinguished from its outcome—the pattern of response acquired by the learning. If, as a result of repeated experience, an individual acquires an unchanging response to an event (for instance, if I know from the drumming noise on a metal roof that it is raining) then that response constitutes an example of Learning Zero. Similarly, a reflex response, which is genetically determined and does not change, also constitutes Learning Zero.
2. Learning proceeds at different levels simultaneously. While a rat is learning to find its way through a particular maze (Learning I), it is also learning something about maze-type problems (Learning II). It does not have to complete one level of learning before proceeding to the next higher level.

The advantage of Learning II is that it enables the learner to narrow down the range of events or elements to which it must attend. Behavior becomes much less random. This results in economy of time and effort: the learner can go directly to the heart of the problem and solve it quickly and efficiently. As long as the Learning II (or its product in the acquired pattern of responses) is valid, the adaptation of the individual to its environment is promoted. But if some change occurs in the type or class of problem so that the effects of the past Learning II are invalidated, then the learner is in serious trouble. Response patterns determined at the level of Learning II are very hard to change. The complex enterprise of psychotherapy has developed in an attempt to change the effects of Learning II.

Learning II has been demonstrated so far in respect to problem-solving activities and the acquisition of skills. It is, however, of particular interest in its importance for character development and for its relation to personality traits. For Bateson, personal characteristics such as honesty, reliability, dependency, and assertiveness are outcomes of Learning II. As he puts it, "If we would define these words more carefully, our definition will consist in laying down the contingency pattern of that context of Learning I which would expectedly bring about that Learning II which would make the adjective applicable" (1972, p. 298).

Since Learning II, which determines much of the interactional life of human beings, dates from early childhood and is unconscious, it is extraordinarily difficult to change. There are two reasons for this.

1. In the circular sequence of the learning process in which feedback from the behavior at time T_1 influences the behavior that will be emitted at time T_2, the earlier behavior is part of the causal sequence and will affect the outcome. This is the case of the self-fulfilling hypothesis. Thus, a person who views the world as hostile is likely to emit behavior that produces a hostile reaction, and thus find reinforcement for his way of seeing the world.
2. Learning II and its effects are not subject to refutation by observation. The person who views the social world as hostile need not change his outlook if he receives friendly and supportive treatment from others. Such behavior can easily be attributed to ulterior motives. What is acquired through Learning II is a way

of viewing events, a way of punctuating a sequence of occurrences; it is not demonstrably right or wrong. In Bateson's words, "There is nothing contained in the propositions of this learning that can be tested against reality. It is like a picture seen in an ink blot; it has neither correctness or incorrectness. It is only a *way* of seeing the ink blot" (1972, p. 300).

Learning III is a "corrective change in the system of *sets* of alternatives from which choice is made." The process of change in Learning II and its relation to Learning III is a complex area of great concern to psychotherapists. It is, however, beyond the scope of our present discussion. I have discussed Bateson's position on this matter elsewhere (Pentony, 1981).

Learning IV is of interest to us because it involves adaptation through genetic change. In Bateson's scheme, genetic change is a continuation of change occurring through learning. It differs in being of a higher logical type for it constitutes change in the population or class rather than in the individual. As with individual learning, it is stochastic in that it requires both a random component and a selective or conservative component which ensures that only certain items of the random are selected for recurrence.

EVOLUTION

Named after Gregor Mendel by his father William Bateson, who was professor of biology at Cambridge for many years and one of the founders of the science of genetics, Gregory Bateson lived in a climate of evolutionary biology from his earliest years. To understand his perspective, it is necessary to take note of some general trends in evolutionary theory.

The problem for the early evolutionists was to provide an explanation for the way some variations, which gave individual members of the species an advantage for survival and hence for reproduction, were sometimes passed on to the next generation and sometimes not. The rediscovery of Mendel's work, which accounted for the resemblances between parents and offspring by a system of separated factors or genes which were shown to sometimes change suddenly from one form to another for no apparent reason, had a profound effect on thinking on this issue.

The early Mendelians saw biological evolution as being dependent on the occurrence of such single new genes which were produced by some "random" process that seemed independent of the environment, but which increased the probability that the offspring would survive. The mutation would be passed on to the offspring, thereby increasing the probability of the survival of such offspring and thus leading to evolutionary change.

It was implicit in this thinking that the genes were relatively few in number, both in the individual and in its population. Such views were gradually developed and given some mathematical form by about 1930.

The work of Theodosius Dobzhansky during that decade showed false the assumption that, in a natural population, most members have almost the same set of genes with only a few variants.

Bateson summarizes the significance of this development:

> Theodosius Dobzhansky's discovery that the unit of evolution is the population and that the population is a heterogeneous storehouse of genic possibilities greatly reduces the time required by evolutionary theory. The population is able to respond immediately to environmental pressures. The individual organism has the capacity for adaptive somatic change, but it is the population that, by selective mortality, undergoes change which is

transmitted to future generations. The *potentiality* for somatic change becomes the object of selection. It is on *populations* that environmental selection acts (1980 pp. 196-97).

The shift in emphasis from mutations to the selective process brought back into evolutionary thinking the concept of the organism as it appeard in nature, that is in the notion of the phenotype. The Mendelians had reduced the organism to its hereditary components or genes. However it is to the organism, and not to the genes, that natural selection is applied.

There is no one-to-one correlation between the genotype which will be selected and the phenotype on which natural selection operates. The phenotype is partly shaped by the environment in which it develops. So one and the same set of genes may produce different phenotypes if they develop in different environments.

Such shaping of the phenotype by the environment constitutes learning and brings us to the relation between learning and evolution. Although Lamarck proposed the inheritance of acquired or learned characteristics at the beginning of the nineteenth century, the weight of evidence and theoretical considerations alike have been against it. However, a strong case for less direct links between the two processes has been made over recent decades. This is based on the argument that the phenotype is partly determined by a process of adaptation to the environment in response to environmental stress. It is important to keep in mind that the *ability* of the organism to adapt is itself genetically determined and varies from individual to individual.

Hence, while the *adaptation achieved* is not transmitted in the genes, the ability to adapt is so transmitted. In this way a strain of organisms may be produced with a high facility for the adaptation. When such a strain has been achieved it may require only a small mutation to convert the learned or somatic adaptation into a genetically determined adaptation. An analogy can be drawn with a gun which is discharged by pressing a trigger. If the discharge mechanism is refined so that the lightest touch on the trigger will fire the gun, a point may be reached where the gun may be discharged by other means (*e.g.,* by dropping it or bumping it against another object).

Bateson sees some research by Waddington with fruit flies as being suggestive in this regard. Flies ordinarily have two wings. However in some members which have a gene called bi-thorax, four wings develop. By intoxicating fruit fly pupae with ethyl ether, Waddington was able to produce four-winged flies in a sizeable proportion of cases. He selected the best examples of such four-winged flies and bred the next generation from them, continuing this procedure for generation after generation.

He put aside a few pupae from each generation before intoxicating the remainder. After some thirty generations four-winged flies began to appear in this untreated group. Breeding from these showed that they were produced by a combination of genes and not by the single mutant gene bi-thorax. Waddington's explanation was that his selective process, operating on a vast scale, had selected out those individuals with the lowest threshhold for the production of the four-wing anomaly.

It will be apparent that, if we follow this line of thinking, learning and evolution appear as continuous stochastic processes. So an organism may adapt to its environment and it may adapt its adaptation to the environment, but when such a series of levels is exhausted, further adaptation must depend upon genetic change. When such genetic change occurs we have an instance of Bateson's Learning IV.

We should note that as we ascend the learning hierarchy, the change produced becomes increasingly irreversible and more deeply buried in our unconscious.

The bringing together of learning and evolution in a single conceptual scheme exemplifies Bateson's quest for unity in living matter. As he expressed it in his last major work, his goal was to discover the pattern that connects all life forms, from the growth of the flower to the thinking of the scientist.

When he chose to work in the broad field of anthropology, he brought with him a mind steeped in evolutionary ideas. As I indicated in my opening remarks, this oriented him toward viewing human interaction in terms of sequential process which, in turn, led him to the notions of circular or reciprocal causation and the consequent hierarchical order in communication.

It was fortuitous that at this stage of his development, he encountered the new ideas of cybernetics which burst onto the scene in the construction of computers and weapon-control systems. His discussions with mathematicians, particularly with Norbert Wiener, who shared something of his interests, opened new horizons for him and gave a structure to his thinking. The remainder of his life was devoted to relating these new mathematical insights to the biological world. It was an exercise that took him across disciplinary boundaries and to places as diverse as jungle villages in New Guinea, back wards of a mental hospital, acquaria for cetaceans and playpens of otters at a zoo.

His primary concern was the nature of mental process or of knowing. He enunciated his credo in the words, "I surrender to the belief that my knowing is a small part of a wider integrated knowing that knits the entire biosphere or creation" (1980 p. 100). Within this frame, evolution and all that it entails becomes formally a mental process.

REFERENCES

Bateson, G. *Naven.* A Survey of the Problems Suggested by a Composite Picture of the Culture of a New Guinea Tribe Drawn from Three Points of View. Cambridge: Cambridge University Press, 1936.

Bateson, G. "Social Planning and the Concept of Deutero Learning." Published as Chapter IV of *Science, Philosophy and Religion, Second Symposium.* New York: Harper & Ross, 1942.

Bateson, G. *Steps to an Ecology of Mind.* New York: Ballantine, 1972.

Bateson, G. "The Birth of a Matrix or Double Bind and Epistemology" in M.M. Berger (Ed.) *Beyond the Double Bind.* New York: Brunner/Mazel, 1978.

Bateson, G. *Mind and Nature: A Necessary Unity.* Glasgow: Fontana/Collin, 1980.

Frank, L.K. "The Problems of Learning" *Psychological Review,* 1976, *33,* 329-51.

Harlow, H.E. "The Formation of Learning Sets" *Psychological Review,* 1949, *56,* 51-65.

Jantsch, E. and Waddington, C.H. (Eds.). *Evolution and Consciousness. Human Systems in Transition.* Reading, MA: Addison-Wesley, 1976.

Maier, N.R.F. "The Behavior Mechanisms Concerned with Problem Solving," *Psychological Review,* 1940, *47,* 43-50.

Miller, G.A., Galanter, E. and Pribram, K.H. *Plans and the Structure of Behavior.* New York: Holt, Rinehart and Winston, 1960.

Milton M. Berger (Ed.) *Beyond the Double Bind: Communication and Family Systems, Theories, and Techniques with Schizophrenics.* New York: Brunner/Mazel, 1978.

Pentony, P. *Models of Influence in Psychotherapy.* New York: The Free Press, 1981.

Reichenbach, H. (Ed.) *The Direction of Time*. Berkeley, CA: The University of California Press, 1956.

Whitehead, A.N. and Russell, B. *Principia Mathematica, Vol. I.* London: Cambridge University Press, 1910.

THE PATTERN THAT CONNECTS

Jeannette P. Maas

ABSTRACT

Bateson asserts that a knowing mental function is embedded in the evolutionary process. This is not pantheism, but a complex immanent interaction of "mind" and nature. The interactions are between inside and outside, and require a "double description," that is, input from both. Bateson discovers that if he is to talk about mind he cannot ignore consciousness; therefore his initial definition of mind as a pattern that connects is not sufficient. This is always the quandary of the reductionist approach. Bateson realizes he needs to write a new book in which he addresses the issues of consciousness. He lets us know he would like to have a hand in the survival of his species, but fears to claim any power to do so.

Bateson says that the premise of *Mind and Nature: A Necessary Unity* is that mental functions are immanent in the interaction of differentiated parts as evolution proceeds. The mental functions, he asserts, are co-evolutionary with the differentiations. Wholes, which are more complex, are constituted by such interactions.

This premise sounds as if it might be related to the mind in nature of pantheistic fame, but such is not the case. Fechner (1946) postulated that nature, and we assume that this is the same nature Bateson is talking about, is a manifestation of "mind." However, Fechner's "mind" was also God's mind, since he said that God's mind and nature are the same events looked at from different angles. Bateson's term "immanent mental functions" is more reminiscent of a body being "lived consciousness" as asserted by Sartre (1956); in other words, Sartre says, "Consciousness *suffuses* the body" (Sartre, 1956). In viewing evolution as an *epistemological* process, Bateson posits intentionality and learning as being "embedded" within the evolutionary process.

The central thesis is that a pattern connects through a meta pattern, a pattern of patterns. The "necessary unity" effected by the patterning reminds us of a mandala laid over a mandala, laid over a mandala, each one adding more complexity without obscuring or destroying the pattern underneath. This unity of patterning cannot be like that of cream added to coffee, for it must not be a homogenous merging. It must not be absorbed by the previusly organized patterns if it is to maintain and preserve each separate pattern, while creating a more and more complex pattern

J.P. Maas is Lecturer in Educational Psychology at The University of the South Pacific in Suva, Fiji.

which is all of one gestalt. In other words, there must be an outside-to-inside relationship if the "meta-pattern" is to provide an organizing or modifying action. Bateson uses the term "meta-pattern" in ways that appear to give it the prerogatives of conscious action, although he does not, until the end of the book, bring up the topic of consciousness. By using the prefix "meta," he infers a more highly-organized or specialized form, and his usage would lead us to believe he is talking about an intentional orientation. The intention appears to be at the level of acting creatively to modify itself as it proceeds.

Bateson uses the term "immanent," *i.e.*, taking place within, but in addition he posits that the individual patterns have to interact with external patterns in complex ways not heretofore recognized. Although Bateson does not elaborate upon this, what has not been recognized is the fact that there is a discontinuity between inside and outside information. He does, however, continue discussing the interactions in explicit terms by saying that the epistemology of the process is not a matter of internal discussion, as for example ones' own mental acts are, but is a matter of the external relationships between inside and outside. To quote, "Relationship is always a product of double description. . . Relationship preceeds. . ." To explain this position, Bateson uses the metaphor of a cyclops-like creature who has one eye and monocular vision. If two of these creatures interact with their two eyes, they will be able to create a binocular view in depth. This double view, he says is what he means by their relationship, one with a double description. What he does not say, as inferred above, is that each of these monocular creatures has a different point of view from the other, and that there must be a discontinuity, in order that each may provide an inside description of its own position, and an outside description of the other's description. Each delivers to the other. Bateson differentiates between this kind of "I-Thou" relationship and the relationship of each creature to the world of things. He spends some time discussing the disastrous consequences of confusing the "I" with the "it," the attributing of human characteristics to the inanimate, and the objectifying of the human as if the human were an inanimate object. He points out that it may do little harm to reify the mountain, but to try to turn the human into a thing is to court the disasters that we see every day under fascistic governments.

As Bateson proceeds, it becomes clear that "knowing" is an integral part of successive differentiations. He uses the example of the starfish, saying that it "knows" how to grow its five arms around its symmetrical core. He defines the progress of epistemology and evolution as "two great stochastic processes" which combine with each other at every step. This is the reason behind the use of the words "mind" and "nature" in his title. He argues convincingly that the mind, as a "pattern," and as a "pattern of patterns" can effect a unity in the developing organism. However, when he comes to the end of his explanations, he finds he is faced with a dilemma. He has not really defined "mind," nor has he said anything about "consciousness." This is a dilemma which must be faced by anyone who attempts to say anything significant about "mind" while using a building-block, *i.e.*, a "bottom-up" approach. Where does this "mind" come from? When does it enter the system? Is it like the steam which begins to develop when the pot boils?

The whole problem is brought into sharp focus when, at the end of the book, he relates a conversation with his daughter who plays the part of devil's advocate. She asks, "Why did you write this book?" The father answers by giving a kind of parable: during the suicidal dash of lemmings to the sea, there should be one lemming taking notes on their passing. The note-taking lemming would also be in a position of saying, "I told you so!" This sounds like consciousness at its best! The daughter won't be satisfied with this. As the conversation progresses, Bateson plays the role of the seeker of enlightenment. He talks as if he has been engaging in a personal yoga, or a work that proposes to lead toward enlightenment. It becomes apparent that the present book is a prologue to a new book, which he will entitle, *Where Angels Fear to Tread*. In this new book, he will explore issues of mind and consciousness. He will ask, "What is the primary definition of mind, the mind that is immanent to the patterning process?" And, "On what sort of surface shall this consciousness be mapped?" And, "What is the relationship of consciousness to beauty?" and "of the sacred to beauty?" and "of the consciousness to the sacred?" As the conversation continues, he gives us a clue to why he wants to talk about where the angels fear to tread. He says, "If I could stop the race of the lemmings to the ocean, I might be accused of being even more arrogant than if I said, 'I told you so.' " Bateson sees the headlong dash of his species into self destruction. At least by implication, he would like to survive. He makes a value judgment that the situation should be eliminated by knowledgeable comment. He fears to claim that he has any power to do anything about it.

The daughter wants to know whether these questions have not already been answered, and Bateson notes that they never have. He notices that historically, many people have tried, but have not succeeded. Bateson believes that when one approaches the questions he wants to address, one will be diverted. It is as if, he says, the hunted gives off a false scent, leading the questioner off down the garden path, after the wild goose, who holds the red herring in its beak!

Bateson comes close to admitting that he has "painted himself into a corner." From a phenomenological point of view, consciousness is more than simple awareness of the world. If one were to address the issues, one would have to take note that there is an awareness of being aware; and an awareness of being an awareness of being aware. This is the analog of Bateson's patterning of patterning, and meta-patterns. As Bateson points out, the Darwinian concept of survival of the fittest is a tautology. How else could one define "fittest" except that it leads to survival? The lemming metaphor leads us to the premise that the "fittest" of all the fit would be to develop a concept of survival, and to start looking for that particular strategy that will do the job. Consciousness *is* the ability to loop back and get information about information and to survive amidst our efforts to survive. This consciousness "loop" frees the patterns and the patterning of patterns from random determinism.

One philosopher of mind and nature who made a beginning at coping with the questions Bateson raises is Teilhard de Chardin (1959). Chardin expressed the view that in the evolutionary process there are nexus points which provide choices. For evolution to proceed from the simple to the complex, the ultimate survival choice must always be in the direction of more and more complexity. Again, we are reminded of patterns laid upon patterns. If the choice is made through the immanence of mind to nature, could we not say that the more complex is the more beautiful to the chooser? But *can* we be both inside and outside at once? There is a veil between the holy and the most holy. We can approach the sacred from the outside, either in the vestments of high priest, or as the mad scientist creating Frankensteins. Or we can approach through immanence and fascination, whereupon examination in retrospect of the experience can come only through symbols and allegories (Corey and Maas, 1976). And here is where the red herrings abound, for those experiences and symbols and allegories are made to be either too sacred to examine and interpret, or are dismissed as nonscientific non-sense.

It is as if one were required to be midwife at one's own birth. We preserve words such as apotheosis, transfiguration, and that most fascinating of all, the *hieros gamos*, or the mystical marriage of energies and opposites, to remind us that although the experiences of immanence seem inexpressible, they can be given a label. These kinds of terms indicate that conditions which occur at the nexus points are both beautiful and sacred.

When we think of nature, we think of the mass-energy side of Einstein's equation. Here the whirlpools of energy and the physical contributions of atoms and molecules provide the raw material to be structured into form and substance. But the "mind" which is going to help effect the "necessary unity" of the pattern of patterns is on the spacing and timing side. Consciousness provides the "room" for the epistemological events to take place.

When we think of evolution, we usually think of the "tree" of more and more complex development in the structuring of the mass-energy dimension. But the epistemological side of the equation is also evolving. We have allegorical evidence of this in the early Sumerian and Akkadian Literature:

> The Elohim said, Look, the earthlings are as one of us, knowing good and bad. Now lest the earthlings take of the tree of life and become as the Elohim, let us send them from the garden....
>
> The Elohim said, Go to, let us go down and see. This is only the beginning of what they will do, and nothing that they propose to do will be impossible for them (Graves and Patai, 1966).

SUMMARY

Bateson has attempted to make a case for the necessary unity of mind and nature. He would like to see "mind" as a "pattern that connects," a special definition of mind. Evolution is seen as an instantiation of meta-level patterns, giving form to more and more complex organisms. Two great stochastic processes combine at every step, creating the necessary interpenetration of patterns and patterns of patterns.

He realizes after he has finished making his case that he has said nothing about consciousness, and that his definition of "mind" is not sufficient. To develop his case further he feels the necessity for writing a new book, *Where Angels Fear to Tread*, in which he will discuss the problems raised by his ommissions. An understanding of the creative, evolutionary significance of consciousness cannot be arrived at through a biologically reductionistic approach.

In trying to relate his life-long efforts to understand the past evolution of our species and the present problem of preserving our threatened biosphere, Bateson raises more questions than he answers. The present paper attempts to bring some of these out into the open in light of the concepts of modern physics and existentialism. If consciousness is to play a part in the evolutionary process, then the influences of spacing, temporalizing, and intentionality must be taken into account.

REFERENCES

Corey, D. and Maas, J. P. *The Existential Bible, a Genesis of Creativity.* Honolulu: NaPali Publishing Co., 1976.

Graves, R. and Patai, R. *Hebrew Myths: The Book of Genesis.* New York: McGraw Hill, 1966.

Lowrie, E. (Ed.) *Religion of a Scientist.* New York: Pantheon, 1946.

Sartre, J. *Being and Nothingness: An Essay on Phenomenological Ontology.* New York: Philosophical Library, 1956.

Teilhard de Chardin, P. *The Phenomenon of Man.* London: Wm. Collins Sons Co. 1959.

SOME CRITICISMS OF *MIND AND NATURE*

Robert A.M. Gregson

ABSTRACT

Bateson's use of concepts in cybernetics and systems theory are critically examined. It is indicated by example that his conceptual grasp of cybernetic theory is not adequate to pursue his attempted analyses. Only with a fuller understanding and use of the quantitative methodology of cybernetics could Bateson have said anything of substantial content and coherence.

The idea that human thought processes have some of the characteristics of closed systems capable of self-regulation is widespread, and indeed might be said to underpin much of modern theoretical psychology, both cognitive and behavioral. In fairness to others who have written and experimented within this wide area, cybernetic ideas about thinking have been dealt with in far more precision and with more rigor and more regard for the fine details than Bateson shows in his book, *Mind and Nature*. See, for example, Frank George (1970) in England, William Powers (1973) in the United States, and many Soviet theoreticians whose work has rarely been translated into English. Cybernetic models of thinking have been around at least since the 1950's. They have become, both empirically and mathematically, complex and are frequently structured hierarchically. I think we have gone so far along this path that a model which was not, at least in some subsystems, closed loop and hierarchical, would have little (if any) *a priori* validity for an experimental psychologist. If we restrict consideration to systems theorists who would be the mathematical counterparts of the psychologists (and some people obviously are in both camps at once), then they have a common language which looks suspiciously like what Bateson is saying. There is no doubt, then, that Bateson is reflecting some patterns in contemporary thought, or what has been contemporary for a couple of decades at least.

The fundamental problem Bateson raises for me is that it is possible *to talk about* cybernetics and systems theory, but not *to do* these things as analytical activities, in ordinary language. Let us try and evaluate his comments in part from his own perspective. In his memorandum, *Time is Out of Joint,* he makes two points that seem to define his stance, though I am not sure that is what he intended. He

---

R.A.M. Gregson is Head of the Department of Psychology at the University of New England in Armidale, Australia.

suggests that the approach whereby we study and evaluate mental phenomena in quantitative terms is both anti-aesthetic and an assumption, and he comments that, "Rigor alone is paralytic death, but imagination alone is insanity." So we had better see if Bateson, in borrowing cybernetics without the intrinsic mathematics of that approach, has lost his rigor and his sanity at the same time, for there is no doubt that his search for examples and parallels to make his points shows an imagination and fluency which promises more than it delivers.

Let us examine five of Bateson's six criteria of his chapter four, where the nature of mind, as he sees it, is necessarily and sufficiently characterized. It is here that he attempts an application of cybernetics.

1. "Mind is an aggregate of interacting parts."

It is true that some mental processes function, intermittently, in apparent autonomy, particularly when they are overlearnt. A long time ago, the British psychologist Charles Spearman observed that if we try to think exactly what we are doing when we ride a bicycle, we start to fall off; forcing overlearnt skills into consciousness can impair their normal execution, which is hardly available to introspection. But the partitioning of mental activity into compartments is what psychologists have to assume in order to get tractable representations; it does not mean that any of these parts of mind are closed systems, and it doesn't mean that we can ever point to system boundaries in tidy fashion. So far, so good.

2. "The interaction of parts of mind is triggered by differences."

Bateson seems to have the oddly naive view that inanimate systems are almost always described only by open causal chains, and that mental events are likewise described by relationships and responses to rates of change. This is where Bateson's failure to understand either differential equations or modern systems theory is horrendously silly in its consequences. His treatment of difference, and the examples he advances, are nonsensical. For example, "It is surprising to find how rare are cases in the inorganic world in which some A responds to a difference between some B and some C" (p. 96). In fact, every electrical circuit used in power generation or propulsion, from an electric clock to a power station, works that way. Every chemical reaction involving transmission across permeable membranes, used in production engineering in abundance, works that way. Every means of transport involves subsystems functioning that way; every common spring or shock absorber works that way; the next thunderstorm on a Fijian summer evening will work that way. Bateson is back to front; what is interesting is how complex systems with feedback will, under dynamic stationarity (which is not sharply defined in non-mathematical language), exhibit the characteristics of a simple input-output causality, which belies entirely the details of their internal functioning.

Let us look for a moment at Bateson's example of his finger moving across a lump of chalkdust on the blackboard and getting a sensation. It is true that sensory input, in most modalities, depends on a change in the level or rate of excitation; this change is local in space and time.

He says, "I am concerned only with understanding how mind and mental processes must necessarily work" (p. 98). He continues, that mind can receive news only of difference. Actually, within some narrow finite ranges of environmental energy levels, the human observer can take in information about identity, level, rate of change of level, rate of change of change of level, and even mixtures of the last three. What is even more interesting is that optimum control of the environment, when the environment itself is subject to dynamic change, may be achieved by the organization using combinations of various sorts of inputs, a principle which is also used in engineering. Further, a shifting from responding to continuous change by making almost continuously changing responses, to making responses which shift in large discrete steps, comes with learning to control and to be economical in that control. The efficient operator knows when to break feedback and go into open-loop behavior, in other words, when to be efficient, when to abandon precisely those system qualities which Bateson thinks are characteristic of mind. Again, in terms of dynamic systems theory, there is no perfectly human, mental, or animate quality in any of the properties which Bateson attempts to discern in mind.

3. "Mental processes require collateral energy."

As we are told (pp. 99–100) that Bateson doesn't understand what "energy" means, and the text indicates that he doesn't understand what "information" means in the context of cybernetics, it is a little disconcerting to see these words still around. About the most one can say of his third principle is that it is either trivial—we metabolize substances in our nervous system while we think—or that it is irrelevant to his thesis. If he does not measure this energy and its rate of dissipation, between points in space and time, and show that this goes with mental activity, then he might as well say nothing.

4. "Mental process requires circular or more complex chains of determination."

Again, Bateson tries to use metaphors about rocks to describe dynamic systems. He would have done better to remember Ludwig von Bertalanffy's adage that the organism is not a crystal but a flame, which is a prettier expression and has the virtue of being succinct.

This section of his chapter, about circular chains, is actually about positive feedback, and how to turn it into negative feedback. His account is oddly incomplete: he tells the story of control theory up to Clerk Maxwell in the 1850's, but doesn't explain that the parts of system theory which are particularly applicable to human behavior derive from Liapunov in the 1880's, Volterra in the 1920's and Andronov in the 1930's, when the notions of stability, controllability and identifiability of systems began to take on precise and testable meanings. The point to grasp is that today the theory of how machines (in the widest and non-mechanistic sense) work is prodigiously more rich and diverse than Bateson's account of mind, and is, at the same time, more precise, testable, and disciplined. We now know that systems which are stable and robust against changes of some sorts, either in their environment or within their own structure, can be defined in ways so as to distinguish between the many cybernetic paradigms that could be applicable to human behavior. Governors on steam engines and switches on walls are parts, sometimes, of cybernetic systems, but not all are good metaphors for biological self-regulation, let alone for the special cases in mental activity.

The advantage of getting away from Bateson's primitive extended metaphors into the abstractions of systems theory, is that we lose the notion that it is the mechanistic hardware, of the environment or of the peripheral nervous system, that matters. Obviously, the way our brains are constructed imposes limits on what we can do and how we can do it; as Bateson noted, Lamarck said this in 1809, but this does not mean that thinking is isomorphic with sensory systems, or with overt behavior during sequences of learning and of forgetting, or of extending and of reducing repertoires of behavior. Bateson advances very general principles of scientific explanation, and then picks explanatory examples which aren't really relevant to his thesis. This suggests to me that he doesn't understand the principles. The cybernetic principles mean very little unless and until there is some quantification of the inputs and the outputs, or at least the probabilities of different classes of inputs and outputs, precisely because the same internal structure or process can exhibit a rich and surprising diversity of outputs for the same inputs, with only minute changes in its internal parameters. Stability in structure and stability in the order and complexity of a living system, are not the same thing as the stability in the simple examples he uses, be they about light switches or dolphins or whatever. The quantification which he rejects as anti-aesthetic is precisely the tool for probing out the distinctions between one sort of cybernetic system and another, and for stopping us from seeing analogies where they are not and to see why changes in overt behavior are not necessarily any evidence of changes in internal processes, but only in internal values of some stored input or state which contributes to a process.

As soon as you get to complex hierarchical systems, such as mental abilities and the thinking that goes with them, then you cannot uniquely identify the form of the internal process from external records of inputs and outputs, from stimuli and response records, from protocols of people thinking aloud, and so on. You can eliminate a great many explanations as much too simple, which is what Bateson does with gusto, but you need a model as well, and you need prior probabilities, in the researcher's view of things, to help choose between explanations. And, ultimately, you have to make predictions which are in principle falsifiable; with cybernetic systems this is not something which you do in words alone, you need numbers.

This problem becomes acute in Bateson's treatment of sensory systems as switches; his mechanistic analogy blinds us to important, fundamental issues (pp. 108–109). For example, for convenience we may, with some loss of information, treat a continuous system as existing in discontinuous time, or the reverse; the former is done in any psychological experiment which is made up of a sequence of trials or discrete observations. This representation in discrete time in a system, or in parts within a system, has nothing necessarily to do with there being switches, and the switch which changes a system from one configuration to another is not at all the same thing as the mechanism which discretizes the analysis by sampling a process at spaced points in time. Bateson telescopes too many subtleties together and loses any power of explanation as a consequence. Sense organs are not part of thinking, nor are they models for thinking, though how they function can, in part, be controlled by signals going out from the central nervous system to the periphery. In short, they are not switches at all but themselves parts of feedback loops with variable structure. They don't switch except at the molecular level; in the time scale of the nervous system and of thinking they are differentiators or integrators. The important thing about the senses is that they transform abrupt changes in inputs into sequences, and can increase the redundancy of input (which makes it resistant to being rubbed out) at the price of losing fidelity. This has biological survival value, indeed Norbert Wiener pointed this out in the case of some particular filters used in time series, and it has implications for those of us who want to construct models of central cognitive processes, but I am not sure it is about thinking. In fact, Bateson is writing about biological systems in a racy way, using undefined words to jump over the difficult bits, but what he says could be true of non-living systems as well, and could be true of behavior without thinking or consciousness ever happening. His extended examples drawn from animal behavior are cases of operant learning experiments devised by psychologists who painstakingly theorized without any reference to consciousness, and didn't need to at the level of analysis involved.

5. "In mental process the effects of difference are to be regarded as transforms of the difference which preceded them."

Any system, mental or otherwise, which persists in time, and has a memory, and can respond to different levels of input, will do this. In fact, it could not do anything else without coming apart at the seams. The problem is to identify the transforms, and again that involves the methodology from which Bateson retreats.

Hans Anderson wrote of an Emperor who had no clothes; I think Bateson has got second-hand clothes, but he has put them on upside down, back to front, or inside out, and the total picture is hardly elegant. The only thing to do is undress the figure and start again from scratch.

REFERENCES

Bateson, G. *Mind and Nature.* New York: Dutton, 1979.
George, F.H. *Models of Thinking.* London: Allen and Unwin, 1970.
Powers, W.T. *Behavior: The Control of Perception.* London: Wildwood, 1974.

THE SYMPOSIUM ON
MIND AND NATURE:
A BRIEF SUMMARY

Victor N. Kobayashi

ABSTRACT

Some of the main concerns brought out by the five panelists in the Symposium on Bateson's *Mind and Nature* which was held at the University of the South Pacific, January, 1982, are briefly summarized by the Symposium Chairman. Gregson's objection to Bateson's neglecting "the intrinsic mathematics" and Diorio's allegation of Bateson's self-contradictions, are balanced by Maas' admiration for the attempt to map the mind from inside and out, and by Booth's assertion that Bateson's marriage of the studies of the sciences and the humanities is the way forward.

The Symposium on Gregory Bateson's book, *Mind and Nature: A Necessary Unity,* featured Michael Booth, Lecturer in Social and Political Theory, Murdoch University, Western Australia; Joseph A. Diorio, Senior Lecturer in Education, University of Otago, New Zealand; R.A.M. Gregson, Professor and Chair, Psychology, University of New England, Australia; Jeannette P. Maas, Psychology, University of the South Pacific, Fiji; and Donald F. Miller, Senior Lecturer in Political Science, University of Melbourne, Australia.[1]

Jeannette P. Maas welcomed Bateson's book, although she was certain that it would be considered subversive by most people today if they understood the ideas presented. Bateson's attempt to construct a map of the "mind" that is both "inside of" and "outside of" mind was a difficult task, full of dangers.

On the other hand, Robert A.M. Gregson found much of Bateson's assertions in the book, particularly the version of cybernetics presented, to be unacceptable. Arguing for more quantitative rigor, his fundamental criticism was Bateson's at-

---

V.N. Kobayashi is in the Department of Educational Foundations at the University of Hawaii, Manoa.

1. Both Maas' and Gregson's papers appear in this volume. Patrick Pentony, Psychology, Australian National University, also submitted a paper, "Gregory Bateson and Cybernetics," but, unable to travel to Fiji, did not participate in the Symposium on Gregory Bateson's *Mind and Nature.* (However, his paper is included in this volume.)

tempt to analyze cybernetic and systems theory events in ordinary language "without the intrinsic mathematics." He said that the quantification rejected by Bateson as "anti-aesthetic," "...is precisely the tool for probing out the distinctions between one sort of cybernetic system and another, and for stopping us from seeing analogies where they are not and to see why changes in overt behavior are not necessarily any evidence of changes in internal processes, but only in internal values of some stored input or state which contributes to a process." Gregson appropriately directed his criticisms to the key chapter in *Mind and Nature,* "Criteria of Mental Process," which Bateson himself considered the "cornerstone of the whole book." Gregson's critique seemed well received by many members of the audience. However, although Gregson's criticisms seemed to be valid (within the epistemological assumptions shared by most scientists who emphasized quantitative data in their studies), it must be pointed out that Bateson's perspective argues *against* such epistemological premises, and calls for a deep restructuring of that epistemology. Space does not permit a full resolution of the disagreement between the two positions, but, briefly, the epistemology favored by Bateson would take into account the human subject, the thinker, involved in the description/observation; Bateson would also regard the subject matter under discussion as basically in the realm of *ideas* about the world. In Bateson's words, from *Mind and Nature:*

> We are discussing a world of *meaning,* a world some of whose details and differences, big and small, in some parts of that world, get *represented* in relations between other parts of that total world. A change in my neurons or in yours must represent that change in the forest, that falling of that tree. But not the physical event, only the *idea* of the physical event. And the idea has no location in space or time—only perhaps in an *idea* of space or time (from Bantam edition, NY, 1980, p. 110, emphasis in original).

Bateson's universe of discourse, although it uses terms and ideas from cybernetics, an area of study he shares with Gregson, nevertheless completely differs from Gregson's universe. Any basic criticism of Bateson must direct itself to the basic premises of Bateson's universe, premises which seem historically related to a non-materialistic, idealistic philosophical tradition and which attempt to bridge the gap between positivism and the realm of the arts and humanities.

Joseph A. Diorio, whose criticisms might also be understood in this light, raised questions about Bateson's view of evolution and learning, and their relationship to the problem of human freedom versus determinism. Diorio argued that Bateson's position was fatalistic and deterministic, yet in his capacity as a Regent of the University of California, in 1978, Bateson had urged the Regents (in a memorandum reprinted in the book's appendix) to act more wisely and in a statesmanlike manner in dealing with the problem of the presently held obsolete epistemologies that "lead to greed, monstrous over-growth, war, tyranny, and pollution" (Bantam edition, p. 241). Diorio believed that Bateson contradicted himself, and he concludes, "If the human race is learning itself into a terminal cul-de-sac, as Bateson seems to complain, then unless the control of learning can be freed from the genetically limited selective process of reinforcement, neither statesmanship nor any other deliberate and deliberative device could have any predictable effect on the outcome."

Donald L. Miller explored Bateson's idea of information being "the difference that makes a difference." Unlike Gregson and Diorio, Miller seemed comfortable with Bateson's universe. In Miller's words:

> But what are ideas? What constitutes information? It is not things in themselves; they do nothing. Rather it is our appreciation, perceptually, conceptually, affectively or morally,

about relations between things, and between ourselves and these things. Such relationships are everything. We cannot observe a thing in itself, or a thing constant over time, or a thing in isolation.

Much of Miller's presentation related Bateson's central idea of *difference* to the concept of *differance* as proposed by Jacques Derrida, the contemporary French thinker.

Michael Booth discussed Bateson as a thinker who brought together the sciences and humanities in a significant way, and identified Bateson as a pioneer in a new field of study, "a field comprising studies of how cultural systems interact with biological entities." He concluded by emphasizing the need for further exploration and development of this field:

> Descartes made one of the inaugural statements of our scientific era by doubting all that was not self-evident. This character of self-evidence led him both to mind and to matter. The humanities and the sciences have been the resultant ruling distinction of our times within the field of human intellect. Many today believe we are at the threshold of a new era based in the study of systems. In these studies natural systems on the one hand are set against human systems on the other. While it is indisputable that human systems have the characteristics of mentality it is increasingly at issue whether mentality should be situated in the physiological systems of brain tissue, or alternatively in the traditional systems of cultural interactions. For me this is a non-issue. Mentality is an outcome of the continuing, dialectical evolution of the interaction between these two. Only by pursuing, as Bateson does, the necessary unity in what biological sciences and the humanities study can human beings develop an understanding of that interaction.

The symposium on Bateson was appropriate for a conference on thinking. Thinking is both a cause *and* effect of evolution. The rather frequently cited cliché that "up until now evolution was unconscious and hereafter may be conscious" is a false dichotomy. Evolution is thinking and thinking is evolution. Nature and mind are evolving together. Bateson helped us to see this unity.

REFERENCE NOTES

Booth, M. "The Necessary Unity of the Humanities and the Sciences," presented at Symposium on Bateson, Conference on Thinking, University of the South Pacific, 1982.

Diorio, J.A. "A Critique of Bateson's View of Evolution and Learning," presented at Symposium on Bateson, Conference on Thinking, University of the South Pacific, 1982.

Gregson, R.A.M. "Some Criticisms," paper presented at Symposium on Bateson, Conference on Thinking, University of the South Pacific, 1982.

Maas, Jeannette P. "The Pattern that Connects," paper presented at Symposium on Bateson, Conference on Thinking, University of the South Pacific, 1982.

Miller, D.L. "Information that Makes a Difference," paper presented at Symposium on Bateson, Conference on Thinking, University of the South Pacific, 1982.

REFERENCES

Bateson, G. *Mind and Nature: A Necessary Unity.* New York: Dutton. 1979. (New York, Bantam, 1980). Pagination of these editions is different.

NAVIGATING BY THE STARS

What shall we say to each other,
You and I,
When these stars leave
Our sky?

When this moon, that sun, yonder comet
That reflecting satellite,
This drying rainbow fades,
Upon what shall we hang our wishes?

How many light houses must we sight
Or, how many sirens must we hear
On this harmonic night,
To know enchantment?

My star, my Southern Cross,
Your northern Pleiades
Our constellation, our galaxy,
Our Universe
You. We? You. You!

You cannot fade, from us.
We are you and you are we.
There is only one circle.
All others
Are but images
Representations.

Farewell Pacific Island Feast

APPENDIX A

APPENDIX A. LIST OF PARTICIPANTS[1]

BARKER, Alan, M.A., Lecturer, Discipline of English, University of the South Pacific, Suva, Fiji.

BISHOP, John Christopher, Ph.D., Lecturer in Philosophy, The University of Auckland, New Zealand.

BODEN, Margaret A., M.A., Ph.D., Professor of Philosophy and Psychology, University of Sussex, Brighton, U.K.

BOOTH, Michael Alfred, M.Sc., Lecturer, School of Social Inquiry, Murdoch University, Perth, Western Australia.

BROSNAHAN, Frank L., D. Litt. & Phil., Professor of English, University of the South Pacific, Suva, Fiji.

BURTON, Leone, Ph.D., Senior Lecturer in Mathematics Education, The Open University, Walton Hall, Milton Keynes, U.K.

CHAND, Dewan, B.A. (Hon.), Principal, Ba Provincial Secondary School, Lautoka, Fiji.

CHURCHLAND, Patricia Smith, B. Phil., Associate Professor, Department of Philosophy, University of Manitoba, Canada.

CONNELL, William Fraser, Ph.D., Mornington, Victoria, Australia.

COSTA, Arthur L., Ed.D., Professor of Education, California State University, Sacramento, CA, U.S.A.

CROCOMBE, Ron G., Ph.D., Professor and Director, Institute of Pacific Studies, University of the South Pacific, Suva, Fiji.

CROWELL, David H., Ph.D., Professor, Newborn Research Laboratory, University of Hawaii, Honolulu, HI, U.S.A.

CROWELL, Doris C., M.A., Curriculum Researcher, Kamehameha Schools, Honolulu, HI, U.S.A.

---

1. In addition to the participants listed, there were approximately 200 other "observers" and "students" who attended the Conference and who contributed in various ways to the success of the Conference.

DALL'ALBA, Gloria A., B.Ed., Science/Mathematics Teacher, Marian College, Launceston, Tasmania, Australia.

DALZELL, Rex Stewart, M.Ed., Dean, Palmerston North Teachers College, Palmerston North, New Zealand.

DASCAL, Marcelo, Ph.D., Professor, Department of Linguistics, University of Campinas, SP, Brazil.

DAVIDSON, Graham R., Ph.D., Senior Lecturer, Center for Behavioural Studies in Education, University of New England, Armidale, Australia.

DAWKINS, Richard, D. Phil., Lecturer, Department of Zoology, Oxford University, South Parks Road, Oxford, England, U.K.

DE BONO, Edward, D. Phil. Medicine, Ph.D., Faculty of Medicine, Cambridge University, Cambridge, England, U.K.

DIORIO, Joseph A., Ph.D., Senior Lecturer in Education, University of Otago, Dunedin, New Zealand.

DROMEY, Robert G., Ph.D., Senior Lecturer, Department of Computing Science, University of Wollongong, Australia.

EDWARDS, John, M.Sc., Lecturer in Science Education, James Cook University, Queensland, Australia.

EDWARDS, Vicki W., Dip.Sp.Ed., North Ward, Australia.

FIRTH, Donald Edward, M. Phil., Lecturer in Mathematics, School of Education, La Trobe University, Bundoora, Victoria, Australia.

FRANCE, M. Honoré, Ed.D., Assistant Professor, Department of Psychological Foundations in Education, University of Victoria, Victoria, British Columbia, Canada.

GALLO, Delores, Ed.D., Associate Professor of Education, Co-director of the Critical and Creative Thinking Graduate Program, University of Massachusetts at Boston, MA, U.S.A.

GIBBONS, John R., Ph.D., Lecturer in Biology, School of Natural Resources, University of the South Pacific, Suva, Fiji.

GIRLE, Roderic A., Ph.D., Professor and Head, Department of Philosophy, University of Queensland, St. Lucia, Australia 4067.

GRABHAM, Kathryn Patricia, M.Ed., Lecturer, Canberra College of Advanced Education, Belconnon, A.C.T., Australia.

GREGSON, Robert A.M., Ph.D., Professor and Head, Department of Psychology, University of New England, Armidale, Australia.

GRIFFIN, Christopher, D. Phil., Lecturer in Sociology, University of the South Pacific, Suva, Fiji.

HELU, I. Futa, 'Atenisi Institute, Nuku'alofa, Tonga.

JANSSON, Laura H., M.A., Sportspsychologist, The Finnish Sports Academy, Finland.

JERSIN, Patricia D., Ed.D., Profesor of Education, California State University, Long Beach, CA, U.S.A.

KACIMAIWAI, Epeli V., Dip. Ed. Admin., Secretary for Education, Ministry of Education, Selbourne Street, Suva, Fiji.

KANHAI, Shiu Narayan, BA, General Secretary, Fiji Teachers Union, Samabula, Suva, Fiji.

KAWHARU, Ian H., D. Phil., Professor and Head, Department of Social Anthropology and Maori Studies, Massey University, Palmerston North, New Zealand.

KAYE, Tom, Ph.D., Reader in Education, University of the South Pacific, Suva, Fiji.

KENNEDY, Cathy, Ph.D., Department of Zoology, Oxford University, South Parks Road, Oxford, U.K.

KISHOR, Nand, M.A., Lecturer in Education, University of the South Pacific, Suva, Fiji.

KOBAYASHI, Victor, Ph.D., Professor of Educational Foundations, College of Education, University of Hawaii, Honolulu, HI, U.S.A.

LAMB, Roger E., Ph.D., Lecturer in Philosophy, University of Queensland, St. Lucia, Queensland, Australia.

LANG, Melvin, Ed.D., Professor of Education, College of Education, University of Hawaii, Honolulu, HI, U.S.A.

LARKIN, Jill H., Ph.D., Assistant Professor, Department of Psychology, Carnegie-Mellon University, Pittsburgh, PA, U.S.A.

LOCHHEAD, Jack, Ph.D., Ed.D., Professor, Department of Physics and Astronomy, University of Massachusetts, Amherst, MA., U.S.A.

MAAS, Jeannette P., Ph.D., Lecturer in Educational Psychology, University of the South Pacific, Suva, Fiji.

MACINTOSH, J.J., B. Phil., Professor, Department of Philosophy, University of Calgary, Canada.

MACKAY, D.M., Ph.D., Department of Communications and Neuroscience, University of Keele, Staffordshire, U.K.

MACRAE, Kristina S., Ph.D., Principal Tutor, Psychology Department, La Trobe University, Bundoora, Victoria, Australia.

MARLAND, Percy W., Ph.D., Senior Lecturer in Education, James Cook University, Post Office, Queensland, Australia.

MAWER, Robert F., M.Ed., Ph.D. Candidate, School of Education, University of New South Wales, Kensington, Australia.

MAXWELL, William, Ed.D., Professor of Education, University of the South Pacific, Suva, Fiji.

MCBEATH, Arthur G., Ed.D., Professor of Education, University of Regina, Regina, Canada.

MCPECK, John E., Ph.D., Assistant Professor of Education, University of Western Ontario, London, Ontario, Canada.

MEEKER, Mary, Ed.D., SOI Institute, El Segundo, CA, U.S.A.

MILLER, Donald F., M.A., Senior Lecturer, Department of Political Science, University of Melbourne, Parkville, Australia.

MWAIPAYA, Paul A., Ph.D., Senior Lecturer in Philosophy, University of Papua, New Guinea.

MURALIDHAR, S., M.Sc.(Ed.), Lecturer in Science Education, University of the South Pacific, Suva, Fiji.

NABUKA, Joeli, B.A.(Ed.), Fijian Teachers Association, Suva, Fiji.

NINNES, Leonard E., Ph.D., University of Edinburgh, Lecturer in Philosophy, Paisley College of Technology, Paisley, Renfrewshire, Scotland, U.K.

PELLETIER, Francis Jeffry, Ph.D., Associate Professor of Philosophy, University of Alberta, Edmonton, Canada.

PERKINS, David M., Ed.D., Co-director, Harvard Project Zero, Senior Research Associate in Education, Harvard University, Cambridge, MA, U.S.A.

PRASAD, Jwala, M.A. (Dip.Ed.), Senior Lecturer in Social Science, Nasinu Teachers' College, Suva, Fiji.

RAM, Hari, B.Sc., Deputy Secretary for Education, Ministry of Education, Suva, Fiji.

SELDON, Rodney Charles, B.Sc., Lecturer, University of Technology, Lae, Papua, New Guinea.

SHARMA, Jagdish P., Ph.D., Professor of History, University of Hawaii, Honolulu, HI, U.S.A.

STEWART, Robert A.C., Ph.D., Reader in Educational Psychology, University of the South Pacific, Suva, Fiji.

SOVAKI, Joeli Kalou, B.A., President, Fijian Teachers Association, Suva, Fiji.

SWELLER, John, Ph.D., Senior Lecturer in Education, University of New South Wales, Kensington, Australia.

TEASDALE, Bob, Ph.D., Senior Lecturer in Education, Flinders University, Adelaide, South Australia.

WHITELEY, Patricia S., M.Ed., Doctoral Student, University of Oregon, Eugene, OR, U.S.A.

WILSON, Daniel C., B.Sc., Bell Labs, Naperville, IL, U.S.A.

WILSON, Derek, Ph.D., Professor of Elementary Education, University of Alberta, Edmonton, Alberta, Canada.

ZWIER, Antonie G., M.A., Doctoral Student, University of Auckland, New Zealand.

INDEX

AUTHOR INDEX

Abelson, R.P., 189
Adler, A., 102, 112
Alexander, H.W., 200, 208
Allen, G.L., 86
Allen, Richard, 177–189
Almy, M., 112
Anastasi, A., 200, 208
Anderson, J.C., 86
Anderson, J.M., 146
Anderson, R.C., 218, 221
Andre, T., 217, 221
Aquila, R.E., 36
Aristotle, 140, 146, 256
Armstrong, D.M., 21–22
Arno, 64, 66
Asimov, Isaac, 108
Atkinson, R.C., 221
Austin, G.A., 221

Bailey, F.G., 64, 66
Baldauf, Richard B., Jr., 127, 129–137
Bandura, A., 221, 224
Barbe, W., 218, 221
Barron, F., 150, 153, 157
Barron, R., 233, 235
Bateson, Gregory, 26, 36, 101, 102, 108,
    112, 255–284
Bateson, P.P.G., 109, 113
Baum, R., 141, 146
Beck, R.J., 82, 87
Beckett, Sir Terrence, 115
Belcher, T., 219, 221
Bell, M., 221
Belshaw, C.S., 58, 66
Bennett, Jonathon, 16, 22
Bergmann, M., 146
Bernstein, B., 47, 55, 57, 63, 66
Bigelow, Julian, 261

Birch, H.G., 46, 56
Bishop, John C., 13–23
Blaut, A.S., 82, 87
Blaut, J.M., 82, 87
Bledsoe, W.W., 245, 250
Bloom, B.S., 214, 219, 221, 222
Bock, R.D., 201, 208
Boden, Margaret A., 227–236
Bohr, Niels, 25
Booth, Michael, 281, 284
Borg, V.R., 221
Bounds, W.G., Jr., 137
Boyer, W.A., 113
Bright, G.W., 108, 110, 113
Broder, L.J., 214, 219
Brophy, J.E., 217, 221, 222
Brown, J.S., 230, 235, 236
Bruner, J.S., 77, 102–103, 108, 113, 221
Bryant, K.J., 87
Bunge, M., 11
Burns, A., 58, 66
Burton, R.R., 230, 235

Card, W.I., 234, 235
Carney, J.D., 140–141, 146
Carpenter, Edmund, 62, 66
Champagne, A.B., 137
Chang, C.L., 244, 250
Chernoff, H., 201, 207, 208
Church, A., 239, 250
Clark, C.V., 194, 196
Clowes, Max, 234
Clunie, F., 59, 66
Cohen, M., 211, 212, 221
Coker, M., 221
Cole, M., 155, 157
Copi, I.M., 140, 146, 177, 189
Cormier, W.H., 137

Costa, Arthur L., 211–222
Crowell, Doris C., 93–99
Curnow, I., 233, 235

Dalzell, Rex, 101
Davidson, Donald, 16, 17, 19, 20, 23
Davidson, Graham R., 79–88
Dawkins, Richard, 8
Davies, P., 26, 36
Davis, O., 216, 221
de Bono, Edward, 115–127, 129, 137
de Finetti, B., 201, 207, 208
Dennett, Daniel C., 14, 17, 19, 21, 23
DeNys, M.J., 26, 36
Descartes, Rene, 142
Dicken, P., 82, 88
Diorio, Joseph A., 281, 284
Dobzhansky, Theodosius, 267
Douglas, M., 63, 66
Dove, K.R., 26, 36
Downs, R.M., 87
Dressel, P.L., 208
Dunn-Rankin, P., 94, 99
Dunne, R., 221

Eccles, Sir John, 6, 11
Edwards, John, 127, 129–137
Einstein, A., 108
Eisner, E., 221
Elzey, F., 216, 222
Emanuel, R., 233
Engel, S. Morris, 146
Engelhart, M.D., 221
Engles, F., 56
Erikson, E.H., 77
Eysenck, H.J., 56

Faust, G.W., 218, 221
Fearnside, W.W., 189
Feigenbaum, J., 238, 250
Feldman, J.A., 238, 250
Feuerstein, R., 214, 221
Feynmann, Richard, 104
Finney, B., 79, 87
Firth, R., 87
Fisk, F., 58, 66
Flanders, N.A., 217, 222
Flew, A., 140, 146
Fodor, J., 14, 23
Foos, P.W., 82, 83, 87
Fooshay, A.W., 222
France, P., 58, 66
Frank, L.K., 265, 269
Freud, S., 56

Fujita, A., 191, 197
Furst, E.J., 221

Galanter, E., 263, 269
Gallo, Delores, 149–158
Galton, Sir Francis, 101–102
Garcia, J., 200, 208
Georgacarakos, G.M., 244, 250
George, Frank H., 275, 279
Gilbert, J.K., 137, 139–147
Gladwin, T., 80, 83, 84, 86, 87
Glaser, R., 199, 200, 208
Gleeson, Michael, 115
Gluckman, M., 66
Good, T., 212, 222
Goodman, N., 177–178, 189
Goodnow, J.J., 221
Goodwin, L.C., 77
Gordon, E.W., 199, 208
Grant, C., 60, 66
Graves, R., 274
Gregory, R.L., 235
Gregson, Robert A.M., 275–279, 281, 284
Griffin, Christopher M., 57–67
Grimble, A., 79, 81, 83, 87
Groen, G., 230, 235
Groos, Karl, 102, 110, 113
Guilford, J.P., 150, 151, 157, 200, 208, 222
Gunstone, R.F., 130, 137
Guttenplan, S., 23

Haddon, A.C., 79, 87
Hafner, James, 177–189
Hage, P., 79, 80, 81, 83, 86, 87
Hagen, E.P., 204
Haggerty, J.B., 113
Halpin, T.A., 146
Hamblin, C.L., 139, 143, 147, 179, 189
Hanna, F.K., 232, 235
Hardwick, D.A., 87
Harlow, H.E., 265, 269
Harlow, H.F., 46, 56
Harmin, M., 222
Harris, A.J., 99
Harris, Richard J., 110, 113
Hart, R.A., 82, 87
Harvey, O.J., 219, 222
Harwood, F., 80, 87
Hayes, J.R., 188, 189
Hegel, G.W.F., 24–37
Heim, 200, 208
Helu, I. Futa, 43–56
Henry, Jules, 108, 113
Herman, J.F., 86

Hill, H.W., 221
Hindman, Darwin A., 113
Hocart, A.M., 59, 60, 64, 66, 104, 113
Hoffman, P.J., 200, 209
Holther, W.B., 189
Hornell, J., 79, 80, 87
Horst, D.P., 135, 137, 204, 209
Howe, J.M., 230, 235
Huck, S.W., 137
Hughes, Robert, 234
Huizinga, J., 110, 113
Hume, David, 16–17, 20, 23
Hunt, E., 200
Hutchins, E., 86, 87

Inhelder, B., 229
Iwamoto, Kaoru, 113

Jacobson, L., 69, 77
Jansson, Laura H., 191–197
Jantsch, E., 269
Jeffrey, R.C., 140, 147, 239, 241, 256
Jessen, K., 197
Johnson, H.W., 146
Johnson-Laird, P.N., 189
Joyce, James, 151

Kahneman, D., 179, 186, 189
Kalish, D., 241, 246, 250
Kant, Immanuel, 29, 33, 257
Kanygin, V., 194, 197
Kareev, Y., 233, 236
Karmiloff-Smith, A., 229, 235
Karotaua, Maara, 77
Kelly, George, 70, 71, 77
Kikau, Eli, 66
King, F.J., 99
Kirasic, K.C., 86
Kirk, Robert, 21–23
Kirshenbaum, H., 222
Klein, F., 211, 222
Klevin, A., 217, 222
Kobayashi, Victor N., 255–259, 281–284
Köhler, W., 46, 56
Kosok, M., 30, 37
Kowalski, R., 244, 250
Kozlov, E., 194, 197
Kozlowski, L.T., 87
Krathwohl, D., 221, 222
Kuhn, M.H., 54, 56

Lane, D., 126, 127
Lazarsfeld, P.F., 207, 208
Lee, R.C.T., 244, 250

Lenat, D.B., 231, 232, 235
Levin, J.A., 233, 236
Levine, S., 216, 222
Levi-Strauss, C., 56, 64, 102
Lewis, D., 79, 83, 87
Lewis, J., 200
Link, F.R., 219, 222
Lipman, M., 143, 147
Lord, F.M., 200, 209
Lowery, L., 216, 219, 222
Lowrie, E., 274
Lumsden, J., 201, 208
Lunneborg, C., 200

Maas, Jeanette P., 271–274, 281, 284
Machado, Corinna, 115
MacKay, D.M., 5–12
Mackenzie, J., 147
Mackinnon, D.W., 149, 157
Macrae, Kristina, 199–209
Maier, Norah, 115, 269, 272
Mannheim, K., 43, 44, 56, 140, 147
Marshall, H., 222
Masia, B.B., 222
Maude, H.C., 80, 87
Maude, H.E., 80, 87
Maxwell, Clerk, 262, 263, 277
Maxwell, William, 101–113
McCleary, G.S., Jr., 82, 87
McCulloch, Warren, 261
McPartland, T.S., 54, 56
McPeck, John E., 163–175
Means, B., 157
Medler, M., 192, 194, 197
Medley, D., 221
Meinong, A. von, 55, 56
Metfessel, N.S., 219, 222
Michael, W.B., 219, 222
Mill, John Stuart, 151, 157
Miller, C.L., 146
Miller, Donald, 281, 284
Miller, G.A., 221, 222, 263, 269
Milton, M., 269
Montague, R., 241, 246, 250
Montessori, Maria, 109, 113
Moor, J., 146
Moore, G.T., 82, 87

Nation, John, 64, 66
Nayacakalou, R.R., 58, 66
Nelson, J., 146
Newell, A., 232, 236, 243, 250
Newton, Isaac, 255
Ng, Kim T., 208

Niedeffer, R.M., 192, 195, 197
Ninnes, Leonard E., 25–37
Nisbett, R., 186, 189
Novick, M.R., 200, 208

O'Connor, J., 71, 77
Olton, D.S., 82, 87
Osborne, R.J., 130, 137
Oscanyan, F.S., 147
O'Shea, T., 230, 236

Papert, S., 229, 230, 236
Parr, A., 55
Patai, R., 274
Pateman, T., 234, 236
Pearce, Chelton, 102, 113
Peirce, C.S., 44, 56
Pelletier, Francis Jeffrey, 237–250
Penfield, W., 11
Pentony, Patrick, 261–270
Perkins, David, 101, 177–189
Piaget, Jean, 35, 37, 110, 113, 216, 218,
        228, 229, 233
Pinneau, Samuel R., 113
Plato, 56
Poling, D.R., 222
Popper, Sir Karl, 6, 11
Pospesel, H., 140, 147
Powers, William, 275, 279
Prather, D.C., 194, 197
Pribram, K.H., 263, 269
Putnam, Hilary, 23

Quine, W.V.O., 19, 23

Rasch, G., 207, 209
Reichenbach, H., 262, 270
Rennie, M.K., 147
Restak, R., 216, 218, 222
Rex, J., 44, 56
Richards, T.S., 141, 147
Riesenberg, S.H., 80, 83, 84, 86, 88
Ritchie, G.D., 232, 235
Ritchie, J., 71, 77
Robinson, M.E., 82, 88
Rogers, C.R., 154, 157
Rosenthal, R., 69, 77
Ross, L., 189
Rowe, M.B., 217, 222
Rushall, B.S., 192, 194, 197
Russell, B., 46, 55, 56, 238, 243, 256, 270

Samejima, F., 207, 209

Sanchez, Margaretta, 115, 116
Sapir, Edward, 61, 66
Sarlemijn, A., 37
Sartre, J.-P., 271, 274
Scarne, John, 113
Scarr, D., 62, 66
Scarr, S., 199, 209
Schank, R., 189
Scheer, R.K., 140–141, 146
Schmid, P., 209
Schubert, Lenart K., 237, 245
Sellars, Wilfrid, 23
Sexton, T.G., 222
Sharp, A., 79, 88, 147
Shaw, J.C., 243, 250
Shiffren, R.M., 221
Shtarkshall, Ronnie, 115
Siefel, A.W., 86
Siekmann, J., 245
Simon, H.A., 186, 189, 209, 232, 236, 250
Simon, J.C., 243, 250
Simon, S., 222
Singer, R.N., 191, 192, 197
Sipay, E.R., 99
Skinner, B.F., 230
Sleeman, D.H., 230, 236
Smith, E.R., 212, 222
Smith, R., 244, 250
Soar, R., 221
Spate, Oscar, 58, 66
Spearman, Charles, 276
Spitz, Herman, 102, 113
Standing, E.M., 109, 113
Staudenmayer, H., 185, 189
Stea, D., 87
Steinaker, N., 221
Stewart, Robert A.C., 66, 69–78
Stich, Stephen, 16, 18, 23
Strasser, B.B., 219, 222
Suchman, J.R., 217, 222
Suonperä, M., 194, 197
Sussman, G.J., 236
Sutton-Smith, Brian, 113
Swassig, R., 218, 221

Taba, H., 216, 222
Tallmadge, G.K., 135, 137
Taylor, C., 35, 37
Terrell, M.D., 199
Thomason, R., 246, 250
Thompson, L., 64, 67
Thornburn, K.S. (now Macrae, K.S.), 202,
        203, 205, 209

Thorndike, E.L., 45, 56
Thorndike, R.L., 204, 209
Thorpe, W.H., 109, 113
Thorton, S., 229, 236
Terrell, M.D., 208
Teilhard de Chardin, P., 273, 274
Tinsley, D.C., 216, 221
Tolman, E.C., 82, 88
Torrance, E.P., 149, 158
Tripp, D., 126
Tversky, A., 179, 186, 189
Tye, K., 211, 222
Tyler, R.W., 212, 222
Tyler, Sidney, 127

Ulich, E., 191, 192, 197
Unestal, L.W., 194, 197

Vanlehn, K., 230, 235
Veldman, D., 137
Vernon, P.E., 200, 201, 208
Vico, G., 48, 50, 56
Volkamer, M., 192, 197

Waddington, C.H., 269

Wallace, J., 200, 209
Walsh, P., 113
Walter, M.A.H.B., 59, 66
Wasserman, S., 215, 222
Weir, S., 233, 236
Weiss, Donald, 21, 23
Weizenbaum, J., 234, 236
Westcott, M.R., 186, 189
Whimbey, A., 219, 222
White, R.T., 137
Whitehead, Alfred North, 238, 243, 270
Wieck, D.T., 146
Wiener, Norbert, 256, 263
Williams, G.H., 146
Williams, Ivan, 81
Williams, T., 65, 67
Wilson, Dan C., 237–250
Winne, P.H., 222
Wood, C.T., 135, 137
Wood, D., 82, 87
Woodrow, H., 200, 209
Wright, J., 211, 222
Wrightsman, L.S., 69, 70, 71, 78

Young, 230, 232, 233, 236

SUBJECT INDEX

Absolute Knowledge, 25, 26
AI (artificial intelligence), 227–236
Alternative argument, 183
Artificial intelligence, educational
    implications of, 227–236
Axiomatic logic, 239

Behavior, intelligent, teaching toward,
    211–222
Beliefs about human nature held by young
    people in the South Pacific, 69–78
Believing, 44–45
Bottom-up approach to reasoning, 140–141
  problems with, 141–142
Brain and will, 9–10
"Brain-story," 5, 7
Brute intentionalism, 18–19
  arguments for, 20–22

Carpenter Effect, 191
Causation, circular, 262
Children, reasoning ability of, 104
Children's Version of the Philosophies of
    Human Nature Inventory
    (C-PHN), 71
Circular causation, 262
Cognitive map as a theoretical construct, 82
Cognitive mapping features of Micronesian
    navigation systems, 79–88
Cognitive maps, as complex
    transformations, 85–86
  Puluwatese schemata as, 81–86
  as spoken sentences, 83–85
Cognitive Research Trust (CoRT),
    163–175. *See also* CoRT
Cognitive Research Trust (CoRT) Thinking
    Program, 115–127. *See also* CoRT
Contradiction, law of, 33–34
Contrary antecedent method, 182

Contrary consequent method, 181
Conversion, reasoning and, 184–185
CoRT (Cognitive Research Trust) Program,
    115–127, 163–175
  attention-directing strategies of, 114–115
  design of, 116
  difficulties with, 120–121
  evaluation of, 125–127
  lateral thinking unit of, 172–175
  methodology of, 118
  objectives of, 116–117
  pilot study using, 129–137
  procedure for, 119, 120
  structure of, 121–125
  theoretical base of, 118
  type of thinking taught in, 117–118
CoRT I (breadth), 122
CoRT II (organization), 122–123
CoRT III (interaction), 123
CoRT IV (creativity), 123–124
CoRT V (information and feeling), 124
CoRT VI (action), 124–125
CoRT thinking lessons, 165–172
  conduct of, 125
  methods of, 130–134
  pilot study, data collection for, 132–133
    results of, 134–136
  subjects of study using, 132
Counterexample, 183
Creative thinking, contribution of
    personality to, 152–153
  factors contributing to, 151–152
  operational definition of, 150–151
Creativity, educating for, 149–158
Critical and Creative Thinking Program,
    153–157
  evaluation of, 156–157
  objectives of, 153–156
Critical epistemology, 187–189

Culture and socialization, Fijian, 60–61
Culture and structure, Fijian, 61–63
Cybernetics, Gregory Bateson and,
    261–270

de Bono's heuristics for thinking, 163–175
Determination, two conceptual levels of, 8
Determinative efficacy of thinking, 6–7
Dialectical style and skills, 187–188
Dialogue and formal dialectic, 143–144
Difference, 32–33
Disconnection, 182
Dualist interactionist position, 6

Ecological level, 50–51
Educating for creativity: a holistic approach,
    149–158
Education, intelligent behaviors as a goal of,
    211–212
Educational implications of artificial
    intelligence, 227–236
Einsteinian space, 108
Epistemological realism, 187
Epistemology, critical, 187–189
    makes-sense, 185–187
Excluded middle, law of, 32–33
External factor method, 182

Fijian culture and socialization, 60–61
    and structure, 61–63
Fijian reactions to the problems of social
    change, 57–67
Fijian social structure, 58–60
Fijian speech codes, 63–65
FIP (First Important Priorities), 167
Formal dialectic, dialogue and, 143–144
Formal logic, Hegel's evaluation of, 27–35
Formal repertoire, 188–189

Game introduction, readiness factor in,
    109–110
Games, limitless number of, 105–106
    scientific, mathematical, and social
    concepts learned through, 108–109
Games children play: powerful tools that
    teach some thinking skills, 101–113
Games—play or experimentation, 104–105
Genetic and environmental factors affecting
    IQ, 102–104
Genius, potential for, 102–104

Harris-Jacobson formula, 95
Hegel on pure thought, 25–37
Hegelian science, entrance to, 26–28

Hegel's evaluation of formal logic, 28–34
Hegel's law of identity, 28–32
Heuristic theorem proving, 237–250
Human nature, measurement of
    philosophies of, 71
Hume's argument from analogy: the
    personification challenge and an
    instrumentalist solution, 16–17

Identity, Hegel's law of, 28–32
Identity of a modern Tongan, 51–55
Ideological level, 51
Indeterminacy problem, 18
Influence of society on the thinking of
    Tongans, 47–55
Information-engineering, 6
Intellectual behavior, models of, 212–214
Intellectual capacity, enhancement of, 212
Intelligence, artificial, educational
    implications of, 227–236
Intelligent behavior, teaching toward,
    211–222
Intentional-linguistic or "I-L" thesis, 15–20
    intentional state explanations and, 15–17
    two arguments for, 18–20
Intentional state explanations and the
    intentional-linguistic theses, 15–17
Intentionalism, brute, 18–19
    arguments for, 20–22
INVENTIVE QUOTIENT, 103
IQ, genetic and environmental factors
    involved in, 102–104
"I-story," 5, 7

Kamehameha Reading Objective System
    (KROS), 93–98
Kamehameha Writing Program (KWP),
    93–98
Knowing, 45
Knowledge, Absolute, 25, 26
    sociology of, 43
KROS, 93–98
KWP, 93–98

Language, thought and, 13–23
Language arts curriculum, systematic
    development of thinking skills
    through, 93–99
"Language of thought," 14–15
Lateral thinking, 172–175
Law of contradiction, 33–34
Law of the excluded middle, 32–33
Law of identity, Hegel's, 28–32
Learning, 45

"Liaison brain," 6
Linguistics, thinking and, 14–15
Literature, oral, Tongan, 49–50
Logic, axiomatic, 239
    formal, Hegel's evaluation of, 28–34
    semantic, 239–241
    speculative, Hegel's, 28
    systems of, 238–243

Makes-sense epistemology, 185–187
Maxwell's Child's Intellectual Progress Scale
    (CHIPS), 103
Measurement of philosophies of human
    nature, 71
Mental ability, high, 101–102
Mental training, 191–197
Micronesian navigation systems, cognitive
    mapping features of, 79–88
Mind and Nature
    criticisms of, 275–279
    symposium on, 255–284
    teaching and thinking and, 255–259
Mnemonic strategies, Puluwatese schemata
    and, 80–86
Mythology, Tongan, 48–50
    interpretation of, 50–51

Nature of thinking, 44–46
Nim, 106–108
Neglected critical distinction, 183

Oral literature, Tongan, 49–50
"Origin of the Coconut," 49

Personal Construct Theory, 70
Phenomenology of Spirit, 25, 26–28, 29, 35
Philosophies of human nature,
    measurement of, 71
Philosophies of Human Nature Inventory
    (PHN), 71
Plato's Dialogues, 46
"Privileged access," 7
Problem-solving strategies, analysis of,
    199–209
Provers, theorem, 243–246
Psychometric testing, implications for, in
    the analysis of problem-solving
    strategies, 199–209
Puluwatese schemata as cognitive maps,
    81–86
    and mnemonic strategies, 83–86
Punishment, 48
Pure thought, Hegel on, 25–37
    science of, beginning of, 35–36

Raven's Progressive Matrices, 201
Readiness factor in game introduction,
    109–110
Realism, epistemological, 187
Reasoning, 177–179
    alternative argument and, 183
    bottom-up approach to, 140–141
    contrary antecedent method of, 182
    contrary consequent method of, 181
    conversion and, 184–185
    counterexample and, 183
    disconnection and, 182
    everyday, difficulties in, 177–189
    external factor method of, 182
    method of investigation of, 179–181
    neglected critical distinction and, 183
    scalar insufficiency and, 182–183
    towards a course in, 144–146
    trouble with, 183–184
Reasoning skills, top-down approach to the
    teaching of, 139–147
Remedial reasoning, 142
Remembering, 46
Repertoire, formal, 188–189
Responsibility, 10
Richmond's and Kicklighter's Children's
    Adaptive Behavior Scale (CABS),
    103
"Rock Matahina," 49–50

Scalar insufficiency, 182–183
Schemata, Puluwatese, as cognitive maps,
    81–86
    and mnemonic strategies, 80–86
Science, secondary, teaching thinking in,
    129–137
    thinking skills in, 130
Science of Logic, 25
Science of pure thought, beginning of,
    35–36
Semantic logic, 239–241
"Sense-certainty," level of, 26
Single-cell activity, 5
SNOBOL, 246
Social change, Fijian reactions to the
    problems of, 57–67
Social identity, Tongan, scope of, 52–53
Social structure, Fijian, 58–60
    speech, and silence: Fijian reactions to the
        problems of social change, 60–61
Socialization, culture and, Fijian, 60–61
Society, influence of, on the thinking of
    Tongans, 47–55
    scope and thought of, 47–48

Society-nature relation, 50
Sociology of knowledge, 43
South Pacific, beliefs about human nature
    held by young people in, 69–78
Speculative logic, Hegel's, 28
Speech codes, Fijian, 63–65
SPITBOL, 246
Sports, psychology of, 191–197
Systematic development of thinking skills
    through a language arts curriculum,
    92–99
Systems of logic, 238–243

Taboos, curses, and sanctification, 47
Teaching, implications for, 10
Teaching and thinking, mind and nature
    and, 255–259
Teaching thinking in secondary science,
    129–137
Teaching toward intelligent behavior,
    211–222
Testing, psychometric, 199–209
Theorem prover, heuristic-based, 246–248
Theorem provers, 243–246
Theorem proving, heuristic, 237–250
    and thinking, 237–238
Theoretical construct, cognitive map as, 82
THINKER: a heuristic-based theorem
    prover, 246–248
    example of, 248–249
Thinking, 199–201
    CoRT and, 163–165
    creative, contribution of personality to,
        152–153
        factors contributing to, 151–152
        operational definition of, 150–151
    de Bono's heuristics for, 163–175
    determinative efficacy of, 6–7
    lateral, 172–175
    linguistics and, 14–15

nature of, 44–46
speed of, in the CoRT exercises, 121
teaching, in secondary science, 129–137
    mind and nature and, 255–259
theorem proving and, 237–238
Tongan society and, 48–50
type of, taught by the CoRT program,
    117–118
Thinking lessons, CoRT, 165–172
Thinking rehearsal and its use, 191–197
Thinking skills, games as teachers of,
    101–113
    in science, 130
    systematic development of, through a
        language arts curriculum, 93–99
Thinking in Tongan society, 43–56
Thought, existence of, without language,
    13–23
    pure, beginning of the science of, 35–36
        Hegel on, 25–37
    scope of, and society, 47–48
Thought unity, 31
Tongan, modern, identity of, 51–55
Tongan mythology, 48–50
    interpretation of, 50–51
Tongan social identity, scope of, 52–53
Tongan society, thinking in, 43–56
Tongan value mobility, 54–55
Top-down approach to the teaching of
    reasoning skills, 139–147
Treatise of Human Nature, A, 16–17
Twenty Statements Instruments, 53

Unity, thought, 31

Value mobility, Tongan, 54–55

Will, brain and, 9–10
Wrightsman's Children's Philosophies of
    Human Nature Scale, 69